THE PRACTICAL BOOK OF CHINAWARE

The Practical Book

of

CHINAWARE

BY

HAROLD DONALDSON EBERLEIN

AND

ROGER WEARNE RAMSDELL

*With 202 halftone illustrations
including 13 in full color,
and numerous drawings*

J. B. LIPPINCOTT COMPANY
PHILADELPHIA AND NEW YORK

TO THE MASTER AND MISTRESS OF HARINGTON HOUSE,
BOURTON-ON-THE-WATER, GLOUCESTERSHIRE,
THIS VOLUME IS DEDICATED
WITH SINCERE FRIENDSHIP AND REGARDS

FOREWORD

This is the only work in one volume that covers the chinaware of all countries. It is a complete compendium for the collector and all in search of information, fully setting forth the essential facts, systematically arranged for easy and ready consultation, and with many cross references and comparisons.

The novice, who delights in the beauties and possession of old china, but knows little about the means of identifying the various kinds he admires or seeks, will find herein the key and a trusty guide for his quest.

The collector of long experience, who is familiar with the characteristics of many different makes of china and is usually able to identify them from personal knowledge without other assistance, will nevertheless find in this volume the necessary data for reference or comparison which few can hope to carry wholly in their heads and for which it is convenient to turn to an handbook. The book has been schemed throughout to make it especially convenient for just this sort of ready consultation. The comparative tables and cross references will be found particularly helpful for this purpose.

"Of making many books there is no end," might well be said of books about chinaware and porcelain in general. The subject has always been peculiarly alluring, and to glance at a bibliography of the books that have been written, dealing with one phase or another of the ceramic art, is positively appalling. In the face of such a multitude of volumes, it may be asked why the authors venture to put forth another. The answer is simple. It is, just because there are so many other books and because none of them covers the ground in the same way.

Many of these books deal with only some one particular kind of china, or with some particular phase of its manufacture. Many others

7

are so highly specialised on the purely technical side of manufacture as to be of little direct value to the average person. Many more are so loosely arranged and so diffuse in generalities that they are almost useless for casual reference; extended search and perusal are necessary in order to get at any specific facts. Many are in foreign languages. Many are out of print. To have even a third of them for consultation would mean a fair-sized library on chinaware alone.

In the present volume it has been the aim of the authors so to marshal the facts and condense the statements that convenience of use may be assured and waste of time through searching in the wrong place avoided. They have endeavoured, so to speak, to reduce the subject to its lowest terms and to present the essential facts in such order and arrangement that all the aspects and interrelations may be quickly grasped. In other words, they have tried to make a usable book, and its usability is its justification.

It has seemed not only advisable but absolutely necessary to set limits of date beyond which the different sorts of china cannot be considered. These limits extend from the beginnings of manufacture to 1840, and they are set for the following reasons. First of all, china, like everything else, suffered from the nineteenth century collapse that befell good design and good taste, a collapse that had become general by 1840. Thereafter, for a long time, there was little made that was worth recording. Second, the fashion for one factory to copy the works of another, though always practised to some extent, had grown so common by this date that individuality was at a discount. Third, were all the modern varieties of china to be included, the bulk of the volume would be unmanageable and much of the matter contained would not interest the majority of readers. Fourth, the characteristics of modern china are sufficiently well known and the different sorts bear enough identification to make notice herein unnecessary.

This book deals only with such china as the person of average means can expect to have, either by way of inherited ownership or by purchase. What are distinctly "museum" rarities are omitted; space devoted to them would little avail most readers. The rarer kinds of Oriental porcelain, therefore, are not considered; besides, they are very fully treated in books exclusively devoted to them. For the same reason—unlikelihood or impossibility of acquisition—various European porcelains are mentioned only in general historical notices and without the detailed discussion bestowed on the varieties of china made more extensively and over a longer period. Such, for example, are the sixteenth century Medici porcelain, made in Florence, and the seventeenth century porcelain made at Rouen. In cases like these the manufacture lasted for only a very short time and comparatively few pieces were made. To-day there are less than fifty authentic specimens of the Medici china known, and the Rouen china is likewise about equally rare. Needless to say, all the known examples of either have been jealously cherished for years past in either museums or well-known private collections, so that there is not the least chance of the china-lover or collector lighting upon anything of the sort by way of a "find."

Following the general introductory matter, the arrangement of this volume goes by countries. First comes the china of China along with the Japanese porcelain; in this division are treated those sorts of Oriental china that exercised a profound influence on early European design and those sorts that found their way to the West in large enough quantities to make them well-known features of domestic plenishing in England and America in previous generations. Amongst these last will be found the so-called "Lowestoft" that never saw the town of Lowestoft. Next follow the china products of the different European countries. Then comes the chinaware of England and America, appearing last so that the reader may see straightway how far foreign influences have or have not affected the art in the forms most familiar to the majority of us.

There are five factors to consider in judging a piece of chinaware—the body or "paste," the glaze, the makers' marks, the manner of decoration and the character of the colours. These are all dealt with in their appropriate places.

In conclusion the authors wish to thank all who have contributed to the making of this volume, but especially William Burton, Esquire, for his many kindnesses in criticism and his courteous permission to quote several passages from his writings; the authorities of the British Museum and of the Victoria and Albert Museum. especially W. W. Wink-

worth, Esquire, A. G. Cook, Esquire, Eric Maclagan, Esquire, Bernard Rackham, Esquire, and William King, Esquire; Doctor Samuel W. Woodhouse, Jr., Esquire, of the Pennsylvania Museum in Philadelphia, Henry Batsford, Esquire, and the directors of the Museums at Worcester and Doccia; and Messrs. Reeves and Turner for the gracious permission to use a number of the marks from Chaffers.

Harold Donaldson Eberlein
Roger Wearne Ramsdell

Broadway, Worcestershire
April, 1925

FOREWORD TO REVISED EDITION

The former printings of this book considered chinaware up to 1840, and ended there. Now that a revised edition is being made, it seems opportune to answer a question, or complaint, at the very outset.

Time and again, readers have asked why the authors did not discuss and illustrate the Staffordshire table services and toilet sets with the blue transfer-printed "willow pattern," or decorations showing English and American views, set in floral borders. Sometimes the complaints of such omission have been quite indignant.

The transfer-printed Staffordshire tableware was not mentioned nor discussed because it is not *china. The subject of this book is porcelain, otherwise known as chinaware. The blue-printed plates, platters, sugarbowls, tureens and the like are* earthenware—*a superior type of earthenware, it is true—and the makers who produced them never pretended they were anything else. Ignorant or unscrupulous antique dealers (there be too many such) may choose to reckon and represent them as china, but that does not alter the fact.*

These transfer-printed Staffordshire table services and toilet sets (colours other than blue were often used), embellished with the "willow pattern," or with English and American views and important buildings, had great charm and one can readily understand the fascination of col-

lecting them. For the wares decorated with American subjects—made especially for the American market—the Staffordshire makers employed the best artists to travel about and make the sketches from which the engravers made the copperplates for reproducing the transfer designs. Incidentally, some of the "willow pattern" and scenic ware came from potteries outside Staffordshire.

So popular in America were the Staffordshire pictorial table sets that two well-known and successful Staffordshire potters undertook to start factories on this side of the Atlantic, in order to produce their wares near an already well-established market. One of them, James Clews, who had made a great deal of the blue-printed ware for export, came over in 1829 and set up an establishment at Troy, Indiana; but the clay there proved unsuitable for the kind of white ware for transfer-printing that he had been making in Staffordshire, and the factory was set to turning out other kinds of earthenware. Mr. Clews later went back to England.

The other Staffordshire potter who came overseas was William Ridgway. At their Hanley pottery, John and William Ridgway had produced a large proportion of the pictorial ware for the American trade, and their transfer-printed decorations, characterised by rich, deep colour, is now highly prized by collectors. Arrived here, William Ridgway "pushed his plans so far as to commence the erection of a pottery on a large scale in Kentucky, which for some reason was never completed."

HAROLD DONALDSON EBERLEIN

CONTENTS

	PAGE
"China-Mania"	25
What Chinaware Is	38
The Making of Chinaware	44
General Advice to the Student of Chinaware	50
Oriental Chinaware and the West	56
Italian Chinaware	102
medici	102
ginori (doccia)	102
venice	109
capo di monte	111
le nove	115
vinovo (torino)	116
rome	116
treviso and este (ferrara)	116
French Chinaware	118
rouen	118
st. cloud	119
lille	123
chantilly	124
mennecy-villeroy	127
vincennes	130
sceaux	136
tournay	138
orléans	140
sèvres	141
bourg-la-reine	153
arras	153
st. amand	154
paris	154
vaux	160
lauraguais	165

	PAGE
STRASBURG	166
NIDERVILLER	168
MARSEILLES	170
LIMOGES	171
VALENCIENNES	171
CAEN	172
HAVILAND	173
AHRENFELDT	175
SPANISH AND PORTUGUESE	177
GERMAN CHINAWARE	179
DRESDEN (MEISSEN)—SAXONY	179
BERLIN—PRUSSIA	186
HÖCHST	188
NYMPHENBURG—BAVARIA	190
FÜRSTENBERG—BRUNSWICK	192
LUDWIGSBURG—WÜRTEMBERG	193
FRANKENTHAL—BADEN	195
ANSBACH—THURINGIA	196
AUSTRIAN CHINAWARE	197
VIENNA	197
HEREND (HUNGARY)	199
SWISS CHINAWARE	200
NYON	200
ZURICH	200
DUTCH AND BELGIAN CHINAWARE	202
AMSTEL	202
WEESP	202
OUDE LOOSDRECHT	202
OUDE AMSTEL	202
NIEUWE AMSTEL	202
THE HAGUE	204
BRUSSELS	205
SWEDISH AND DANISH CHINAWARE	207
MARIEBERG	207
RÖRSTRAND	209
GUSTAVSBERG	210
UPSALA-EKEBY	212
COPENHAGEN	213

CONTENTS

PAGE

ROYAL COPENHAGEN 213
BING AND GRØNDAHL 216

RUSSIAN AND POLISH CHINAWARE 219
ST. PETERSBURG 219
MOSCOW 219
KORZEC 219

ENGLISH CHINAWARE 221
BOW 221
CHELSEA 228
WORCESTER 236
DERBY 243
LONGTON HALL 247
LIVERPOOL 248
LOWESTOFT 249
PLYMOUTH 253
BRISTOL 255
NEW HALL 258
PINXTON AND TORKSEY 259
CHURCH GRESLEY 260
CAUGHLEY 261
COALPORT 263
SPODE 266
MINTON 271
DAVENPORT (LONGPORT) 274
WEDGWOOD (ETRURIA) 275
NANTGARW 278
SWANSEA 280
ROCKINGHAM 282
WIRKSWORTH 283
MADELEY 284
LANE DELPH (MASON) 286
CAULDON (RIDGWAY) 289
ROYAL DOULTON 289
BELLEEK 291

AMERICAN CHINAWARE 293
NORTH CAMBRIDGE 293
PHILADELPHIA (SOUTHWARK) 294
BERGEN (NEW JERSEY) 295
NEW YORK 296

	PAGE
PHILADELPHIA (TUCKER)	296
LENOX	298
SYRACUSE	300
PICKARD	302
LAMBERTON	303
CASTLETON	304
BIBLIOGRAPHY	307
INDEX	311

ILLUSTRATIONS

Grouped by Country at the End of the Book

COLOUR PLATES

PLATE

1 Chinese "Imari" Platter
2 A. *Famille Rose* Octagonal Plate
   B. *Famille Verte* Plate
3 Japanese Imari Platter
4 A. Sceaux Ice Pail
   B. Ginori Oval Platter
5 A. Dresden Plate, "Kakiyemon" Manner
   B. Sèvres Green Covered Jar
6 A. Bristol Tray
   B. Lowestoft Cup and Saucer
7 Worcester Platter
8 A. Eighteenth Century Chinese Powder-Blue Vase
   B. Caughley Mug

HALFTONES

9   Table of Characteristic Contours
10 Characteristic Types of Decoration
11 Covered Blue and White Ming Jar
12 A. Blue and White Ming Bowl
    B. Blue and White Ming Platter
13 Sea-Green Celadon Vase
14 A. "Rice-Grain" Cup and Saucer
    B. Blue and White Pierced Cup
    C. "White Ware" Prunus Blossom Cup
15 Blue and White Prunus or "Hawthorn" Jar
16 "Batavian" Vase, "Dead-Leaf" Brown Glaze
17 A. Blue and White K'ang Hsi Bowl
    B. Blue and White Ming Plate

17

PLATE

18 A. and B. Two Eighteenth Century Blue and White Plates
19 Eight-Sided K'ang Hsi Bowl
20 Eighteenth Century Polychrome Tray
21 K'ang Hsi Bowl, Nankin Yellow Ground
22 A. K'ang Hsi Polychrome Plate
   B. K'ang Hsi Plate, *Jouee-Head* Border
23 A. Plate with Red Bat Decoration
   B. Eighteenth Century Octagonal Plate
24 A. Blue and Gold Cup and Saucer, Eighteenth Century
   B. Seventeenth Century Cup and Saucer
25 A. K'ang Hsi Plate, "Mandarin" Figures
   B. Eighteenth Century "Jesuit" Plate
26 A. Eighteenth Century Plate with Waved Rim
   B. Chinese "Lowestoft" Mug
27 A. Chinese "Lowestoft" Beaker Vase
   B. Chinese "Lowestoft" Covered Jar
28 A. Small Chinese "Lowestoft" Bowl
   B. Chinese Green "Lowestoft" Sauce Boat
29 "Lowestoft" Helmet Cream Jug and Sugar Bason
30 A. "Lowestoft" Cup, Black Decoration
   B. "Lowestoft" Saucer, Transfer Imitation
31 A. Eighteenth Century "Lowestoft" Teapot
   B. "Lowestoft" Teapot, Brown Monochrome
32 A. Apple-Green "Lowestoft" Platter
   B. "Lowestoft" Dish, Strawberry Decoration
33 Chinese "Lowestoft" Platter
34 Chinese "Medallion" Punch Bowl
35 A. Eight-Sided Hizen Polychrome Bowl
   B. Kutani Pear-Shaped Polychrome Bottle
36 Bowl of Medici China
37 Ginori Platter, 1737
38 A. Ginori Ice Pail, "Dresden" Manner
   B. Ginori Soup Plate, Moulded Rim
39 A. Ginori Platter, Chinese Peony Decoration
   B. Ginori Covered Dish, Modelled Ornament
40 A. Ginori Plate, "Empire" Style
   B. Ginori Plate, Oriental Decoration
41 A. Ginori Neo-Classic Urn-Shaped Jar
   B. Ginori Neo-Classic Chocolate Pot

PLATE

42 A. Ginori Sweetmeat Dish, with Medallion
    B. Ginori Tureen on Legs

43 Ginori Modelled Figures

44 A and B. Ginori Cups and Saucers, Monochrome
    C. Ginori Reproduction of Capo di Monte Figure

45 A. Capo di Monte Cup
    B. Naples "Pompeian" Tureen and Platter

46 Le Nove Jardinière

47 A. Venetian Cup and Saucer
    B. Venetian Tray with Shaped Rim

48 A. St. Cloud Moulded Flower Pot
    B. St. Cloud "Prunus" Blossom Teapot

49 A. St. Cloud Jar, Blue Baroque Decoration
    B. St. Cloud Jar, Polychrome Reliefs

50 Chantilly Gravy Boat, "Kakiyemon" Manner

51 A and B. Chantilly Flower Pot and Lobate Dish
    C. Chantilly Oval Pierced Fruit Dish

52 Mennecy-Villeroy Vase

53 A. Mennecy-Villeroy Covered Jar
    B. Mennecy-Villeroy Covered Dish

54 Three Vincennes Vases

55 A. Tournay Flower Pot
    B. Arras Flower Pot, Blue Decoration

56 A. Sèvres "Directoire" Cup and Saucer
    B. Sèvres Diapered Cup and Saucer

57 Sèvres "Vine and Trellis" Teapot

58 A. Sèvres Octagon Plate
    B. Sèvres Flare-Top Cup and Saucer

59 Sèvres Jug, Empire Shape

60 A. Sèvres Cup and Saucer, Empire Shape
    B. Sèvres Cup and Saucer

61 Blue and Gold Bowl and Ewer

62 A. Caen Jug, Empire Shape
    B. Empire Jug, All Gold Decoration

63 A. Niderviller Flower Pot
    B. Valenciennes Covered Sugar Bason

64 A. Dresden "Onion" Pattern Soup Plate
    B. Dresden Cup and Saucer, Typical Flowers

PLATE
65   A. Early Dresden Chocolate Pot
      B. Early Dresden Jug
66   A. Dresden Figure of Lace Maker
      B. Dresden Jardinière
67   A. Nymphenburg Flower Pot
      B. Höchst Sauce Boat
68   A. Berlin Tea Caddy
      B. Ansbach Teapot
69   Ludwigsburg Tureen
70   A. Vienna Milk Jug, Empire Shape
      B. Nymphenburg Cup and Saucer
71   A. Herend Tray with Pierced Rim
      B. Copenhagen Soup Tureen
72   A. Bow Blue and White Plate, Chinese Manner
      B. Bow Blue and White Sauce Boat, Chinese Manner
      C. Bow Sauce Boat, Rococo Manner
      D. Bow Sauce Boat, "White Ware"
73   A. Bow Mug with Bulging Base
      B. Bow Globular Teapot
74   A. Bow Pierced Fruit Dish
      B. Bow Plate, Moulded Rim
75   A. Bow Vase in the White
      B. Bow Vase, Cobalt Ground
      C. Bow Candlestick, Modelled Figure
76   A. Bow Pierced Fruit Dish and Stand
      B. Barrel-Shaped Chelsea Mug
77   Chelsea Oblong Octagonal Platter
78   A. Chelsea Fluted Chocolate Pot
      B. Chelsea Eight-Sided Vase
79   A. Chelsea Flower Holder
      B. Late Chelsea Covered Sugar Bason
80   Bing & Grøndahl Porcelain Figure
81   A. Worcester "Imari" Teapot
      B. Worcester "Imari" Plate
82   Late Worcester Landscape Plate
83   A. Worcester Blue and White Bowl
      B. Worcester Plate, Shaped Reserved Panels
84   Worcester Chocolate Pot, "Mandarin" Figures
85   Worcester Vase, Late Period

PLATE

86   Worcester Chocolate Pot, Domed Lid
87   Worcester Soup Plate, Green Monochrome
88   Early Worcester Apple-Green Mug
89   A. Derby Oval Butter Dish
     B. Derby Vase, Blue Ground
90   A. Derby Plate, Flowered Border
     B. Derby Plate, "Imari" Manner
91   A. Derby Arabesque Cup and Saucer
     B. Derby Bowl
92   Plymouth Covered Jar, Chinese Shape
93   Plymouth Mug, Swelling Base
94   A. Plymouth Mug
     B. Plymouth Sauce Boat, Rococo Shape
95   Bristol Chocolate Pot, Domed Lid
96   A. Bristol Pear-Shaped Chocolate Pot
     B. Bristol Figure of *Autumn*
97   A. Bristol Plate with Birds and Butterflies
     B. Bristol Plate with Flowers and Ribbons
98   A. Lowestoft Small Bowl
     B. Lowestoft Mug, Cornflower Decoration
99   A. Lowestoft Butter Boat
     B. Lowestoft Cream Jug
     C. Lowestoft Pierced Fruit Basket
100 A. Caughley Saucer, Blue and Gold Decoration
     B. Caughley Two-Handled, Covered Cup
101 A. Spode Oblong Sugar Bason
     B. Caughley Oval Sugar Bason
102 A. Spode Covered Butter Dish
     B. Spode Stone-China Plate
103 Spode Oval Dish, Transfer Printed
104 A and B. Spode Butter Dish and Tray
105 A. Spode Vase, "Imari" Decoration
     B and C. Spode Cup and Saucers, "Imari" Manner
106 A. New Hall Cup and Saucer
     B. New Hall Straight-Sided Teapot
107 A. Swansea Vase, Modelled Flowers
     B. Pinxton Jardinière
108 Modern Wedgwood Plate and Bouillon Cup and Saucer

PLATE

109 A. Nantgarw Plate, Flower *Motifs*
    B. Nantgarw Plate, Reserved Panels
110 Nantgarw Plate, Bird *Motif*
111 A. Coalport Cup and Saucer
    B. Nantgarw Inkpot, Empire Shape
112 A. Coalport Butter Dish in Tray
    B. Coalport Cylindrical Vase
113 A. Rockingham Sugar Bason
    B. Rockingham Jug
114 A. Liverpool Cup and Saucer
    B. Longton Hall Vase
115 A. Tucker Shell-Shaped Dish
    B. Tucker Jug, Characteristic Shape
116 A. Tucker Sugar Bowl, c. 1830
    B. Tucker Coffee Pot, c. 1830
117 Large Tucker Water Jug, Typical Shape
118 A. Small Tucker Plate
    B. Vase-Shaped Tucker Jug
119 A. Fragment of Southwark Porcelain
    B. Oriental Teapot and Cups, Seventeenth Century
120 A. Blue Staffordshire Plate
    B. Liverpool Jug, c. 1800

DIAGRAMS

FIG.
                                                                          PAGE
1 Characteristic Chinese Porcelain Shapes   81
2 Characteristic Chinese Porcelain Shapes   82
3 Characteristic Diaper Patterns used in Chinese Porcelain   89
4 Characteristic Diaper Patterns used in Chinese Porcelain   90
5 Characteristic Diaper Patterns used in Chinese Porcelain   91
6 Typical Emblems used in Chinese Porcelain   92
7 Typical Emblems used in Chinese Porcelain   93

THE PRACTICAL BOOK OF CHINAWARE

"China-Mania"

"China-mania" was an epidemic that once held the whole of Europe in polite and beneficent thrall. Its furore was as great as "tulip mania," but longer-lived; for the results of both we have cause to be thankful. Chinaware was the "new toy" of the Western world from the middle of the seventeenth century until the eighteenth was well advanced. During all that time the enthusiasm for Oriental chinaware maintained an intensity that we of to-day, accustomed as we are to the finest porcelains of East and West, find it hard to understand. However much we may sincerely delight in rare or beautiful chinaware, the keenness of our admiration for porcelain as porcelain—porcelain as the embodiment of certain physical properties—is somewhat blunted by constant association. We have been used to it from infancy. We take it as a matter of course; it is a familiar incident of everyday life. Even though we may treasure no especially noteworthy porcelain amongst our own household possessions, we know it well in the collections of museums. To our seventeenth century forebears, however, the wondrous quality of the porcelain substance was a revelation that provoked unmeasured delight. They straightway recognised porcelain as the most patrician product of the potter's art and paid homage to its worth.

But, over and above the charm of an hitherto almost unknown substance of exquisite delicacy and refinement, which extended trade with the Orient had placed within their reach, there were combined with it the marvels of glowing, brilliant colour, the engaging patterns of decoration, and a beguiling novelty in the diversity of shapes. It is no wonder that chinaware won an instant hold upon their affections. Personal whim and the behests of fashion doubtless played their parts at first in establishing the sway of chinaware, but its own intrinsic excellences made so strong an appeal to common-sense and good taste that the permanency of its place could never afterwards be in question.

We are so used to chinaware as a part of the daily machinery of polite life that it is an effort to envision the way of things before china cups and saucers, plates, platters and dishes became commonly accepted table plenishings. The nobility and gentry had table services of silver or pewter, pewter of course being much the more abundant. At the same time, there was a certain amount of Delft pottery in use. Even amongst the less well to do there was usually a plentiful garnishing of pewter, while the hinds were content with simple and substantial earthenware that would come under the head of crockery.

The habit of drinking tea, coffee and chocolate, which came into vogue about the middle of the seventeenth century and gained headway with amazing rapidity, gave the initial impetus to a general introduction of chinaware and supplied the stimulus for its popular acquisition. So long as ale was a prevalent breakfast beverage, or meet for polite tween-meals refreshment in the afternoon, the most fastidious could be quite content with mugs and tankards of silver or pewter. But these new exotic drinks required something different. Imagine drinking tea out of a pewter tankard! The glamour would be gone and the flavour would be annihilated. Tea pre-eminently, and coffee and chocolate in scarcely less degree, demanded the association of porcelain both for the sake of the flavour and also on æsthetic grounds. It was natural that these foreign potables should be accompanied by vessels deemed appropriate to their serving in the countries of their origin. This was peculiarly true in the case of tea, the subtleties of whose taste and fragrance could so easily be destroyed by contact with a wrong substance. Fashion prescribed dainty cups of porcelain, later designated "China ware" from the place of its provenance, although "Gombroon ware" was an earlier name to which we shall have occasion to allude hereafter.

Fashion having set the seal of its approval upon tea-drinking and the use of porcelain therefor, the chief devotees of fashion accordingly employed tea tackle of the choicest chinaware they could come by. The emulative instinct in humanity has ever been the same. What the leading devotees of fashion did, that other folk imitated as fast as they could. And thus the use of teacups and their related accompaniments became one of the foremost means of causing a general, popular and intimate acquaintance with the worth and desirability of chinaware. The old table services of pewter or silver were not summarily abandoned the instant china teacups came into the house, but once the possessors of porcelain tea equipage learned to appreciate the elegance and manifold fascination of chinaware—and this they did very soon—it was only a short time before other items of chinaware multiplied with amazing rapidity until its possession became a positive mania and complete table services of porcelain became the pride of their owners' hearts. Queen Mary was a sincere admirer and ardent collector of chinaware and her example had much to do with firmly fixing its hold upon popular esteem. China-mania and the Queen's precedent were responsible for evolving a new article of furniture—the hooded china cabinet with glass doors that made its appearance as a distinctive mobiliary item of the William and Mary period. This gave an opportunity to display, without undue ostentation, the choice pieces of porcelain that china-lovers delighted to acquire.

What was true in England was also true in the American Colonies. The Colonists were always alert to know exactly what was going on in the Mother Country, even to the minutest detail in the current fashions of clothing. Whatever elegancies of domestic appointment came into general favour in England were sure to appear a very little while afterward in the houses of affluent Americans in New England, the Middle Colonies and the South, for they were prospering and wealth was increasing apace as the result of their industry, initiative and commercial activity. Their circumstances, growing yearly easier, enabled them to gratify their tastes for the refinements of life and to order from London merchants whatever luxuries within reason they desired.

Before the seventeenth century came to a close, there was an appreciable amount of good china to be found in and round about Boston, Philadelphia and New York, and throughout the great plantations of the South. In the early years of the eighteenth century the quantity of china arriving at American ports waxed steadily more and more, and from the middle of the century onward the stream of both Oriental and British porcelain imported reached such volume as to justify in great measure the assertion that the "history of the production of English china can be traced as easily in New England as in old England." It would have been truer if the writer here quoted had said, "America" instead of "New England"; New England, though well supplied, had by no means a monopoly of the good things, for much of the best china, both Oriental and British, was to be found in Philadelphia, New York and the South. There was an especially large quantity in Philadelphia and its neighbourhood.

We must bear in mind, however, that the early distribution of china-ware in the American Colonies was by no means uniform. While the seaports and places within easy reach of them secured the coveted porcelain with little delay, and while the planters of the South and the manorial families of the Hudson lightly set aside the obstacles of distance and inconveniences of transportation to obtain any luxuries they wished, in the ordinary run of events the generality of people who lived in the less accessible portions of the country did not acquire very much chinaware until a somewhat later date than the more favoured folk who enjoyed ready communication with the shipping centres. For example, it was not until 1757 that "Maple Grove" was built at Marlborough in Ulster County, in the Province of New York. Madame du Bois, the mistress of "Maple Grove," is said to have used the first complete dinner service of china in that neighbourhood, "and curious housewives from the country round about came journeying thither to gaze with interest on this unwonted piece of luxury." The du Bois dinner service, nevertheless, could scarcely have been the first in the county for polite, wealthy, luxury-loving Kingston-on-Hudson must surely have cultivated and gratified the taste for porcelain long ere this. At the same time, to instance the differences in date of porcelain penetration in the Colonies, there are the dainty handleless teacups of Chinese porcelain from which William Penn sipped his Oolong when he visited some of the substantial Friends of Philadelphia in the latter part of the seventeenth century. These little teacups are still treasured by the descendants of the original owners. Fine china, too, doubtless formed part of the equipment of Pennsbury, in Bucks, for the Proprietary, despite Quaker principles, had an exquisite taste and was not averse to a degree of dignified courtliness that permitted him to make his journeys between Pennsbury and the infant City of Brotherly Love in a stately barge with its due complement of rowers.

In France the popular vogue of porcelain as a utilitarian household accessory, apart from its presence in the form of rare *objets d'art*, received its initial impetus from the dictates of stern necessity. On two occasions, once after the ruinous war of 1691, and, again, after the famine of 1709, Louis XIV, and the nobles of France were obliged to send their silver plate to the Mint in order to obtain badly needed funds in a period of economic tension. To take the place of melted and minted plate, table services of faïence became the fashion, but it was a fashion followed under stress of compulsion and, directly circumstances permitted, the *noblesse* got new plate again and abandoned the faïence. No matter how beguiling its decoration, it was *earthenware* and they could not forget the quality of its body which, to their minds, seemed rustic and lacking in elegance. They had not the English habit of tea-drinking and Chinese tea equipage made little appeal to them. Fine jars, vases and bowls of Oriental porcelain they could and did appreciate, but it was not until they could obtain dinner services of Western china, or Oriental services made after Western patterns, that they became really enthusiastic "China-maniacs" and willingly supplanted silver plate on their tables with choice porcelain.

Although little or nothing was known in Europe of the technical aspect of making porcelain before the sixteenth century, when various attempts were made with more or less success in Italy, to be followed by further successful essays in the latter part of the seventeenth century in France, and although the vogue of porcelain cannot be said to have become generally popular until the second half of the seventeenth century, when the rapid growth of trade with the Orient and the activities of the various East India Companies, English, Dutch and French, brought the elegancies and charms of chinaware within the reach of ordinarily well to do people, it must not be imagined that porcelain was unknown or unvalued in the West at a much earlier date. As a matter of fact, it was known and highly esteemed for centuries before it became subject of common interest and aspiration, but it was of such rare occurrence and so precious that few besides princes and kings, or the greatest nobles, could hope to possess a piece of it.

Though it is not at all impossible that returning Crusaders may now and then have brought back with them from the East a bit of porcelain, just as they brought back spices, plants and fur-lined night-clothes, there is no definite and indubitable evidence on this score. We must be content to date the authentic history of Europe's concern with Oriental porcelain from the year 1447. Then it was, so we are told by Mathieu de Coussy, the historian of Charles VII, that a letter addressed to the Sultan of "Babylon," bespeaking favour towards French commerce in Levantine seaports, concludes with a request for a present of porcelain to be conveyed to the King of France by his ambassador: —"Si te mande par le dit Ambassadeur un présent à savoir trois escuelles de pourcelaine de Sinant, deux grands plats ouvertz de pourcelaine, deux touques verdes de pourcelaine, deux bouquetz de pourcelaine ouvré," and then the customary polite salutations. The *touque* was a vessel or oval vase; the *bouquet* was a bottle with handles. What value was attached to porcelain may be imagined when it was thus solicited in a diplomatic communication as a present from one monarch to another. Thence onward we find instances, now and again, where the porcelains of the Orient were collected and highly prized by the kings and greatest nobles of Europe. An inventory of the year 1586 shews us that Francis I of France had amongst his treasures "vases and dishes of porcelain, curiously wrought." We know, too, that the Medici had rare specimens of Eastern porcelain considerably prior to this, while it seems to have found its way to Venice at an even earlier date. In 1567 Queen Elizabeth possessed a much esteemed gift in the shape of a "poringer of white porselyn and a cup of green porselyn." Similar porringers and cups of porcelain were in the possession of some of the great nobles of England not long after, and in the Victoria and Albert Museum there is a splendid octagonal ewer of blue and white Chinese porcelain with exquisite silver mountings bearing the hall-mark of the year 1585. Cairo was the Mediterranean port to which much of the precious porcelain came overland from China, and thence, during the early period, it went through various channels to different parts of Europe where it was eagerly sought.

In the Palace of Versailles there was a Chinese room where were kept the rarest pieces of porcelain presented to Louis XIV, or purchased by him. In 1686 this collection was much enriched by the magnificent porcelains presented to the Grand Monarch by the King of Siam and delivered with great pomp by the Siamese ambassador, but long before this vases, jars, bowls and platters of Oriental porcelain had become familiar objects of decoration not only in the palaces and great houses of France but in England, Italy, Spain, Holland and other countries as well. In fact, ever since the beginning of the seventeenth century the increased development of trade with the Orient had tremendously broadened the acquaintance with porcelain and stimulated appreciation of its value and beauty. As early as the year 1660 there were various merchants in Paris dealing especially in fine porcelain and they were well patronised by a clientèle of amateurs and collectors.

In England, however, it was left for the introduction of tea, coffee and chocolate drinking to popularise and give impetus to the acquisition of china by the general public who had hitherto regarded possession of the precious substance as peculiarly the privilege of the very wealthy. "Gombroon ware" gave place to "China ware" just a little before or about the time of this marked spread of popularity. Up to about 1640 porcelain was called "Gombroon ware" in England from the English trading post at Gombroon, on the Persian Gulf, whence the Chinese porcelains were sent to England; after that, when the East India Company had obtained a concession in Canton, the name for porcelain was gradually changed to "China ware." And not a little of the early "China ware" brought to England consisted of the thin, handleless teacups and the various objects associated with them, as already pointed out. Directly the passion for china was implanted in the popular taste—and a supply was forthcoming to meet the demand—it spread like wildfire. We hear of Mistress Nell Gwynne time and again going down to the docks and poking through the cargoes of newly arrived East Indiamen in order that she might have the first pick of anything that pleased her fancy. Doubtless she gathered in many a choice bit of porcelain on these piratical forestalling jaunts and her practice, we may be sure, not a few others followed as closely as they could. It needed only the example of Queen Mary a few years later to clinch the ardent desire for chinaware on every hand.

To shew how the consuming taste for china continued unabated through the eighteenth century, and how it not only swayed all ranks of society but also aroused genuine enthusiasm amongst men as well as women, we may cite an amusing incident that occurred about 1765. A ship, in whose cargo was a large quantity of Oriental china, went ashore on the Cornish coast. Presumably it had been intended to smuggle the china and escape the customs duties, for when the customs agents boarded the wreck, as soon as the weather permitted, the ship's company had gone and taken all the papers with them. The chief customs agent, finding some choice teapots and other pieces of china that he greatly admired, in the course of his examination, and regarding them as a professional perquisite, stowed the whole lot in his capacious knee breeches preparatory to going over the side. As he was gingerly descending the ladder to get into the waiting dory, one of his comrades, impatient to be off, bade him make haste and playfully paddled him on the seat of the breeches with the blade of an oar—to the utter ruin of the concealed china and an astounding loud crash!

Horace Walpole was no less enthusiastic a "China-maniac" than the Cornish customs gauger, but it is not recorded that he ever had such a disastrous disappointment in his collecting efforts. He had a good collection of different sorts of china at Strawberry Hill and was always on the alert to add to it, soliciting his friends when they were travelling abroad to bring him back representative pieces from the various Continental china manufactories. In 1785 he writes to Sir Horace Mann, then in Italy:—

"On reading over your 'Florentine Gazette,' I observe that the Great Duke has a manufacture of porcelain. If any of it is sold, I should be glad if your nephew would bring me a single bit, a cup or other trifle, as a sample. I remember that, ages ago, there was a manufacture at Florence belonging to a Marquis Ginori, of which I wished for a piece, but could not procure one. The Grand Ducal may be more obtainable."

What he seems really to have had in mind was a piece of the Ginori china which he had previously failed to procure, for the Ginori china had then attained great fame but there was no Grand Ducal manufacture. But it is not surprising to find Horace Walpole falling into confusion over such tiresome things as facts. The beauty of china, however, strongly appealed to him and he was constantly seeking some new type to gratify his insatiable taste. And Horace Walpole's attitude was a good index to the popular passion for china, the "china-mania" that affected all ranks of society.

America was not a whit behind England in appreciation of good china and eager desire to possess the best, whether of Oriental or European origin. It was no uncommon thing to send special orders for complete dinner services to the East, and to wait patiently, or impatiently, for the execution of the commission with monograms or armorial bearings on each piece. The vast treasure of fine old china preserved all along the Atlantic seaboard bears eloquent witness not only to the prevalence of widespread "china-mania" in America, but also to the knowledge and discriminating taste of those who first secured this goodly heritage. When a ship laden with china was lured by the wreckers to destruction on the Barnegat sands, the "beach" china, as it was called, found a ready and profitable market amongst purchasers who either knew not whence it came or, at any rate, asked "no questions for conscience sake." But most of the china made its entrance in a regular manner and if anyone cares to examine the old shipping invoices they will gain an amazing but fairly accurate idea of the amount of porcelain it took to satisfy, even partially, the demands of American "china-mania."

With all the enormous demand for Oriental china, it was but natural that attempts should be made in the West to produce the same material, comparable with the Eastern prototypes in substance and decoration. These attempts began in Italy in the sixteenth century. More successful and enduring essays were made in France in the seventeenth century. The eighteenth century saw successful and permanent manufactories of china in England, France, Italy, Germany and Austria. The earlier attempts resulted in what is known as "soft paste" porcelain, an approximation to the Oriental ware that has much to be said in its favour. During the eighteenth century, beginning with Saxony, European potters mastered the secrets of making "hard paste" or the so-called "true" porcelain of the same quality and characteristics as the Chinese. Thence onward both "soft paste" and "hard paste" china were made in the West, as well as the "bone china" manufactured in England, a substance holding a middle ground between the "soft paste" and "hard paste" porcelains. In America some attempts to produce china were made in the eighteenth century, but though these attempts in one or two instances resulted favourably so far as the quality of the porcelain was concerned, they were not commercially successful and came to an untimely end. It was not until the early years of the nineteenth century that china was successfully and profitably produced on American soil.

Between 1840 and the fore part of the twentieth century, there is little good to be said for either English or American chinaware.

After achieving a blaze of glory in Philadelphia's Tucker & Hemphill china, American china-making went into total eclipse. It was to be many long years before there would emerge from the darkness anything really significant in which later generations could take honest pride.

In 1902, when the White House was restored and renovated under President Theodore Roosevelt,

"he determined that the china which was to be purchased then for the new state dining room must be a home product and for several months he swept the country from Maine to Texas and from Florida to California to find a pottery which was equipped to take the Executive order for a state dining set. . . . At that time it was simply out of the question. There were no American kilns producing china of the quality required."

It was not until 1918 that the occupants of the White House could get a satisfactory "state dining service," designed "by an American artist, made from American clay at an American pottery, burned at American kilns and decorated by American workmen."

In this general condemnation of English and American china, the strictures apply to the "outward and visible" aspect of the articles produced, not to the composition of the porcelain body nor to the purely technical processes of manufacture. It was an era of deplorably bad taste, and the chinaware then produced merely reflected the spirit of the age.

Technically speaking, it was a period of progress. On both sides of the Atlantic there were endless mechanical improvements to facilitate the potters' labours and to ensure uniform quality of product through the processes employed. In England the bone porcelain formula, with only slight variations or corrections at the several factories, maintained a china body of unimpaired excellence. In America there was widespread experimentation; some satisfactory true porcelain bodies were arrived at but, at the same time, so many modifications were tried and introduced that it was often hard to tell what was porcelain and what was not, or when.

Even before 1840, much English china was showing a kind of tumid pomposity (both in shape and decoration) that fitted in with the general *milieu* of the age. As the nineteenth century advanced, the chinaware (both purely utilitarian and also what purported to be ornamental) reflected the increasingly decadent taste of the period—bad enough when expressed in wholly English manner, worse when uninspired Continental devisements were freely adopted. Each factory borrowed indiscriminately—"appropriated" and "pirated" would be better terms—both shapes and types of decoration.

On the Continent, for the most part, things were equally bad. While Worcester, for instance, in the late Victorian Era, was proudly turning out ingeniously contrived and expensive monstrosities, Sèvres, only a little while before, had been launching new colours of such nauseating hue, with dinnerware decorations so potent in emetic value, that it must have taken a strong stomach to sit at the table with them. (So appalling were these productions that one person who had inherited a lot of them, only a few years ago wisely used the several pieces as targets for pistol practice.)

Almost the only china products not engulfed in this maelstrom of intricate abnormality were some of the perennially-favourite traditional types, the steady demand for which, from people who refused to acquire a "reefined" taste in the current vogue, dictated their continuance as sound commercial policy. These, and a few simple and inexpensive types of "cottage" ware, chiefly represented the unspoiled residue from a great china-making past.

In America, after the discontinuance of Tucker & Hemphill china in 1838, the picture was equally dismal. From the ferment of experimentation carried on, there occasionally emerged something creditable, but few of these creditable achievements had any permanence. There were porcelain door-plates, with dainty polychrome floral decorations and gilding, but these soon went out of fashion. The *Jersey City Porcelain and Earthenware Company* discontinued porcelain-making shortly after they had shown "a small porcelain bowl, with heavy gold band," at one of the Franklin Institute exhibitions in Philadelphia; porcelain-making appears not to have been resumed there until about 1850, when the *Jersey City Pottery* is said to have been making porcelain, but of what sort is not specifically recorded. In the middle and late nineteenth century some creditable porcelain is said to have been made at Greenpoint, Long Island. Just before the War Between the States, a little porcelain was made in South Carolina, but the War put an end to that venture. At Bennington, in Vermont, "Parian" pitchers and similar objects were produced, which well deserve the praise collectors bestow on them. Just after the middle of the nineteenth century, Trenton began potting and eventually advanced to china-making; while Baltimore, Boston and East Liverpool, Ohio, could all claim some success in the production of porcelain. But the china made in all these places rarely rose superior to the prevalent execrable taste of the day.

To counterbalance sporadic excellences, there were the horrible pre-Raphaelite vases, pre-Raphaelite polychrome tiles and similar porcelain aberrations in which the arbiters of "æsthetic" taste delighted in the sentimental "peacock-feather-sunflower-cattail-Oscar Wilde" era. Above all, there were the ubiquitous ornamental spittoons that the learned ceramist, Dr. E. A. Barber *(Pottery and Porcelain of the United States)* seemed to feel bound to enumerate, if not indeed to commend, as amongst the conspicuously important articles of manufacture by maker after maker. These revolting "decorative" cuspidors were a sorry index to far-spreading vulgarity and bore unpleasant witness to the persistence of that bestial addiction to spitting that Mrs. Trollope and Dickens (and our own writers, too) had been mercilessly flaying for seventy-odd years. Under the circumstances, one can understand the existence of large "decorating" establishments in New York and other cities, whose proprietors imported chinaware "in the white" and then overloaded it with "splendacious" and glittering embellishments for wealthy patrons; and the wealthy patrons often ordered large dinner services in duplicate.

However, in spite of all the unprepossessing outward manifestations, the welter of banality and aggressive hideosity that marked the late Victorian and Edwardian days was not wholly barren of useful results. The china-makers in America were gaining technical proficiency; when the world-wide epidemic of diseased imagination had run its course, the American porcelain potters were in a position to apply their skill in creating chinaware that has just claims to consideration in the matter of design and decoration as well as excellence of body.

What Chinaware Is

China, or chinaware, is porcelain. It is not to be confounded with *pottery*. Porcelain, though first evolved from pottery, is a thing beyond and apart from it. And pottery is not porcelain.

It is quite true that porcelain is made by potters, and that a mechanical and decorative kinship exists; that its making is included within the scope of the fictile art along with the making of pottery; and that the ultimate perfection of porcelain's manufacture was developed from the processes of pottery making. But porcelain is the highest, the most precious and the most highly organised expression of the potter's art.

And it is something still more than that. Porcelain is a thing separate and distinct from pottery, because there is a fundamental difference between the body of porcelain and the bodies of all the various sorts of pottery and earthenware. This radical difference is manifest through a combination of certain well-defined physical properties which porcelain *has,* and which the divers kinds of pottery and earthenware *have not.*

Porcelain is called china, or chinaware, because China is the land of its origin and first manufacture. For centuries it was exported thence to other countries, until the secrets of its composition and manufacture were discovered. Even after that, and when the porcelain manufactories of the West were competing with Chinese products for public favour, export of the "china of China" continued in great volume and still maintains an appreciable place in Oriental commerce.

THE DISTINGUISHING PROPERTIES OF PORCELAIN

First, it is important to remember that porcelain is composed of a *clay* that is burnt or fired at intense heat in a furnace; it is not a *glass* or vitreous substance that has been molten.

There are two fundamental things to be considered in studying porcelain: (1) the body of which it consists or the *paste,* as it is called and, (2) the *glaze,* that is to say, the transparent vitreous or glassy substance with which the body or *paste* of the object, platter, cup, vase or whatever it may be, is coated. When the paste or body is left unglazed, as is often the case with medallions, busts or small groups of sculpture, it is spoken of as *biscuit.* The term *biscuit* is also used to designate in general the pieces of porcelain, of whatever type, before they have been glazed. In the making of Chinese porcelain, there is, as a general rule, no "biscuit" stage; the fluid glaze is applied directly to the air-dried clay vessel and glaze and body are fired at one and the same operation.

The two essentially distinctive qualities possessed by porcelain, the qualities that differentiate it from other products of the potter's art, are (1) the *whiteness of its body,* not merely on the surface but clean through the substance, as it appears when broken; and (2) its *greater or less degree of translucency* where the body is at all thin. The edges of thin plates or saucers, thin lips, and mouldings, when held against the light, should be translucent. Bowls, cups, and not seldom the whole body of plates and saucers should be translucent, when subjected to this test against the light, unless the body is of unusual thickness.

Oftentimes, too, when the edge of a bowl or plate is struck it will give forth a clear, bell-like note.

In addition to the whiteness and translucence of porcelain, there is a peculiarly distinctive manner in which its glaze reflects the light, while to the touch the surface is smooth and soft as nacreous shell lining.

THE DIFFERENT SORTS OF PORCELAIN

Porcelain is classified as *hard paste* porcelain and *soft paste* porcelain. There is also a third porcelain composition known as *bone* porcelain, which occupies a more or less middle ground between the *hard paste* and *soft paste* types. It is the fashion in some quarters to refer to hard paste porcelain as *true* porcelain while soft paste porcelain and bone porcelain are termed *artificial* porcelains. However, all three have so much in common, and all three are so widely separated in every respect from other fictile bodies, that it seems much wiser, on the

whole, much fairer, and much less provocative of confusion and mis-
understandings to adopt the former classification of *hard paste, soft
paste* and *bone* porcelain.

HARD PASTE PORCELAIN

Hard paste porcelain is distinguished by its *hardness,* its *high resistance to heat,* its *resistance to acids* and its *impermeability to staining
fluids,* its *close, compact texture,* its *complete vitrification,* its *translucence,* the nature of its fracture when chipped or broken which is
conchoidal or *shell-like,* very much like the fracture of a piece of flint,
and its *clear, bell-like note* when sharply struck. When we speak of
complete vitrification it means that the several elements in the composition of the porcelain body are so thoroughly blended and compacted
by the intense heat of the firing that the substance appears dense and
absolutely homogeneous and is hard and smooth to the touch. This
quality is readily apparent in the "biscuit," at the points of fracture
where glazed porcelain is chipped or broken, and on the bottom edges
of foot-rims that are free from glaze. Complete vitrification also implies that, since the glaze, in the intense heat of the firing, has become
virtually part and parcel of the body which it covers, it cannot be
chipped off and separated from that body in flakes.

The *materials* of which *hard paste* porcelain is made are, first, *kaolin*
or china-clay, a white earthy substance which is a product of decom-
position of the felspar contained in granitic rocks; and, second, *petuntse*
or china-stone, which contains felspar, the silicate of alumina and potash, or sometimes soda. The felspar is closely allied with granite, or
kindred rock, in a somewhat weathered condition and is frequently
associated with more or less quartz and mica. The china-clay or kaolin
is not fusible, even at the highest temperatures to which the kiln can
be brought; the *petuntse,* china-stone or felspar *is* fusible at an high
temperature. William Burton, one of the greatest living authorities on
porcelain and porcelain technique, notes that "at the high temperature
to which the porcelain is exposed during the firing a gradual chemical
interchange takes place between the various silicates composing the
mixture. The *fusible* silicates, such as the felspar and mica, begin to

melt and attack the free silica and the kaolin, and when the changes are complete we get a dense, hard, white porcelain, quite translucent if sufficiently thin. . . . However intensely fired the body may be, it never becomes transparent or clear like a piece of glass, for the glassy silicates that result from the fusion are penetrated through and through with opaque needles or rod-like crystallites." The deflections and diffusion of the rays of light through this vitreous fused body produce the soft translucence so highly prized in fine porcelain. In other words, the melting of the fusible china-stone in the kiln to a glassy substance that holds the non-fusible china-clay or kaolin in suspension produces the marked translucent and vitreous character of hard paste porcelain. The china-clay or kaolin has been aptly likened to the bones of the porcelain body, while the fusible china-stone is the flesh. To carry the simile one step further, the glaze may be likened to the skin.

All hard paste porcelain has not a body or paste of identically the same composition. The character depends upon the proportions of china-clay or kaolin, on the one hand, and of *petuntse* or felspar, on the other, that enter into the mixture before it is shaped and fired. The larger the amount af kaolin, the harder and more infusible the finished porcelain. The great plasticity of the clay mixture when it contains an high percentage of kaolin renders the utmost care necessary to avoid mishaps before drying and firing. As much as 65 per cent. of kaolin can be used in the mixture. When there is an high percentage of kaolin, the resulting porcelain is said to be of "severe" type; when the percentage is much lower the porcelain is said to be "mild." To the "severe" type belongs much of the earlier hard paste porcelain of Sèvres and most of the German porcelain. China of this type may possess admirable utilitarian qualities, but as a substance it is apt to be harsh to the sight and cold and hard to the touch. The china of China belongs to the "mild" type, and so does much of the porcelain made at Sèvres in recent years. Irrespective of decoration, the mild porcelain is much more delightful to see and more sympathetic to the touch. In every way it is far more mellow and satisfactory. The reader can have no better object lesson in this respect than by comparing a piece of German porcelain with a piece of Chinese; the latter is mellow, lovable and seductive, the former is brutally hard and unsympathetic. Incidentally, the severe porcelain does not lend itself nearly so kindly to decoration as does the milder type.

SOFT PASTE PORCELAIN

Soft paste porcelain is sometimes called *artificial* porcelain because some of the materials entering into its composition were substitutes for the materials used in the making of Oriental porcelain which, from the very outset, was the acknowledged model for imitation. These substitutes were arrived at as a result of conjectures regarding the nature of Oriental china and experiments on the part of European porcelain pioneers to approximate the qualities displayed by Oriental models.

Soft paste porcelain is distinguished from hard paste porcelain by the *softer whiteness of its body,* sometimes distinctly creamy in tone, and by its usually greater *translucence,* though whiteness and translucence are qualities common to all porcelain. It is also distinguished by the nature of its fracture, when chipped or broken; the unglazed portion of the body thus exposed is granular and chalky. The break or chip, too, is apt to be straight and not conchoidal or flint-like as in the case of hard paste porcelain. The substance, furthermore, is much softer and yields readily to filing. Sometimes the translucence of soft paste porcelain is slightly tinged with yellow. Soft paste porcelain has not as great resistance to heat as that possessed by hard paste china.

The *materials* entering into the composition of soft paste china are, first, a white-firing clay, and, second, a fusible silicate such as a frit of glass, sand or broken and pulverised china. When deposits of kaolin were discovered in Europe, the kaolin was made use of.

Most of the early European china was soft paste porcelain and, in nearly all cases it possesses a rarely mellow quality that much of the hard paste china totally lacks. The loveliest and most highly prized old Sèvres china was all of soft paste.

In the process of firing in the kiln the artificial silicates melt, envelope and partly dissolve the clay so that, as Burton points out, "again a material is obtained in which a clear transparent base holds in suspension white and opaque particles, and such substances consequently exhibit something of the soft translucence that distinguishes the porcelains as a class."

BONE PORCELAIN

Bone porcelain, as noted before, may be said to hold a middle ground between hard paste and soft paste porcelain, representing, so to speak, a compromise between them. The *materials* of which the body or paste consists are mainly kaolin, felspar, *petuntse* or china-stone—whichever name you choose to apply to it—and, thirdly, a quantity of bone-ash. This composition was discovered and the process developed in England from about 1750 onward. As Burton aptly points out, "we may regard English bone-porcelain, so far as the body of the ware is concerned, as a true porcelain paste which has been rendered more fusible by the addition of a large proportion of calcium phosphate in the form of bone-ash."

In its distinguishing qualities bone porcelain likewise occupies an intermediate position between the hard paste or natural felspathic porcelains, on the one hand, and the soft paste or artificial glassy porcelains, on the other. It is not generally so white as the hard paste, but more white than the soft paste. Also, it is not quite so hard, nor so impermeable to the action of acid or staining fluids, as the hard paste body, but it is harder and less permeable than the soft paste. Although it holds comparatively a middle ground between the two, yet in its qualities it somewhat more closely resembles the hard paste. In its fracture it is more akin to the hard than to the soft paste. It has the durability of the hard paste and the softer quality of the soft paste glaze.

The Making of Chinaware

If the reader wishes to follow up in detail all the intimate minutiæ of porcelain manufacture, and to become acquainted with all the technical processes, the books noted in the bibliography at the end of the volume had best be consulted. As we are chiefly concerned here with the aspect of the finished product, it must suffice to point out a few of the salient facts connected with the transformation from the original elements to the ultimate stages of decoration.

After the materials are finely ground, washed and filtered, they are mixed in the desired proportions and the plastic clay is thoroughly worked and kneaded to ensure uniformity of texture. The clay may, perhaps, be "short" and inclined to crumble, or it may be highly plastic and "fat," as is apt to be the case when there is present in the mixture an high percentage of kaolin. The nature of the clay and its degree of plasticity necessarily somewhat determine the methods by which the articles to be made are shaped.

A lump of clay may be "thrown" on the potter's wheel and gradually shaped by the manipulation of the potter's thumbs and fingers as the wheel revolves. This method implies an object of circular form and a proper degree of plasticity on the part of the clay. Again, objects may be moulded, the clay being pressed firmly into moulds of the desired shape. Fluted articles, articles with raised patterns or perforations, and such members as the handles of cups, the handles and spouts of teapots, and the handles and knobs of tureens and vegetable dishes must all be moulded as well as lids, the generality of plates, all plates and platters of form other than circular and, as a rule, most articles with the exception of such jars, bowls and vases of circular form as can be shaped on the potter's wheel. Statuettes and figures, of course, are moulded, unless shaped by the casting process which, however, was unknown in the East. Handles, spouts, knobs and embellishments in high relief, such as figures and flowers, are moulded separately and then attached in their proper places with "slip." "Slip" is a fluid mixture of the clay body, of a thick cream-like consistency. After the separately moulded members are attached in their proper places, the articles are set away to dry until the time comes for them to be fired. Many objects of elaborate and complex shape have to be built up of a number of separately moulded parts.

In casting porcelain a thick "slip" is poured into a plaster-of-Paris mould. The water is absorbed or drained off, and when the clay has dried and hardened to the right extent to hold its shape, the plaster mould is removed.

When the ware has been carefully dried, it is fired. In China it was customary, with a great deal of the porcelain, to apply the fluid glaze directly to the surface of the air-dried object and then subject it to only one firing at intense heat. Much hard paste porcelain in Europe, however, had a preliminary firing at a dull to full red heat. This "half baked ware" was afterwards glazed and subjected to a firing at the full temperature necessary, which served to make the glaze become virtually part and parcel of the body. In England the bone pastes were first fired at the most intense heat. Afterwards they were glazed and fired only to a temperature sufficient to melt the glaze and make it adhere inseparably to the body. The same method was followed for firing and glazing soft paste porcelains.

With the exception of underglaze colours, all coloured decoration with enamel colours and all gilding are applied after the article has been through its second or glazing firing and these overglaze enamels and gilding must be fixed by an additional firing at little more than a clear red heat, a temperature much lower than is needed to melt the glaze.

THE GLAZE

The term "glaze" is really only another form of the word "glass," and there is not a great deal of difference in chemical composition between the glaze on the surface of china and the glass which we daily see and handle.

The glaze is a very important factor, not only so far as the aspect of porcelain is concerned, but also as one of the cardinal items of identification. There are many variations of glazing and some of these are peculiar to certain kinds of china; all of them add their quota of individuality and distinction to the ware of which they form the skin. The different glazes vary in their quality which the sense of touch distinguishes as well as in the appearance they reveal to the sight.

The glaze is transparent and ordinarily colourless, or almost altogether so, so that the white body or paste beneath is perfectly visible. In some of the early Chinese porcelains the decoration is effected by the use of one or more coloured glazes, but such glazes are the exception rather than the rule. In still other cases the glaze, although perfectly transparent, is slightly tinged with a greenish, bluish or yellowish tint which, whether intentional or not, often enhances the beauty of the general effect. In some of the old Chinese blue and white porcelain the glaze has a slight bluish tinge which acts as a pleasant bond between the white of the body and the blue of the decoration.

In China the glaze was made of the pure *petuntse* or china-stone, sometimes softened with a little lime, and was applied in a thin fluid state to the air-dried but still unfired objects. They were then fired at an intense heat and finished at one firing, the glaze becoming thoroughly incorporated with the body. In Europe and Japan it was customary to fire the pieces first at a moderate heat of between 600 and 900 degrees Centigrade. Afterwards they were covered with the coating of glaze and subjected to a second firing at the full temperature of from 1350 to 1500 degrees Centigrade, the heat required by hard paste porcelain. Thus the porcelainisation of the body and the fusion of the glaze took place simultaneously.

An accurate mental picture explanatory of this process is most happily conveyed by Burton, in his *Porcelain: Its Nature, Art and Manufacture.* He says:—

"It will be readily conceived that under such circumstances the melting glaze, containing fusible ingredients similar to those used in the body, will also attack and partly dissolve the outer layer of the body substance, and we may picture to ourselves a piece of glazed porcelain of the first class as consisting of many layers of different silicates, some of them of excessive thinness and none of them sharply defined, ranging from the outer skin of the glaze, which in perfect pieces is always the clearest, down to the body itself, which is a felted mass of minute crystalline rods imbedded in a more glassy substance. Only by forming some such mental picture, which is in harmony with the knowledge obtained by a microscopical examination of thin slices of the material, can we understand where the distinctive beauty of porcelain resides. When light falls upon a piece of true porcelain it penetrates these successive layers, which, so to speak, filter, soften and subdue it, so that the lowest depths shimmer and glisten with the light they reflect to the observer's eye through the sucessive envelopes of more translucent substance."

The process of glazing was different for the soft paste or glassy porcelains and for bone porcelain. The unglazed articles were fired up to a temperature of 1100 to 1150 degrees Centigrade. They were then coated with a glaze that was virtually a glass, rich in lead oxide or borax, and subjected to a second firing, at about 1000 degrees Centigrade, a temperature sufficient to melt and fuse the glaze. Of such glazes Burton observes:—

"Glazes made in this way are always thinner, more transparent and brilliant, more 'glassy,' in a word, than those in the first class for hard paste porcelain, and from their nature and method of formation they lack the subtle depth and unctuous richness of the latter, because they affect the light less as it passes through them."

THE DECORATION

China may be decorated in two ways. *First,* the decoration may be contained in the body of the piece itself and consist of *engraving, embossing, perforations* or fretwork, or of *applied reliefs.* All of these devices are perfected before glazing. This may be called decoration in the white. *Second,* the decoration may be accomplished by means of colours or gilding.

These methods may be employed singly or in combination.

DECORATION IN THE WHITE. Decoration in the white is effected by engraving or incising patterns in the body of an article before it is fired, or the patterns may be impressed by the mould in which the article is first shaped. The engraving or incising process is exemplified in such pieces as the Oriental ware decorated with the rice-grain *motifs*. When patterns are embossed in low relief, they are made by the moulds or, when higher relief is desired, patterns are produced by painting with thick "slip" (a thick fluid form of the clay) upon the surface of the previously air-dried article. When the slip painting, in turn, has dried, the article is ready for glazing and firing. Sometimes the piece of porcelain is first covered with coloured glaze and fired, and then painted with white slip, thus necessitating a second glazing and firing. In certain cases these slip painted reliefs are as delicate as lacework. Examples of the low embossed or raised patterns are to be found in the basketwork now and again found on the rims of plates. Perforations or fretwork, in such instances as plate rims, fruit baskets and the old Chinese porcelain lanthorns, often supply a distinctive decoration. Separately moulded reliefs, such as rosettes for the intersections of fretwork, sprigs, flowers and the various sorts of figures employed as knobs and handles are attached with slip to the body of the piece before glazing. In much of the old Chinese Fuchien porcelain these moulded decorations in the white are very beautiful and not infrequently of an elaborate nature.

DECORATION IN COLOUR AND GOLD. The colours used in decorating china are of two sorts, the *underglaze* colours applied before glazing and firing, and the *enamel colours* and gold applied after glazing. Enamel colours and gold thus applied require a second firing to make them fuse with the glaze and become permanent.

The most substantial and reliable underglaze colour is blue, made from cobalt. In the old blue and white ware of China the decorations were painted with this blue on the air-dried bodies of the articles which were subsequently glazed and fired. At a comparatively early date the Chinese developed also an underglaze red. This was difficult to produce, however, and the secret of it was afterwards lost. Another underglaze red followed later but was never nearly so much used as the blue. Underglaze blue was likewise commonly employed by the European makers of porcelain. An underglaze rose was invented in England in the eighteenth century. Foreign potters frequently speak of it as "English pink," and it has been very extensively used. Somewhat later a few other underglaze colours were developed on the Continent and, about the beginning of the nineteenth century, the range of these colours was increased by a good underglaze green and some other colours that were not so pleasing. After all is said and done, blue was the one reliable and serviceable underglaze colour that could always be depended upon and was almost exclusively used, although in many cases overglaze blues likewise occurred.

The overglaze enamels were easy to manipulate and remarkably varied effects were produced with a comparatively limited palette, although by the eighteenth century the Chinese had devised an adequate chromatic range much ampler than the colour resources at their command in earlier times. In Europe, too, especially in France, during the eighteenth century, the colour possibilities were greatly enriched. Enamel colours on the glaze of hard paste porcelain often stand up perceptibly from the surface of the glaze, for the glaze is so hard that the enamel colours, which require a comparatively low temperature for their firing, do not thoroughly fuse with it. On the other hand, enamel colours applied over the glaze of soft paste porcelain very often melt into and become thoroughly incorporated with it so that their presence above the surface of the glaze is neither visible to the eye nor palpable to the touch and you feel nothing but the soft glossy coating of glaze. This absorption of the enamel colours by the glaze both protects them and adds to their lustre.

The third way of applying colour decoration to china is by the use of coloured glazes, previously mentioned. The glaze may be of one colour over the whole of a piece, as in the case of the old Chinese Celadon ware, or glazes of several different colours may be applied to different parts of the same article. This method was used in adorning some of the old Chinese wares. In some cases a piece covered with a single-coloured glaze was further embellished with designs painted upon its surface in enamel colours.

General Advice to the Student of Chinaware

It has been pointed out in the Foreword that there are five factors to keep in mind when judging a piece of china—(1) the body or paste of which it is made; (2) the glaze that covers its surface; (3) the kind of article and its contour; (4) the manner of its decoration; and (5) the mark affixed by its maker. The latter is often lacking as there are a great many pieces of old china that are altogether unmarked.

In the foregoing section, on the making of chinaware, the properties of the paste or body and the nature of the glaze have been explained. It is necessary to state very emphatically, however, that the reader cannot expect to gain a sufficient and accurate knowledge of china merely from books. It is absolutely essential to *see* and to compare the various sorts in order to acquire and cultivate a proper appreciation of the outstanding characteristics that distinguish one kind from another.

Language alone is inadequate to describe and fully define all the subtle variations of quality, colour and texture that enter into consideration and cannot be disregarded. The statement of facts must be complemented by *sight* and *touch,* or at any rate by sight, when it is not possible to handle and feel of the actual objects. The habit of close, critical observation must be encouraged.

The English language is fully as capable as any other—and more capable than most—of expressing the nice differences of quality that appear in the paste, the glaze and the colour of the several sorts of china. Nevertheless, there are many variations quite perceptible to the eye that cannot be adequately described in words, for no matter how carefully weighed or meticulously couched the phraseology may be, you can never be sure that the same words or expressions are going to convey identically the same impressions to two different minds.

For example, we may be obliged to describe the pastes of two different kinds of china as *white* and the glazes as *transparent*. There are no other terms by which to designate them. Furthermore, both whites may be of a creamy tone. The term "creamy white" as accurately describes one as the other, so far as words can convey a definitely exact idea, and yet when we see examples of the two pastes side by side we can readily distinguish a difference between one "creamy white" and the other "creamy white." The one "creamy white" is just as much "creamy white" as the other and just as much entitled to the term. The only way in which these differences can be expressed verbally—and it is an insufficient and clumsy way, at best—is to establish some basis of comparison and to say that the paste of A is not so creamy white as the creamy white paste of B. This method must needs be purely arbitrary, and the arbitrarily chosen norm of comparison cannot be a constant, invariable quantity, definitely fixed with mathematical exactitude, but will inevitably vary according to each individual conception.

It is plain, therefore, that acquaintance and familiarity by sight, and acquaintance and familiarity by touch also if it be possible, must accompany and complement the knowledge conveyed verbally. The verbal descriptions constitute an indispensable guide and an equally indispensable check; from the visual and tactual acquaintance comes the real knowledge and likewise the real pleasure.

This intimate acquaintance it is not hard to gain. Outside of one's own personal possessions in the way of china, there is always the opportunity to inspect and study the china treasures of one's friends, who are almost always pleased at the interest and appreciation manifested; there are the antique shops where you are at liberty to scrutinise as closely as you will; and, above all, there are the museums whose collections exist for the purpose of being studied.

Too much stress cannot be laid upon the importance of using the opportunities provided by the museums. You rarely have the chance to touch and handle the museum specimens, it is true, but they are generally well displayed for the purpose of close inspection; they usually have the advantage of indubitable authenticity and therefore serve as representative and trustworthy standards of comparison; and, finally, there are the curators to give such additional information regarding the specimens as you may require. This help they are there to give. It is a part of their duty, and a duty that is almost always cheerfully and graciously discharged.

In the matter of colour and methods of decoration, and likewise in the matter of characteristic contours, a study of the museum specimens will be quite as helpful as it is in the particulars of paste and glaze. With respect to colours, modes of decoration and characteristic contours the experience you gather with keen observation from the wares in antique shops and amongst the possessions of your friends will be even more broadening than the results of museum study, for the museums, no matter how large and complete their collections may be, cannot be expected to display every type of every phase of chinaware ever produced. Such a display would be manifestly impossible. What they aim to do is to shew in each instance the essential characteristics. Having grasped these essential characteristics, it is part of the fascination and stimulus of chinaware study to detect them, trace them and collate them in their manifold combinations which you are certain to meet with from time to time.

The marks of chinaware are often the least reliable sources of identification. While the marks, in many cases, may be accepted as trustworthy, there are many other instances in which they are positively deceptive. Time and time again the marks were deliberately forged, or else made so closely to resemble the marks found on the products of some other factory that there was obviously an intent, on the part of the makers, to deceive the public. Then, again, not a few marks have been applied at some period long subsequent to the date of manufacture. The question of authenticity of marks will be dealt with in each of the ensuing sections.

Both the fashioning and decorating of china are pre-eminently imitative arts. Many of the early Chinese shapes were imitated from earlier bronze vessels. When china began to be made in the West, Chinese shapes were universally imitated. One factory imitated another in its wares. And just so was imitation carried on in endless ways throughout the practice of the whole art. It was precisely the same with decoration. Chinese types were imitated in Japan, and when any decorator initiated a new method in Japan his style was copied in China. The West copied both with avidity, and when the decorators of one European factory originated something different from what had been done before, it was not long before most of the other factories were putting forth products decorated in almost exactly the same manner.

Despite this promiscuous imitation, certain general types of decoration became so to speak crystallised and their pronounced characteristics were unmistakable whether the pieces of porcelain on which they appeared were made in China or Japan, Bow or Worcester, Chantilly or Dresden. Very often there was just enough of the element of individual or local interpretation to add a flavour of varied interest without destroying or obscuring the identity of the mode. The more important of these families of decoration that occur almost universally will be recognised in the key-plate of decorative types (PLATE 10). Other types, less conspicuous perhaps but none the less well-defined, are noted here and there with references to examples on which they occur.

The contours of china objects are of great significance, more, indeed, than many people imagine. Quite apart from the skillful technique required for producing shapes of a certain description and the mastery of the art implied in their successful achievement, the contours indicate sundry other things. For instance, plates with rims, although they may have been made in China, were unquestionably made for export to the West. The Chinese prefer plates or dishes of a modified or flat bowl contour devoid of rims. Again, there are certain national tastes and preferences betrayed in the shapes of chinaware, some shapes being peculiarly characteristic of France and others just as peculiarly characteristic of England while, of course, there are numerous contours unmistakably Chinese which have persisted through the centuries and inspired numberless derivations in the West (v. Figs. 1 and 2).

But there is still another aspect of contour that ought not to be overlooked. While there are many shapes that have been repeated indefinitely from early times and continue to-day in unabated popularity, nevertheless the prevailing trend of "collective" contour, as exemplified by a number of different pieces of any one date, plainly reflects the design tendencies that made themselves felt everywhere in every branch of art at different well-defined periods.

If we care to make a few comparisons, we can easily see these successive design influences manifested in china contours—the swelling rotundity and symmetrical vigour of the Baroque age, when the making of European porcelain was first established upon a permanent basis; the sinuous whimsicalities and polished graces of the Rococo period; the restraint and delicacy of the Neo-Classic dominance; and, finally, the downright severity and bold insistence of the later Neo-Grec era. (PLATE 9).

Although shapes of early date may enjoy permanent favour—such, for instance, as various types of teapots (PLATE 9)—so that we cannot assume that they were made at this or that period merely on account of their contour, we *do* know, however, that certain shapes first made their appearance at certain epochs and not only enjoyed universal contemporary popularity but were also embodiments of the spirit of design dominant at that time. As striking instances of this sort of thing, the Ginori tureen (PLATE 42, B), with oval body and straight, tapering fluted legs clearly betokens the Neo-Classic feeling that pervaded every field of design in the latter part of the eighteenth century; the Derby teapot (PLATE 9, D), has a shape eloquent of Neo-Grec supremacy and echoes the contour of silver plate made at the period; the Mennecy vase (PLATE 9, J), could not have been designed before the Rococo influence of Louis XV's reign was paramount; and the Saint Cloud vase (PLATE 49, A). is plainly indicative of Baroque inspiration in the background of its maker's mind. And so it goes throughout the whole history of chinaware. The key-plate (PLATE 9), of representative period contours, affords a basis for illuminating comparisons on this score.

Finally, a word of advice about acquiring china. If a piece appeals to you by the quality of its shape and the beauty of its decoration, and if you can get it at a fair price, it is worth buying for the joy and satisfaction it will give you to possess it. Study its characteristics and settle its identification, if there is any doubt in your mind about its origin, at your leisure. On the other hand, if you are seeking a specimen of some particular make and date, and if you are not fully satisfied that the piece is what it more or less appears to be, have no hesitation in consulting a museum curator about it and settling the doubt in that manner. A museum curator of ceramics who knows his subject, and is thoroughly conversant with all the niceties of paste and glaze, will be able to give you an unbiassed attribution and, in most cases, will do so quite cheerfully. This is a precaution that is worth taking, especially if the piece in question happens to be of a sort much sought after and likely to command an high price. After all, however, while there is a certain satisfaction in acquiring a piece of highly-prized ware, prized by the professional connoisseur because of its origin and rarity, there is infinitely more satisfaction to the average person in getting something that appeals because of the intrinsic beauties it embodies. Acquaintance with and appreciation of the varied and beautiful qualities to be found in chinaware, it is one of the prime objects of this volume to stimulate.

Oriental Chinaware and the West

THE CHINAWARE OF CHINA

HISTORY. To China, the original source and home of chinaware, we naturally turn first in our survey of the porcelain art. Without knowing something of the story of china-making in the Celestial Empire, we cannot understand what took place in the development and fashioning of porcelain in the Western world.

In this section keen collectors of very old and rare Chinese and Japanese porcelains, and the habitual frequenters of museums, will miss not a few varieties of Oriental china with which they are more or less familiar. These varieties are omitted from detailed consideration and likewise from the scheme of illustration not through oversight, intentional slight nor any lacking appreciation of their manifold excellence, but because of their rarity and the great difficulty or unlikelihood of their acquisition by the average person. Furthermore, setting aside the very early wares of rare occurrence, certain choice products of later date were, and still are, eagerly sought after by the Chinese and jealously retained in China so that they almost never find their way out of the country. At the same time, vast quantities of Chinese porcelain, from the seventeenth century onward were made expressly for export. These "exports wares" were those that most profoundly influenced the porcelain of the Western world and those, likewise, that have always been most familiar to Occidentals. It seems wiser, therefore, to leave the virtually unattainable sorts to special treatises and to concentrate attention chiefly on those kinds of Oriental china more commonly met with and more possible of acquisition.

Although we are told in some quarters that the manufacture of porcelain began in China before the Christian era, there are no authentic specimens known of earlier date than those produced during the period of the Sung Dynasty (960–1279, A.D.), and these are extremely rare, although imitations and reproductions are by no means uncommon.

In surveying the history of Chinese porcelain, it is necessary to keep in mind the chief periods into which it falls under the various sucessive Imperial dynasties. The following table of dynasties and dates will prove useful as a memory peg and for general reference.

SUNG DYNASTY, 960–1279

YÜAN OR MONGOL DYNASTY, 1280–1367

MING DYNASTY, 1368–1644

CH'ING (TSING) OR MANCHU DYNASTY, 1644—Fall of Empire in Modern
Times

Emperors of the Ming Dynasty

Hung Wu	1368–1399
Chien Wên	1399–1403
Yung Lo	1403–1425
Hung Hsi	1425–1426
Hsüan Tê	1426–1436
Chêng T'ung	1436–1450
Ching T'ai	1450–1457
T'ien Shun	1457–1465
Ch'êng Hua	1465–1488
Hung Chih	1488–1506
Chêng Tê	1506–1522
Chia Ching	1522–1567
Lung Ch'ing	1567–1573
Wan Li	1573–1620
T'ai Chang	1620–1621
T'ien Ch'i	1621–1628
Ch'ung Chêng	1628–1644

Emperors of the Ch'ing or Manchu Dynasty

Shun Chih	1644–1662
*K'ang Hsi	1662–1723
Yung Cheng	1723–1736
*Ch'ien Lung	1736–1796
Chia Ch'ing	1796–1821
Tao Kuang	1821–1851

In addition to the list of the dynasties with their dates, the *emperors* of the Ming and Ch'ing dynasties, with their dates also, are given because of the generally accepted custom of speaking of old Chinese porcelain as belonging to the reigns of Wan Li or of K'ang Hsi rather than designating them merely as of the Ming or Ch'ing periods. In fact, the porcelains of the Ch'ing period are seldom or never spoken of as Ch'ing porcelains, but almost invariably are designated in a more specific manner by the name of the reigning Emperor. This usage of terminology doubtless owes its origin to the intense interest in the manufacture of porcelain shewn by the successive Emperors and to the patronage bestowed on the factories whose choicest wares were commissioned for the Imperial household.

It is altogether unnecessary to attempt to commit to memory all the foregoing dates. It is quite sufficient for the average person to remember the chief periods—Sung, Ming and Ch'ing—and their dates, and also the dates of K'ang Hsi and of Ch'ien Lung, in the Ch'ing Dynasty, before whose names asterisks are set. It was during the reigns of K'ang Hsi and Ch'ien Lung that porcelain-making received especial impetus.

THE SUNG DYNASTY

Burton summarises the distinguishing characteristics of the Sung porcelain as simple, and sometimes clumsy, in shape; the body never white, but at best greyish in colour, and occasionally drab or even reddish-brown; the walls of the pieces thick and rarely possessing the quality of translucence; the glazes imperfect and uneven in their distribution, displaying bubbles and drops; and the decoration attained by the use of coloured glazes but never by painting under the glaze.

The significant wares produced during the Sung period were the *Ju yao* (*yao* means "ware"), whose pale green surface was compared to the lightest jade and was said to feel like "congealed lard" to the touch; the *Kuan yao* of the twelfth century, with a crackled green or blue glaze; the *Chün Chou yao* with its blue glaze dappled with purple or plum-coloured splotches; and the *Lung ch'üan yao*.

Unless one is specialising in ancient Chinese porcelains, which are to be found only in the best museums and a few of the most famous private collections, and are quite unobtainable, the last named variety is the only one that needs to be considered. It is the old Celadon ware, so highly prized in the Middle Ages, and was exported in considerable quantities to India, Persia, Egypt and other parts of Asia and Africa, a small amount finding is way to Europe from the merchants of Cairo. It is this Celadon that has had so many imitations and reproductions and the genuine pieces of which are so valued to-day.

It was called Martabani ware in Persia because it was shipped from the port of Moulmein on the Gulf of Martaban, in Burmah, and by this name it was at one time more or less known in Europe. The name *Celadon,* by which it is now generally known, was later applied in allusion to the grey-green dress of the shepherd Céladon who appeared in d'Urfé's *Astrée.*

From the earliest times it was universally esteemed and admired for its beauty and was also looked upon with superstitious veneration because it was commonly believed to possess the magic property of changing colour on being brought into contact with poisoned food or drink. The protection it was thus supposed to afford against poison naturally increased the high regard in which it was held. The "Warham Bowl" bequeathed to New College, Oxford, by Archbishop Warham in 1530 is a piece of this ware.

The body of Celadon porcelain is heavy and thick and the pieces are covered with a coloured glaze, sea-green, grey-green, olive-green, blue-green or grass-green. The glaze may be either plain or crackled, but the smooth plain glaze is more usual. Although a certain amount of the Celadon ware is undecorated, the pieces generally exhibit more or less embellishment under the glaze, the decorations consisting of vigorously drawn floral *motifs* (PLATE 13) and occasionally landscapes and Taoist figures. These decorations are executed in relief, incised, engraved, or stamped into the paste, and were fashioned before the pieces were glazed and fired. The glaze is never so thick that the decoration does not shew through very plainly and the increased thickness of the glaze along the lines of the relief or the incisions often increases the depth of colour at those points.

The other notable ceramic product of the Sung period—the one exception previously mentioned before commenting on the characteristics of Celadon—is the *Ting yao* made at Ting Chou in Chihli, a product that came nearer to fulfilling the modern ideals of porcelain quality and excellence than anything previously made.

It is known in the West as *fên Ting* ("rice-flower Ting") or *pai Ting* ("White Ting"), has a thin white or yellowish-white body, and is somewhat translucent and resonant when struck. The decoration consists of delicate ornament, either incised or moulded, and the soft, whitish, tender glaze, more or less dull and opaque, sometimes gathers in "tear-drops" of a straw-coloured tinge. It may be regarded as the immediate ancestor from which sprang the finest subsequent developments in the manufacture of porcelain.

About 1126 the manufacture of *Ting yao* was transferred from Ting Chou to Ching-tê Chên, a place destined under Imperial patronage to become the greatest porcelain-making centre of the world.

YÜAN DYNASTY

During the eighty-odd years of the Mongol or Yüan Dynasty's rule in China, the development of porcelain, to a certain degree, was substantially encouraged in one place at least, and the most esteemed product of the period, the *shu fu yao,* made by Imperial command at Ching-tê Chên, it is generally conceded was a direct outcome from the earlier *Ting yao* and an improvement upon it. It was, in fact, a perfect porcelain of pure composition, *hard, white, translucent* and *resonant.* It was a splendid and perfected vehicle ready for the later steps of painted decoration in colour.

MING DYNASTY

With the Ming period, during which all the arts were encouraged and flourished, we mark a notable advance, for painted decoration in colour, both monochrome (PLATES 11 and 12), and polychrome, now appears with its manifold fascination, whereas formerly coloured glazes had supplied the sole chromatic resource.

However admirable and praiseworthy may have been the previous achievements in the making of porcelain, it is with the coming of the Ming Dynasty that we enter upon the "first really great period of

Chinese porcelain." With the exception of the Têhua factory in the province of Fuchien, whose ware will by-and-by receive specific notice, the manufacture of porcelain was now concentrated at Ching-tê Chên, all the other Sung factories having either wholly disappeared or sunk into utter insignificance during the troublous times of the Mongol domination. As a matter of fact, Ching-tê Chên became the Imperial manufactory, directly under the control and constant supervision of State officials, and it enjoyed generous Imperial patronage throughout the ensuing centuries.

This concentration of the resources and the talent of all the most skillful potters, together with the support of keenly interested and appreciative rulers, naturally conduced to developments undreamed of before. Earlier experience was treasured and the best of the preceding wares were reproduced, while new technical methods were devised and new forms of decoration were evolved.

Nearly all the fine Chinese porcelains, from the beginning of the Ming period onward, with which we are familiar in Europe and America have come from the kilns of Ching-tê Chên at one stage or another of its remarkable career, although in some instances the articles made there were decorated at other places, such as Canton, before being exported to the china-loving West. The only significant exceptions are the "white wares" (PLATE 14, C), of Fuchien, for in some way the factory at Têhua managed to retain its identity and independent existence despite the centralisation of all other efforts at Ching-tê Chên.

The first advance in colour decoration was to fashion the design with the different members of the pattern isolated by raised lines in the body. The spaces within these lines were then filled with glazes of different colours. The process seems to have been suggested by the method used for executing designs in cloisonné enamel. Pieces of this sort, attributed to the beginning of the Ming period, are heavy and oftentimes clumsy both in shape and material. The raised lines, defining the different portions of the pattern, are left unglazed and virtually silhouette the figures; the ornament usually consists of diaper patterns, flowers, animals or human figures, boldly drawn and rather crudely, while the glazes used are generally of three colours—ochre yellow, turquoise blue and purple, although an opaque white glaze is sometimes employed also. Contrary to the usual Chinese practice, pieces of this sort appear to have been first fired to a biscuit stage and then decorated with the coloured glazes afterwards, the second firing for the glazes being at a much lower temperature than the first.

The very thin, delicate and translucent white porcelain, developed and refined under the Mongol Dynasty from the *Ting yao* of the Sung period, also was further elaborated in its refinement until the so-called "bodiless" porcelain was produced. This fragile triumph of the potter's daring, patience and adroitness is commonly known as "egg-shell" porcelain and has been made practically without interruption from the reign of Yung Lo, 1403–1425. In the finest specimens of this sort of porcelain the substance of the body or paste is so thin that it seems as though there could be no clay left between the inner and outer layers of glaze.

Notwithstanding the exceeding thinness of this ware, many specimens were enriched with intricate designs incised with a steel tool in the air-dried paste before it was glazed and fired. The best early egg-shell pieces bearing designs executed in this manner were usually of pure white and the ornament was barely visible beneath the glaze unless they were held up against the light or filled with liquid. There is a very early white bowl of this ware in the British Museum with five-clawed dragons traced in white slip under the glaze. When this delicate bit of porcelain is held up to the light the dragons appear like a water-mark in paper.

Another method of decorating this thin white porcelain, requiring the utmost delicacy and deftness of handling, was contrived at about the same time. This is known as the "rice-grain" decoration (PLATE 14, A) where small pieces the size and shape of a grain of rice are cut out of the thin walls of the piece so that the little piecings form the pattern desired. This is done whilst the body is in its air-dried state; it is then glazed and fired, the glaze filling the piercings and leaving them absolutely transparent.

The perfect production of such articles eloquently testifies to the degree of technical proficiency the Chinese potters had reached by the beginning of the fifteenth century.

The production of blue and white ware (PLATES 11 and 12), with the decorations painted in underglaze blue, is the next epoch-making event in the history of Chinese porcelain. Painting with underglaze blue seems not to have been practised to any appreciable extent in China prior to the beginning of the fifteenth century, and it is not at all impossible that the Chinese may have derived this method of decoration from the Persians who had made use of it centuries previously.

The underglaze blue pigment is made from cobalt and the native Chinese supply of this material is of an impure and inferior sort, the presence of manganese and other impurities producing a dull, greyish tone. The cobalt used by the Persians, on the other hand, was very pure and brilliant in colour. Early in the fifteenth century the Chinese seem to have obtained their supply of cobalt from the Persians, or from the people of some other Moslem country, for they always speak of it as Mohammedan blue.

This rich sapphire blue appears in the blue and white porcelain of the reigns of Hsüan-Tê (1426–1435) and of Ch'êng Hua (1465–1488), the early Ming porcelain most highly prized by the Chinese connoisseurs themselves, while the blue and white of the reign of Yung Lo (1403–1425), with its inferior grey-blue, the Chinese collectors consider poor by comparison.

The supply of Mohammedan blue failed in the latter part of the fifteenth century and the Chinese potters were driven back upon their own native materials, with a resultant change in the character of the colour, a change decidedly for the worse. However, during the reign of Chêng Tê (1506–1522) a further supply of Mohammedan blue was obtained and the blue and white ware of this period is exceptionally fine.

This Mohammedan blue was used in two shades (PLATES 11 and 12), and there was absolute harmony and balance between the blues in their distribution and between them and the tone of the glaze. This complete harmony of colouring is one of the factors that renders the old Ming blue and white so delicious in quality and so satisfying. The blue painting of the later Ming period, about the time of the reign of

Wan Li, is not graduated nor shaded (PLATE 12, A), but applied throughout with the full pigment. Consequently, at its greatest intensity, it produces an almost overwhelming impression; at its best, its decorative effect is amazingly fine.

Early in the Ming period, too, the Chinese potters succeeded in producing a wonderfully beautiful underglaze red from oxidised copper. At first it was used as a ground or solid all-over colour for the outside of such articles as bowls and cups. but later came to be employed for painting designs (PLATE 23, A), and was then covered with an especially fine white glaze. An early Chinese connoisseur, in describing a piece of porcelain decorated with this deservedly famous underglaze red, speaks of "three red fishes on a white ground, pure as driven snow, the fish boldly outlined and red as fresh blood, all with colour so brilliant as to dazzle the eyes."

A few, but only a few, examples of porcelain bearing this underglaze red are to be found in collections on both sides of the Atlantic. Later in the Ming period this excellent red disappeared and its place was taken by another red, an inferior on-glaze colour derived from iron.

In the latter part of the sixteenth century, or the beginning of the seventeenth, as the Ming dynasty was nearing its end, variety in the design and technique of colour decoration comes more and more into evidence. The beginnings of polychrome decoration seem to have been well on their way by the reign of Chia Ching (1522–1567) for the efforts of the preceding reign (Chêng Tê, 1506–1522) in that direction were continued and we find polychrome decoration in reserve on a monochrome ground. There were also some designs wrought altogether in gold on a solid-coloured ground of red or green.*

---

* As early as the reign of Ch'êng Hua (1465–1488) definite attempts at polychrome decoration seem to have met with a degree of success. Hannover calls attention to the effects produced by the use of different-coloured glazes in combination on the same piece, and also points out incipient efforts at *painted* polychrome decoration, instancing several pieces recorded and commented upon by Chinese connoisseurs and antiquaries, to wit, a wine-cup with a border of green leaves and red grapes and likewise one of the so-called "chicken-cups," a cup on which chickens, insects and flowers are depicted in natural colours. Of these no examples are extant and we must rest content with the recorded statement. Pointing to this as a new colouristic development, Hannover observes: "Here, evidently, is one of the earliest attempts in the direction of the so-called *wu ts'ai*, the complete five-colour brush painting of the later Ming period."

By the time of Wan Li (1573–1620) we find firmly established the practice of painting with enamel colours on the finished fired glaze, these on-glaze paintings being fused into the surface of the glaze by re-firing at a temperature lower than that of the initial firing.

There were two well-recognised schemes of polychrome decoration with enamel colours painted on the glaze—the three-colour scheme and the five-colour scheme. The first, known to the Chinese as *San ts'ai*, was a combination of green, purple and yellow. In the time of the Emperor Wan Li this scheme was amplified and became known as the Wan Li *wu ts'ai* or five-colour scheme, consisting of the green, purple and yellow already mentioned, in addition to underglaze blue and the on-glaze red, derived from iron oxide, that had taken the place of the earlier copper red. From the conspicuous presence and frequent predominance of vigorous green in these three- and five-colour schemes of enamel-painted decoration, many of the pieces so decorated are classified as belonging to the *famille verte* (PLATE 22, B), which reached its fullest expansion early in the reign of K'ang Hsi.

Although Chinese porcelain, to some degree, had been exported for centuries previously, during the fifteenth and sixteenth centuries this export trade increased steadily and rapidly until, by the end of the sixteenth century, there was not only the Persian, Indian and Egyptian trade to be considered, but whole cargoes of blue and white ware were sent to Europe. As we shall see, a little further on, the trade relations with foreign countries caused a profound reaction upon Chinese porcelain both in form and in the manner of decoration.

CH'ING OR MANCHU DYNASTY

The political disturbances that attended the passing of the Ming Dynasty and the establishment of the Ch'ing Manchus were unfavourable to any material progress at the Ching-tê Chên factory, but when order was restored and the Emperor K'ang Hsi was securely set upon the throne in 1662 there began the golden age of Chinese porcelain. During the reigns of K'ang Hsi (1662–1723) and of his two successors, Yung Cheng (1723–1736) and Ch'ien Lung (1736–1796), Chinese porcelain reached the high-water mark of its development in technical perfection, the grace of forms produced, variety of output, and beauty of decoration. Both K'ang Hsi and his grandson Ch'ien Lung took a deep interest in the porcelain factory and their intelligent patronage was an important factor in assuring the triumphs scored during this long period of uninterrupted prosperity and progress.

It would be easier to enumerate the sorts of porcelain that were *not* made during this epoch than to chronicle all the divers kinds that were produced. Nearly all of the earlier types that distinguished preceding centuries were duplicated in addition to the output of the wares that especially characterised the eighteenth century. It is just as well to bear in mind that the great bulk of the Oriental porcelain with which we are acquainted, both in private possession and in museum collections, in Europe and America alike, was made at Ching-tê Chên, in the prolific eighteenth century and the latter part of the seventeenth and falls under the general classifications of either K'ang Hsi or Ch'ien Lung china.

Without entering into a full catalogue of the distinctive K'ang Hsi and Ch'ien Lung products of Ching-tê Chên, which will be noted in the ensuing sections, we should remember that within the limits of this period, besides the well-known varieties of blue and white ware, the Chinese potters put forth the sorts of porcelain known as the *famille noir,* the *famille verte* (PLATE 22, B), in its ultimate development, and the *famille rose* (PLATE 22, A), the last named the most beautiful of all the groups designated by their distinctive methods of colouration. To this era also belong the "powder blue" porcelains (PLATE 8, A), and that large and highly diversified group generally called "Lowestoft" (PLATES 25–34), which was made to the order of foreign merchants and decorated, oftentimes with armorial bearings or monograms (PLATES 27, 28, B and 31, B), for individual customers in England and America. This last mentioned type of chinaware has been mistakenly termed "Lowestoft" although by far the greatest part of it was never within miles of the little East Anglian town whose name the general public, aided and abetted by many antique dealers, insist upon attaching to it.

The facts about the so-called "Lowestoft" china, made and decorated in China, have been set forth plainly and often. Nevertheless, china-lovers time and again still evince such hazy notions about the subject that it seems advisable to stress anew the points that ought to be kept in mind.

First of all, unfortunate nomenclature has caused no end of confusion. Only recently, a lady who has a goodly quantity of this beautiful Oriental porcelain—choice pieces, all of it—was visibly hurt when it was referred to as "so-called 'Lowestoft'" and continued upset until it was fully and carefully explained to her that there was nothing spurious about her prized possessions, which were really far finer than anything that ever came from the little East Anglian pottery whose name unfortunately has wrongly and quite illogically become attached to some of the most exquisite products of the Chinese potters' art.

To call it "Chinese 'Lowestoft'" does not help very much. It would be far better to call it "East India Company" china, or simply "East India" china, as it was once very generally called, because the several East India Companies were mainly responsible in the first place for its getting to Europe and America. Even after a brisk China Trade grew up independently between the United States and Canton, the term "East India" china continued long in use in America. How the name "Lowestoft" came to be attached to a kind of chinaware with which the Lowestoft pottery had only the remotest, and shadowy—one might almost say furtive and dishonest—connection, is set forth in the "Lowestoft" section.

We know that Chinese porcelain tea sets, coffee sets, dessert services, dinner services, vases, jars and other objects of occasional use or ornament found their way to England in considerable and increasing quantities from the second half of the seventeenth century onward. These shipments included the "export" porcelain of the contemporary types and also, in due time, the so-called "Chinese 'Lowestoft.'"

At exactly what time chinaware of these several types, and especially the Oriental "Lowestoft," first appeared in the American Colonies, it is hard to say. Of course, after the establishment of direct trade between America and China, the quantities of chinaware brought hither from the Orient appreciably increased. It is easy enough to name the date when such direct trade began and to mention the American ports that subsequently engaged most actively in the China Trade, but long prior to the beginning of this immediate commerce—and far earlier that many people imagine—Oriental "Lowestoft," as well as other types of Oriental chinaware, inevitably came to America; for whatever luxuries and elegancies of household appointment England had, we know well-to-do Colonials also had in Philadelphia, Boston, Newport, Providence, New York, Charleston and in the great country houses of Maryland and Virginia.

In Camden, New Jersey, is still preserved the little Oriental china tea set, with decorations in underglaze blue and red, from which William Penn drank when he went to have tea with Friend Cooper; that fixes the date not later than 1701, when Penn went back to England, never to return to his "Holy Experiment." How much earlier Friend Cooper had the tea set is not known. And this is only one of numerous similar instances of carefully treasured porcelain heirlooms.

In 1720, the Emperor K'ang Hsi licensed certain Canton merchants to deal with the "foreign devils," as all foreigners were generally called by the Chinese. This Imperial consent to trade carried sundry restrictions and conditions. For one thing, the Chinese merchants had to be responsible for the devils' good behaviour while they were on Chinese soil, and for their payment of customs dues. The Canton merchants who had these trading licenses

"promptly built a series of thirteen establishments on the bank of the Pearl River, between the river and the high walls of the city in a section that was already considerably built up but was not regarded as a part of Canton proper, being without the walls. These they leased to foreign merchants, generally the East India Companies, and here all foreigners resided and also carried on their business, being strictly circumscribed in their daily life by Imperial regulations that forbade them to pass the gates of Canton, to go upon the river, to ride in sedan chairs, or to have Chinese servants."

These thirteen buildings the Chinese called "hongs," meaning *places of business;* the European called them "factories."

The chinaware made at Ching-tê Chên was sent four hundred miles to Canton, where the Agents at the Factories bought and shipped it to England and the Continent. From the Ming period onward, porcelain-making centred in Ching-tê Chên. The Imperial porcelain factory was there and besides, there were numerous factories in private hands. In fact, the concentration of the industry at Ching-tê Chên left no other porcelain factories in China to be particularly considered, except at the small and relatively unimportant centre of Tehua in Fukien province, where the *blanc de Chine* was made. How tremendous must have been the porcelain output at Ching-tê Chên, one can infer from the description of it given by Père d'Entrecolles in the time of the Emperor K'ang Hsi:

"The town was then about four miles around, with a population of about a million people, all, practically speaking, connected in some way or other with the porcelain industry. As mentioned, there had previously been 300 kilns; now there were 3000, which, especially in the evening, gave the place a characteristic appearance of its own. To anyone coming from the surrounding mountains, it would look as if the town were on fire. And it happened occasionally that it did catch fire; for the kilns were a constant source of danger, and large portions of the town were repeatedly burned down. In the southern part stood the Imperial factory established by the first Ming Emperors. But, in addition, there were innumerable private factories in the town, with an enormous export trade . . ."

A good deal of the china was sent "in the white" (undecorated) from Ching-tê Chên to Canton. There, the Agents at the Factories could choose from samples such decorations as they wished. Then the Canton painters, who were many and skillful, painted the decorations and the china was refired in the Canton enamelling kilns before shipment.

This practice soon led to sending out to the Agents of the Factories in Canton special orders to be filled for individual customers in Europe. Designs to be copied often accompanied these orders for dinner services, dessert services, tea sets and the like. These designs sent out from Europe affected both decorations and chinaware shapes. Some of the articles required—such as tureens, cream jugs or pierced fruit baskets—were wholly foreign to Chinese usage and it was necessary to supply models for the potters at Ching-tê Chên to work from. In this way European shapes of both china and silver came to be reproduced in Chinese porcelain, shapes that were altogether non-Chinese.

In the matter of decoration, the sketches sent out were in colour, so

that the Chinese enamel-colour painters had adequate chromatic guid-
ance. They not only copied the *motifs* of the Renaissance arabesques
and border scrolls, ribbons and knots, the dainty floral swags and sprigs
of Bow and Bristol, the scattered posies of Meissen and other familiar
European devices, but also faithfully reproduced the heraldic charges
and tinctures for the sets of armorial china.

From both England and the American Colonies went orders for dinner services of armorial china, and these orders were carefully fulfilled.
In the British Museum is preserved an example of a set of Oriental
armorial china made as early as 1731, along with a sketch of the design
and the correctly emblasoned arms sent out for reproduction, and the
shipper's invoice, dated at Canton at the time of shipment thence. This
set would undoubtedly be classified in the category of armorial Chinese
"Lowestoft."

As a variant or alternate to the armorial blasonings, there were monograms and cyphers, which occupied the same place in the arrangement
of the decoration as the heraldic achievements would have taken. The
border decoration of the heraldic china was often quite simple and the
undecorated surfaces of the porcelain with its slightly grey-blue tinge,
and frequently the rippled or "orange-peel" texture of the glaze, made
an effective foil for the vigorous colouring of the heraldic blasons.

To facilitate the ordering of sets of Chinese tableware, the East India
Companies at Canton sent "pattern chests" of china to their home offices. Customers could then pick out from these what they wished to
order. The single pieces in these sets often showed a number of patterns for decoration to choose from; for instance, one plate might exhibit four distinct designs, each quarter of the plate being decorated
with a different pattern. These sample pieces are rarely seen nowadays,
but once in a long while they do turn up.

Notwithstanding all the special orders sent out to China, and all the
decorated chinaware shipped thence to Europe to meet the general demand, a considerable quantity of undecorated chinaware ("in the white"
or "in blank") was exported and found its way to both England and
the Continent. English and Continental china painters then decorated
it with designs in enamel colours and it found a ready market. Not

only was some of the "East India" or Chinese "Lowestoft" china decorated in this way, but some of the *blanc de Chine* or white ware of
Tehua in Fuchien (never intended to be decorated in colour) met with
similar embellishment—quite superfluous, if not indeed impertinent, in
the latter case—for European customers. This over-decorated ware is
spoken of as "clobbered."

When direct commerce between China and the United States started
up right after the close of the Revolutionary War, special orders from
America for Chinese "Lowestoft" greatly increased in number. One
stimulus to the enlarged American demand lay in the fact that Oriental
chinaware now cost less than it did when it had to be carried first to
England and then reshipped, with all the incident duties and other
charges. The captains and supercargoes of ships in the American China
Trade were constantly bringing back dinner services, dessert services,
tea sets and punch bowls in fulfillment of the commissions personally
entrusted to them.

The *Empress of China,* sailing from New York in February, 1784,
bound for Canton, is reputed the first American ship to have engaged
in the direct China Trade, although Captain Walter Sims—a retired
sea-captain who bought China Hall, on the Delaware above Philadelphia, on the departure of Andreas Everardus van Braam-Houckgeest
for Holland—is said to have brought the first Chinese "Lowestoft"
tableware direct from China to America in 1772. (This latter statement
and date are interesting, but need verification.)

By 1789 fifteen ships flying the American flag were trading to Canton.
Illuminating data on the American China Trade will be found in K. S.
Latourette's *Voyages of American Ships to China, 1784–1844,* published
in the "Transactions of the Connecticut Academy of Arts and Sciences,"
Volume XXVIII. The China Trade was at its height in the late eighteenth century and in the early years of the nineteenth. Much of the
best, and certainly the greatest quantity, of Chinese "Lowestoft" came
in to grace American households during the Federal era while Duncan
Phyfe was making furniture and Latrobe and his pupils were building
houses and public edifices that rivalled the contemporary Regency creations in the Mother Country.

In 1788 Washington's celebrated "Cincinnati" dinner service arrived, a very large service presented by the Society of the Cincinnati to their former esteemed commander and first president. The central decoration of each piece was the angel of fame holding the emblem of the society; there was a rich "Fitzhugh" border in blue. This set, of course, was one of the very numerous special orders sent to China.

As J. A. Lloyd Hyde truly points out in his excellent book, *Oriental Lowestoft,* "by the beginning of the nineteenth century, there was little left of Chinese influence but the paste and the glaze" in the Oriental porcelain exported. The shapes of tableware had been completely adapted to European and American requirements. As for decoration, not only were the "ornaments designed and placed in a way that was quite foreign to the Chinese taste," but the *subjects* chosen for the main emphasis of decoration were themselves wholly of Western inspiration and were either intended to mark the memory of some historic event or else reflected the characteristics, tastes and habits of those for whom the chinaware was made.

One of the most illuminating instances of this total shift to Western inclinations in decoration can be seen in a very large—and unique—set of tableware, made and decorated in China on explicit order from America, and sent to Philadelphia in the height of the "Lowestoft" period. (PLATE 33.) The porcelain has unmistakably all the physical characteristics of Chinese "Lowestoft"; the decoration does not fall into any category of the familiar "Lowestoft" types, heraldic, floral, marine or otherwise. About 1808, a young Quakeress, possessed of an urge to sketch, drew a spavined cow obviously afflicted also with the colic; standing beside the dolorous animal, the farmer; the background, a cottage, trees and other rural properties. To her brother, who was going supercargo on a ship in the China Trade, the artist entrusted this masterpiece with orders to have it reproduced entirely in black on a large set of tableware. The Chinese decorators, evidently feeling the embellishment was a bit too sombre, tried to lighten the gloom by putting a thin band of burnished gilding on the rim of each piece. After a year's lapse, during which the Quaker artist and her spouse had been getting "principled" to plainer and plainer views, when the supercargo brought the complete set of chinaware back and showed them a plate with the gilded rim, artist and husband gave one severe, disapproving look, said, "Much too gay for a plain Friend," and gave supercargo brother the whole set. Most of it remains in the possession of three of the supercargo's descendants.

Fox-hunting, horse-racing and cock-fighting were sports dear to the hearts of our eighteenth- and early nineteenth-century forebears. Punch bowls and other pieces of chinaware became appropriate vehicles of sporting subjects, and designs were sent out to China, along with the orders, so that the Chinese porcelain-painters could correctly depict the desired scenes, generally enclosed within round or oval medallions, the rest of the decoration on rims and the like following customary usage in colouring and detail. An excellent example is the celebrated Tally Ho punch bowl the members of the old Gloucester Fox Hunting Club (which became the parent of Philadelphia's renowned City Troop) presented to Captain Samuel Morris, at some time prior to 1797; on one side of it a huntsman is taking a fence, on the other his long-necked barb is jumping a ditch.

Besides the hunting and other sporting "Lowestoft" china, there were sets with masonic devices; marine subjects lent themselves kindly to pourtrayal by the deft Chinese painters, and punch bowls with ships in full sail on their sides were in much esteem; occasionally decorations carried unmistakable political allusion; and specific events were sometimes recorded, as in the sets of tableware known to have been made to commemorate Washington's death.

In April, 1796, Andreas Everardus van Braam-Houckgeest, that extraordinary Dutch diplomat, traveller, and long-time resident of China, landed in Philadelphia with his *entourage* and a cargo of Chinese treas-ures, bringing with him a tea set of Chinese "Lowestoft" he had especially had made and decorated as a present for Mrs. Washington.

"In the centre of each piece appears a medallion of gold bearing the monogram M.W. in square architectural lettering, encircled by a wreath of green leaves, beneath it on a flowing ribbon the motto: *Decus Et Tutamen Ab Illo*. From this central motif radiate the shafts of a sunburst which, terminating in fifteen points, lead the eye to the corresponding fifteen links of a circular chain, thus explaining the motto. In each of these links is the name of one of the fifteen states forming the Union in 1792. Around and about it all, toward the outer edge of the china, is a serpent painted in blue and gold, holding its tail in its mouth, a symbol of unity."

Some pieces of this set are still in the White House, and a descendant of van Braam-Houckgeest has a specimen. The design has been twice copied in France (on French china); once for the Centennial in 1876, and once for the Chicago World's Fair in 1893.

"Lowestoft" punch bowls, with appropriate and highly individual decorations executed on them, were favourite objects for special orders. One such is the three-gallon Pennsylvania Hospital Punch Bowl, presented to the Hospital by Joseph Saunders Lewis in April, 1802, and still carefully preserved in Philadelphia. On opposite sides of the exterior, enclosed in long ovals, is repeated a view of the Hospital, painted in colours. The circular "English Views" (one of them, at least, happens to be American) on the other two sides are done in sepia. The festooned rim is in dark blue and orange, picked out with gold.

Another especially noteworthy punch bowl is that made for Colonel Richard Varick, of New Jersey, now preserved by the Washington Association of New Jersey, at Morristown. The decoration consists of a most meticulously and minutely reproduced copy of the Colonel's certificate of membership in the Society of the Cincinnati. This, of course, is necessarily in black, but all the accompanying symbolic devices are in brilliant colour and gilding so that the total effect of the decoration is exceptionally rich. The generous eight-gallon punch bowl, presented to the Corporation of the City of New York in 1812 by General Jacob Morton, has the arms of the City of New York on one side of the exterior, with the arms of the United States on the opposite side; on the other two sides, between the heraldic devices, are views of the city. The whole interior of the bowl is covered with a view of New York City from Brooklyn, done in full colour.

An even larger "Lowestoft" punch bowl is a greatly cherished possession of the "State in Schuylkill," more commonly known in Philadelphia as the "Fish House," the oldest social club with an uninterrupted existence in the English-speaking world. In 1822 (the club was then ninety years old), one of the members, Captain Charles Ross, a Philadelphia shipping merchant in the China Trade, gave the club this mammoth bowl (it holds nine gallons) that he had had made in China. Inside the bowl, near the gilded rim at the top, are swimming appropriately a number of perch painted in black. This bowl is dedicated to holding the justly famed Fish House Punch, that innocent-tasting but insidious brew. It was from this punch bowl that the Marquis de la Fayette was regaled when he was the club's guest on July 21st, 1825.

The border line between Chinese "Lowestoft" and much of the other contemporary Chinese porcelain is so faint, and the misnomer itself subject to such flexible interpretation, that it is often somewhat puzzling to say just what is, and what is not, to be reckoned Chinese "Lowestoft." One sometimes feels that Nankin and "Fitzhugh," for example, ought to be included in the so-called "Lowestoft" family, in spite of the highly specialising tendency of many collectors; they are certainly the closest of kin. The chief difference is that, whereas the sundry types and subtypes of Chinese "Lowestoft" have to a greater or less degree embodied Western ideas in the matter of decoration, both Nankin and "Fitzhugh" have retained intact (almost without exception) their purely Chinese manner and *motifs* of decoration. Being both made and decorated in underglaze colours at Ching-tê Chên, they escaped the impress of Western decorative impulses to which the porcelain decorated in enamel colours at Canton was subjected.

The familiar blue and white Nankin, or Nankeen, china seems to have got its name in part from the place of shipment—no porcelain was made at Nankin—in part, also because the Chinese themselves always called ware with this decoration "Nankeen" and were in the habit of using that name as a badge of distinction.

For the name "Fitzhugh"—applied to chinaware decorated with a trelliswork, split-pomegranate and butterfly border, the central composition consisting of four separate groups of flowers and symbols symmetrically arranged about a medallion charged with a monogram—divers explanations are given. One is that the first person to order a set of china thus decorated was named Fitzhugh. Another is that "Fitzhugh" is a corruption of Foo Chow—so pronounced by a New England sea-captain's wife when answering a question about the Chinese port whence her husband had brought in a lot of chinaware of this type. "Fitzhugh" besides being decorated in blue, occurs also in sepia, brown, bright green and orange-red. The name seems to be wholly of American application.

The blue and white Canton ware, so popular in the United States in the early nineteenth century, owes its decoration to adaptations from earlier Nankin designs. Much of it, made in the factories at Shao King west of Canton, where the Canton ginger-jars were made, is of coarser paste than the wares of Ching-tê Chên, and the decoration of the later Canton is often carelessly done.

The so-called "Medallion" china—completely covered with reserved panels in which multi-coloured mandarin figures and domestic scenes usually alternated with bird and flower compositions, with foliated and floral bands and borders, in which gold and green predominated, separating the panels—was a type of "export" ware that became popular in America about the late 1820's and continued in favour for a long time thereafter.

For detailed consideration of other types of Chinese porcelain (of the late seventeenth, eighteenth and early nineteenth centuries) which the china-lover is likely to meet with outside of museums, the reader is referred to the Bibliography.

THE BODY. The body or paste of the oldest Chinese porcelains is heavy, opaque, crude and often full of impurities to such an extent that many authorities are disinclined to consider it truly porcelain. It is not until well on towards the end of the Sung period that a body appears which all agree is undeniably porcelain, a body *hard, white, translucent* and *resonant.*

It is worth noting that the Chinese themselves apparently attach no particular value to the quality of *translucence,* which we set so much store by. In their estimation, *resonance* is of far greater moment in judging the physical merits of a piece.

The body or paste of Chinese porcelain is by no means of uniform quality, even at any one period. All sorts of variations are to be found from the coarse greyish, reddish or yellowish pastes of the very early period to the fine *pure white, hard, translucent* and *resonant* body of the egg-shell or "bodiless" porcelain perfected in the early Ming period. Furthermore, we know that at Ching-tê Chên, in the early part of the eighteenth century, various grades of porcelain were being made at the same time. The finest was composed of equal parts of kaolin and *petuntse,* while in the composition of an inferior kind there were four parts of kaolin to six parts of *petuntse.* The least proportion of kaolin that could be used was one part to three parts of *petuntse.*

In many pieces of the purest Chinese porcelain the walls are thick so that the paste is not translucent except at the thinnest parts. The colour of the paste is affected by the purity or impurity of the ingredients entering into the composition, and also by the peculiarities of different local formulas which regulate the proportions of the ingredients employed in mixing the clay. The later paste for the finest wares of the Ching-tê Chên factory, during the reigns of K'ang Hsi and Ch'ien Lung, is pure milky white, while the paste of Fuchien is characterised by a creamy or ivory tinge (PLATE 14, C), and the finest pieces betray a slightly pinkish or rosy glow.

The term "soft paste" is often heard in connexion with Chinese porcelain. The term thus applied is absolutely misleading as to the nature of the porcelain in question. There was never any soft paste porcelain made in China. The so-called "soft paste" of the Ch'ing period seems to have been compounded with such a proportion of fusible ingredients that it might be porcelainised at a lower temperature than the ware whose body was compounded in the usual way. The modification appears to have been caused by the addition of steatite or soapstone. Unlike the majority of Chinese porcelain, which was fired and glazed at one operation, the so-called "soft paste" porcelain was first fired to the biscuit stage, then painted with its decoration, coated with a lead glaze and fired again at a temperature lower than that of the first firing.

It is highly probable that this was the variety of porcelain mentioned in his letters by the Jesuit, Père d'Entrecolles to whose admirable account we are indebted for much of our information anent the manufacture of Chinese porcelain. He states that this kind of china was remarkably light in weight and that the painted decorations resembled paintings on vellum in their neatness and precision. These are qualities that mark the so-called "soft paste" Chinese porcelain whose surface is somewhat pitted or stippled in appearance and of a pale greyish tint.

The body colour of a good deal of old Chinese porcelain with blue decoration, or with decoration in which blue predominates, as in the imitations of the Japanese Imari ware, appears to be of a slightly bluish tinge like the colour of very poor skimmed-milk from which every atom of cream has been extracted. This tinge is not the body colour but is caused in reality, by the presence of smalt (pulverised cobalt glass) in the glaze, and was purposely introduced for the general harmony of colour. When such a piece is chipped or broken, or where it is not wholly covered by the glaze, the body or paste will be found to be hard, smooth and white.

THE GLAZE. The characteristic composition of the glaze of Chinese porcelain, and the manner of its application, have been noted in the section on The Making of Chinaware. There are, however, certain amplifications of the statements made there that must be added at this point.

Manipulation of the glaze unquestionably causes a great measure of the beauty and charm of not a few types of old Chinese porcelain. In certain types, indeed, the body is merely a vehicle to give shape and stability while the glaze plays the rôle of both decoration and finish. The glazes were often wholly responsible for the colour effects and were either applied to the whole piece in one coating or several different glazes were applied at different places in order to produce varied patterns and colour results.

The crackled glaze, which is so highly esteemed and which occurs in varied forms that constitute decorations in themselves, was in all likelihood the result of accident in the first instance. The crackling was caused by the glaze cooling and contracting more rapidly than the body underneath it, thus breaking into sections separated by fine surface lines or cracks.

Having discovered the cause of this phenomenon, the potters turned it to good account and were soon able to produce crackled ware at will and, what was more, even to regulate the size of the crackle which came to be designated as large, medium and small, the last being graduated from the size of trout scales down to a semblance of fish roe. The effect of the large and medium-sized crackling was sometimes accentuated by rubbing either red pigment or India ink into the minute cracks.

Vari-colored or "transmutation" glazes were at first the result of accident but were soon brought wholly under the potter's control. As these glazes, along with the other coloured glazes, some of which have already been mentioned, were really decorations quite as much as they were the bodily finish and protection of the ware, they will be more fully noticed under Types of Decoration.

The glaze is transparent and, when perfectly applied, is evenly distributed over the whole surface of an article. It is only on pieces where the mechanical technique is not perfect that the glaze runs and collects in "tear-drops."

When quite pure and perfect, the glaze is colourless and absolutely smooth of surface. When it shews a slight tinge of colour, this tinge is either the result of intent or else caused by some impurity in the composition of the glaze.

The slightly dappled, vellum or matt-like appearance of the glaze on the so-called "soft paste" Chinese porcelain has already been noted. This dappled or matt-like surface of the glaze is often to be seen also on the so-called "Lowestoft" china.

There is a monochrome coloured glaze seemingly peculiar to the Ming period. It is a smooth glaze uncracked, coated over a grey or white crackled porcelain, and is much esteemed in tones of green.

ARTICLES MADE AND CONTOUR. The articles commonly made of porcelain included vessels for temple or sacrificial use, the vessels for domestic shrines, all manner of writing paraphernalia, every description of vase, jar and bowl for flowers—for the Chinese are an essentially flower-loving people and require a large supply and variety of such things—wine-cups, trays, teapots, tea-caddies, teacups, plates, platters, bowls, bottles, drum or barrel-shaped garden seats, flower-pots, lanthorns, fish-bowls, covered jars for sweetmeats or ginger, plaques for the embellishment of furniture, figures or statuettes, and an whole host of minor odds and ends.

Besides these, there were the table services and other miscellaneous articles made for general export to Europe and America, and oftentimes made to the special order of individual patrons.

The native Chinese shapes of the earliest porcelain pieces were in many cases derived from still earlier bronze or brass articles, such as various bronze temple vessels, and they perpetuated the forms of their prototypes. These pieces usually possessed grace and directness of contour; they were always interesting. A number of the characteristic Chinese shapes are given in the accompanying line cuts.

Increasing trade relations between China, on the one hand, and Persia and India, on the other, especially from the beginning of the fifteenth century onward, resulted in a multiplied variety of contours. Persian and Indian shapes were gradually adopted—although the Chinese have ever been notoriously conservative—and became in time a part of the Chinese contour *répertoire,* while certain other shapes were employed almost exclusively for articles manufactured for export to the countries just mentioned and apparently made little appeal to native Chinese taste. Some of the representative Persian shapes adopted and naturalised by the Chinese potters are shewn on the accompanying pages, especially in Figure 2.

In addition to the shapes obviously derived from bronze vessels and continued in pottery and porcelain, there were other naturalistic shapes, suited to plastic rendering, that the potters devised and perfected at an early date. Early in the Ming period, along with the severe contours of ancient bronzes translated into porcelain, we find lively imitations of animals, fruit and flowers. The potters displayed great aptitude in adapting these forms to expression in their own medium.

When Oriental china began to be shipped in large quantities to Europe, a certain reflex influence set in from the Western purchasers. It was not long before the customers of the different East India companies gave orders to be fulfilled in China, and accompanied these orders with patterns and designs of what they desired to have executed for them at the factory of Ching-tê Chên. These commissions the Chinese cheerfully and obligingly fulfilled oftentimes giving the new articles they were fashioning a peculiarly Oriental (PLATE 25, B) interpretation, but

FIG. 1. Characteristic Chinese porcelain shapes

FIG. 2.   Characteristic Chinese porcelain shapes

for their own use and pleasure they held to the time-honoured forms to which they had been accustomed and never really adopted the Western shapes as they had some of those derived from Persia several centuries previously.

TYPES OF DECORATION. The types of decoration for Chinese porcelain during the period with which we are chiefly concerned—that is, from about the middle of the seventeenth century to a little before the middle of the nineteenth—were exceedingly varied, and it will conduce to a comprehensive grasp of the subject if we follow for the most part the classification made many years ago by Sir Wollaston Franks when he arranged the collection in the British Museum. This classification is so logical and all-inclusive that it has very generally been followed as a standard ever since. The classification makes five main divisions and is as follows:

A. *Decoration depending on the Glaze alone.*
    1. Glazes plain white or creamy.
    2. Coloured Glazes uniform in tint.
    3. Flambé and other Glazes, varying locally in Colour, but the whole applied at the same time.

B. *Decoration in Slip, generally white, over the Glaze.*

C. *Decoration with Underglaze Colours.*
    1. Copper-red.
    2. Cobalt-blue. (This includes all the "blue and white" ware.)

D. *Glazes of more than one Colour, painted on the previously fired biscuit.*

E. *Decoration with Enamel Colours over the Glaze.*
    1. Coral.
    2. *Famille noire.*
    3. *Famille verte.*
    4. *Famille rose.*
    5. Chrysanthemum and Peony.
    6. "Mandarin."
    7. "India."
    8. Chinese Imari and Kakiyemon.
    9. Reserved Panels in Ground Colour.
    10. Jesuit.
    11. "Lowestoft."

The foregoing classification does not make a separate division of modelled decoration found on white ware especially the white ware of Fuchien (PLATE 14, C), already referred to, with ornaments modelled in high relief and applied; neither does it make a separate division for patterns engraved in the paste before firing and glazing and subsequently enriched with enamel painting over the relief.

A. *Decoration depending on the Glaze alone.*

1. *Glazes plain white.* This does not mean the ordinary ware made for subsequent decoration in colour, but the finer-textured pieces with an ivory-like appearance, whose beauty of form and mellow, ivory-like colour constitute their charm (PLATE 14, C). China of this sort, which usually occurs in rather small objects, is ordinarily known as *blanc de Chine.*

In this section may also be classed crackled ware, with a transparent colourless glaze over a white body or over a coarser greyish paste.

2. *Coloured Glazes uniform in tint.* Reference has already been made to the skill with which the Chinese potters contrived glazes of various colours, the colour being inherent in the glaze itself and produced by the materials in its composition. Besides the Celadon glaze (PLATE 13) and its greyish and greenish variations already noted, often with underglaze engraving, there were glazes of various turquoise shades, royal blue, deep blue, blue verging almost to black, *sang de boeuf,* mule's blood, pigeon's blood (a glaze approaching ruby red), liver colour, tomato red, ruby, coral, lilac, pink, lavender, *clair de lune,* crushed strawberry, purple, peach bloom, "dead-leaf" brown and sundry other gradations of brown, *café au lait,* tea-colour, Imperial pale yellow, lemon yellow, straw colour, orange and grey.

The glazes known as "soufflé" and "jasper" belong in this monochrome-glaze class. The "soufflé" glaze may be of any colour. The name refers to the mechanical *manner* in which the effect is produced. Jacquemart, quoting and translating Père d'Entrecolles, says: "This is how it is obtained. The colour, made of the proper consistency, is placed in a tube, one end of which is covered with a close gauze; by blowing through the other end, little drops filled with air are precipitated upon the enamel. These burst when coming in contact with the sides of the piece, and reduce themselves into little contiguous circles, forming a network like the finest lace. Sometimes the soufflé colour is blue, more often of a carmine red, which, at first sight, gives to the piece the appearance of a violet-like enamel. This decoration often fails; the little drops do not burst, but form, on the contrary, into little veins, which run half-melted into the starch-blue glaze. Hence results a peculiar decoration very agreeable to the eye —jasper, not less sought after than the soufflé itself."

3. *Flambé and other Glazes, varying locally in Colour, but the whole applied at the same time.* In these splashed, mottled or *flambé* glazes —"transmutation" glazes, the Chinese call them—the varied effect is largely dependent upon chemical changes that take place in the substance of the glaze itself during the firing process and often produce striking contrasts and modulations of colour. One type of transmutation glaze of the "Chünyao," so say the Chinese connoisseurs, ought to be "red as cinnabar, green as the plumage of the king fisher, and purple, brown and black as the skin of the egg-plant."

B. *Decoration in Slip, generally white, over the Glaze.*

Porcelain decorated with devices in slip over the glaze was usually of a strong-coloured ground so as to throw the pattern in white slip into stronger relief. This sort of decoration was applied mostly to vases, jars and bowls.

C. *Decoration with Underglaze Colours.*

This sort of decoration was painted on the air-dried body *before* the application of the glaze and *before* firing.

1. *Copper-red.* Reference has already been made to the old copper-red decoration, and also to the later iron-oxide red under glaze.

2. *Cobalt-blue.* This class includes all the enormous family of "blue and white" ware. The white porcelain supplies the ground; the decorations are in blue alone. The most usual types of decoration found in "blue and white" ware are:

   a. *Miscellaneous* (PLATE 17, A), including dragons, flowers, birds, animals, landscapes, pagodas, shaped panels or medallions, bridges, mountains, trees, fishes, fishermen in punts, insects, baskets and pots of flowers, houses, hunting scenes, pheasants on rockeries, peonies, bamboos, peony and lotus scrolls, asters, magnolias, and sundry other subjects.

   b. The prunus or so-called "hawthorn" (PLATE 15) blossom pattern, executed either in blue on a white ground or in white on a blue ground.

   c. The "Mandarin" (PLATE 12, B) type, so-called because the chief subjects are figures, usually of persons belonging to the Mandarin class. Under this division should also be placed the tall, willowy ladies standing beside vases of flowers, irreverently known as "long Elizas." The seventeenth-century Dutch traders called them "lange Liszen" and the term, translated as "long Elizas," has clung ever since (PLATE 17, B).

> *d.* "India" china. This large class includes all the porcelain made for export to Europe and America and is characterised, to a great extent by shapes that are essentially European (PLATES 17, B and 18), such as tureens, vegetable dishes, sauce boats, gravy boats and cream jugs. The decorative *motifs* are virtually the same as in the preceding classes.
>
> It might be well, however, to add to this class the china made for export to Persia (PLATE 12, A), and India on which scrolls, flowers, tree and other devices were used that were not at all Chinese but essentially Persian in character and derivation.

3. *Powder-blue.* Powder-blue porcelain (PLATE 8, A), was decorated with a solid coating of cobalt blue that was *blown,* not brushed, upon the air-dried body before glazing and firing. This method of application in minute drops of fluid pigment imparted the powdered appearance.

4. *Mazarine blue.* This is a blue in which the ground is solid and has not the mottled aspect of powder blue, hence the different name to distinguish the two types.

It should be added that with both powder blue and mazarine blue there are often reserved spaces or panels in white (PLATE 8, A), so that the blue does not wholly cover the surface of the piece. Various devices occur in these reserved spaces, and are rendered either wholly in blue or else in polychrome.

On much blue and white china the decoration is rendered in several shades of blue (PLATES 11, 12 and 17), usually two, but sometimes more. Attention must also be directed to the great variations that occur in the quality of the blue—it may be a pure cobalt colour, or blackish, greyish, or even almost purple at times. The pale silvery blue might be especially characteristic of one period, while the full-bodied blue would be equally characteristic of another.

D. *Glazes of more than one Colour, painted on the previously fired biscuit.*

Allusion has already been made to this method of decoration in the section on *History*.

E. *Decoration with Enamel Colours over the Glaze.*

This division includes a broad range of distinct and well-recognised types of decoration. They are:

1. *Coral-red,* the *motifs* being rendered in red alone (PLATE 23, A), on the white porcelain, or the ground colour being coral-red with devices in gold.

2. *Famille noire,* so-called because the ground is either a lustrous green-black glaze or enamel, while the decorative *motifs* appear in white, green, yellow and brown. The usual subject is the prunus blossom, and the colouring is always restrained.

3. *Famille verte* (PLATE 22, B), so-called because the prevailing or dominating colour is a vivid enamel leaf-green. The other colours are underglaze blue or on-glaze blue, an iron red, purple and yellow. While the green dominates, it does not necessarily monopolise the colour scheme. The subjects depicted are largely historical—emperors, eminent scholars, famous warriors, statesmen, and scenes from celebrated plays and romances. Floral *motifs* and *genre* scenes are also of frequent occurrence.

4. *Famille rose* (PLATE 2, A), so-called because a beautiful rose-colour a later addition to the porcelain painter's palette, is a conspicuous colour and often imparts the prevailing tone. Along with this distinctive rose-colour all other colours, many of them hitherto new to Chinese porcelain, were freely used so that the *famille rose* is *par excellence* the polychrome class. The *famille rose* began to dominate about the second quarter of the eighteenth century and continued in high favour till the early years of the nineteenth. All manner of subjects are represented in the *famille rose* decoration and the drawing is usually of the greatest delicacy and refinement.

5. *Chrysanthemum and Peony* (PLATE 20). This class is sometimes so designated because of the well-defined type of decorations in which chrysanthemums or peonies, or both together, are the dominating *motifs.* This type occurs in both the *famille rose* and the *famille verte.*

6. *"Mandarin" china* (PLATE 19). This class has the same *motifs* as already noted for the "blue and white" "Mandarin" group, the difference being that they are in polychrome.

7. *"India" china* (PLATES 22, A, 24, 28, 29, 31). The same distinction applies here as in No. 6.

8. *Chinese Imari and Chinese Kakiyemon.* This group consists of imitations of the Japanese Imari and Kakiyemon types. There was such a demand from Europe for these Japanese wares that the Chinese saw their market being injured by Japanese competition and therefore

promptly produced types of the same sort. The red, blue and gold Chinese Imari (PLATE 1), is often much finer and more beautiful ware than the Japanese originals. The Chinese Kakiyemon (PLATE 20), also, is exceedingly beautiful.

9. *Reserved Panels in Ground Colour* (PLATE 21). This class occurs also in the powder-blue division, the *famille verte,* and the *famille rose.* The polychrome devices in the shaped reserved panels are usually flowers, birds, figures or landscapes. A great deal of china with divers shades of brown glaze and reserved panels with blue decoration (PLATE 16) was exported to Europe by the Dutch merchants and is generally known as "Batavian" ware.

10. *Jesuit china,* so-called because it was decorated with scriptural or ecclesiastical designs supplied by the Jesuit missionaries. The "Baptism" plate (PLATE 25, B), shews a good example of such decoration. The renderings were purely Oriental, as may be seen by looking at the writhing cherubs in the border which more resemble malignant animals than celestial creatures.

11. *"Lowestoft"* (PLATES 26, 32). Under this head comes all that great body of china exported to Europe and America throughout the greater part of the eighteenth century, decorated with armorial bearings, monograms and cyphers, bearing numerous small polychrome flowers, thoroughly European and not at all Oriental in character.

In casting up an enumeration of the foregoing, we must not overlook the importance to general decorative effect of the scroll borders (PLATES 18, B, 22 and 25), and, even more, of the many varied diaper patterns (Figs. 3, 4 and 5, and PLATES 2, B, 18, A and 20), that were employed for the enrichment of rims and borders and, often enough, composed whole grounds, imparting a rich texture full of interest in both colour and line. These diapers occur constantly in almost all classes.

In point of decorative interest, we cannot attach too much importance to the diaper patterns in the embellishment of Chinese porcelain. Some idea of the rich variety to be achieved by their use may be gathered from a careful scrutiny of the examples given in Figures 3, 4 and 5. And these are only a portion of the *répertoire.* When employed in monochrome, as on the blue and white chinaware, they afford a fascinating enrichment; expressed in a variety of colours, they cause the porcelain to glow with vibrant life. To the apt use of diapers is attributable no small part of the charm of Oriental china.

FIG. 3. Characteristic Diaper Patterns used in the decoration of Chinese porcelain

FIG. 4. Characteristic Diaper Patterns used in the decoration of Chinese porcelain

FIG. 5. Characteristic Diaper Patterns used in the decoration of Chinese porcelain

Amongst the many subjects that appear in the decoration of Chinese porcelain, besides the *motifs* already mentioned may be numbered symbols (PLATES 17, B, 19 and 12, B), emblems, charms, characters, lozenges, coins, rhinoceros horns, fillets, sugar cane, bamboo, storks, tortoises, fir-trees, cocks, mirrors, fish nets, bats (PLATE 23, A), mythical animals, such as kylins, swastikas, sceptres, chess boards, rats and vines, squirrels, arrows, three-legged toads, musical instruments, drums, horses, oxen, hares, monkeys, sheep, dogs, boars, lions, tigers, elephants, deer, foxes, camels, cats, ducks, pheasants, quails, peacocks, parrots, butterflies, bees, silkworms, and endless fruits, plants, flowers and trees, every one of which has some symbolical significance. The peculiar figures termed "symbols," Sir Wollaston Franks notes, "are generally eight in number, although the individual forms are apt to vary." The number eight is favourably regarded by the Chinese, doubtless because of the *Pa-kwa* or eight mystical trigrams and also because it is a number whose units can be arranged symmetrically. These sequences of eight may be classed in three chief divisions: (1) the emblems of the eight immortals, which are of Taoist origin and not of very common occurrence; (2) the eight

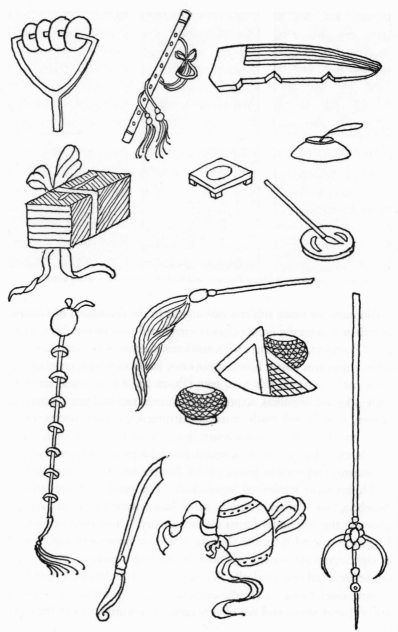

FIG. 6. Typical emblems or symbols used in the decoration of Chinese porcelain

FIG. 7. Typical emblems or symbols used in the decoration of Chinese porcelain

lucky emblems of the Buddhists, which are to be found in every possible place and manner of expression; (3) the *pa-pao* or signs of the eight precious things. These last vary widely in their expression and seem not to be connected with any particular religion.

Symbols or emblems can usually be distinguished from other ornaments by the fillets or streaming ribbons entwined about or attached to them. In ordinary life fillets are narrow strips of red cloth which the Chinese tie round or attach to any object they think has the efficacy of a charm. These fillets typify the rays or aura emanating from the charm and are to a charm what the nimbus is to a saint or deity. A number of characteristic symbols or emblems, with fillets attached, are shown in Figures 6 and 7.

The symbolism of Chinese decoration is inexhaustible. There is a story wrapped up in every piece of Chinese ornament and there is not a cup, saucer, plate or vase that will not repay investigation on that score alone. You can eat your dinner from a Chinese plate and along with each morsel of beef or mutton you can also trace a romance or get a lesson in Confucian morals, if you care to read the language of the symbols before your eyes.

THE MARKS. The marks on Chinese porcelain may occur in three classes—date marks, hall and other allied marks, and symbol marks. The date marks may be in both plain and seal characters. Marks usually are found on the base of a piece and most commonly are painted in blue. On some of the later pieces they are in red. They may also be engraved in the paste or stand out in relief.

Little reliance can be placed upon them, for they have been habitually forged and misapplied, and it is more than likely that falsified marks have been made, over and over again, to the order of exporters. This practice has gone on for centuries. By the average person the mark on a piece of Chinese porcelain may as well be considered merely an interesting item of decoration and naught else. The mark may tell the truth, but more probably it tells a lie. Under ordinary circumstances, it is much safer and more satisfactory to disregard the mark and judge a piece by its more visible and tangible qualities. If you are really concerned about the mark, go to an acknowledged expert in Chinese porcelain and he can tell you what the mark *says* and also what he *thinks* the piece really *is*. His opinion will be worth considering.

JAPANESE CHINAWARE

HISTORY. Japanese porcelain is thought to have had its beginning with the handiwork of a certain Gorodayu Go-Shonzui. It is related that he visited China at the beginning of the sixteenth century and worked for five years in the factories of Ching-tê Chên. When he learned all he could in that time, he returned to Japan, taking with him a supply of porcelain materials from China, and made a number of pieces of blue and white porcelain. Not knowing where there were deposits of kaolin and *petuntse* in his native country, he had to stop making porcelain when his materials gave out.

In the opening years of the seventeenth century Risampei, a Corean potter settled in the province of Hizen, so the story goes, discovered the necessary kaolin and *petuntse* in the neighbourhood of Arita. Kilns were established at Hyakken and it is probable that blue and white ware was made there. The kilns were afterwards moved to Arita to be near the source of supplies.

The use of brilliant enamel colour on Japanese porcelain is inseparably associated with the name of Kakiyemon. Kakiyemon was connected with the works at Arita and, according to the story told, he and a companion, Tokuemon, set out to China in 1646, bent on discovering the secret of Chinese enamel colours. At Nagasaki they chanced upon the captain of a Chinese junk who gave them the information they sought and thus saved them the trouble of a long journey. They went back to Arita and it was not long after this that Kakiyemon originated the beautiful manner of decoration known by his name. After Arita, other porcelain factories were established in the same province, such as Nabeshima and Mikawachi, under the control of the great feudal lords and not a little fine porcelain was produced at these places.

In the provinces of Kioto, Owari and Kaga other porcelain factories sprang up and various sorts of wares were made, restrained in character with delicately drawn designs in underglaze blue or else decorated with a few enamel colours in a reticent manner and with excellent

good taste. The Japanese always greatly admired the old Chinese Celadon wares, and these also they used as models for their work.

One of the dominant characteristics of Japanese porcelain is its reticence of colouring and design. The decoration was always kept well
within bounds and exuberance of composition was virtually unknown.
It is not fair to judge Japanese taste in porcelain design by the Imari
ware made for export. If anyone is to be blamed for the crudities and
vulgarity that often appear in such ware, it is the Dutch traders who
suggested that what the Japanese porcelain-makers had done extremely
well should be "improved" by mussing up the design and adding heavy
blobs of colour. A great portion of the Imari ware that found its way
to the West was of a description that the Japanese would not counte-
nance for their own use, and it was made only for export at the behest
of the Dutch East India merchants.

Some of the most distinguished porcelains of Japan were produced at
the different factories in the latter part of the eighteenth century and
first half of the nineteenth. As there was no one important centre of
porcelain production, like Ching-tê Chên in China, there was not only
great diversity of individual style in the wares made at the several factories, but there was also much difference in the quality of the paste and
glaze. The output during this period was not large, except in the few
instances where the porcelain was made almost solely for export, and
for that reason the quality in more than one of the factories was maintained at a rather high standard.

THE BODY. In general, the quality of the body in Japanese porcelain
was not so good as that which distinguished the ware made at the great
factory of Ching-tê Chên in China. The Japanese paste was more glassy-
looking and seemed of thinner consistency. Compared with the Chinese pastes, it appeared to lack the finer qualities that go to make a
really excellent body. For one thing, it seems as though the materials
for the Japanese paste had not been prepared in the same careful, scru-
pulous and patient manner as the Chinese. Furthermore, the clay mixture apparently was not so plastic as the Chinese and perhaps because
of this failing it was customary to fire the ware to a biscuit stage before
glazing and then fire it a second time after glazing. There was also

oftentimes a tendency for the pieces to warp and crack in the firing. The result of all these conditions was that much of the Japanese porcelain seems thick and clumsy when compared with Chinese porcelain of the same period.

The paste of the Imari commercial ware was thick, heavy and coarse and the body of the early Kutani porcelain was greyish and seemingly composed of impure materials. On the other hand, the paste of the Hirado porcelain, with which great pains were taken, was of rich, fine solid quality and clean white, closely resembling Chinese paste. The Nabeshima body, too, which was carefully prepared, was of good, clean, dense texture and wholesome colour. Likewise, the later Kutani paste was milky white, though somewhat soft in substance. The early Arita paste with the Kakiyemon decorations was of a beautiful creamy white which made an admirable foil for the coloured enamel embellishments. The paste of the Owari porcelain, though milky white was of a rather soft, chalky nature. At several of the factories very fine egg-shell porcelain was made and for this purpose the paste had to be most carefully prepared, so that it exhibited the qualities we naturally look for in porcelain of an high order.

THE GLAZE. The glaze commonly used, especially the glaze of the Imari commercial wares, which contained an appreciable quantity of lime, was almost always minutely pitted so that it presented a semblance to fine muslin. It was less solid than the Chinese glaze and this musliny aspect from tiny bubbles seems to have been caused by incomplete fusion. In colour it had often a cold greyish tinge. Its whole appearance is very different from the close texture and oily sheen of the Chinese glaze. By way of contrast, the glaze of the Hirado porcelain, made from more carefully prepared materials, has a velvety, lustrous aspect. The Nabeshima glaze and the later Kutani are both of good quality, though the latter shews a somewhat dull surface.

ARTICLES MADE AND CONTOUR. There has never been as great diversity in the articles made by the Japanese as there was in porcelain of Chinese manufacture. While the Japanese made plates, platters, bowls, cups, saucers, teapots, jars and vases and, for their own use, such articles as incense boxes, incense burners, rice bowls, wine-cups, and the various things required for the elaborate tea ritual, they were not in the habit of making dinner, tea, coffee and chocolate sets, with all the etceteras for the Western market, as the Chinese did. There were also the human figures, grotesques, birds, and animals which were made in large numbers.

The contours, almost without exception, are simple and straightforward and, to a certain extent, shew the influence of Chinese shapes.

TYPES OF DECORATION. The types of decoration commonly practised included painting in underglaze blue, painting with enamel colours, gilding, ground colours, coloured glazes, ribbing, piercing and fretwork. The Japanese palette was limited to a comparatively few enamel colours, and nearly all of their *motifs* shewed reticence and restraint in treatment. Many of the subjects were treated in a purely conventionalised or symbolic form, a circumstance that rather enhanced their decorative value than otherwise.

Religious subjects supplied not a few themes for decoration. There were also landscapes and river scenes, the beloved mountain Fujiyama, animals, birds—in the depiction of which they were peculiarly successful—fishes, mythical creatures, flowers, trees and sundry symbols.

The local specialities in decoration are noted in the section devoted to the individual factories.

THE MARKS. The marks on Japanese porcelain usually indicate the names of the factory and the potter. The name-mark of the Japanese Emperor is sometimes added. These marks may be incised in the paste, impressed in the paste with a seal or stamp, or painted either in underglaze blue or with enamel colours. Much of the best Japanese porcelain is altogether unmarked. The Japanese marks are far more to be relied upon for accurate information than are the Chinese, except the marks on Japanese ware made solely for export. These last are purely fantastic inventions.

ARITA CHINA—1605 TO PRESENT DAY

HISTORY. This factory was established when Risampei, the Corean, found porcelain materials near Arita. Its most beautiful and famous product was the Kakiyemon ware (cf. PLATE 5, A), named for the painter who devised this means of decoration in a few colours—iron-red sometimes verging to orange, lilac, a fine enamel-blue, grass-green, and dull gold—and with a limited range of *motifs* comprised in a sparse composition of dragons, phœnixes, tigers, fluttering birds, quails or partridges, bamboos, pines or plum trees.

The red, blue and gold Imari ware (PLATE 3), so-called from its place of export—was also made here, the patterns being largely derived from old brocades; hence the term "brocaded."

Blue and white ware, decorated chiefly with diapers and scrolls, was made at Arita, the underglaze blue being of a rather poor, muddy quality. Celadon porcelain, too, was produced; likewise very exquisite egg-shell porcelain, decorated with underglaze blue or with enamel colours.

NABESHIMA (OKAWACHI) CHINA—
c.1660–c.1868

HISTORY. This factory, also in the province of Hizen as well as Arita, was established under the patronage of the feudal lord about 1660. The paste and glaze of this china are, in many instances, better than the paste and glaze of Arita.

A type of china was made here whose decoration closely resembled the Kakiyemon ware of Arita. Another sort had decorations in underglaze blue, less brilliant than the Chinese blue. Celadon porcelain was likewise made. The favourite decorative *motifs* for the blue and white china were cherry-blossoms, hydrangeas, peonies, chrysanthemums and other floral subjects, along with conventionalised birds and butterflies, in conjunction with conventional scrolls and diaper patterns. The ware was not marked but had a comb pattern encircling the footrim. This same comb pattern is sometimes seen on Kaga porcelain.

HIRADO (MIKAWACHI) CHINA—1712–1868

HISTORY. This factory was established at Mikawachi in the province of Hizen, under the patronage of the feudal lord. In 1750, Matsura, the lord of Hirado converted it into a private factory and from then until 1830 the finest porcelain in Japan is reputed to have been made there.

The paste and glaze were of a quality far superior to anything produced in the other factories.

The painted ware was decorated altogether in underglaze blue and the drawing exhibited exquisite delicacy. Some of the ware shewed engraving and modelling in the paste, delicate piercings and frettings were employed, and egg-shell pieces were also made. Modelled figures, too, were fashioned and glazed with coloured glazes.

KUTANI (KAGA) CHINA—1664-1750; 1779-1822; 1832 TO PRESENT DAY

HISTORY. The Kutani factory in the province of Kaga was established by the feudal lord of Daishoji in 1664. Several different sorts of ware were made. One was distinguished by a beautiful green glaze, along with soft greenish blue, purple and yellow glazes, disposed in scrolls, diapers and floral patterns over outlines traced in black on the biscuit. Another sort was painted with red, green, blue, yellow and purple enamel colours, along with silver and gold. Landscapes, flowers, a single bird on a twig, and similar naturalistic subjects (PLATE 35) supplied the themes together with symbolical ornaments and diaper patterns. In still another sort, red was predominant. The decoration of red scrolls and diapers was disposed in panels containing landscapes, mythical animals and flower *motifs* in green, yellow, purple and red. A subdivision of this variety had a red ground colour, with patterns wrought in gold, silver, bright green, yellow and purple. The making of these wares came to an end about 1750. After that date several revivals took place, one of which had a red ground colour whereon the patterns appeared in gold.

KIOTO CHINA

There were not a few porcelain-makers of great ability and good taste who flourished in Kioto at one time or another from the middle of the eighteenth century down to the end of the period with which this book deals. Eisen, who worked about 1760, was the first of these. The wares they made were of excellent quality and beautiful in decoration, but as none of their products exercised a material influence on chinaware in the Western World, the reader desirous of pursuing the subject further is referred to books treating especially of Japanese porcelains.

Italian Chinaware

MEDICI CHINA
FLORENCE—1580-1613 (?)

HISTORY. Francesco I de' Medici, Grand Duke of Tuscany, in 1580 established at Florence a manufacture of soft paste porcelain. The factory was in the Boboli Gardens. Bernardo Buontalenti played an active part in this undertaking, and it is said that soon after its inception porcelain vases and other articles, of the finest quality, were produced and decorated in blue. This was the first European porcelain of which we have any certain knowledge and of which undoubtedly authentic examples exist.

Fewer than fifty authentic pieces are now known to be in existence. These comprise vases, dishes, bowls, (PLATE 36), plates, cruets, bottles, flasks, basons and ewers. They are all in museums or else in well-known private collections.

The mark, painted in blue, consists of the dome of the Cathedral in Florence, above a capital F, occasionally with slight additions or variations.

The manufacture was discontinued in the early years of the seventeenth century.

GINORI OR DOCCIA CHINA
DOCCIA, BY SESTO, NEAR FLORENCE—1735 TO PRESENT DAY

HISTORY. The Marchese Carlo Ginori, in 1735, founded the porcelain factory at Doccia, an estate belonging to his family at Sesto, about six miles from Florence. As a Tuscan, he had all the initiative, readiness for enquiry and hard-headed common-sense characteristic of his race. Endowed with both energy and tenacity of purpose, he chose to follow the old Tuscan tradition that strongly sanctioned mercantile, industrial and agricultural activities on the part of the nobility. Through application and diligence he occupied a prominent position in Florentine affairs and became a senator. As part of the services he rendered the State there were sundry special commissions, entrusted to him in view of his sterling capacity, public spirit, and the confidence reposed in him by the Grand Duke.

At one time he was engaged in reclaiming a part of the Maremma, a formidable task that meant draining a section of the waste, malarial marsh lands and converting them to purposes of productive farming. This involved much canal cutting, road making, bridge building, the planting of settlers from various quarters, and the establishment and care of divers industries. Along the coast, he exerted himself to develope coral fisheries, attracting thither Neapolitans skilled in their conduct. By well-directed efforts he also materially furthered the interests of Tuscan shipping.

In one place, where the conditions seemed suitable, he introduced Angora goats, hoping to promote the manufacture of cashmere shawls. What measure of success rewarded this venture we know not, but the attempt was indicative of Ginori's alertness and determination to make the most of every opportunity for improvement that offered. While Governour of Livorno—he had then embarked on his porcelain-making experiments—at his own expense he sent a ship to the East Indies expressly to fetch some of the clay and other materials used by the Chinese in making porcelain.

The Marchese Ginori was a man of cultivated tastes and was readily susceptible to the "China-mania" that had taken Europe by storm. He was also blessed with prevision or prophetic imagination. Whether his ambition was fired by the memory and knowledge of the Medici porcelain, previously made in Florence, and by a laudable desire to renew and develope in his native country an enterprise so gratifying to his sense of beauty, or whether, as a result of his enquiries and observations, convinced that Italy possessed the materials requisite for an industry he foresaw would have a fruitful issue, it is impossible to say. In all likelihood both motives played a part in forming his ultimate determination. At all events, he set up his kilns and started the making of porcelain at Doccia. Quite apart from the character of the chinaware produced, the success of this establishment, which has continued in active operation to the present day, is remarkable because it was never assisted by Government subsidies or patronage as were so many other ventures of a like sort in other countries, with the exception of England and America.

Going to Vienna on a diplomatic mission, in 1737, the Marchese Ginori there met Karl Wandhelein, a chemist who had previously had some considerable experience in the manufacture of porcelain. Him Ginori engaged to come to Doccia and direct the nascent industry on which he had embarked two years before. Along with Wandhelein it is said—apparently with sufficient foundation—there came to Doccia one or more artists from Vienna or Saxony. Even the very early products shew the presence of someone experienced in design. Both the founder and his successors made it a point not only to have the ordinary workmen trained in modelling and decoration, but also to have their children taught these arts as well so that the traditions of the factory might pass on from generation to generation. In a way Doccia was really a little school of industrial art. Whoever the first modellers and decorators may have been, they were followed by a series of experts as competent as we should expect Florence to produce. The factory museum at Doccia, in which there is a complete chronologically arranged record of production, testifies to the prowess of these assistants.

Wandhelein appears to have been a capable director and in due time, though not until many costly experiments had been tried, the factory was enabled to place its products on a commercial basis. It has been said that eighteen years elapsed before the venture began to bring in any appreciable returns of profit. This statement, however, altogether lacks authentic substantiation. Whatever difficulties may or may not have had to be surmounted, this we know—the industry, from the very outset, was supported by the enterprise, energy and enthusiasm of Ginori alone.

The china made at Doccia exhibited many phases of style and decoration and in nearly all of them it is possible to recognise easily the sources of inspiration in different sorts of china made elsewhere. Some of the influence is distinctly Chinese, as was the case in nearly all china factories during much of the eighteenth century. This was natural for the art of chinaware was essentially a Chinese art and it was to be expected that Chinese precedents should be held in high esteem. Besides, the china art is an imitative art. Even the Chinese copied or adapted many of their early porcelain forms from bronze, brass and other metal shapes and, despite their proverbial conservatism, in much of their later ware they did not scruple to make use of elements derived from outside sources. Again, many of the influences to be discerned in the Ginori china are plainly of European origin. The Doccia factory was founded about ten years before Bow and Chelsea, five or six years before Vincennes, and only a few years later than St. Cloud and Chantilly, yet the impulses received from the greater French porcelain factories and some of those in England can be detected without difficulty, to say nothing of the strains derived from Dresden and Vienna. In regarding this reflex action exerted upon the output of Doccia by the work of other factories we must, however, remember this. Through former centuries Italy had lavishly supplied other countries with inspiration in all the arts; the eighteenth century was pre-eminently a period of borrowing back the commodity she had so freely given forth aforetime. Nevertheless, Italian hands always managed to give an individual twist of interpretation to borrowed *motifs,* imparting a distinctly national flavour. So it was in the making of Ginori china, and in this characteristic lies much of its charm. Again and again we find a strongly individual adaptation of several distinctive methods of borrowed decoration combined on one piece. Early in the nineteenth century the Ginori family bought many of the moulds from the Capo di Monte factory, at Naples, along with the right to use the Capo di Monte mark on reproductions made from these moulds.

The Doccia factory until a recent period remained wholly under the control of the Ginori family. Since a corporation was formed and an amalgamation effected with the Richard company, of Milano, the Ginori family have retained a controlling interest.

THE BODY. During the early years, the body or paste used was what they called *masso bastardo,* a composition which Brongniart places amongst the "hybrid" or *soft pastes,* apparently taking exception to the quantity of magnesia and the clay of Monte Carlo. In speaking of the kaolins of Campo and Chiusi, near Porto Ferraio on the Island of Elba, he notes that they are talc clays rather than true kaolins. He therefore designates the early Ginori china "hybrid" or *soft paste* porcelain, reserving the term "true" or *hard paste* porcelain for the later products. Although Brongniart is loath to count the *masso bastardo* as hard paste, nevertheless it was certainly not soft paste in the French sense nor the "bone" porcelain made in England. From the very start, Doccia followed the hard paste ideals of Dresden and Vienna, and there was never a distinct period of soft paste development as there was in France. Whatever may have been the imperfections of materials and composition, judged by Dresden standards, the *masso bastardo* seems to have been as "true" porcelain as some of the old Chinese bodies that have always been accounted hard paste.

The cost of importing clays and minerals from Germany would have been prohibitive; the Ginori factory, therefore, used native materials as closely as possible approximating the qualities of the kaolin and felspar used at Dresden. The paste made from these materials had a slightly greyish tone and a smooth texture.

When the deposits of kaolin and felspar were found at St. Yrieix in the south of France, these materials were used and the paste became a pure white. Since that date the characteristic Doccia paste has been white, hard, translucent and resonant.

THE GLAZE. The early glaze was soft, unctuous and exceeding mellow, but not always evenly distributed, sometimes shewing a tendency to run. The later glaze was clear, brilliant and absolutely even in distribution, both glaze and body being technically perfect.

ARTICLES MADE AND CONTOUR. Almost from the outset Doccia has made all manner of tableware, vases of all sorts, candlesticks, sconces, all the various accessories for writing and dressing tables and figures and groups in biscuit. About the middle of the eighteenth century flowers were extensively modelled and naturalistically coloured. As the century advanced the pieces in biscuit were not confined to busts, figures and groups, but clock cases, table garnitures, vases and many other items were fashioned in the same substance.

The contours during the early days were to a great extent of Rococo type (PLATE 39, B), with occasional interpretations of Oriental shapes. From about 1765 onward the contours were predominantly of Neo-Classic inspiration (PLATE 41), while at the end of the century and in the fore part of the nineteenth the shapes shewed the impress of Neo-Grec and Empire styles.

TYPES OF DECORATION. At an early date in its history Doccia was using a varied array of decorative processes—moulding (PLATE 38, B), modelling (PLATE 39, B) in relief, painting in underglaze blue and with enamel colours on the glaze, and gilding. The decorative *motifs* and methods were in part Oriental (PLATE 39, A), as they were in nearly every European porcelain factory at some period of its career, in part taken from the types in vogue at Dresden (PLATE 38, B), Sèvres, Vienna, Worcester, Naples (PLATE 42, B), and other factories whence pronounced styles had issued from time to time. So many sources of inspiration were drawn from that it would be hard to fix upon any one style as peculiarly characteristic.

In the earliest Doccia period, from 1735 to 1765, some of the china had no coloured decoration at all (PLATE 39, B), or else only reddish brown lines on the edges of rims. From the first, underglaze blue decoration was used, often with Chinese floral *motifs*. On-glaze colours very soon made their appearance, and the *reds, rose,* light *apple-green,* and *mulberry* were especially good. The first piece made at Doccia with polychrome decoration dates (PLATE 37) from 1737 and is an oval platter with a narrow guilloche of deep mulberry and light green at the edge of the rim, a narrow band of orange next, then sprays of flowers on the broad rim; the central subject is a turbanned Turk with purple overrobe, green sleeves and coral-red underrobe, with an equally polychrome cock on the grass beside him. To this period also belong the first polychrome floral decorations in the manners of Chantilly (PLATE 38, A), and Dresden; there were likewise gaily-coloured Tyrolese *motifs,* rather crudely rendered. Prunus blossoms and sprigs modelled in relief, inspired by the Fuchien white ware, adorned some of the early.pieces without coloured decorations. Now and then these reliefs were accentuated with colour and gilding. A few of the early prunus blossom reliefs were emphasised with colour schemes of gold, red and black on the plain white surface. Modelled flowers, fruits, birds, leaves, and animal heads, in an wholly European manner, were commonly applied as handles and knobs and accented with colour. There were perforations and fretwork for fruit baskets and stands, while not a few plates and platters were embellished with moulded impressions of basketwork (PLATE 38, B), and floral patterns on the rims.

In the second period, 1765 to 1780, we note the Dresden and Chantilly flowers (PLATE 38, A), a reversion to Chinese peony (PLATE 39, A) and chrysanthemum subjects, the appearance of Wedgwood cameos and medallions (PLATE 42, A), reflections of the current Sèvres manner, polychrome flowers recalling those of Mennecy (PLATE 4, A), and Sceaux, and not seldom may be seen two or three methods happily combined in the decoration of one piece.

From 1780 to 1815 Neo-Classic *motifs* (PLATES 41 and 42, B) were very much in the ascendant, with a strong trend towards the Pompeian and Etruscan types of the Capo di Monte china. Ground colours were more frequent, sometimes several of them in combination; vertical stripes, geometrical figured bands, coral-red bands dotted with gold, on pieces otherwise without decoration; Sèvres corn flowers, reserved panels on ground colours, with flowers, fruits, figures, birds or landscapes; ribbon and flower patterns; polychrome landscapes and landscapes *en camaïeu* (PLATE 44); rims with heavy ground colours overlaid with rich gilding in Classic *motifs,* and surrounding elaborate architectural subjects (PLATE 40, A), or mythological *motifs;* a prevalence of Pompeian and Etruscan features; and a more lavish use of gilding are the characteristics that especially mark this period.

THE MARKS. The marks used at the Doccia factory varied more or less at different periods. That of most common occurrence was the six-pointed star in one form or another. The six-pointed star and the star with many points are usually in red; the double triangle, which is really a variant of the six-pointed star, is often in gold on the finest pieces; the mullet with the double triangle may be found in blue or gold on pieces of exceptional quality. Capo di Monte reproductions, made from the purchased Capo di Monte moulds, bear the crowned N of Capo di Monte.

VENICE CHINA
VEZZI, 1720–1740; COZZI, 1764–1812

HISTORY. The first successful attempt to make porcelain in Europe is believed to have been in Venice about 1470. It is recorded that a certain Maestro Antonio, an alchemist, made bowls, vases and other small articles which were said to be of a very light and translucent porcelain, quite as good as, or even superior to, the porcelain of "Barbary." In 1508 a payment is recorded for seven bowls of *porcellana contrafacta,* which evidently means imitation porcelain. It is more than likely that this ware made by Maestro Antonio was soft paste porcelain. None of it is known to exist; nothing further is known of its making. The earliest European porcelain of which visible evidences remain was the Medici porcelain made in Florence.

The next venture at porcelain-making in Venice was in the eighteenth century. The brothers Vezzi, wealthy goldsmiths, had acquired patents of nobility. Having determined to establish an hard paste porcelain factory, in association with two other Venetians of rank, they employed Christoph Conrad Hunger as director and began operations in 1720. Hunger had previously worked at Dresden and at Vienna, and had the reputation of being the ablest porcelain expert of the day. Some workmen from Dresden are also believed to have been employed. The kaolin for the Vezzi china is said to have been brought from Saxony, but this seems highly improbable. The chinaware made was of very superior quality and closely resembled the wares of Dresden. Francesco Vezzi died in 1740 and the factory was discontinued.

From 1758 to 1763 there appears to have been a small porcelain factory conducted by a man named Hewelche and his wife, supposed to have come from Dresden. Little is known about this undertaking, and virtually nothing can be stated with certainty.

In 1764 Geminiano Cozzi established a soft paste porcelain factory near San Giobbe in Venice and made a great variety of beautiful wares. The enterprise proved a great commercial success and the factory did a flourishing business until 1812, when it was discontinued.

THE BODY. The hard paste of the Vezzi china was never a cold staring white, but of a somewhat warmer, creamier tone than Dresden china. It was, too, a little more glassy in appearance. Soft paste was also made by the Vezzi. The soft paste of the Cozzi had a slightly greyish tinge.

THE GLAZE. The Vezzi glaze was good, clear and very like that of Dresden. The Cozzi glaze was of excellent quality, but more satin-like and mellow.

ARTICLES MADE AND CONTOUR. The articles made at the Vezzi factory included not only the usual varieties of tableware, vases, flower pots and other ornamental objects, but also a number of figures and statuettes. During the term of Hunger's directorship, 1720 to 1725, the contours closely followed Dresden precedents. After Hunger's departure, the Dresden lead was less closely followed and the contours became more florid and more characteristic of the mid-eighteenth century Venetian phase of the Rococo manner.

The Cozzi factory also produced an highly diversified range of wares, over and above the usual table services and kindred articles of universal demand. Figures and groups, both glazed and painted, and also in the biscuit, were regularly made. By the time the Cozzi factory started, 1764, the excesses of Rococo design had passed so that the contours chiefly reflected the Neo-Classic trend, but with that mellowness and occasional whimsicality often imparted by Italian hands.

TYPES OF DECORATION. At the Vezzi factory, moulded or impressed ornament, modelled and applied ornament, pierced ornament, painting in underglaze blue and with on-glaze enamel colours, and gilding were all constantly used. The *motifs* were commonly figures, flowers (PLATE 47), landscapes, harbour scenes, country scenes, birds, monkeys, and scrolls. Oriental *motifs* were often employed and were sometimes curiously blended with Venetian *motifs*. During the late period an iron-red was a favourite colour, although underglaze blue and a full palette of enamel colours, along with gilding, were in use throughout the entire period of the factory's existence.

At the Cozzi factory, all the same decorative processes were in use. The *motifs* were in large measure the Neo-Classic versions of those mentioned in connexion with the Vezzi factory, and other purely Classic devices pertaining especially to the later period, although some pronounced *chinoiseries* were still used, the taste for which seems to have lingered. In colour, there was a predilection for iron-red by itself, although all colours were in general use. Some of the decorations were in gold alone. The gilding done at the Cozzi factory was especially fine.

THE MARKS. During the period of Hunger's directorship at the Vezzi factory, 1720–1725, the pieces were unmarked. From 1725 to 1740 the mark in red or blue varied from "V" to "Venezia" with all manner of intermediate abbreviations. The mark of the Cozzi factory was an anchor drawn in red, blue, or gold, sometimes with the painter's initials above it. It is possible that the letter "C" may also have been used.

CAPO DI MONTE CHINA—1743-1821

CAPO DI MONTE—1743-1759
PORTICI—1771-1773
NAPLES—1773-1821

HISTORY. The Capo di Monte porcelain factory was established by Charles III, King of Naples, and installed in the palace of Capo di Monte in 1743, where it continued in operation till 1759, when Charles III succeeded to the throne of Spain and left Naples. This porcelain factory was a matter of the deepest interest to the King, and tradition says that he often worked in it with his own hands. At the annual fair, in the piazza before the palace, the products of the factory had a special stall and the King was furnished daily with a list of the sales made and the names of the purchasers. When Charles left Naples in 1759 he took with him to Madrid the best models and moulds, and about forty of the most skillful workmen.

From 1759 to 1771 operations were suspended. Then King Ferdinand IV re-established the works in the Villa Reale at Portici. In 1773 the factory was again moved and set up in Naples, where it continued to work under State direction and support until 1807, when it was sold to a company. It was closed in 1821.

THE BODY. During the first period, only soft paste porcelain was made, and the body was yellowish, greenish, bluish or dead grey in tone, the colour shewing considerable variation. The tinge was not always pronounced, and the ware was translucent.

From 1771 to about 1806 both soft and hard paste bodies were used. After 1806, or thereabouts, only hard paste was produced. The hard paste was pure white, hard, translucent and generally of excellent quality.

THE GLAZE. The glaze of the soft paste was soft, rich and satin-like to sight and touch. The hard paste glaze was clear and brilliant without being glittering.

ARTICLES MADE AND CONTOUR. The common impression of Capo di Monte china is onesided and quite erroneous. People ordinarily think of it as a sort of ware much over-decorated with small figures modelled in high relief (PLATE 45, A), and further accentuated by lavish gilding and vigorous colouring in which pink, rose and purple are dominant. This manner of ware was peculiar to Capo di Monte, it is true, but it was by no means the only thing made there. A few of the pieces responsible for this impression may be genuine, but most of those ordinarily met with are counterfeits, manufactured by the gross to sell to gullible tourists. And by no means all of these counterfeits are made in Italy. As a matter of fact, a great many other and very different things were made at the royal factory, but unfortunately they are almost altogether unknown.

During the first period, besides tableware, vases, jars, flower pots, sconces and the like, there were made numbers of small snuff-boxes, patch-boxes, inkstands and similar articles on which it was possible to lavish the modelled and highly coloured decoration just mentioned—the kind of decoration that ninety-nine people out of an hundred associate with the name of Capo di Monte. Then, too, special pieces such as consoles, mirror-frames, clock-cases and chandeliers were made. All of these creations were agreeable to the Rococo taste of the age and were generally of more or less pronounced Rococo contours.

During the second period a number of biscuit pieces were put forth in addition to the wares previously enumerated. The contours, especially in the case of tableware and vases, became far more restrained and shewed the increasing influence of Neo-Classic conception. Painted decoration on the flat surface began visibly to triumph over applied modelling.

During the last period, when the factory was in Naples, all the preceding wares were made in considerable quantity, but there was a tendency to increase and emphasise the production of biscuit pieces. With Pompeii and Herculaneum as immediate sources of inspiration at the very doors, it is not surprising to find the Classic trend in contour becoming more and more pronounced.

TYPES OF DECORATION. Both for painted decoration and for decoration modelled and applied, we find great plenty of marine *motifs*—shells, dolphins, periwinkles, coral, fishes and the like. It has been suggested that some of these popular shell forms more than likely inspired the shell salt-cellars not long afterwards made at Bow. There is certainly a striking similarity between the Bow shell salt-cellars in plain white and the plain white shell forms made at Naples. Not a little of the early Capo di Monte china was wholly without colour; the modelled forms were not suggested by the white ware of Fuchien, but the general type probably was. Some of the white undecorated pieces, without modelled and applied ornament, are very simple and exhibit much dignity and charm of contour.

A number of pieces were painted with Oriental *motifs* interpreted in a very European manner. These were soon succeeded by unmistakably

European themes in the way of natural flowers, fruits, birds, figures, pastorals, love scenes, landscapes and harbour scenes. Oftentimes the decorations were painted *en camaïeu,* crimson, bluish-violet and black being especially favoured for this purpose. Small landscapes and harbour scenes were often thus rendered in monochrome, either enclosed within panels and medallions or unenclosed.

Towards the latter part of the century and in the early years of the nineteenth two strong tendencies became apparent—first, a disposition to substitute painting and colour on a flat surface, whether in the form of ground colours, carefully executed Classic *motifs* or landscapes and harbour scenes of a general character, for modelled, applied and coloured ornament; second, a pronounced bias in favour of the *motifs* directly derived from Pompeii and Herculaneum (PLATE 45, B). To the latter tendency we are indebted for the so-called "Pompeian" china which supplied an impulse felt throughout Europe. The cameos and medallions were rendered with exquisite taste, and these as well as the arabesques exercised a profound influence on the china decoration of the age. From the time the factory was transferred to Naples, the revived Classic style in both contour and decoration was followed almost exclusively. There were also many local incidents of sea and mountain, including the various moods of Vesuvius, introduced into the decoration. Grey, green, blue, yellow and Pompeian red were some of the ground colours much used and these, sometimes along with touches of black, afforded admirable foils for Classic subjects in panels and medallions, or for the reserved panels enclosing flowers, birds, country scenes or harbour views. The gilding was always notably good.

THE MARKS. During the first period the mark was the Bourbon fleur-de-lys, impressed in the paste or painted in blue. It was also occasionally applied in red or gold. In the later periods the mark was "N," usually surmounted by a crown, but sometimes without. It was commonly in blue, but now and again it occurred in red or else impressed in the paste. While the factory was at Portici the marks "R. F." and "F. R. F." occur. The genuine Capo di Monte ware with modelled and applied figures is generally unmarked, and the flesh tints are exquisitely soft; the Ginori reproductions of the same ware are usually marked with the crowned "N" or otherwise and the flesh tints have a stippled appearance.

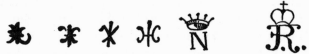

LE NOVE CHINA—1762-1835

HISTORY. In 1761 or 1762 Pasquale Antonibon began to make soft paste porcelain at Nove, near Bassano, in his faïence factory. Antonibon had the fortunate faculty of being able to attract men of talent to work with him, and the results of this are manifest in the china. The Antonibons, father and son, made soft paste porcelain until 1802, when the factory passed out of their hands till 1825. The factory then reverted to the former owners and they continued to produce porcelain till 1835. After that time only faïence and divers other sorts of earthenware were made.

The chinaware issuing from the Nove factory possesses great artistic distinction (PLATE 46). The paste was a beautiful creamy white and the glaze was mellow and clear. There was great diversity in the matter of decoration. The jardinière illustrated (PLATE 46), is clearly in the manner of Sèvres. Flower decorations are numerous, oftentimes in polychrome, occasionally in green and gold, now and again in purple. Ground colours were used very frequently and were always good. Birds, landscapes, Classical and mythological subjects likewise appear as *motifs*. The factory is said to have made figures in biscuit.

The mark was "Nove," either with or without a six-pointed star in blue or red or, sometimes, in gold. Occasionally the star occurs without the name. Some of the Nove China, between 1802 and 1825 when the factory was in the hands of Giovanni Baroni, has the initials "G. B." above the name "Nove."

VINOVO CHINA—1776-1820

HISTORY. With the assistance of Pierre Antoine Hannong of Strasburg, Giovanni Brodel established an hard paste porcelain factory at
Vinovo, near Torino, in 1776. Brodel found Hannong a most difficult
person to work with and retired from the business in 1778. In 1780 it
was sold to Dr. Gioanetti, an eminent chemist. Under him the factory
produced a considerable quantity of china up to 1815, when Dr. Gioanetti died. Under his successor the business declined so rapidly that the
factory was closed in 1820.

The paste at first was of a yellowish tone and the glaze was often
defective; the later ware was of fine grain and had an excellent white
glaze. The decorations, though not distinguished, were pleasing and
the colours were good. Flowers, polychrome and monochrome, garlands and ribbons, medallions, landscapes, flowers and arabesques in
gold, and numerous *motifs* of Classic provenance make up the repertoire. In general style the Vinovo china resembled the wares of the
independent Parisian factories of the late eighteenth century.

The mark was "V" with a cross above it, in either underglaze blue
or on-glaze blue; occasionally the mark was incised, or else applied in
black, brown, red, or gold. In exceptional cases the "V" may be omitted or the cross may be omitted.

ROME PORCELAIN—1790-1831

HISTORY. The hard paste porcelain made by Giovanni Volpato at
Rome from 1790 to 1831 was restricted to groups and figures in biscuit.
They were copies from antiques and the sculptures of Canova.

TREVISO AND ESTE CHINA

HISTORY. At Este, between Padova and Ferrara, a soft paste porcelain factory was established in 1780 which made both tableware and
figures in biscuit. Little is known about it, but the few pieces that can

be traced to Este display merit. The Este mark may be the word "Este" accompanied by a date or may be of the form shewn in the cut.

In the latter part of the eighteenth century a small quantity of soft paste porcelain was made at Treviso, consisting mostly of tableware. The pieces are marked "Treviso" with G.A.F.F., or F.F., in addition.

French Chinaware

History. The earliest manufacture of porcelain in France, of which we have any reasonably sure knowledge, was that established under letters-patent by Louis Poterat in 1673 at Rouen.

In 1664, it is true, Louis XIV had granted to Charles Reverend a patent for the making of porcelain in Paris, and there are several allusions in works of the time apparently indicating that in or near Paris attempts to produce porcelain were made before 1670. There are several specimens of early work, too, which it seems impossible to identify as the products of either Rouen or St. Cloud. These seem to indicate the existence of a short-lived enterprise whose records have been lost. It is, therefore, the manufacture inaugurated by Poterat at Rouen that we must regard as the first authenticated production of porcelain in France.

The letters-patent issued to Poterat in 1673 granted him an "exclusive monopoly for the fabrication of plates and dishes, pots, and vases of porcelain like that of China . . . for the period of thirty years." This privilege was conferred in consideration of his foreign travels and diligent application whereby he had mastered the technical secrets enabling him to establish a new industry in France. An official report, made at the instance of M. de Pontchartrain in 1694, discloses the facts that porcelain was made at the factories of both Louis Poterat and his father; that the works were well kept; and that although they possessed the secret of making porcelain, very little of it was made, most of the output consisting of faïence. Louis Poterat died in 1696 and the conduct of the works then fell to his brother. The latter, however, seems to have been incapable of continuing the business successfully and the making of Rouen porcelain was discontinued.

The Rouen china was soft paste porcelain and the body, of a rich, creamy quality, has a slightly greenish hue. The glaze is less "glassy" in appearance than the glaze of much other soft paste porcelain and exhibits a very pale sea-green tinge.

There are only about fifty pieces of Rouen china known to be in existence, and almost all of these are decorated altogether in blue, although a few specimens exhibit other colours in combination. One piece in the museum at Rouen shows a decoration in blue, green and red. The blue is darker, denser and often greyer than the blue usually seen on other early soft paste porcelains, and the colour seems to have been applied not *under* the glaze but *on* the raw glaze before it was fired.

It is noteworthy that the decorations were invariably in the contemporary French manner of ornament that characterised the reign of Louis XIV. It is all the more remarkable that no *motifs* of direct Chinese provenance occur when we remember that the making of porcelain was an openly avowed imitation of Chinese methods, was stimulated by Chinese examples, and that in nearly every other case Chinese types of decoration were borrowed and applied without hesitation.

SAINT CLOUD CHINAWARE—c.1696-c.1773 (?)

HISTORY. "I saw the potterie of St. Clou, with which I was marvellously well pleased, for I confess I could not distinguish betwixt the pots made there and the finest China ware I ever saw. It will, I know, be easily granted me that the painting may be better designed and finished (as indeed it was) because our men are far better masters of that art than the Chineses; but the glazing came not in the least behind theirs, not for whiteness, nor the smoothness of running without bubbles. Again, the inward substance and matter of the pots was, to me, the very same, hard and firm as marble, and the self-same grain on this side vitrification. Farther the transparency of the pots the very same. . . . I did not expect to have found it in this perfection, but imagined this might have arrived at the Gomron ware; which is, indeed, little else but a total vitrification, but I found it far otherwise and very surprising, and which I account part of the felicity of the age to equal if not surpass the Chineses in their finest art.

They sold these pots at St. Cloud at excessive rates, and for their ordinary chocolate cups askt crowns a-piece. They had arrived at the burning on gold in neat chequere works. He had sold some tea equipages at 100 livres a sett. There was no moulding or model of China ware which they had not imitated, and had added many fancies of their own, which had their good effects and appeared very beautiful."

Account of a Journey to Paris in the Year 1698, by Doctor Martin Lister, published in London, 1699.

Besides this testimony to the merits and charms of Saint Cloud chinaware by the eminent Doctor Lister, who had accompanied the Duke of Portland to Paris on a diplomatic mission and was afterwards physician to Queen Anne, there is the witness of royal interest in the works and appreciation of its products. *Le Mercure Galant,* in October 1700, contain this notice:

"I have forgotten to write to you that the Duchesse de Bourgogne, when she had passed through St. Cloud and turned along the riverside to visit Madame la Duchesse de Guiche, made her carriage stop at the door of the house where the MM. Chicanneau have had established for some years now a manufactory of fine porcelain, which without doubt has not its like in all Europe. The princess found pleasure in seeing several pieces of very good shape made on the wheel. She saw some others painted in patterns that were more regular and better done than those of the Indian porcelain. Then she went to see the faïences being made in the manufactory, and afterwards MM. Chicanneau conducted her into their office, where she saw quantities of fine and beautiful porcelains in their perfection, with which she was so pleased that she promised to come again. She did not leave without shewing her satisfaction by the gratuities she gave to the workmen."

Established as it was under the shadow of the Château de Saint Cloud, the factory seems not only to have enjoyed a measure of interest and patronage from the Duc d'Orléans, but also to have attracted not a little favourable notice from the King and the great personages of the Court on their comings and goings between Versailles and Paris, and its success in a commercial sense was probably in large measure because of these advantageous circumstances.

The establishment at Saint Cloud began, it appears, as a faïence factory. By 1670 it was important enough to be given a large commission for orange pots and flower vases for the gardens of Versailles, as well as being called upon to supply numerous other decorative requisites from time to time. Its wares justly deserved their high reputation.

Antiquarian research has discovered that there was a painter named Chicanneau in Poterat's factory at Rouen and it is thought that he there first found out the secrets of porcelain-making and then carried them to Saint Cloud. At all events, the letters-patent of 1696—from which year we may date the official manufacture of porcelain at the Saint Cloud factory—granted by Louis XIV to "Barbe Coudray, the widow of Pierre Chicanneau, and to Jean-Baptiste, Pierre and Geneviève Chicanneau, brothers and sisters, children of the aforesaid Coudray and the aforesaid Pierre Chicanneau, and the undertakers of the faïence and porcelain works established at Saint Cloud," mention the porcelain-making experiments of Pierre Chicanneau the father, note his success in producing pieces approximating Chinese porcelain in excellence, and state that the children have carried on the work and, prior to the year 1696, "have arrived at the point of making porcelain of perfect quality."

Historical data regarding the porcelain works of Saint Cloud are not plentiful in contemporary French memoirs, but it appears that off-shoots of the establishment at Saint Cloud were started in the faubourg St. Honoré and in the faubourg St. Antoine in Paris, where similar wares were produced, by members of the Chicanneau family. These splits were seemingly caused by family dissensions with ensuing legal processes and great expense. It is said that the factory at Saint Cloud was destroyed by fire in 1773 and that the owners, thanks to long wrangling and law costs, had not money enough to rebuild it. This misfortune presumably put an end to the manufacture of Saint Cloud china. The Saint Cloud works, however, can boast the distinction of having been the first French enterprise of the sort that succeeded in maintaining a long continued existence.

THE BODY. The china of Saint Cloud is one of the soft paste porcelains. It has a cream-like yellowish tinge, and where chipped or broken the fracture shews a close, regular granular texture.

THE GLAZE. The glaze is clear and shews very few bubbles to break its evenness. It is more brilliant than the Rouen glaze and has a very slight creamy tinge. Blisters rarely occur. There seems also to have been some use of coloured glazes for there is in the Victoria and Albert Museum a little water jug, with attached cover, moulded top and bottom, with an overlapping scale or pineapple skin *motif,* and covered with a pale green glaze, evidently made in emulation of the old Chinese Celadon ware.

ARTICLES MADE AND CONTOUR. The articles most commonly made at the Saint Cloud factory included cups, saucers, jugs, teapots, coffee pots, chocolate pots, tea, coffee and chocolate services, trays, dishes, plates, platters, tureens, sugar-bowls or basons and tableware generally, knife handles, statuettes, grotesques, vases, bowls and flower-pots.

Porcelain figures are said to have been first fashioned at Saint Cloud and, between 1710 and 1724 under the direction of Dominique Chican-neau, "all other kinds of imaginable things." Grotesque figures and branched candlesticks in the form of tree trunks appeared, it is stated, as early as 1731, but these branched candlesticks mentioned by contemporary writers seem not to have survived.

The contours of the various pieces were at first mainly of Chinese derivation for European china-makers at the outset, almost without exception, tried to reproduce both Oriental shapes and Oriental decoration as nearly as they could in order to compete with the china imported from the East.

Later there was a gradual modification and an addition of shapes less distinctively Chinese and more European in character. It is worth noting that at Saint Cloud the same contours and the same decorations were continued in use over a long period of time.

METHODS AND TYPES OF DECORATION. White pieces with modelled ornament (PLATE 48, A), were produced in fairly numerous quantity, evidently inspired by the white ware of Fuchien (PLATE 48, B), which was greatly admired in Europe. These pieces depended for their charm on the moulded and applied ornaments and included such objects as small figures or statuettes, knife handles, cups, saucers, covered jars, jugs, bowls and sugar dishes, and flower-pots. Prunus blossoms and sprigs in relief (PLATE 48, B), flowers, sprays and rosettes appeared on the porcelain surface.

While the plain white ware decorated with applied reliefs (1) met with favour, a great many of the pieces bearing moulded reliefs were also enriched with patterns in underglaze blue, (2) the colour decoration being so disposed as to accentuate the value of the modelling (PLATE 49, B). (3) A few of the pieces with modelled reliefs were decorated with red, yellow, purple, green and dark brown along with the blue. (4) Pieces of Chinese shape, but without moulded reliefs, bore polychrome decorations, for the most part in designs closely copied from Chinese models. (5) A later development employed European designs, blue and polychrome, in the lighter and more graceful *motifs* of the Baroque manner (PLATE 49, A), that characterised the reign of Louis XIV; these appeared first on pieces of Chinese shape. Together with these patterns and modified shapes, (6) a more flowing manner of modelled reliefs came into use, the combination resulting in what was, perhaps, the most typical phase of Saint Cloud chinaware.

THE MARKS. The marks were carelessly used and are not certain guides. A sun pressed into the paste was the first mark. A later mark consisted of the letters S C, in blue, with a small cross above and the letter T underneath. In company with this mark are often found numbers or detached letters, which may be the numbers of certain patterns or the initials of the decorators. Sometimes these blue initials are surrounded by little crosses. A fleur-de-lys is said to have been used sometimes but some doubt exists on this score.

LILLE CHINAWARE—c.1711-?

HISTORY. In 1711 Barthélemy Dorez exhibited to the Mayor and Council of Lille specimens of porcelain that he and his nephew, Pierre Pélissier, had fashioned; at the same time he sought permission to set up a porcelain factory in connexion with his faïence establishment and likewise asked certain concessions. The Council granted his petitions and subsidised his works, the subsidy being regularly continued till 1720 by which time the undertaking seems to have been firmly on its feet. The brothers Dorez offered to sell their enterprise to the King who, however, declined to buy it but gave them certain privileges and exemptions that could not infringe the rights of the French East India Company nor offend the Duc d'Orléans who was patron of the Saint Cloud factory. These privileges did not include permission to open a warehouse in Paris for the sale of their wares, and without this outlet they had not a sufficient market to maintain their enterprise. The manufacture of Lille porcelain was discontinued not long afterwards, but it is not known in exactly what year this occurred.

The products of the Lille factory were chiefly confined to imitations of the wares of Saint Cloud, and it is often difficult to distinguish with any degree of certainty between the pieces issuing from the two establishments, especially when sufficient marks of identification are lacking. The chief difference between the porcelain of Lille and that of Saint Cloud seems to have been that the former lacked the finish and interest of decoration shewn by the Saint Cloud china, and that the glaze shewed a greater tendency to blister. The paste was the same at both Lille and Saint Cloud.

The mark D occasionally appears on pieces decorated in blue, as well as the mark Æ. The mark L, accompanied by a cross, may indicate Lille or it may be one of the varied marks employed at Saint Cloud.

L   D+.   L

CHANTILLY CHINA—1725-1789

HISTORY. The Prince de Condé, lord of the château and domain of Chantilly, was the patron of the porcelain factory and provided the funds to enable Ciquaire Cirou to carry out experiments. Letters-patent were issued to Cirou in 1735, and therein it is set forth that, for the ten years preceding, he had endeavoured at Chantilly to make porcelain of the same quality as the Japanese; that he had excelled the Dresden porcelain; and that he purposed selling his wares not only in France but abroad as well. In view of these declarations, the King accords Ciquaire Cirou licence, for twenty years, to make at Chantilly all manner of china in imitation of Japanese porcelain.

The Prince de Condé was an eager connoisseur and had collected a number of fine examples of Imari ware. In this collection were some excellent specimens of Kakiyemon decoration, and these seem particularly to have inspired much of the early Chantilly decoration—very appropriately, indeed, as imitation of the Japanese porcelain was avowedly one of the chief objects proposed by Cirou. (PLATE 50.)

Chantilly never took the lead in originating new styles. The factory was started with the ideal of good imitations, and its successive directors contented themselves with producing admirable adaptations of the successive styles put forth elsewhere. Nevertheless, despite any evidence of originality, the work of Chantilly possessed great distinction and charm, and its appealing beauty ensured constant popularity so long as the factory lasted. It continued until 1789, on the eve of the Revolution, and, after the time of Cirou, was under the directorship of Antheaume, Potter, de Baynal and Lallement in order.

THE BODY. The body of Chantilly china was a soft paste, very like the paste of Saint Cloud, of an even granular texture, with a mellow, creamy or slightly yellowish tinge. It seems, however, to have been more solid and stable in the firing, inasmuch as large flat pieces, such as platters, could be made successfully. These appear not to have been put forth at Saint Cloud.

THE GLAZE. There were two distinct types of glaze used at Chantilly, one during the early years of the factory's existence, the other adopted at a later date. The early Chantilly glaze contained oxide of tin which gave it a milky-white, opaque quality that not only enhanced the brilliancy of the decorations but also imparted a strongly individual aspect to the ware and increased its resemblance to the Japanese prototypes.

Subsequently, in order to meet the demand of competition with Sèvres and Mennecy-Villeroy, this glaze was abandoned and a transparent glaze adopted in its stead.

ARTICLES MADE AND CONTOUR. The chief products of the Chantilly factory included dinner services, tea and coffee sets, cabarets or solitaires, trays, jugs, statuettes, grotesque figures, flowers, birds, sconces and candlesticks, modelled bouquets, knife handles, ink-pots and writing paraphernalia in general, boxes, caskets, powder boxes, vases, pomatum pots, snuff boxes, patch boxes, covered jars, and various other objects of common use.

At first Japanese forms were largely used as models, and many of the platters, dishes, trays and sugar bowls were of lobate form which seems to have been especially favoured. Chinese types of contour, too, were considerably followed, not only for tea services and articles of tableware but also for the modelled figures and grotesques.

At the same time a great many distinctively French forms were adopted and executed with consummate delicacy, refinement and charm. Subsequently, the work done at Sèvres supplied not a little material for imitation and the Chantilly renderings were in no wise inferior to their models.

TYPES OF DECORATION. The types of decoration characteristic of Chantilly china include the polychrome Kakiyemon *motifs* (PLATE 50), of flowers, sprigs and birds; the more stayed and conventionally disposed Imari *motifs* with dominant blue, red and gold; Chinese polychrome *motifs;* underglaze blue decorations of flower sprays (PLATE 51, A and B), modelled and applied ornaments for white ware, and modelled flowers and figures for knobs and handles on tableware, which were decorated with colour; little scattered flowers and sprays in imitation of the Dresden manner; compositions of fruits, flowers and birds in a clear green etched with black; polychrome flowers, fruits and birds like those used at Sèvres; embossed patterns of basket-work and other *motifs* for plate rims and necks of jugs; perforations (PLATE 51, C), and the yellow, blue, green, and rose grounds in the style of Sèvres, with the accompaniment of gilding, reserves, and multi-coloured flowers. These last, it may be added, were so successfully carried out that it is virtually impossible to tell many of them from Sèvres pieces of the same description unless the marks be examined.

THE MARKS. The usual mark employed at Chantilly was a carefully drawn hunting horn applied in on-glaze red. Late in the eighteenth century the same mark appears in blue, oftentimes accompanied by letters and figures meant to specify different individual pieces. The fact that instances occur where the Chantilly mark has been removed and the Sèvres mark substituted by falsifiers shews how close was often the resemblance between the two wares.

MENNECY-VILLEROY CHINA—
1735-1773 OR 1774

HISTORY. The factory of Mennecy-Villeroy was started in 1735 by François Barbin under the patronage of the Duke, Louis-François de Neufville de Villeroy, one of the great nobles of the Court of Louis XV. Apparently the venture was undertaken, and porcelain was manufactured, without the authorisation of royal letters-patent. Royal sanction, it seems, was not granted until 1748, and then it was restricted with stipulations that Barbin must not employ any workmen who had ever worked at Vincennes and that he must not imitate the wares made there.

The earliest pieces made at Mennecy were imitations of Saint Cloud china. Somewhat later, the opaque tin glaze of Chantilly was used and Chantilly wares were copied. At length the factory found itself, so to speak, and developed a manner of its own. Although the creations of Vincennes and Sèvres were closely imitated, nevertheless a certain individual character was imparted to the Mennecy china.

Jean-Baptiste Barbin, who had succeeded his father as director of Mennecy, was himself succeeded about 1766 by the MM. Jacques and Jullien, who not only managed the works but became its owners as well. One was a painter and the other a sculptor. In 1773 or 1774 the factory of Mennecy-Villeroy came to an end after venturing to make pieces in biscuit besides producing some of the most fascinating china of the eighteenth century, of much artistic excellence.

THE BODY. The Mennecy-Villeroy porcelain had a soft paste body of a yellowish or dark ivory tinge, and was made in emulation of the Saint Cloud body. The faint yellowish or amber tone gave it a peculiarly mellow quality and rendered it a warm and sympathetic ground for the coloured decoration applied to its surface.

THE GLAZE. The glaze of the earliest efforts is faulty and uneven, and although the technical short-comings were soon remedied, there was rarely or never quite the same perfection of finish in this respect that characterised the work of several of the other contemporary factories. At one time an opaque glaze was used, much like the early Chantilly glaze which, however, it did not equal.

ARTICLES MADE AND CONTOUR. Amongst the articles made at the Mennecy-Villeroy factory the modelled pieces in biscuit deserve special mention because of their artistic excellence and because of the initiative implied in undertaking them. An advertisement of March, 1766, announcing the coming sale of the factory and its stock of wares—this was just before Jacques and Jullien became the proprietors—enumerates "cups, saucers, antique vases, groups, pedestals, mustard-pots, gravy-boats, dishes, covered dishes, cruet-stands, powder-boxes, sugar-boxes, sugar bowls for the table, and fruit baskets of various forms."

Besides these, the factory customarily made a varied assortment of pieces including flower pots, pot-pourri jars, milk jugs, coffee and chocolate pots, teapots, water jugs, ewers and basons, wall brackets and sconces, small clock cases, mirror frames, candlesticks, statuettes, snuff-boxes, pomatum pots, patch boxes, knife handles, and sundries for household embellishment or use upon writing tables or dressing stands. There seems to have been a marked preference for vertical rather than flat pieces, and consequently plates and platters were comparatively rare products.

During the sway of the Chinese taste the Mennecy factory made use of a number of Oriental shapes, but most of its products exhibit purely European contours. Those in the Rococo manner shew much grace and charm, patricularly the pieces of simpler character, although some of the more elaborate efforts (PLATE 9, J) were rather overdone in their tortured intricacy.

The knobs on the lids of tea, coffee and chocolate pots, sugar bowls (PLATE 53), and covered dishes, and the handles of tureens and dishes, were well modelled and daintily picked out with colours.

Types of Decoration. The Mennecy types of decoration, at the out-set, were patterned after the early methods of Saint Cloud and Rouen, use being made of the characteristic *lambrequins* of the latter factory wrought in blue. Then followed decorative painting in bright, glow-ing reds, greens, yellows and blues in the subsequent manner of Saint Cloud and Chantilly, both in the Kakiyemon vein and in the more realistic French and Saxon styles (Plate 48). The most characteristic Mennecy decorations were those patterned after the modes of Vin-cennes and Sèvres, although the Mennecy decorators always managed to impart a certain individuality to the pieces they put forth. Chinese as well as Japanese *motifs,* of course, were employed to some extent, but the greater part of the decorations were wholly European in char-acter.

Occasionally Sèvres ground colour processes were followed, such as using a *bleu du roi* ground enriched with "partridge eye" diapering, gilding and polychrome flowers in reserve. A number of cups, saucers, snuff-boxes and other small articles were produced which displayed pastoral scenes and figures after the fashion of Watteau and Lancret, executed with exquisite finish.

A purplish rose colour was characteristic of Mennecy decoration (Plate 52), and occurs very frequently, while yellow, rose, lilac and blue are rather predominant in the flower painting. As gilding was a jealously maintained prerogative of the royal factories, and was forbid-den Mennecy, so that there were times when it could not be practised extensively or openly, it was necessary to find some substitute to use as a finish for certain schemes where gold would ordinarily have been em-ployed. This substitute is discovered in the yellow, blue and, more especially, the rose-coloured lines with which the mouldings, edges (Plate 52), and other suitable points were habitually embellished. These colour lines add greatly to the charm of the decoration and we may now be glad that gilding was banned.

Polychrome painting of flowers and other *motifs* was also proscribed by royal letters-patent as the sole privilege of Vincennes and Sèvres. Although there were long periods when this regulation was not en-forced, and when the other porcelain factories employed colour as freely as they pleased without molestation or interference, there were also occasions when the privilege was insistently maintained. At such times there was no choice but compliance and Mennecy, Chantilly and Saint Cloud had to be content for a season with monochrome decoration until the lines were relaxed again. About 1766 there was such a period of stringency. When the anti-polychrome regulation was enforced, the factories other than Vincennes and Sèvres were at liberty to use any one colour desired in decorating a piece of china, and flowers, birds, and other *motifs* were all presented in blue, yellow, rose or mauve, as the case might be, *en camaïeu* as the method was called. Not a few of these decorations *en camaïeu* are very beautiful and possess great distinction.

THE MARKS. The unmistakably Mennecy mark consisted of the letters D. V. (presumably signifying Duc de Villeroy). On the earlier work, this mark was painted in enamel colour; later it became customary to scratch or engrave it on the paste before firing. On some of the Sèvres imitations the two crossed "L's" of Sèvres are *painted* beside the D.V. incised in the body.

D.V.

VINCENNES CHINA—1740-1745-1756

HISTORY. The porcelain factory at Vincennes owed its inception to three fugitives from Chantilly—the brothers Dubois, painter and sculptor, who had been dismissed for flagrant ill conduct, and one Gérin. Having secretly got possession of the Chantilly processes, they set about the manufacture of porcelain on their own account. About 1740 they disposed of some of their products in Paris and, as a result, obtained the interest of M. de Fulvy through whose good offices the King granted them permission to occupy some buildings adjacent to the château of Vincennes. M. de Fulvy also got them a grant of money. They took into partnership a man named Gravant, who likewise had knowledge of porcelain-making processes and was ready to invest a considerable sum in the enterprise.

The porcelain they made appears to have been unreliable in quality at first and a large proportion of their pieces got spoiled in the firing. Much of the trouble was directly attributable to the general ill behaviour and drunkenness of the brothers Dubois—there seems to have been no fault with their formulas or processes—who eventually made off, leaving a disorganised and bankrupt concern on Gravant's hands. Gravant, however, had mastered all their porcelain secrets and succeeded in winning the substantial support of M. de Fulvy and a number of courtiers and financiers so that he was able to put the factory on its feet for the time being.

In 1745 a company was formed, with privileges granted by the King who himself took a direct and lively interest in the undertaking and aided it financially. Under these favourable auspices the staff was strengthened by the addition of the most competent people it was possible to secure. Hellot, a distinguished chemist, took charge of the chemical management; Duplessis, a goldsmith and sculptor, supervised the modelling; and the artist Bachelier, along with Mathieu, the King's enameller, took charge of the decorating.

Although the financial condition was always precarious until the factory ultimately became a royal establishment, artistic success crowned the efforts put forth and so distinguished were the achievements that early in 1748, when the Queen received an handsome presentation vase from the factory, the Dauphine Marie-Josèphe, "a finished diplomatist, ordered a similar vase as a present for her father, Frederick Augustus, Elector of Saxony, to shew him that the Vincennes porcelain was quite equal to that of Dresden." All the great nobles of the Court became ardent patrons of the works, and plans were laid for increasing the volume of the output in view of the demand both in France and abroad. The memoirs of the Duc de Luynes mention naïvely that "the English want only white porcelain, but as they might use this to paint upon, they [the pieces of porcelain] are sold just as dear as the painted ones."

Triumphs of marvellous production continued without cease. One of the notable achievements was the fashioning of porcelain flowers that possessed the utmost verisimilitude to the living blooms and were immensely popular. From the memoirs of the Marquis d'Argenson we learn that:

"The King has ordered from the Vincennes works porcelain flowers, naturally painted, with their vases——more than 800,000 livres worth——for all his country houses, and especially for the château of Bellevue of the Marquise de Pompadour. Nothing else is spoken of in Paris, and truly this unheard of luxury causes great scandal."

Also, Soulavie, in his memoirs of the Duc de Richelieu, writes:

"Madame de Pompadour, doing the honours of her residence to the King, displayed before his eyes a whole flower garden. She expected him one day in this charming château of Bellevue, which had cost him so much, and when he entered it, she received him in an apartment at the far end of which was a hot-house with an immense flower bed, although it was a hard winter. As fresh roses, lilies and pinks predominated, the enraptured King could not sufficiently admire the beauty and the sweet scent of these flowers. But nature had been made game of. These vases, flowers, roses, lilies, pinks and their stems—everything was porcelain—and the sweet perfume of these heavenly flowers was the effect of their essences, volatilised by art."

The fashionable world went quite mad over these porcelain flowers, and for a time the major part of the factory's business lay in filling orders for them.

Notwithstanding all these outward successes, the factory was just beginning to work at a small profit when the deaths of both M. de Fulvy and his brother threw the financial affairs of the company again into complete chaos so that it was necessary, in order to avert catastrophe, to appeal for the more direct aid of the King. The outcome of the negotiations was that in 1752-3 the factory of Vincennes was declared the *"Manufacture Royale de Porcelaine"* and became an institution directly under the King's protection and support. As such, it continued until it was merged in the royal manufactory of Sèvres in 1756.

THE BODY. The Vincennes body was a soft paste, regarding the composition of which there are extensive historical data, as well as detailed descriptions of the processes employed. The earliest paste produced by the brothers Dubois was prepared presumably according to the Chantilly formula, but its appearance was slightly greyish and its behaviour in the kiln was not invariably satisfactory. As already explained, much of the trouble was because of negligence. Evidently some change in the composition of the paste was made or else greater care was exercised in its preparation about the time of the reorganisation after the flight of the Dubois brothers. The quality was noticeably improved and brought to a pure, mellow white. Hellot said of it, "M. Gravant's paste [the old paste of Vincennes more carefully prepared after the departure of the Dubois element] produced a biscuit of the same grain as that of the Chantilly porcelain, but much whiter . . ."

This beautiful white soft paste body, possibly with a few slight modifications subsequently introduced by Hellot, continued in use during the whole life of the Vincennes factory.

THE GLAZE. The glaze of the Vincennes porcelain was throughout of a beautifully clear, transparent quality. In some of the very first pieces made it is possible to find flaws, usually concealed, however, by the adroitly painted decoration, but at an early period in the factory's career these imperfections were successfully eliminated.

ARTICLES MADE AND CONTOUR. The articles made at Vincennes fill a rather varied and comprehensive list. Furthermore, they may be divided into two grades, the ordinary tableware and usual articles of household enrichment and utility, on the one hand, and the elaborate pieces upon which special efforts were bestowed, on the other.

The first named class included bowls, jugs, sugar-bowls or boxes of several different sorts, cups and saucers, plates, platters, dishes, butter-dishes, soup tureens, mustard pots, cheese dishes, jardinières, watering-pots, flower-pots, tea, coffee and chocolate pots, vases, candlesticks, covered jars, cabarets, flower-holders, sconces, clock cases, mirror frames, patch boxes, snuff boxes, powder boxes, cream jugs, fruit baskets, sweetmeat dishes and many like articles of common requirement. A few statuettes, decorated in colour, may also be placed in this category.

To the second belonged the modelled flowers (PLATE 54), made and coloured to approximate life, the groups and busts in biscuit produced during the royal period, with vases and other objects of special importance.

Elegance and purity of contour were distinguishing characteristics of the Vincennes china throughout the greater part of the factory's existence. Even from the very outset, there was apparently little recourse to definitely characteristic Oriental shapings in the way of direct imitations. A certain amount of Oriental influence there was bound to be, but there seems to have been a prevailing tendency to develope contours in a national vein. As soon as Duplessis became a member of the staff, he bestowed great attention on the modelling and many of the products were marked by those subtle and delicate refinements of line (PLATE 54), that we are accustomed to associate with the best instances of eighteenth-century French design in all branches of art. Many of the pieces had straight sides and flaring tops or displayed a pleasant blending of oval and lobate forms. Subtlety and simplicity were happily combined, and it was not until the passion for producing pretentious "shew pieces" became an overmastering motive and ran away with discretion that many of the contours became unduly elaborate and intricate in their Rococo complexities.

TYPES OF DECORATION. In the letters-patent issued when the factory was in its infancy it was explicitly set forth in unmistakable terms that the purpose of the enterprise was the manufacture of porcelain *after the style of Saxon porcelain.* Of course the main hope back of this expressed aim was that the porcelain of Vincennes should equal or excel the porcelain of Dresden in point of paste and glaze, but the desire for superlative excellence of decoration was by no means of trifling import.

Amongst the very early pieces are examples with scattered flowers and insects, in the Dresden manner, adroitly painted in polychrome to conceal imperfections in the body or glaze, in the fashion previously noted. The products of Vincennes, and of its successor Sèvres, are noteworthy for the almost complete absence of Oriental *motifs* in their decoration as well as in their contour. The tendencies were always peculiarly European and French. One of the few instances of the employment of Oriental decorative *motifs* occurs in the prunus sprigs and blossoms in relief on early products that displayed no colour save reticent bandings and a few touches upon such moulded features as handles.

Enormous pains were taken to ensure the perfect naturalistic colouring of the modelled flowers and bouquets that were so popular, whether the flowers appeared as separate creations in the form of detached bouquets and sprays or were applied as attached embellishments (PLATE 54), to the body of a vase or dish or the branches of a sconce.

Flowers, likewise, were painted with equal care on the surface of the porcelain and were as meticulously executed as were the modelled blossoms. Sprays of flowers thus painted formed one of the favourite types of decoration. At the outset gold was not used, but as the secret of gilding porcelain was bought from a Benedictine friar when Gravant, supported by M. de Fulvy, reorganised the establishment after the Dubois *dèbacle,* gilding soon made its appearance on Vincennes china and played an increasingly conspicuous rôle in the decoration as time went on. When the factory became a royal undertaking, the right to use gold was considered its special prerogative and other factories, as already noted, were forbidden to use it or put it on their china.

Under the chemists Hellot and Macquer, many new colours were added to the porcelain decorator's palette so that with everything from bright red and carmine, soft rose and lilac, to all gradations of greens, yellows and blues at their disposal the china painters suffered no limitations. One result of this unrestricted colour range was that subtle shadings and greater naturalism in floral renderings supplanted the earlier conventionalised treatment.

Much use, too, was made of ground colours with spaces in reserve in which were polychrome knots of flowers, birds, figures and landscapes. The most important and famous ground colour, *bleu du roi,* appeared just before the middle of the century. This splendid underglaze colour was so intense that it usually had to be modified by a network of gilded lines, or some similar device to break it up. Several years afterwards, Hellot devised the turquoise blue, an enamel or onglaze colour that was peculiarly characteristic of the later decoration of Vincennes and the subsequent decorations of Sèvres.

Besides the types of decoration hitherto mentioned, there were delicate interlaced ribbon patterns in conjunction with minute diaperings, tiny flowers, birds and gilding. There were also piercings, fretwork, and embossings, as well as the more prominent moulded work of rims, handles and knobs, all of which afforded opportunities for manifold enrichment with colour and gold.

Birds of brilliant and varied plumage often appeared as the chief items of polychrome decoration and were, indeed, characteristic of one well-recognised Vincennes type. Small landscapes, woodland and pastoral scenes, in the finished and somewhat minute manner of the day, were employed with great frequency either on shaped panels in reserve or without the accompaniment of any surrounding ground colour. Again, both woodland scenes and flower subjects were painted *en camaïeu,* the edges or rims of pieces so decorated being enriched with a line of gold. Yet another type of decoration consisted of leaves, flowers, sprays and garlands, or of arabesques, painted in gold on the white body of the china.

THE MARKS. Up until the time when Vincennes became a royal factory there seems to have been no definitely recognised mark, although a few pieces of early style bear either the two interlaced L's or two L's standing by themselves with a point between.

When the works came under the direct control of the King, it was ordered that the mark should thenceforward be the royal cypher, the familiar interlacing L's, of which that on the right is reversed. Pieces for the King's personal use, or intended as royal presents, sometimes displayed a fleur-de-lys above the cypher. From 1753 onward it was customary to date the pieces by a letter between the L's, the date letter for 1753 being A, and so onward.

SCEAUX CHINA—1749-   ?

HISTORY. At the instance of one Jacques Chapelle—a versatile person who, amongst other accomplishments, possessed a knowledge of china-making—a company for the manufacture of porcelain was formed at Sceaux in 1749. The nucleus for this enterprise was a faïence factory already well established. Through the good offices of the Duchesse du Maine, Chapelle engaged to secure royal consent for the manufacture of porcelain.

All arrangements had been made down to the least detail, and the work-people engaged were ready to start work, but the expected royal consent failed to materialise. The privileges already granted Vincennes presented one obstacle, and another still more serious was the opposition of Madame de Pompadour. Consequently, for the time being, the new organisation had to be satisfied with making a species of faïence called *Faïence Japonée*.

In 1763 the MM. Jacques and Jullien—the same who acquired Mennecy in 1766—took over the establishment and, in 1772, Richard Glot became director, Jacques and Jullien then concentrating all their interests at Mennecy. Although royal consent was lacking, porcelain was undoubtedly made at Sceaux, surreptitiously, perhaps, but none the less certainly, from the time Jacques and Jullien began to manage the works.

The Duc de Penthièvre, High Admiral of France, became patron of the factory in 1775 and, shielded by his puissant influence, they dared to make porcelain quite openly, although not until 1784, when the Vincennes-Sèvres monopoly was somewhat modified, did they obtain the full right to employ polychrome decoration and gilding. Such decoration, however, they had probably made use of long before.

The Body. The soft paste body was the same as that of Mennecy, which is quite natural considering the intimate connexion in personnel that existed between the two factories, Jacques and Jullien directing both Sceaux and Mennecy simultaneously for several years.

The Glaze. The glaze of Sceaux, likewise, was identical with that of Mennecy.

Articles Made and Contour. The articles made at Sceaux were, in general, the same as those made at Mennecy and included all those things incidental to the furnishing of tables, dressing stands and writing tables, as well as divers other accessories for house embellishment. The contours, too, bore a close resemblance to those of the factory with which there were such intimate relations.

TYPES OF DECORATION. As might be expected, under the circumstances, there was an obvious similarity between the methods of decoration employed at Sceaux and those in vogue at Mennecy. There is this to be said, however. The flower and bird designs, which were particularly favourite *motifs* in both places, were often better conceived and more deftly executed at Sceaux, a fact that gives the Sceaux china a special touch of distinction. During the period when the use of gilding was denied, rims, borders and edges usually displayed a finish of rose-colour (Plate 4, A), in lieu of gold, the effect of which is very engaging.

THE MARKS. The usual mark shews the letters S X incised in the paste, although many pieces which it is reasonable to attribute to Sceaux shew no mark at all.

S X

TOURNAY CHINA—1750-

HISTORY. Although Tournay is now in Belgium, the products of the Tournay factory are included under the head of French china because Tournay was under French rule when the porcelain made there won its reputation.

Peterinck began making porcelain at Tournay in 1750, and the work prospered so much that a few years later the factory employed a large force of work-people and put forth a very considerable volume of wares.

There were two grades of china produced at Tournay, one including pieces of the finest character that could compare favourably with the output of any of the other French porcelain factories, the second being inexpensive and well calculated for all ordinary domestic use. Both kinds were produced simultaneously over a considerable period, but after a number of years the finer grade was discontinued. The ordinary grade is still made there.

THE BODY. The soft paste body of Tournay china was of somewhat different composition from that used at the French factories already considered, and it required a much shorter time for firing. In colour it has not the noticeable yellowish or amber tinge characteristic of the Chantilly or Mennecy body, but it is not so white as the soft paste body of Vincennes or Sèvres. It is also somewhat more porous in texture than the others.

While the usual processes of moulding and throwing were followed in shaping the pieces at Tournay, the process of casting (v. section on The Making of Chinaware) was also used. This process, it is believed, was first employed in the Tournay factory.

THE GLAZE. The Tournay glaze is clear, transparent, beautifully smooth and evenly distributed, without runnings or "tear-drops."

ARTICLES MADE AND CONTOUR. Amongst the articles of the finer ware were vases, flower-pots, tableware and table garnitures, tea, coffee and chocolate services, candlesticks, sconces, and the sundry elegancies of equipment for writing and dressing tables. The second grade included table services also, and all the articles of everyday domestic utility for which porcelain was suitable. In the matter of contour, both Oriental and European models afforded a basis for adaptation.

TYPES OF DECORATION. One of the most favourite types of decoration consisted of flowers, either scattered in the Dresden manner or else grouped in sprays and more organised compositions. These were very carefully executed, and the factory was particularly fortunate in the use of an excellent iron oxide red.

When the fashions set by Sèvres had become all-prevalent, the Tournay decorators followed suit with admirable ground colours and polychrome *motifs* in reserve (Plate 55, A). The Tournay factory was successful not only in producing a good underglaze *bleu du roi* but also in imitating other items of Sèvres embellishment, such as the "partridge eye" device, diapers and reticulations of gold, and birds of brilliant plumage along with the floral *motifs* and ribbon patterns.

Little landscapes and woodland scenes in the pastoral manner of the day were largely made use of as well as figures, the latter in the form of cherubs or *amorini* or else as compositions based on Classic precedents. Both landscapes and figure subjects often appeared *en camaïeu*, as a rule, however, in conjunction with a certain amount of gilding.

The commoner wares were chiefly decorated with flowers, either

scattered or arranged in sprays or connected garlands. These decorations were executed, for the most part, in blue, although polychrome
painting was employed to some extent.

THE MARKS. The mark of the finer grade of Tournay china consisted of two crossed swords accompanied by four crosses, and was
applied either with gold or in on-glaze colour. The inferior grade bore
only workmen's individual marks or some factory symbol indicating
the pattern of the piece.

ORLÉANS CHINA—1753-1811 (?)

HISTORY. The Orléans porcelain factory, under Sieur Gerréault, began its career in 1753 with the Duc de Penthièvre as its patron, the
same nobleman whom we have already met extending his protective
interest to the factory at Sceaux, although his patronage at Sceaux was
not exercised till many years later.

This venture was authorised by the Council of State and was distant
far enough from Paris not to be perpetually harassed by the opposition
of neighbouring competitors and claimants of exclusive privileges. Up
until 1770 the factory produced soft paste porcelain; after that date all
its products were of hard paste. The factory continued in operation
until 1811, it is known certainly, and may have gone on for some years
longer. A good deal of china must have been produced, but it was
very fragile. Consequently, it is comparatively rare.

THE BODY. The Orléans soft paste body was highly vitreous, very
translucent, white in colour, and of beautiful quality. The hard paste
body used after 1770 was extremely vitreous or glassy at first and exceptionally brittle, but the composition later became more satisfactory.

THE GLAZE. The glaze on both the soft paste and the hard paste
bodies was very brilliant and glassy and lacked the sympathetic mellowness displayed by the glazes of such factories as Chantilly, Mennecy, or Sceaux.

ARTICLES MADE AND CONTOUR. Table services, tea, coffee and chocolate sets, and pieces of kindred use composed the principal output, although a certain number of statuettes and vases were also produced. The contours were chiefly of European character, well shaped, and with all the moulded details impeccably designed and executed. During the hard paste period the prevalent Neo-Classic forms made their appearance.

TYPES OF DECORATION. In the soft paste period the decorations were often in the form of scattered flowers done in underglaze blue. The other type chiefly employed consisted of bouquets, knots and garlands painted in polychrome and enriched with gilding.

During the hard paste period scattered flowers and garlands composed the usual decorative *motifs* and gilding was also used.

THE MARKS. The marks of the early period consist of a label above the letter C. At some time early in the nineteenth century the mark became a round vignette with the word "Orléans." It was applied in gold or in on-glaze colour.

SÈVRES CHINA—1756 TO DATE

HISTORY. The first chapter of the history of Sèvres is the history of Vincennes, which we have already traversed in detail. One of the shareholders of the factory of Vincennes, realising full well the more or less precarious financial condition of the establishment, endeavoured to interest Madame de Pompadour in its affairs, hoping that her intervention might be instrumental in placing everything on a firm footing.

Madame de Pompadour, who was a person of great good taste and felt a deep concern in everything connected with the welfare of art in France, promptly took the matter up and straightway proceeded to fasten the King's interest more securely and directly on the development of the royal porcelain manufactory. A piece of ground was selected at Sèvres, and, to make a long story short, in due time the necessary buildings were erected and the Vincennes establishment with its whole personnel transferred there.

The trying experimental stages attending the early years of any enterprise had all been passed through. Sèvres began with an already complete background of ripe experience and established tradition and, so far as processes were concerned, there was an absolutely clear path ahead to spring full-grown into fame and the glories of superlative achievement. There were defects in the organisation and management of the factory, it is true, and these were serious enough to have landed an establishment without royal support in total bankruptcy, but the King's interest and pocket, both manipulated by Madame de Pompadour, bridged over the difficulties and made it possible to produce china of unparalleled excellence and beauty.

Madame de Pompadour manifested no less solicitude about the design and quality of the factory's products than she did over the ways and means of maintenance. Her tastes in the matter of the designs followed and executed can readily be traced; her care for material prosperity can be judged from the following extract, taken from the memoirs of the Marquis d'Argenson where it is recorded that:

"Madame de Pompadour talks about nothing but the great advantage that the State will derive from the manufacture of porcelain in the Saxon fashion, and even in having excelled the Saxons in it. A royal shop for the sale of this porcelain is opened in the rue de la Monnaie, and there is exhibited a service which the King is going to send to the King of Saxony as if he wanted to bid him defiance, and provoke him by shewing him that he had even excelled his porcelain manufacture. At one of the King's suppers the Marquise de Pompadour said that those who did not buy as much of this porcelain as they could afford were not good citizens, to which someone answered that, 'Since the King had bestowed so many donations in the encouragement of this manufactory, those at Charleville and at St. Etienne for the manufacture of weapons, useful to us in another way, are neglected, and three-quarters of the work-people go over to foreign countries.'"

Financial difficulties, however, continued. Most people found the ware too expensive, especially as they could buy Dresden porcelain and Oriental china at a much lower figure. At last, in November 1759, in order to save the situation, the King undertook the whole monetary responsibility of the works, an edict was issued ordering the factory to be administered for His Majesty, and the shareholders were paid off with interest-bearing notes, properly secured. Thus did the factory of Sèvres become crown property.

At the instance of M. Boileau, who had grown up with the business management of Vincennes and had contrived to make himself absolutely indispensable, the Lieutenant-General of Police put forth an edict forbidding all persons to make, model, paint or gild porcelain, or to sell the same, under the severest penalties. This edict likewise forbade manufacturers of so-called common porcelains, who had hitherto enjoyed certain privileges, to use gilding, to make figures, flowers, or other modelled pieces except as embellishments for their own wares, or to employ any colour other than blue, applied after the customary Chinese patterns, for decorating their products.

This, of course, called forth a stormy outburst of indignation and protest. Factories like Mennecy and Chantilly enjoyed the patronage of powerful nobles whom the King did not wish to offend and, furthermore, he saw the unwisdom of ruining a number of factories and causing needless unemployment. Accordingly, by another decree, set forth in February 1766, the making of porcelain in imitation of the Chinese was permitted, but the managers of the factories were straitly charged in the decoration of their china to use no colour other than blue, except they chose to paint a piece wholly with some other single colour *en camaïeu*. They were likewise forbidden to use gold, or to make statuettes or ornaments in high relief out of porcelain, either glazed or unglazed. These monopolistic restrictions explain why Chantilly and Mennecy china of a certain period was decorated either in blue, or in some other colour *en camaïeu,* and without the grace of gilding.

In spite of these drastic measures that crippled the liberty of other factories, Sèvres still laboured under money troubles and the King was ultimately obliged to meet deficits from his privy-purse. If some of the energies and talent had been turned to making more china for the average market, instead of concentrating almost all efforts on magnificent regal productions, there would have been more substantial profit and less anxiety. Nor need artistic excellence have suffered in the least. Chantilly and Mennecy, to mention no others, produced beautiful chinaware of a quality and price not prohibitive to the purse of those who could afford reasonable luxury. And they found profit in doing so.

As it was, the management of Sèvres, inspired by extravagant notions of splendid ostentation, pinned their faith mostly on effulgent *chefs d'œuvres,* cabinet pieces marvellous to behold, but quite beyond ordinary reach. "Most of the pieces appear to have been intended for the King's service, for the furnishing of the royal palaces of Versailles, the Trianon, Marly, Bellevue, Meudon, St. Germain, and Fontainebleau. He used them as presents for his relatives, his friends, his courtiers and his ambassadors. They were also made use of as diplomatic presents, sometimes, perhaps, as diplomatic bribes." Naturally, when the commercial considerations were either wholly eliminated or else so minimised that they counted for naught in the grand total, it required a kingly purse to meet the costs of production, and even the kingly purse was not always adequate to the demands without a good deal of pinching and paring. When the royal purse was utterly depleted and Louis XV, like his predecessor, had to send all his silver to the mint, then Sèvres made wares for popular consumption and prospered.

The early sumptuous period of Sèvres soft paste porcelain lasted from 1756 to 1769. In the latter year began the manufacture of hard paste porcelain conjointly with the soft paste. A great quantity of the factory's productions were still of the magnifical type and, so it seems, of equally magnifical price. To encourage the artists responsible for the designs and decoration, and also to help the sales, the King had exhibitions of porcelain every year in the Palace at Versailles. These he not only attended in person, but he actually played the part of shewman and salesman. A contemporary source gives us a lively picture of these occasions:

"Every New Year's Day they bring into the galleries at Versailles the newest and choicest pieces of Sèvres porcelain, which the King himself distributes among his great lords for their money; he fixes the prices himself and they are not cheap. We presume that the price must be pretty high on account of the financial situation, but we shall speak about that later on. It is certain that some of the noble lords are not ashamed of taking a cup, or some little ornament, when they think they are not observed. Seeing a count take a cup in this way, Louis XV sent to him next morning the cashier from Sèvres with the saucer that he had been unable to take, and a bill for the pieces. One day the King saw that an *abbé* refused to purchase a piece on account of its price, but in order to persuade him the King immediately promised him a benefice."

In time the wealthier public gradually became educated up to the price of the wares of Sèvres and collectors bought the choice vases, flower-pots and figures, both glazed and in the biscuit, on the production of which the ablest sculptors, painters and modellers of the day had spent their best efforts, but popular requirements were still too little considered, and the factory was usually run at a loss or now and then barely managed to pay expenses. These latter occasions were of rare occurrence.

When Louis XVI succeeded to the throne, royal interest in the factory was continued unabated, both on the part of the King himself, who took deep pride in the Sèvres achievements, and also on the part of the Queen, for Marie Antoinette dearly loved the graces which the painters, the sculptors and the modellers so beguilingly expressed, and often visited the works. The story is told that one day the Queen, on looking at a quantity of recently decorated porcelain, deplored the fact that she saw abundance of roses, tulips, daffodils and other flowers of all colours save blue, a colour to which she was very partial. Hettlinger, one of the directors, at once thought of using the cornflower as a decoration to please the Queen, and thenceforth it became vastly popular as a *motif,* not only at Sèvres but at all the other porcelain factories as well.

The King's enthusiasm was very obviously attested both by his continuance of the annual exhibitions in the Palace at Versailles and by the active part he took in the preparations for them, on which occasions he was sometimes more of an hindrance than an help, as we may gather from a letter written by Hettlinger:

"I have already said that an exhibition of porcelains takes place at the end of every year up to the day of the 'Three Magi.' It is held at the Royal Palace, but the public are allowed to come and examine and buy the pieces. The King occupies in Versailles, besides the State rooms, the *Petits Appartements,* where he passes his private life. Three of these rooms are cleared of their furniture, and the porcelain pieces are exhibited on tables. This year he did not wait until the arrival of the work-people, but must himself be unpacking the pieces, breaking not a few, and mixing every-thing up so that it took us hours to put it straight. The King delights in his manufactory at Sèvres, and he said to one of his confidants, 'Our brave Sèvres men will soon be here. I must make haste to shoot some game.' "

But royal interest in the prettinesses of the work did not help matters much, and certainly did not assist the financial management. Fifteen years before Louis XVI succeeded to the throne, the materials requisite for making hard paste porcelain had been found in France, endless experiments had been carried out, and a number of hard paste porce-lain factories had sprung up in various parts of the kingdom, although hard paste was not made at Sèvres until some years after the native materials had become available.

These recently established hard paste porcelain works were forging steadily ahead and were seriously affecting the market of Sèvres. Al-though there were still in effect the restrictive edicts that gave Sèvres a virtual monopoly of fine porcelain-making in France, and clipped the wings of private enterprise, those edicts were not rigorously enforced. There was laxity on the part of government officials, there were eva-sions on the part of the newly arisen factories and, what was most significant of all, some of the greatest nobles of the realm and, indeed, members of the royal family, had lent their names and active patronage to divers of these independent ventures even when they were not finan-cially interested in their success, as they were in more than one instance.

Things gradually went from bad to worse in the business affairs of Sèvres, until at last the King was obliged to retrench and greatly curtail the staff which, of course, only made the position of the independent factories stronger. Even under these disadvantageous conditions, mar-vellous work was performed in the royal factory and triumphs of porce-lain design and decoration were produced right up to the very eve of the Revolution.

During the Revolution the factory was in sorry plight and so were the workers, but under the Napoleonic *régime* order was restored and the establishment was again put on its feet, for Napoleon saw in it a means of contributing to the splendour and outward display of pomp about which he was so solicitous and which he knew how to use to such good purpose. In this era much magnificent but over-elaborate porcelain was produced. The great physicist Brongniart became director and bent his energies to perfecting the hard paste body. It was at this time, in the early years of the nineteenth century, that the making of the beautiful soft paste porcelain at Sèvres was definitely abandoned.

The factory of Sèvres has grown into a great national institution and has rendered invaluable services to the porcelain art. In the museum at Sèvres are admirable and comprehensive collections of china which it is well worth while for any china-lover to inspect.

THE BODY. In the section on Vincennes china the early story of the soft paste body was told. After the factory of Vincennes was removed to become the foundation of the Sèvres factory, the chemical staff of Sèvres were constantly conducting experiments, and whenever there was a chance to effect an improvement, the improvement was straightway made, until the paste was brought to absolute perfection—*pure milky white, hard,* and *translucent.*

This perfect body, with its tender translucence, continued to be used without a competitor for favour until 1769, when hard paste was added to the list of products. Oftentimes the walls of the soft paste pieces were thinner at Sèvres than they had been made at Vincennes; this increased their translucence and also their fragility. The soft paste in the biscuit pieces sometimes shews a very pale amber tinge, which adds a warm glow and mellowness to the general aspect.

The hard paste produced underwent the same constant and rigid scrutiny as the soft paste had undergone at an earlier date, and the same revision of formulas for its composition. It was the tendency of the chemists in charge to aim at technical perfection rather than sympathetic quality, beauty, or adaptability for decoration. The soft paste was the most perfect vehicle ever achieved for decorating, far more so than the hard paste. But much was sacrificed in the endeavour to reach technical perfection in the hard paste, and there was a tendency to make it too "severe"—cold, hard, metallic and glittering in quality.

Brongniart, who abandoned the manufacture of soft paste porcelain, bent his efforts toward making the hard paste conform absolutely with the hardest type of Chinese porcelain. Under Brongniart the hard paste was made harder than previously, and the type he introduced is still employed for table services. It was not until late in the nineteenth century that this attitude was at all modified. The Sèvres hard paste body is absolutely *white, hard, translucent* and *resonant* and needless to say, flawless.

THE GLAZE. The glaze used at Vincennes had been brought to perfection before the removal to Sèvres. It had a lustrous, luscious richness, and at Sèvres it was maintained at its highest state of clarity, colourless transparency, glassy smoothness, and evenness of distribution.

The glaze used on the first hard paste porcelain made at Sèvres, and continued down to 1800, was calcareous, that is, it had chalk or lime in its composition, and was much less glossy than the glaze of the soft paste porcelain. As a matter of fact, it was relatively opaque, and hence the early hard paste exhibits a pearly whiteness. This early glaze was an especially kindly medium for colours and for enamels in relief. Brongniart changed this glaze for one made from the natural pegmatite of St. Yrieix, near Limoges, and it is this later glaze that so often seems glittering and unsympathetic.

ARTICLES MADE AND CONTOUR. Apart from the objects *de luxe,* the "shew pieces," to which reference has already been made, the modelled flowers, the splendid vases and other ornaments intended for the King's service or to be given as presents to foreign monarchs and ambassadors, the wares made at Sèvres number dinner services of both simple pattern and the more elaborate designs of Duplessis, trays, sugar-bowls, inkstands, jardinières, tea, coffee and chocolate services, milk jugs, table garnitures, sconces, candlesticks, basons and ewers, tobacco and snuffboxes, patch boxes, covered jars, watch cases, buttons, cane-heads, thimbles, perfume and pomatum pots, needle-cases, *bonbonnières,* bowls, pot-pourri jars, gravy-boats and sauce-boats, vases of a dozen different styles, fruit baskets, dessert services, clock cases, cups and saucers, plaques or panels for furniture—these in the reign of Louis XVI—small flower jars, and jewel caskets. Besides these there were the portrait medallions, busts, groups, and figures of biscuit porcelain modelled by the most eminent sculptors.

As previously pointed out, the contours followed at Sèvres were distinctly French. It is the nature of the French genius, even when a model is admittedly drawn from some foreign source, so to assimilate and adapt it and endow it with new individuality that it wholly ceases to be what it was and becomes a new thing instinct with Gallic character. Whatever inspiration in contour was derived from Oriental sources was so reshaped in the hands of the Sèvres designers that it became French in the transmutation.

During the reign of Louis XV the contours of Sèvres porcelain were a faithful index to the prevalent trend and spirit of contemporary design as we see it reflected in architecture, furniture and painting. Subtle shapings and curves were the order of the day, and we find these elements accommodated to chinaware, as well as everywhere else. Long before Louis XVI came to the throne, however, a change of taste had set in and superseded the well-recognised Rococo manner that we particularly associate with the reign of Louis XV.

A strong tendency toward greater purity and simplicity of line was unmistakable. The chinaware of Sèvres promptly registered all the changes of style from the exuberant fancies of the Rococo mode to the more austere forms of Neo-Classic provenance. Without loss of grace, the many playful curves and subtle shapings gave place to straight lines or restrained flaring contours (PLATE 58, B). When the Directoire and First Empire came, the urbanity and suave but cheerful dignity of Neo-Classic contours yielded, in turn, to the aggressive and insistent severity of robust Neo-Grec forms (PLATES 59 and 56, A), inspired by newly-quickened archæological enthusiasms. In short, whatever was the dominant attitude in the minds of Frenchmen toward matters of style and design, that attitude was straightway mirrored in the products of Sèvres whose design was a peculiarly sensitive index to every slightest variation of national taste.

TYPES OF DECORATION. The types of decoration that characterised the porcelain of Sèvres, notwithstanding their manifold variety, reflected the procession of style influences just as surely and accurately as did the contours. We find the Rococo manner, at its best, exemplified from about 1756 to 1769. Before this, however, there were indications of the coming change, and during the reign of Louis XVI the spirit of the decorations manifested an altogether new aspect. Delicacy, elegance and restraint succeeded to exuberant and playful fancy, to be in turn ousted by the incisive severity of the Directoire mode which was soon to be followed by the ostentatious pomp and circumstance of the Empire fashion. All of these epochs had their own well-defined preferences in both colouring and the character of decorative *motifs*, and these preferences were interpreted in the china of Sèvres no less than in every other visible manifestation of decorative art.

It must be remembered that Sèvres had fallen heir to all the decorative developments of Vincennes and had only to go on amplifying and adding to the stock of thoroughly organised tradition acquired by inheritance at the outset. There were, to begin with, the various types of flower and bird painting followed by the Vincennes decorators and there were the wonderful ground colours that the Vincennes chemists had already devised. To these colours, in 1757, was added the beautiful *rose Pompadour,* popularly and *wrongly* called *rose du Barry.*

The development of the Sèvres style of decoration was the natural outgrowth of the methods in vogue at the Vincennes factory. There was no break in the tradition. It was a continuous progression, to a large measure in the hands of the same men. The chief difference to be noted, so far as the early work of Sèvres is concerned, is that the decorations in many instances gradually became richer and more sumptuous than those customarily employed at Vincennes and new colours and gradations of colour were added.

The *bleu du roi,* as previously mentioned, was too intense and vibrant to use in large masses alone and was ordinarily modified by fine gilded reticulations in a regular pattern, by vermiform gold lines, by the "partridge eye" *motif,* or by a circular diaper in gold. Besides the *bleu du roi,* the Sèvres blue and turquoise blue as ground colours, there were *rose Pompadour* (just mentioned), apple-green (PLATE 5, B), grass-green, lilac, daffodil yellow, claret colour, a pale canary yellow which was developed at a rather late date, brown tortoise shell and green tortoise shell grounds, and the underglaze chrome green, which last was developed during the Empire and, although striking, cannot be considered beautiful or in any way worthy to be compared with the earlier grounds.

The panels reserved on the white ground of the porcelain, in conjunction with these ground colours, were surrounded and defined with

gilded or coloured scrolls or bands of ribbon. In the case of one jardinière, now preserved in the Wallace Collection, with a ground colour
of *rose Pompadour,* the oval reserved panel is surrounded with a broad
green ribbon touched with gold. On these reserved panels were customarily painted with the utmost delicacy woodland scenes, pastorals,
groups of figures, harbour scenes, military subjects, scenes of society,
gallantry or love, and a diversity of mythological subjects, or else they
were decorated with flowers in polychrome or birds of gorgeous plumage. Although subjects of this sort had been marvellously well executed
at Vincennes, at Sèvres there was a marked increase in the delicacy and
refinement of presentation. This is not to be wondered at when a number of the ablest artists of the time were constantly employed—such men
as Le Guay, Lecot, Dodin, Armand, Aubert, Bouillat, Mérault, Sioux,
Chabry, Pithou, Bouchet and Rosset, to name only a few of them.

The modellers and sculptors were no less distinguished in their pro-
fession. There were Duplessis, Falconet, Bachelier, Le Riche, Perrotin
and Levaux, while in modelling the originals for the biscuit portrait
busts and groups there were such men as Pigalle, Clodion, Caffieri,
Boizot, Julien and, above all, Pajou. Many more names of painters,
sculptors and modellers might be added to the list, did space permit,
but if anyone wishes to pursue the details further on this score a complete roll may be found in the bulletins of the Sèvres museum.

When ground colours were not used, with reserved panels for the
elaborate painted decorations, rims, bands or other parts of grounds
were sometimes filled with diapers of lattice (PLATES 56, B and 57), or
trellis work or with "partridge eye" forms composed of sea-green or
bright blue dots in conjunction with minute gold dots on the white
ground of the porcelain to give additional texture and enrichment.
There were also landscapes and country scenes executed on a white
ground *en camäieu* in crimson, rose, blue or rose mulberry, with gilding on the rims and at other appropriate places.

Not a little of the tableware was decorated with flowers in polychrome, scattered or in bouquets (PLATE 56, A and B), and often the
scattered flowers were very minute. There were also garlands, festoons
and wreaths (PLATE 58, B), of both flowers and foliage (PLATE 60, B),
while fruit was often used on dessert services. Armorial bearings like-

wise played an important part in the decorations, along with mono-grams and cyphers.

Besides tiny forget-me-nots, little cornflowers and rosettes set at the intersections of latticework (PLATE 56, B), there were graceful arabes-ques (PLATE 58, A), patterned after those of Pompeii or adapted from the frescoes of Raphael; there were medallions with cameo heads and figures; there were rectangles, ovals, octagons, hexagons, and panels of other shapes filled with Classic figures; there were country scenes and peasant figures (PLATE 60, A); there were innumerable border patterns with scrolls, cartouches, cornucopias and various symbols and attributes, and there were elegant Etruscan *motifs*.

The Directoire brought Phrygian caps and an host of Roman republi-can and Imperial *motifs,* while the Empire brought a brief dominance of Egyptian themes and a larger and more permanent following of Greek and Roman devices supplied by Percier and Fontaine.

The gilding was always excellent (PLATE 60, B), whether the whole design was painted in gold or whether the gold was employed as an enrichment, either flat or burnished. The "jewelled Sèvres" with trans-parent raised enamels laid on gold that appeared like inlaid jewels on the surface of the porcelain, was one of the triumphs of combined gild-ing and enamelling.

THE MARKS. The Sèvres mark was the royal cypher, the two "L's" interlaced and facing each other. The date letter or letters stood between the two L's and afford an accurate means of dating the pieces.

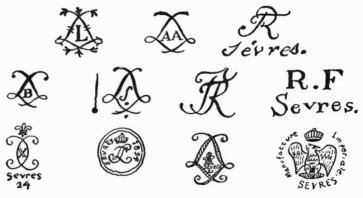

BOURG-LA-REINE CHINA—1774-1788

HISTORY. The factory at Bourg-la-Reine, not far from Sceaux, was founded in 1774 by the MM. Jacques and Jullien who have appeared twice before, once in connexion with Sceaux and once as the managers of the factory at Mennecy-Villeroy. The Bourg-la-Reine factory was started under the protecting patronage of the Comte d'Eu, and it is believed that Jacques and Jullien embarked on this new enterprise upon relinquishing the works of Mennecy-Villeroy, either through sale or upon the expiration of a lease.

Considering who were the heads of the factory, it is to be expected that the wares produced at Bourg-la-Reine should be substantially the same as those of Sceaux and Mennecy. The china produced at those two places commanded a ready market and the work of Bourg-la-Reine was merely a continuation of the earlier work of Jacques and Jullien. When the pieces are unmarked it is well-nigh impossible to distinguish between the products of the three factories.

Nearly all the edges of the Bourg-la-Reine pieces have a line of rose-colour. Very few were gilded, and those so decorated were probably amongst the latest products after the inhibitions respecting gilding had been removed. The pieces of Bourg-la-Reine china that are marked have the letters B. R. incised in the paste.

B. R.

ARRAS CHINA—1782-1788 (?)

HISTORY. In 1782 the Arras factory was undertaken by two ladies named Deleneur. They were previously faïence dealers in Arras and engaged in the manufacture of porcelain at the instance of the Governour of Flanders and Artois, who supplied the necessary funds. This he did partly because of his jealousy of Tournay, partly because of the extensive importation of English china, which he wished to stop.

The body was a soft paste, yellowish white in colour, somewhat resembling the paste of Mennecy or Sceaux. It was chiefly decorated in blue (PLATE 55, B). The mark consists of the letters A R painted in underglaze blue and occasionally a painter's initial appears alongside.

Competition was too keen and other wares were cheaper so that the factory was not profitable and was abandoned after five or six years.

AR

SAINT-AMAND-LES-EAUX CHINA—
1815 TO DATE

HISTORY. Dorchies Herbo, a Fleming, started the porcelain factory of Saint-Amand-les-Eaux in 1815 and produced a fine white soft paste body. Counterfeiters of porcelain have often availed themselves of this ware to dress up with decorations and sell as specimens of the old soft paste Sèvres. Along with Tournay, the factory of Saint-Amand-les-Eaux is the only establishment that has continued the making of soft paste porcelain to the present day. The common porcelain of this factory is painted with simple designs in underglaze blue.

PARIS CHINA

HISTORY. From about 1760 onward, but chiefly in the later years of the eighteenth century, a number of porcelain factories sprang up in Paris and in its immediate suburbs. They were engaged chiefly in the manufacture of hard paste porcelain, consequent upon the discovery of the necessary materials in the south of France, and were able to pursue their course comparatively unmolested, partly through diplomatic evasion, partly through the laxity of enforcing the regulative edicts that prevailed during the reign of Louis XVI. They unquestionably infringed the prerogatives claimed by Sèvres, but this infringement was generally connived at by those in authority and was actively encouraged by many of exalted station, in one case even by the Queen, Marie Antoinette, herself.

Of these minor factories, many of which produced admirable china both in point of structure and tasteful decoration, those most worthy of attention were Vincennes (not to be confounded with the old Vincennes factory which was merged in Sèvres), the *"Manufacture du Comte d'Artois,"* the factory of Vaux, the Fabrique de la Courtille, the Fabrique de la rue de Reuilly, the Fabrique de Monsieur at Clignancourt, the Fabrique de la Reine, rue Thiroux, the Fabrique du Duc d'Angoulême, rue de Bondy, the Fabrique de la rue Popincourt, and the Fabrique du Duc d'Orléans.

The products of these factories are always turning up and most of them are so excellent (PLATES 61 and 62, B), that anyone might well rejoice at getting them. Nor is this excellence to be wondered at when we remember that not a few of those men who started these factories, or directed them, had gained their knowledge and ability, both technical and artistic, in no less a training school than the factory of Sèvres.

When the deficits of Sèvres were appallingly large in the reign of Louis XVI, and it was well-nigh impossible for the King to find the wherewithal to maintain the works at their full capacity, he was obliged to reduce the staff. Every reduction sent adrift men who were capable of making and decorating porcelain in the manner of Sèvres and, when the enforced retrenchment deprived them of their wonted employment in the royal factory, it was only to be expected that they should seek an outlet for their experience elsewhere and carry on the kind of work for which they were best fitted.

Started as these factories were, late in the century when the passion for hard paste porcelain was strong and when France now had the materials within her own territory whereby she could equal the long-envied products of the German factories and secure the same commercial advantages, it was the most natural thing in the world that they should all pursue the making of hard paste porcelain.

As all these factories were in operation late in the century, the china they made exhibited the contours and decoration characteristic of that epoch when restraint and reticence began to take the place of the more florid exuberance that had previously prevailed. In contour, purity of line, and in decoration, the disciplined elegance of Neo-Classic *motifs* contribute a charm that distinguishes much of the chinaware put forth by these establishments. Their wares may be less famous than the products of other better known factories, but they are none the less beautiful and deserving of sincere appreciation.

VINCENNES (HANNONG) CHINA—
1767–1786 (?)

HISTORY. Before Sèvres engaged in the making of hard paste porcelain, and while experiments with that end in view were being eagerly pursued, negotiations were carried on with the Hannongs, a family of Strasburg potters who unquestionably possessed the secrets of making hard paste porcelain and produced it first at Strasburg and afterwards at Frankenthal. These negotiations do not shew M. Boileau, the guiding spirit of the management at Sèvres, in a very creditable light. Boileau, having obtained Hannong's secrets and pumped him dry of every item of useful information, not only refused to live up to his stipulated agreements but acted with the greatest harshness, persecuted the Hannongs, and made it impossible for them to manufacture porcelain within the kingdom of France. The whole affair was a piece of inexcusable trickery and sharp practice.

In 1767 permission was granted a certain Maurin des Aubiez to set up a faïence factory at Vincennes, and this permission to make faïence was a little later extended to make use of the old soft paste porcelain and manufacture hard paste porcelain *so long as he did not trench upon the privileges of Sèvres.* "Maurin des Aubiez" may have been a name assumed by Hannong or it may have been the name of a silent partner. At any rate, in a document of 1771, Hannong is mentioned as director of the establishment.

In 1772 Hannong left Vincennes to take charge of the porcelain works belonging to the Comte d'Artois. The next indication of the continuance of the Vincennes hard paste porcelain factory was in 1784, when the Sieur Lemaire, evidently making porcelain there at that time, made a protest against the restrictive edicts. When King Louis Philippe visited the Sèvres factory, many years after, he said that while he was still Duc de Chartres he had given his protection to Hannong in setting up the establishment at Vincennes. No mention of the factory occurs after 1786.

THE BODY. The body of the porcelain attributed to this obscure Vincennes venture is a very vitreous hard paste with a slight yellowish tinge, and it somewhat resembles several of the earlier soft paste products.

THE GLAZE. The glaze is often uneven and defective.

ARTICLES MADE AND CONTOUR. The articles made seem to have been chiefly tableware of a purely utilitarian character. The contours had no particular individuality beyond reflecting the trend of contemporary taste in such matters.

TYPES OF DECORATION. Little painted flowers in polychrome formed the usual decoration. The rose and violet colourings are apt to be faded from over-firing.

THE MARKS. The marks "H" and "P.H." in underglaze blue indicate origin at this factory. Pieces marked "L P" under a ducal coronet, in underglaze blue, are also supposed to have come from the Vincennes works.

FABRIQUE DU COMTE D'ARTOIS CHINA—
1769-1810

HISTORY. This factory, in the faubourg St. Denis or the faubourg St. Lazare, began operations about 1769. Pierre Antoine Hannong, leaving Vincennes, became the director here in 1772. Hannong's direction not proving satisfactory from a business point of view, he was removed, and, at the instance of one of the proprietors, the Marquis d'Osson, Barrachin was made director about 1775. It was then that the factory secured the patronage of Charles-Philippe, Comte d'Artois, the brother of Louis XVI. At the same time it obtained the privilege of using the title *"Manufacture du Comte d'Artois."* With a capable direction and staff, and under distinguished and powerful patronage, it now entered upon a prosperous career.

In 1782 Bourdon-Desplanches was director and performed the achievement of firing an ovenful of china with coal in the presence of the municipal authorities, the Sèvres chemists, and a gathering of savants.

The success of this feat made a deep impression, for it meant the saving of a vast quantity of wood fuel which it was becoming all the time more and more difficult to get. Bourdon-Desplanches was rewarded with a subsidy of 3000 livres in recognition of his important accomplishment.

After the restrictive edict of 1784, the factory sought permission to continue making biscuit pieces, busts and other modelled products as well as to go on painting china in all colours and decorating it with gold, on condition of using coal altogether for firing. The petition was granted, provided the gold decoration did not wholly cover any one piece, and provided the biscuit pieces produced were not more than eighteen inches high.

The factory kept on in prosperous working till about 1793. After the worst of the Revolutionary violence and disorder had passed by, the factory resumed its activities, and, under the successive direction of Huet, Benjamin and Schoelcher, maintained operations until 1810 when it was at last discontinued. It was one of the most important of the independent Paris factories and produced a great deal of porcelain of the highest quality.

The Body. The hard paste body for the first few years exhibited a slightly yellowish or amber tinge, similar to the paste of the Vincennes factory while Hannong was its director, and was very vitreous. When Bourdon-Desplanches became director the character of the body changed, shewed a pure milky white colour, and was in every way of admirable quality so that it compared favourably with the hard paste body made at Sèvres. The biscuit pieces, likewise, were of excellent character.

The Glaze. Under Hannong's directorship the glaze was pitted and displayed many imperfections. When the quality of the body was improved, the glaze also was perfected so that it was clear, transparent and evenly distributed.

Articles Made and Contour. From the very beginning of the factory's career it turned out a large quantity of ware which seems at first to have consisted chiefly of table services and similar utilitarian articles. Under the management of Bourdon-Desplanches the scope of the products was broadened so that virtually everything was made for which there could be any demand, including a great number of biscuit pieces both in the form of portrait busts and also the statuettes and groups in the manner of those produced at Sèvres.

The contours in general plainly shewed the influence of Neo-Classic design that marked the reign of Louis XVI and some of the forms closely imitated those of Sèvres which set the fashion in such things.

TYPES OF DECORATION. The decorations of the earlier products were generally more or less scattered polychrome flower subjects in the execution of which a reddish-violet colour was conspicuous, this same colour being employed in a thin line to finish the edges and rims of tableware.

Under Bourdon-Desplanches the types of decoration experienced as marked a change as did the character of the paste and the glaze. Landscapes and Classic figure subjects were freely used. Many of these were executed *en camaïeu,* a soft grey being much employed for that purpose. Arabesques in the Pompeian manner frequently entered into well-disposed compositions. Carefully executed bouquets and garlands of small flowers in polychrome also supplied a popular *motif* and the blue cornflower decoration, originated at Sèvres, likewise entered into the schemes. The gilding was excellent and judiciously used, even when it occurred in lavish measure.

The chemist of the works devised a blue porcelain paste that could be advantageously employed for work of a decorative character without the addition of gilding or painting, but the usual methods of producing ornamental effects were commonly followed.

THE MARKS. Pieces produced while Hannong was director shew the mark "P.H." applied in underglaze blue. The later marks, after Charles-Philippe became patron, were either the letters "C P" interwoven, or the same letters standing beneath a crown of a Prince of the Blood. Ordinarily these marks were enclosed in a vignette and were applied in red or some other colour, painted on the glaze.

VAUX CHINA—1770- ?

History. Records regarding the porcelain factory at Vaux, near Meulan, are by no means as full as might be desired. In 1770, an hard paste porcelain factory, managed by Sieur Moreau, was in operation there. It has been said that Hannong had some concern with the founding of this establishment, but apparently there is nothing whatever to warrant such a statement. Certainly the character of the china produced would not tend to confirm such an opinion, for wherever Hannong was in control the porcelain produced seems to have been of inferior quality, while the porcelain of Vaux had a splendid white body, the wares were excellently potted, and the gilding and painting, executed in the prevalent manner of the time, left nothing to be desired. The mark used was two crossed "V's."

FABRIQUE DE LA COURTILLE CHINA—
1773-1794

History. Locré established the Fabrique de la Courtille, in the rue Fontaine-au-Roi, in 1773 with the express intention of imitating the porcelain made in Germany. Almost from the outset this factory made a large quantity of china, including tableware, a considerable number of shew pieces such as large and important vases, and a number of biscuit groups and busts.

About 1784 Ruffinger joined forces with Locré and the establishment gained such a conspicuous position that in 1787 it was numbered with the works that were of enough importance to be allowed to operate, although they enjoyed no specific authorisation. It was in this factory, in 1790 or thereabouts, that the process of casting was first employed in France in the making of hard paste porcelain. In 1794, presumably owing to the disturbances of the Revolution, the business came to an end. It seems to have been revived later, but only china of a very com· mercial type was made.

The Body. The body was an excellent and pure white hard paste and the biscuit was of equally good quality with the glazed ware.

The Glaze. The glaze was clear and brilliant.

ARTICLES MADE AND CONTOUR. Fine dinner services, tea, coffee and chocolate services, dessert services, candlesticks, sconces and all the usual small articles in common demand at the time were made; also ornamental vases and fine modelling in biscuit ware.

TYPES OF DECORATION. The decorative repertoire embraced arabesques in the Pompeian manner, often on coloured grounds, little flowers and other *motifs* in the style of the period for tableware, and modelled ornament. In connexion with the bases of biscuit ware there were sometimes vermiform applications in white slip, and some of the later porcelain produced was painted like agate.

THE MARKS. The mark was two crossed torches; the biscuit pieces bear the same mark or else the words "Locré à Paris," or "Fabrique de la Courtille."

FABRIQUE DE LA RUE DE REUILLY CHINA— (1774) 1781–1800 (?)

HISTORY. In 1774 a porcelain maker named Lassia sought leave to establish a porcelain works on the rue de Reuilly, in the faubourg St. Antoine, and registered the factory mark "L." Although this date occurs as a possible beginning, there seems to have been no very considerable production of chinaware till somewhere about 1781 when Cadet, Guettard, Lalande and Fontanieu testified to the fire-resisting qualities of Lassia's porcelain. The factory was jointly directed by Lassia and Chanou when it protested against the restrictive edict of 1784. In this same year Chanou left Lassia and set up a factory of his own. Four years later, in 1788, Lassia sought to obtain the exclusive right to make stoves and mantel-pieces of porcelain, but was not successful in his quest. When the factory was discontinued is not definitely known, but it was not in operation in 1800.

THE BODY. The body was of hard paste, hard, white and of excellent quality.

THE GLAZE. The glaze was clear and evenly distributed and compared well with the glaze of other contemporary wares.

ARTICLES MADE AND CONTOUR. From Lassia's application for exclusive right to make porcelain stoves and mantel-pieces, it is evident that the factory essayed unusual things to a certain extent, in addition to the usual articles of manufacture. There were also produced in quantity tableware, tea and coffee services and vases. The contours were of the prevailing Neo-Classic type.

TYPES OF DECORATION. This factory made extensive use of grounds produced with on-glaze enamel colours. A yellow ground of this sort was especially characteristic. Many pieces were also decorated in admirably executed gilding on a white ground. The *motifs* most commonly used were flowers, and arabesques of Classic and Renaissance character and the designs were well adapted to the pieces.

THE MARKS. The mark of this factory was an "L" in underglaze blue or else painted in gold on the glaze. The mark of the independent works started by Chanou, when he left Lassia, was "C.H." in red on the glaze. Pieces of his work are rare, but they are of good quality and the decorations are well painted.

L   ℒ

FABRIQUE DE MONSIEUR, À CLIGNANCOURT CHINA—1771- ?

HISTORY. Pierre Deruelle established an hard paste porcelain factory at Clignancourt in 1771, and apparently carried on work there for three or four years without official authorisation. In 1775 he sought government recognition for his enterprise and gave the required notification to the authorities at Sèvres. At this time he likewise secured the interest of Monsieur, the King's brother, as patron along with the right to style his factory "Fabrique de Monsieur."

De Moitte became the director of the works and a very considerable output of excellent chinaware was made, the factory continuing in active operation until after the Revolution. Indeed, so admirable was the quality of the porcelain in body and glaze, and of such superior character were the gilding and the painted decorations, that the wares could well hold their own in comparison with the work of Sèvres. As a matter of fact, a number of pieces were decorated in the fashions reserved by royal edict to Sèvres, and marked with the crossed and interwoven L's of Sèvres beneath a prince's coronet.

This led to a police investigation, the seizure and confiscation of the pieces so decorated and marked, and the imposition of an heavy fine upon Deruelle. The authorities had no inclination to mitigate the rigours of the law, for the pieces in question were so good that they could readily be mistaken for the work of the royal factory. The contours, the decorations and the gilding of all the chinaware made at the Fabrique de Monsieur were in the Neo-Classic style that dominated the period.

The mark borne by the earliest china produced by this factory was a windmill. After Monsieur became patron, a monogram composed of his initials, L.S.X., was painted in red on the glaze, sometimes with the addition of a prince's coronet above it. Other marks also occur—the interwoven initials of Monsieur including a D, a D beneath a prince's coronet, and an M beneath a coronet, all three were used and applied in red or gold on the glaze.

FABRIQUE DE LA REINE, RUE THIROUX
CHINA—1778- ?

HISTORY. Andrè-Marie Leboeuf established an hard paste porcelain factory in the rue Thiroux in 1778. His wares immediately met with such phenomenal success that in the following year he was heavily fined for trenching upon the privileges reserved to Sèvres in the matter of certain processes and the style of decoration. Of all the factories that may be considered as competitors with Sèvres, Leboeuf's was the one of which the Sèvres management had most cause to be jealous and apprehensive. If Leboeuf's work is closely compared with that of Sèvres, it can be seen at a glance why the authorities of the latter establishment were greatly disquieted.

After his uncomfortable experience with Sevres and the police authorities, Leboeuf secured the protecting patronage of the Queen, who gave him the right to mark his china with her monogram or initial. She gave him further encouragement by ordering from him some of the china for her dairy at Versailles, and also various choice pieces which she gave to her friends as presents. From this royal patronage and the great popularity his work enjoyed, Leboeuf's china came to be known as "Porcelaine à la Reine." After the Revolution the works passed into other hands.

Both the letter A, in underglaze blue, and A beneath the Queen's crown, in either red or gold on-glaze, appear as marks on this truly beautiful china.

FABRIQUE DU DUC D'ANGOULÊME, RUE DE BONDY CHINA—1780- ?

HISTORY. Under the protection and patronage of Louis-Antoine, Duc d'Angoulême, Guerhard and Dihl opened an hard paste porcelain factory, in 1780, in the rue de Bondy. Dihl, a man of broad scientific attainments, is credited with being the first to establish a complete palette of colours that could be used for the decoration of hard paste porcelain.

This factory successfully reproduced all the under-glaze coloured grounds used at Sèvres and all the colours for on-glaze painting. In addition to tableware vases and ornaments of exquisite quality and enriched with the most elaborate decorations, there were made a great many excellent biscuit pieces.

Previous to the Revolution the pieces were marked G.A., occasionally set in an oval vignette with a coronet above it, in red or gold on the glaze. After the Revolution the pieces were signed "Dihl" or "Guerhard and Dihl, Paris," the mark being applied in various ways.

FABRIQUE DE LA RUE POPINCOURT
CHINA—1760- ?

HISTORY. About 1760 Lemaire established an hard paste porcelain factory in the rue des Amandiers, Popincourt. Nast, the elder, bought the factory in 1783 and it afterwards passed to his sons. Both beautiful tableware and ornaments were produced in considerable quantity, and there were also modelled some exceedingly creditable biscuit pieces. The body and glaze were the same as those of the other hard paste factories operating in and near Paris at the time. The contours and the decorations were all in the Neo-Classic manner of the period. When the pieces are marked they bear the word "Nast" in red on the glaze.

FABRIQUE DU DUC D'ORLÉANS CHINA—
1784-1806

HISTORY. This hard paste porcelain factory, established in the faubourg St. Antoine in 1784, in 1786 secured the patronage of Louis-Philippe, Duc d'Orléans and was hence known as the Fabrique du Duc d'Orléans. Not a little good porcelain, well decorated and of some variety, was made there, comparing very favourably with the chinaware produced at the other independent factories in the neighbourhood of Paris. There seem to have been two marks, either one of which might be used—the letters L.J., interlaced, or the letters O.M. In contour and decoration this chinaware followed first the fashions of the reign of Louis XVI, and later the more severe manner of the Directoire period and the Empire.

LAURAGUAIS CHINA—1758- ?

HISTORY. The Comte de Brancas-Lauraguais was deeply interested in hard paste porcelain experimentation and, having made successful trials with the kaolin and felspar found near Alençon, began to make porcelain in the west of France about 1758. The paste was at first coarse and brownish in colour and the glaze was very defective. Later, however, the quality of his porcelain was improved although biscuit pieces shewed a somewhat grey hue. The ware was rather simply decorated in blue. The mark was "B L" interlaced and applied in underglaze blue. The factory was chiefly important on account of its early date and the part it played in the experimental period of French hard paste.

STRASBURG CHINA—1745-1754; 1766-c.1780

HISTORY. The making of hard paste porcelain at Strasburg was carried on at several different periods. Paul Antoine Hannong, a faïence maker, early in the eighteenth century pursued experiments in making hard paste and, in 1726, is said to have presented the Strasburg Corporation with a service of plates, salad dishes and platters of fine white porcelain of his own production. When he died in 1739 he was reputed the first person to have made true hard paste porcelain in France. Whence he obtained the necessary kaolin and felspar is not known but he got enough to establish material evidence that he could make what he claimed. The one indubitable piece of his making is of a greyish paste with a good white glaze and decorations painted in pale rose.

His son, Paul Hannong, who continued to operate the faïence factory, began to make hard paste porcelain in 1745, believing that the ancient privileges guaranteed Strasburg when it was joined to the Kingdom of France would protect him against any action that might be brought by the porcelain makers of Saint Cloud and Vincennes. Several experienced porcelain makers, one a refugee from Meissen and the other lately come from the china factory at Höchst, joined forces with Hannong and before long the Strasburg factory was putting forth a goodly quantity of tableware, flower-pots, and numbers of the little

painted groups and statuettes for which eighteenth century people had
such a passion.

This venture at Strasburg aroused the fears and animosity of the
management at the Vincennes factory who tried to enforce the privileges that had been granted them. Hannong therefore applied for
letters-patent, but his petition producing no result, he went to Paris
and, in his anxiety, appealed to Boileau the director of the Vincennes
factory, offering to treat for the sale of his secrets. The negotiations
came to naught, partly because the materials required by the processes
were not then believed to be obtainable in France, partly because Hannong demanded a cash payment and an annuity which the Vincennes
factory was not prepared to pay.

But Boileau had succeeded in getting possession of Hannong's
secrets, and having done so he treated him abominably, securing an
order prohibiting Hannong from manufacturing any more porcelain at
Strasburg and requiring him to dismantle his oven within a fortnight.
Only through the good offices of the Maréchal de Noailles did Hannong gain permission to finish the work he had actually on hand. It
was after this episode that Hannong, with the support and encouragement of the Archduke Charles Théodore, established the hard paste
porcelain works at Frankenthal.

The second active manufacture of hard paste porcelain at Strasburg
began in 1766 under Joseph Adam Hannong, the son of Paul, who
had remained in charge of the faïence factory when his father went to
Frankenthal. His main object was a large commercial output rather
than the making of ornamental wares. In this policy he was successful
up to 1780 when the manufacture was discontinued.

THE BODY. The hard paste produced at Strasburg under Paul Hannong, in the 1745-1754 period, was very white but only moderately
translucent; the paste of the second period, under Joseph Adam Hannong (1766-1780) was a somewhat heavy, thick substance of a slightly
tawny or yellowish tone.

THE GLAZE. The glaze of the first period was apt to be imperfect,
unevenly distributed, and exhibited a pitted or spotted surface; the
glaze of the second period was also defective and irregular in surface.

ARTICLES MADE AND CONTOUR. In the first period the articles chiefly made were tea, coffee and chocolate services, dinner sets and ornamental flower-pots, with a certain number of the popular polychrome statuettes and figure groups; in the second period the output embraced articles of the same sort, with the addition of some pieces in biscuit.

The contours in general followed the simpler contemporary shapes of Dresden, with a trend towards Neo-Classic forms during the second period.

TYPES OF DECORATION. In the first period the manner of decoration resembled that of the flowered Strasburg faïence, and to hide the glaze defects little flowers and insects were disposed seemingly at random. The colours most used were rose, purple and bluish green, without gilding. In the second period, the same *motifs* of scattered flowers and insects were often used to conceal defects of glaze. There were also Chinese *motifs*, flowers, and small country scenes or figures with an entourage of vegetation. Besides purple, carmine, indigo blue, green, yellow and pale rose, a characteristic bright red was used. Edges and mouldings were often lined with violet carmine. Gilding was rarely used.

THE MARKS. The mark of the first period, under Paul Hannong, was "P.H." either in capitals or cursive letters, in underglaze blue or, occasionally, in rose or brown on-glaze colour; the mark of the second period, under Joseph Hannong's directorship, was "J-I" in underglaze blue, often accompanied by figures indicating special patterns. The biscuit pieces bore "H" in the paste.

$$\mathcal{P}H$$

NIDERVILLER CHINA—1765-c.1850

HISTORY. The manufacture of hard paste porcelain was begun in 1765 at Niderviller by the Baron Jean Louis de Beyerlé, one of the King's Counsellors. The porcelain enterprise grew out of the faïence works that Baron de Beyerlé had established in 1754. Kaolin was brought from Germany until Baron de Beyerlé bought some of the first kaolin mines at St. Yrieix.

In 1780 General the Comte de Custine acquired the works and François Lanfrey became manager. The sculptor Lemire, who had worked at Lunéville with Cyfflé, came to Niderviller and modelled exquisite vases, shepherdesses, children, cupids and sundry other figures in the Louis XVI manner. Many of them were made in biscuit and materially contributed to the profit and reputation of the works. Lemire conceived the notion of creating in connexion with the factory a school of modelling and design for apprentices, a scheme attended with most admirable subsequent results. When the Comte de Custine died, Lanfrey continued as director and eventually became the owner. After Lanfrey's death, a M. Dryander became director. The factory continued working till the middle of the nineteenth century.

THE BODY. The paste at first, under Baron de Beyerlé, was white and highly translucent; afterwards, under the ownership of Comte de Custine, it was less vitreous but of an equally pure white.

THE GLAZE. The glaze of the Niderviller factory was of the best quality and brilliant, closely resembling the contemporary glaze used at Sèvres.

ARTICLES MADE AND CONTOUR. Besides a great quantity of beautiful tableware, tea and coffee services, vases and all the other items of usual demand, there were produced the numerous biscuit pieces that gave Niderviller a special fame. The contours of the chinaware were at first reminiscent of the manner of Dresden; later, the forms were more typically French and the Neo-Classic contours of the reign of Louis XVI were followed by the Neo-Grec shapes of the Empire period.

TYPES OF DECORATION. The earliest Niderviller china was decorated very much in the styles current at Dresden. There were numerous flower subjects, landscapes, polychrome or en camaïeu (PLATE 63), figures, and oftentimes scenes were drawn from La Fontaine's fables, the composition being enclosed within a geometrical frame or border while scattered flowers adorned the outlying ground of the porcelain. Purple, carmine and rose were colours much in favour and there was comparatively little gilding. Later, the styles current in France were more freely followed and many of the favourite flower subjects were painted with great delicacy. The cornflower *motif,* introduced at Sèvres, supplied the basis for much exquisite decoration. Porcelain flowers were likewise made in the Niderviller establishment and admirably coloured. Gilding was more largely used in the later work.

The Marks. There were no regular marks during the years of Baron de Beyerlé's ownership, although a "B" or "A and N" interlaced, and impressed in the paste, are said sometimes to have been used. Under the Comte de Custine, the mark was first the letters C and N interlaced, and later it appeared as two C's crossed beneath a count's coronet. In 1792 occurs the mark "N," or the words "Nider" or "Niderviller" in underglaze blue. Lanfrey's mark was C.F.L. interlaced, in underglaze blue. When the biscuit pieces and statuettes are marked, it is with "Niderviller" impressed.

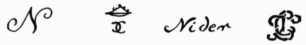

MARSEILLES CHINA—1778- ?

History. Experiments in the making of hard paste porcelain began at Marseilles in 1765. The actual manufacture on a commercial basis seems to have started about 1775 or, perhaps, earlier in the faïence works of J. G. Robert. The earlier ware is generally thick and heavy, with a body and glaze of yellowish grey tinge. This china was commonly decorated *en camaïeu* in a burnt siena colour, the decorations being done rather crudely.

The later ware exhibits a white body and the monochrome decorations are of much better character. Later still, the Marseilles china had a white body and good, clear glaze, and was well decorated with flowers in the manner of Mennecy and Sèvres. The colours especially favoured were rose, blue, and a greenish blue, the last of which was decidedly characteristic of the factory.

The marks of this factory were R., J. R. and, occasionally, F. R., in underglaze blue.

LIMOGES CHINA—1783 TO PRESENT DAY

HISTORY. The Limoges chinaware of modern fame started from a not very brilliant beginning. By an edict of 1783 Massié, Fourniers and Grellet were authorised to manufacture hard paste porcelain, the registered mark of the establishment being C. D. In May 1784 Louis XVI purchased the factory to be used as a branch of Sèvres and the son of M. Grellet, one of the three promoters of the first undertaking, became the director, continuing in that post till 1788 when he was succeeded by M. Alluaud.

The work done at this factory was not very important. During the eighteenth century the paste was of an ivory colour and the decorations usually consisted of little flowers whose colouring was not particularly distinguished although the ware was agreeable enough in its way.

The scheme of a branch factory for the establishment at Sèvres seems not to have worked very well and the factory was afterwards sold. The works are still in operation and producing excellent ware.

The fame of Limoges china is really due to M. Charles Haviland who established works in 1840 to make porcelain for the American market. By his energy and well-directed enterprise he developed the industry to the highest state of perfection in manufacture and the reputation of Limoges china is eminently well deserved.

When the branch establishment was disposed of by Sèvres, it was continued by M. Alluaud and is still in existence under the name of Pouyat and Alluaud. The paste and glaze were perfected, the body being a pure white, and a full palette of on-glaze colours was used. Much of this improvement was effected by the end of the eighteenth century.

VALENCIENNES CHINA—1785-1797

HISTORY. In 1785 Sieur Fauquez and M. Lamoniary obtained authorisation from the Council of State to open a factory at Valenciennes for the making of common or fine porcelain, after the manner of the porcelain of the Indies, and a local monopoly of manufacture was granted them for ten years, provided they fired their ovens with coal. The paste was pure white and the body and glaze of the best quality. The contours and decorations reflected the styles current at the period. The decorations were executed in a manner consistent with the quality of the china (PLATE 63, B). In addition to the tableware and ornamental articles, there were produced some good groups in biscuit.

There was also a common and cheaper grade of porcelain made and decorated in blue after the fashion of the commoner wares of Tournay. The works were finally closed in 1797.

The mark on the pieces of the fine ware consisted of the letters L. V. interlaced. The commoner wares were marked with the name "Valenciennes" or some abbreviation of it.

CAEN CHINA—1798-1808

HISTORY. The hard paste porcelain factory of Caen was founded in 1798 and, with the kaolin and felspar obtained from the neighbourhood of Limoges, produced chinaware of excellent quality in both body and glaze. The Caen chinaware enjoyed great and well-deserved popularity, but the disturbed economic conditions of France in the early nineteenth century compelled the factory to close in 1808.

The contours of Caen china were those characteristic of the Directoire and Empire periods, and many of the shapes shewed much elegance and grace. The decoration was of the highest order in point of design, painting and gilding. A pleasant yellow ground colour was especially characteristic. The beauty and general type of this china may be judged from the jug illustrated (PLATE 62, A).

The mark was "Caen" printed in red within a cartouche.

caen

HAVILAND CHINA—1842 TO PRESENT DAY
(AMERICAN WORKS OPENED, 1936)

HISTORY. Since 1839 the Haviland name has been inseparably associated with the story of chinaware.

In 1839, David Haviland was a New York importer of English china. One day a customer came to him to match a cup; the cup bore no mark, but was evidently of French origin. Much impressed by the fine quality and beauty of the ware, Mr. Haviland determined to be the first to introduce it in America as a regular import. With this in view, he crossed the Atlantic and started his quest for the cup's source in France. "Finally, after following many fruitless leads, the search ended in Limoges."

From Limoges, then, David Haviland began to import the china produced in the different small factories that had grown up there since the end of the eighteenth century. His satisfaction in realising an ambition, however, was short-lived. Difficulties soon arose because of the wide divergence between French and American taste and requirements. The Limoges factories were of limited capacity and their owners were unwilling to make American shapes and decorations. Indeed, so far as decoration went, the little Limoges factories had hitherto sent the greater part of their output "in the white" to Paris to be decorated there.

Unwilling to accept defeat, David Haviland determined to take a bold step. "He resolved to move to France, build a factory in Limoges and there make china in accordance with his own ideas."

"Once settled in that city, he created models of the types of services he wanted to manufacture and while these were being developed, he built and organised his own decorating shops. In these were installed everything necessary to change the product from plain to decorated ware."

The new factory began to operate in 1842 under the name of Haviland & Company.

But even after this, Mr. Haviland's undertaking had far from plain sailing at first. The Haviland innovations aroused undisguised hostility. French artisans, strongly attached to their own long-established ways of doing things, openly resented the introduction of new methods and "staged demonstrations of protest when they saw apprentices being instructed" to work in a manner at variance with the old routine. Opposition, however, gradually subsided and the new factory soon began to make chinaware in larger quantities than ever before produced at Limoges.

About 1850, Charles Field Haviland, a nephew of David Haviland, came into the china-making industry, gave his name to, and continued the French Alluaud factory which had eventually succeeded to the business and traditions of the establishment first founded in 1771 by MM. Grellet, Massié and Fourniers. This factory continued under the Haviland name until about 1880.

About 1892, Theodore Haviland, a son of David Haviland, built his own factory, "one of the largest and best equipped in Limoges." Not only was every advantage taken of the most modern technical and mechanical developments, but the ablest artists were retained to direct the decoration of the china. It was subsequently decided that "certain shapes and patterns" of chinaware "could best be made" in America and, after thorough mechanical equipment, and with moulds and designs from the Limoges factory, in 1936 the American Haviland china factory began to produce fine tableware. The firm of Theodore Haviland & Co. now operates both the Limoges and American works.

In 1939, the Theodore Haviland factory, that had been started at Limoges in 1892, purchased the old establishment of Haviland & Co., founded by David Haviland, thus combining in one business all the Haviland china-making interests that had figured in Limoges for a century.

It is not too much to say that Haviland enterprise and constant adherence through the years to the best traditions of china-making have contributed more than any other factors to the deservedly high repute of Limoges china and the fame of that city as a great ceramic centre. In this connection, it is worth noting that the Havilands in Limoges first introduced the use of chromolithography in the decoration of chinaware, a process now employed by nearly all china-manufacturers on both sides of the Atlantic.

The Haviland china has always had a fine felspathic body, highly vitrified, and bearing an admirable glaze. The decorative processes now chiefly employed for the tableware are hand-painting, transfer printing from chromolithographic decalcomanias, and gilding of sundry sorts.

There are two Haviland marks or "backstamps" now in use—one for ware produced at the Limoges factory and one for the china made at the American factory. The French mark consists of "Theodore Haviland" in block lettering, above "Limoges" in smaller block letters, over the word "FRANCE" in Roman capitals. The American mark has the name "Theodore Haviland" above "New York," all in Old English or "blackletter" capital and small characters, and the whole enclosed within a lobate cartouche. Beneath the cartouche, in small Roman capitals are the words "MADE IN AMERICA."

AHRENFELDT CHINA—1896 TO PRESENT DAY

HISTORY. The story of Ahrenfeldt china begins with importing, goes on to decorating and finally advances to full manufacturing status.

In 1831, Charles Ahrenfeldt was a chinaware importer in New York City. A chinaware enthusiast, with keen appreciation of the properties of fine china, he was also well aware of the trends of American taste and fully realised that the various contemporary porcelains imported from Europe often failed in point of decoration to satisfy the requirements of the American market.

Convinced that he could remedy at least some of the causes of dissatisfaction, he went to France in 1848 and set up as a decorator at Limoges, where he eventually became a conspicuous figure in the china industry. He procured chinaware "in the white" from the small Limoges manufacturers and had it decorated according to his directions. For this work, he engaged the best artists he could find, and by planning and creating "unusual treatments for offering to his customers in his home land" he enjoyed a good business and high esteem until his death at the age of eighty-four.

In 1894, just after his father's death, Charles Jules Ahrenfeldt opened a decorating establishment of his own in Limoges. At the same time, he started to build a factory so that he could make his own chinaware. On the completion of this factory in 1896, Charles Jules Ahrenfeldt not only continued but greatly expanded the work of china-decorating his father had started. With thoroughly modern equipment and the most advanced technical methods of manufacturing, his establishment soon ranked amongst the foremost factories in Limoges and put forth a fine type of chinaware for whose embellishment some of the most versatile artists in Limoges supplied designs.

The felspathic, highly vitrified body of Ahrenfeldt china is a sympathetic vehicle for the types of decoration on which the factory has always placed great emphasis. In 1928, the factory produced a special ivory china body known as "ivoire de France."

While much of the Ahrenfeldt decoration has followed traditional or conservative trends, from 1925 onward there has been definite encouragement to the creation of designs in accord with the "modern" genius, and not a few artists who are professedly exponents of modernism have contributed to the factory's *répertoire* of decoration.

The Ahrenfeldt china mark or "backstamp" is a decorative label or oblong cartouche enclosing the word "FRANCE," in italic capitals, above "Charles Ahrenfeldt," also in italics, with "Limoges" underneath in slightly smaller italics.

Spanish and Portuguese Chinaware

MADRID (BUEN RETIRO) CHINA—
1759-1808 (1812)

HISTORY. The royal porcelain factory of Buen Retiro, at Madrid, was established in 1759 by Charles III, when he became King of Spain. This establishment was an offshoot, or, perhaps, it might be better to call it a transference of the porcelain industry undertaken at Capo di Monte by Charles when he was King of Naples. As we have previously seen, in the story of Italian china, porcelain-making was a darling project of Charles, upon which he spent great sums of money. When he inherited the kingdom of Spain and left Naples, he brought with him most of the skilled workmen and much of the equipment from Capo di Monte, and the inauguration of the new industry in Spain was a matter of the greatest solicitude to the royal patron.

For the first thirty years the porcelain produced was reserved for royal use and disposal, and even after 1789, when a part of the china was allowed to be sold to the public, the sale was not large because of the high price asked for the wares which were nearly all extremely elaborate. Consequently, even in Spain, the Buen Retiro china is exceedingly rare. Outside of Spain it is scarcely known at all.

At Buen Retiro both soft paste and hard paste porcelains were made in great diversity of forms and the fashions of Capo di Monte or Naples, Sèvres, Dresden, and Wedgwood were extensively followed, often with added elaboration and magnificence according to the Spanish taste of the day.

When the French entered Madrid in 1808 they took possession of the china factory and did much damage. After that, although some porcelain was produced in a desultory way, nothing of note was achieved and the factory, which the French had converted into a fortification, was destroyed by Wellington in 1812.

Various marks were employed, amongst them fleur-de-lys and crowns used either by themselves or in conjunction with letters and monograms.

. . . .

At different times, subsequent to the establishment of the Buen Retiro factory, china of a simpler but pleasing character was made at Alcora, Moncloa and Gerona, but these factories were small and their output was very limited. Nor did they endure any length of time.

. . . .

In the latter part of the eighteenth century a small quantity of porcelain was also made in Portugal, both at Oporto and Lisbon. Specimens of Portuguese china are of even rarer occurrence than Spanish china. Buen Retiro was the one important establishment in the whole Peninsula, and both Spanish and Portuguese china are so infrequently met with that specimens need scarcely be considered by the collector as possibilities of acquisition.

German Chinaware

DRESDEN (MEISSEN) CHINA—
1710 TO PRESENT DAY

History. To Johann Friedrich Böttger, erstwhile Berlin apothecary's prentice, belongs the credit of discovering in Europe the secret of making hard paste porcelain.

From childhood Böttger had shewn such interest in chemistry and aptitude for experiment that he was destined for the pursuit of medicine. Accordingly when he was sixteen years old, he was set apprentice to a Berlin apothecary. He straightway plunged into all manner of alchemistic studies, and soon his proficiency in that mysterious lore was bruited about. The impecunious King of Prussia, we are told, hoping and believing that Böttger might have mastered the secret of the philosopher's stone and so be able to transmute the baser metals into gold, was about to seize him and make use of his knowledge. Getting wind of the King's design, Böttger fled to Saxony and, as it turned out, "jumped from the frying pan into the fire."

Augustus the Strong, King of Poland and Elector of Saxony, was quite as much in need of funds as the King of Prussia, and here was a gold-maker fallen into his very lap. He seized Böttger and set him at work to make gold, with the help of a good laboratory, capable assistants and ample working funds. Of course the task ended in failure, as it needs must, but the chemist Tschirnhausen suggested to the King that Böttger's services and knowledge of chemistry, along with the laboratory and apparatus, might be used to better purpose in the cause of industry. More gold was to be got by promoting manufactures in Saxony than by the fantastic chasing of moonbeams. Faïence factories were rising and prospering in other parts of Germany; why should there not be a faïence factory in Saxony, and why should it not be a source of substantial profit?

The King hearkened readily to this suggestion. Böttger and Tschirn-hausen were premitted to change the object of their work and, instead of labouring to metamorphose iron into gold, they examined and ex-perimented with clays and earths. As a result, in 1708 Böttger suc-ceeded in producing the famous red stoneware that was so hard it could be polished on the lapidary's wheel.

The manufacture of the stoneware proved profitable and satisfied the King, at any rate for the nonce, but by this time Böttger had set his mind on solving the riddle of Oriental porcelain which had hitherto baffled its European admirers and he pursued his experiments with unremitting zeal. At last, in 1709, after the death of his collaborator Tschirnhausen, he was able to shew the King a few specimens of what was indubitably true porcelain. As yet, it was unglazed, but Böttger very soon devised the glaze, so that 1709 may be regarded as the dawn of hard paste porcelain-making in the Western World.

In January 1710 the Meissen porcelain factory was established by Royal Patent. The works were equipped in the castle of Albrechtsburg overlooking the town of Meissen, a few miles west of Dresden. There the secret processes of manufacture could not be spied upon by prying eyes. These processes were most jealously guarded and for long after-wards the workmen employed were virtually prisoners. In the castle of Albrechtsburg the works remained until 1863, when they were re-moved to ampler quarters.

At the Leipzig Easter Fair, in 1710, were exhibited some specimens of the new porcelain, and a few weeks later Böttger shewed the King the first painted pieces. But though the factory was established by Royal Writ in 1710, there was still much necessary experimental work to be carried on, and it was not until some years later that the manu-facture of porcelain was put on a commercial footing. From 1710 to 1713 at Meissen only the red stoneware was produced for sale. At the Leipzig Easter Fair, in 1713, the Meissen china was first exposed for public sale, and from that time onward its repute increased with amazing rapidity. By 1716 the manufacture, as a commercial enter-prise, was well on its way.

Böttger died in 1719. Notwithstanding the repute already acquired by the porcelain of Meissen and the rapidly increasing sale of the wares, the financial affairs of the factory were in great disorder and a royal commission was set to deal with the situation. The difficulties were soon adjusted and, in 1720, Johann G. Herold, the painter, who had worked in the Vienna factory under du Pacquier, came to direct the work at Meissen. He was one of the greatest masters of his time, and under his influence the products soon shewed amazing improvement. Some years later, Johann Kändler, the modeller, joined the Meissen staff, and through the work done and the inspiration supplied by these two men the china of Meissen reached the height of its glory.

In 1759 and 1761 Frederick the Great looted the Meissen factory when he occupied Dresden, and carried off a great quantity of the best moulds and models to Berlin, whither as well he transported many of the experienced workmen. This interruption marked the end of the most distinctive, and perhaps the finest, period of Meissen porcelain.

When work was ultimately resumed, new influences that eventually became dominant were already beginning to make themselves felt, and the old creative spontaneity and enthusiasm were gone. About 1764 the painter Dietrich introduced the nascent Neo-Classic spirit into Meissen design, and as this influence became more and more manifest in both contour and decoration, the products of Meissen lost much of their erstwhile individuality, displayed an increasing likeness to the creations of other factories, and betrayed a tendency to follow rather than to lead, with a perceptible bias for the ways of Sèvres.

When Count Marcolini became director in 1774, the Neo-Classic style became paramount in all the new creations of Meissen and continued to dominate shapes and decoration alike until what have been called the "frigidities" of the Empire style succeeded at the dawn of the nineteenth century.

In 1814 Kühn became director and numerous technical improvements were introduced, the firing was done with coal, and the composition of the body was simplified. The earlier wares had grown valuable by this time and were largely reproduced, which was fortunate, as all power of fresh creation had apparently become dormant. The factory was moved from the old fortress of Albrechtsburg in 1863.

In its new environment it has made great advances commercially, but "has added little or nothing to the progress of art."

THE BODY. The body, at first, was thick and clumsy and the pieces were often warped or fire-cracked. The paste exhibited a slightly yellowish tinge, "which Böttger himself regarded as a fault, but which most people nowadays would doubtless prefer to a colder and over-white tint." Owing to lack of quartz or felspar in the composition —alabaster was used instead—the early paste is not particularly translucent. By a series of experiments and modifications, the paste was brought to a pure, hard white at an early date and the translucency was increased.

THE GLAZE. The early glaze produced by Böttger was thick but of even distribution, and it was clear, transparent, and ordinarily free from flaws. The later glaze was of thinner body and more brilliant in its general appearance.

ARTICLES MADE AND CONTOUR. It was only during the initial or experimental period under Böttger that the output of Meissen was at all restricted in variety. Even then, there was considerable diversity in the tea, coffee and breakfast services, the cups and saucers, the small vases and flower pots, and the less ambitious sorts of tableware and decorative accessories. The factory was still young when it began to put forth all kinds of tableware, vases, and every sort of decorative accessory, as well as the figures that were originated there, the modelled flowers, and the busts, figures and groups both glazed and in biscuit (PLATE 66, A).

The contours, at first, were more or less experimental. Shapes were adopted from Chinese models, from metal forms, from faïence, and from whatever source seemed likely to yield material for adaptation. But through all this initial stage, the plastic quality of the material was never for one moment lost sight of, and when Kändler came to Meissen he had only to carry on and amplify a tradition already firmly rooted.

Under his direction the shapes, from whatever source they had been derived in the first instance, began to display both local individuality and an unmistakably European character. He was imbued with the

Rococo conceptions of his day and delighted in embodying in porcelain forms the subtle curves and moulded scrolls so characteristic of the manner. Both the bodies of the pieces and the decorations modelled and applied to them responded to this impulse. He developed the Rococo schemes to such a degree of exuberance that he has sometimes been regarded, though wrongly, as the originator of the mode. He was, nevertheless, an ardent exponent. He also introduced shapes with well-defined architectural mouldings, which was a departure from Chinese precedent.

From 1764 onward, the Rococo contours more and more yielded place to the restrained Neo-Classic shapes, and these, in due order, at the turn of the century, gave way before the modes of the Empire.

TYPES OF DECORATION. The very early types of decoration practised at Meissen included moulding in low relief (PLATE 66, B), modelling in high relief; piercings and fretwork, in the latter of which Böttger and his modellers displayed the greatest daring and dexterity alike; painting in enamel colours with a rather limited palette; and painting in gold alone, which meant arabesques and "gold Chinamen" on a flat surface, or Chinese and floral gilt reliefs raised from the flat ground of the white porcelain. The "gold Chinamen," as they were called, were Chinese figures and attendant *motifs* painted in gold in silhouette on the white porcelain, and made a very interesting and effective decoration. Underglaze painting in blue was employed, but in Böttger's time the results were not at all satisfactory. The blue pigment ran and occasionally formed bubbles, behaviour probably caused by impurities in the cobalt. Nevertheless, persistent efforts were made to overcome the difficulty, and eventually the trouble was altogether eliminated and underglaze blue decoration became one of the customary processes. China decorated in underglaze blue with the "Strohblumen" and "onion" patterns (PLATE 64, A), was exceedingly popular and was made in large quantities. These patterns—especially the former—were so much admired in Denmark and so much copied at Copenhagen that in time they came to be known as "Copenhagen" patterns, although they really originated at Dresden.

With Herold's name are associated the introduction of the Japanese Kakiyemon decoration (PLATE 5, A), which was afterwards widely copied all over Europe and was known in England and America as the "old Japan" pattern; the introduction of armorial services; and the popularisation of naturalistic flowers, arranged either in organised compositions or else scattered at random in sprays and single blossoms (PLATES 65, B and 64, B), sometimes with the addition of insects here and there in the intervals between them. Flowers and insects thus arranged had the advantage of concealing any chance flaws in body or glaze. This type of decoration, also, was almost universally copied and has always been regarded as peculiarly characteristic of Dresden (PLATE 64, B). It was not long *needed* at Dresden for purposes of concealment, but was continued on account of its beauty; many other factories, however, found it not only attractive but most useful in hiding imperfections. The draperies of the figures were often pyed with minute blossoms (PLATE 66, A), after the manner of the East India printed cottons, a fashion of decoration akin to the "scattered flower" *motif*.

During Herold's time likewise the "brocaded" Japanese Imari ware, with its strong reds, blues and gold, furnished a popular decorative theme, while dragons and other distinctly Chinese subjects afforded a wealth of material of which the china painters fully availed themselves. Despite the use of these Oriental themes, however, the tendency towards purely European methods of decoration (Baroque gold pattern, PLATE 65, A), was constantly growing stronger. The "German flowers" rendered in naturalistic manner were followed by landscapes with ornate borders; by Rococo scrolls and other characteristic Rococo forms, expressed either in colour and gilding or by moulded reliefs accentuated with colour and gold; by modelled flowers, birds and other objects, used as knobs and handles and realistically coloured; by Watteau-like panels and arabesques; by landscapes in monochrome (PLATE 65, A); by diapered borders borrowed from Oriental china; and by ground colours with reserved panels in which appeared naturalistic flowers, birds of brilliant plumage, figures, landscapes and pastoral scenes.

Although the trend was away from the employment of Chinese

themes, sometimes the reserved panels in coloured grounds, instead of containing the *motifs* just enumerated, were quatrefoil or lobate-shaped and enclosed Chinese subjects in polychrome.

The usual ground colours were pale violet, light blue, purple, brick-red, apple-green and sea-green, while a yellow which varied from straw colour to deep lemon was particularly successful. Some success attended the experiments in coloured bodies, and grey, blue, mauve, cream and grey-brown were produced. A "dead-leaf" brown-coloured glaze was also occasionally used.

By the time the Dresden factory suffered pillage at the hands of Frederick the Great, the Rococo influence, both in contour and decoration, had not only crowded out almost every trace of Oriental elements but, in many directions, had reached the most extravagant developments.

After the resumption of work, the Sèvres influence became steadily more perceptible in the manner of decoration, and the usual complement of Neo-Classic forms and *motifs*—already noted in connexion with the products of the French factories—dominated the day until they were ousted by the more aggressive expressions of the Empire mode. Much of the china made at Dresden during the period of Neo-Classic supremacy was very beautiful, but it was no longer distinctive of the place in its decoration as the earlier wares had been.

THE MARKS. The early Dresden china was marked with the letters K. P. M.—meaning *Königliche Porzellan Manufactur*—with occasional variations to K. P. F. and M. P. M. These marks date from about 1719; much of the earliest ware was altogether unmarked. About the second quarter of the century the crossed swords from the Saxon arms appeared as the mark; they were at first painted in on-glaze blue and afterwards, when they had learned better how to manage it, in under-glaze blue. Concurrently with the crossed swords the royal cypher, composed of the letters A. R. in monogram, was used on the royal porcelain. About this time, too, appeared the staff of Æsculapius. After the Seven Years' War and the resumption of work at Meissen, a dot was placed between the crossed swords. With the period of Count

Marcolini's directorship, which began in 1774, a star was set between the crossed swords.

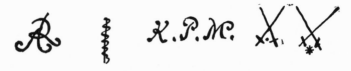

BERLIN CHINA—1750 TO PRESENT DAY

HISTORY. With the help of runaway workmen from Höchst, the hard paste porcelain factory at Berlin was started under Wilhelm Caspar Wegeli in 1750. Some excellent tableware and also figures inspired by those of Meissen were made here, but business difficulties and lack of sufficient interest on the part of the King, who seemed to feel that Wegeli's china was not distinguished enough in character to suit his ambitions, drove Wegeli to give up the works in 1757. Under Reichard, who succeeded him, little advance was made. In 1761 Gotzkowski took the works which then acquired all the loot from Meissen and a number of Dresden workmen. It was Frederick the Great's ambition that the Berlin china should equal or excel the products of Meissen and Gotzkowski's management becoming involved in financial embarrassment, in 1763 the King himself took over the establishment and became sole owner. Thereafter the factory continued as a royal enterprise.

Frederick had no intention of keeping the factory merely as an expensive plaything. He was determined it should pay for itself, and not only pay for itself but make a profit. He accordingly adopted some drastic measures towards this end. The Berlin lotteries were compelled to distribute 10,000 thalers' worth of china annually, no Jew could obtain a marriage certificate till he had bought a set of Berlin china, and in various other ways the sales were assiduously pushed. These methods put the factory on its feet as a business concern and it entered upon a course of prosperity that continued up to World War II.

THE BODY. At first the Berlin china was made of materials from Passau and, owing to impurities, the paste shewed a yellowish-grey tinge, but about 1771 with materials from Silesia and Halle a paste was produced that was very hard, dense of texture and a cold white in colour. These qualities have been maintained ever since.

THE GLAZE. The glaze was hard, clear, brilliant and technically perfect, but the "severe" character of both paste and glaze made it impossible to secure the bright, glowing colour that could be secured with the less refractory glaze of soft paste porcelain.

ARTICLES MADE AND CONTOUR. For some time the wares produced consisted chiefly of dinner services, tea, coffee and chocolate equipages, and breakfast sets, along with a few figures, glazed and decorated. Later the wares shewed more variety and elaboration and a number of ornate vases and other decorative accessories were produced, as well as figures in biscuit.

Although the methods of Meissen manufacture were followed and Meissen workmen and decorators employed, Frederick's admiration for French art dictated the following of French forms and the Rococo style consequently flourished at the Berlin factory in a most pronounced manner, although not with quite the same extravagance sometimes displayed under Kändler's inspiration at Meissen. Nevertheless, some trivial grotesqueries were indulged in, such as making lace decoration by coating lace with porcelain slip, the lace being burned out in the firing and leaving the pattern behind it. Late in the century the Neo-Classic mode made itself felt in contour as well as decoration and, in due time, the Empire manner succeeded.

TYPES OF DECORATION. Underglaze blue decoration was much used in the early days of the factory, and moulded low reliefs in the form of ribbing, scrolls and basket-work patterns were exceedingly favoured. The early colour schemes were simple and the palette limited. Often enough a scheme was carried out with only rose colour and grey, red, black and gold or red, green and gold. The palette was subsequently enlarged. The rose-colour of the Berlin china was highly characteristic as Frederick the Great was very partial to it, but the paste and glaze used were of too "severe" a type ever to get the same beautiful *rose Pompadour* that appeared on the soft paste porcelain of Sèvres. Landscapes, figures and floral subjects (PLATE 68, A), were frequently painted in monochrome, and for these rose-colour was much used as well as in the combinations with other colours. Diaper borders, often in the form of a small scale pattern which the Germans called *"mosaik,"* were freely employed and for these, again, the characteristic rose-colour was favoured. Small scattered flowers, or small flowers in garlands, wreaths and festoons furnished much of the decoration in connexion with these diapered rose borders; likewise, larger flowers in organised composition were not seldom seen. There were also a number of coloured grounds with reserved panels in which appeared flowers, birds, landscapes and figures. The fashions of Sèvres were by no means without their visible influence, especially in the latter part of the eighteenth century when the Neo-Classic mode was paramount. Transfer printing made its appearance about the end of the eighteenth century.

THE MARKS. The mark during the factory's initial period under Wegeli's direction was a W in underglaze blue, with the strokes of the letter crossed. Under Gotzkowski the mark was a crudely formed G. When the factory became a royal possession the mark was a sceptre, adopted in allusion to the sceptre borne by the Electors of Brandenburg as Grand Chamberlains of the Empire, or sometimes the orb and cross above the letters KPM. Later, the two sceptres of the Hohenzollerns were used, crossed saltire-wise, thus resembling the crossed swords of Saxony.

HÖCHST CHINA—1746-1796

HISTORY. At the faïence factory of Höchst, a town governed by the Archbishop-Elector of Mainz, attempts to produce hard paste porcelain were made as early as 1720 but no success attended these efforts until 1746 when A. F. von Löwenfinck, a painter who had left Meissen, brought thither the secrets of porcelain manufacture. For a number of years the Höchst porcelain venture had a chequered career. Until about 1760 it seems to have been as much engaged in making faïence as in producing porcelain. Although some progress had been made and some creditable porcelain products achieved, the undertaking was hampered by financial difficulties, and it was not until 1778, when the Prince-Bishop himself took over the factory that satisfactory conditions prevailed. Most of the work produced at Höchst closely echoed the traditions and practices of Meissen, but in two particulars the factory may claim distinction —the quality of the figures modelled by Johann Peter Melchior and others, which gave the establishment great repute, and the characteristic use of two very beautiful enamel colours made from gold, a light transparent rose largely employed in figure-painting and a rich carmine extensively affected in rendering monochrome landscapes and scenes. Political conditions about the end of the century had a disastrous effect upon the fortunes of the factory and it was closed in 1796.

THE BODY. The paste of the early porcelain made at Höchst had a greyish tone. It was not long, however, before the body was brought to the chalky white colour common to most German porcelains.

THE GLAZE. The glaze at first was greyish and marked by some flaws. This, too, was soon improved and made clear and brilliant.

ARTICLES MADE AND CONTOUR. Apart from the making of tableware and the other usual items of decorative requirement, Höchst is famous for its admirable figures, groups and portrait medallions, both glazed and in biscuit, modelled by Melchior and a succession of other capable artists.

Following the lead of Dresden, the shapes of the chinaware for some time were preponderantly in the Rococo manner, although the Neo-Classic impulse was manifest in the later productions.

TYPES OF DECORATION. Besides the use of the two distinctive colours already mentioned, and their application in the manner pointed out, the types of decoration practised at Höchst included most of the Dresden repertoire with its moulded ribbings, basket-work, Rococo scrolls and other low-relief ornament (PLATE 67, B) raised in the paste; fretwork and piercings; "German flowers," "Indian flowers," scattered flowers and flowers in compositions, garlands, wreaths and festoons; diapered or *"mosaik"* borders; Chinese *motifs* of different sorts; landscapes, figures and scenes; ground colours and reserved panels with birds and flowers; and the later complement of arabesques and Classic elements.

THE MARKS. The mark was a wheel of six spokes, a device derived from the arms of the Archbishop-Elector, often topped with a crown or the Electoral hat, and frequently accompanied by a monogram or initials. Occasionally the wheel has only five spokes. Up to about 1770 the mark was impressed in the paste, or else painted in black, brown, purple, iron-red, or gold. After 1770 the mark almost always appeared in underglaze blue. For the most part, the biscuit pieces are unmarked.

NYMPHENBURG CHINA—1747-1862
(SINCE 1862 CONTINUED IN PRIVATE HANDS)

HISTORY. Under the Elector of Bavaria, Max Joseph III, an hard paste porcelain factory was established as a State enterprise at Naudeck, in 1747, with the aid of the expert, Joseph Jacob Ringler, from Vienna. Ringler left before the work of establishment was fully accomplished and the factory did not get into thorough working order, capable of satisfactory and continuous production, until 1753. In 1761 the factory was transferred from Naudeck to quarters that had been especially prepared for it adjacent to the Palace of Nymphenburg near Munich, and by the name of Nymphenburg it has always been known. Under the patronage of the Elector Max Joseph, the royal factory flourished exceedingly and, in 1765, employed two hundred workmen. The next Elector, however, felt no especial interest in the making of porcelain and from 1777 to 1799 the manufacture languished and the working force of the factory was cut down so that it can scarcely be said to have done more than barely exist. In 1799 the succeeding Elector determined to restore porcelain-making to its former importance and new life was infused into the establishment. In 1800 some of the best workmen from Frankenthal were employed and the output of the factory was greatly increased. In 1862 the establishment ceased to be a royal factory and passed into private hands. The manufacture is still carried on.

THE BODY. The body is a paste of excellent quality, white, hard and of dense, smooth texture.

THE GLAZE. The glaze, likewise, is of unexceptionable quality, perfectly distributed, clear and brilliant.

ARTICLES MADE AND CONTOUR. The articles made include all the customary "useful" tableware and the usual decorative adjuncts, but the making of such chinaware was thrown somewhat into the background by the stress laid upon figures and groups which were of the greatest excellence. The sculptor Melchior came to Nymphenburg and remained there till his death, producing some of his finest figures which contributed much to the factory's fame. Apart from the figures, glazed and in the biscuit, the only special feature of Nymphenburg manufacture is to be found in the food warmers made there.

In the matter of contour the Nymphenburg china followed fairly closely the fashions current at Dresden.

TYPES OF DECORATION. Underglaze blue painting was little, if at all, practised at Nymphenburg and was virtually unknown. Moulding and modelling in high relief were both employed and the raised and modelled parts were accented with colour. Flowers (PLATE 67, A), birds and landscapes supplied the usual *motifs,* as elsewhere. Landscapes and peasant scenes were often painted in monochrome and for this purpose copper green was a rather favourite colour. The Nymphenburg decoration is marked by great naturalism and delicacy of painting. From about 1800 it is also characterised by elaborate and well-executed figure-painting. It then became a practice to decorate the chinaware, and especially vases, with minutely finished copies of famous pictures in the Munich galleries and although this sort of ornamentation was exquisitely rendered, the taste that dictated the practice is decidedly questionable. Much Nymphenburg china of the period is certainly over-decorated. After 1815 not a little of the painted decoration was performed in Munich.

THE MARKS. The usual mark was some form of the Bavarian coat of arms, although the six-pointed "seal of Solomon" now and then occurred with letters or figures at the points. Initial letters were also used in conjunction with the marks just mentioned.

FÜRSTENBERG CHINA—1746-1753-1888

HISTORY. The hard paste porcelain factory of Fürstenberg was established by the Duke of Brunswick in the castle of Fürstenberg on the Weser. The factory was organised in 1746 by Baron von Langen with the aid of the "arcanist" Glaser from Bayreuth, but nothing of any moment was accomplished until Bengraf, an expert from Höchst arrived in 1753, so that manufacture may really be said to have begun at that date. The factory flourished and produced a large output, but its best period really began about 1770. Fürstenberg was the one German factory that ever used any of the English china as models. The work of Bow and Chelsea furnished not a little inspiration. This connexion was doubtless because of close family ties existing between the royal family of England and the Dukes of Brunswick. After a period of decline during the Napoleonic wars, the factory gained renewed life and was continued in operation till 1888.

THE BODY. The early paste of the Fürstenberg china was greyish or yellowish in tone owing to impurities in the materials, which came from Passau. Later, this tone was eliminated and the paste was of the same cold white colour and density of texture as the Dresden china.

THE GLAZE. The early glaze was greyish and full of small black specks. The later glaze was clarified, ridded of its imperfections, and rendered clear and brilliant.

ARTICLES MADE AND CONTOUR. Tableware, decorative accessories such as vases, sconces, candlesticks and the like were made in large quantity at Fürstenberg, and also a great many figures, groups and statuettes, both glazed and in the biscuit.

It seems to have been the policy at Fürstenberg to use the wares of nearly all other factories as models so that little of a distinctive nature in contour can be ascribed to Fürstenberg china. The chronological succession of Rococo forms, Neo-Classic forms and Empire forms can be traced concurrently with the vogue each commanded in other places.

TYPES OF DECORATION. Accessory to decoration, great use was made at Fürstenberg of moulded raised patterns, such as basket-work, ribbing, fluting, and "webs of Rococo scrollwork in low relief." Perhaps to conceal the imperfections of paste and glaze in the early ware, moulded excrescences from the surface were often greatly exaggerated, and this exaggeration was characteristic. Piercing, fretwork and modelling in high relief were also practised, the modelled and applied reliefs which served as knobs and handles being coloured and gilt.

Sea-green and underglaze blue were probably the only two ground colours used. A great deal of purple or rose-carmine appeared in the painting, both monochrome and polychrome. Iron-red was also a favourite monochrome colour. All manner of subjects supplied *motifs* for decoration, but the drawing of flowers, birds, figures and even of landscapes appeared to have been copied from portfolios of engravings rather than to have been inspired more directly by nature. The smooth surfaces customary during the Neo-Classic period, when there was more austerity of form and some renunciation of brilliant colour, fostered an improvement in the painted decoration. During this period there was an observable tendency to make use of Wedgwood models, just as there had been an earlier following of Bow and Chelsea, and also to pattern after the manner of Sèvres.

THE MARKS. The mark was a capital F in script, painted in underglaze blue. The biscuit pieces were marked with the running horse of Brunswick impressed in the paste.

LUDWIGSBURG CHINA—1758-1824

HISTORY. With the assistance of the "arcanist" Ringler, who has already appeared on several other occasions, Carl Eugen, Duke of Würtemberg, established the hard paste porcelain factory at Ludwigsburg in 1758. The factory was maintained by liberal subsidies and highly creditable work was produced, but after the death of Duke Charles in 1793 a decline set in and the manufacture was finally given up in 1824.

THE BODY. The Ludwigsburg paste was made of impure materials from Passau and, in consequence, always had a yellowish-grey tinge very different from the glistering, strident white of the Dresden body. Incidentally, though not considered so technically perfect, it is much mellower and more pleasant to look at.

THE GLAZE. The glaze was of fine quality, transparent and clear.

ARTICLES MADE AND CONTOUR. All the usual kinds of tableware and decorative accessories were made, and likewise groups, figures and statuettes both glazed and in biscuit. The contours ranged from those prevalent in the Rococo age to the later Neo-Classic and Empire forms.

TYPES OF DECORATION. Patterns moulded in low relief, in the usual devices previously mentioned in connexion with the wares of other German factories, played an important part in Ludwigsburg decoration, and likewise modelling in high relief, the attached reliefs being coloured and gilt. The painted decoration was of excellent quality and the *motifs* embraced landscapes, figures, flowers (PLATE 69), wreaths, garlands, birds and butterflies, and occasionally exquisitely painted beetles were also introduced. Lilac was a favourite monochrome colour and sometimes small scattered flowers were thus presented. The modelling and decoration of the figures were of rather exceptional merit.

THE MARKS. The usual mark was the cypher of the reigning duke surmounted by a ducal crown. The cypher of Duke Charles was two C's, back to back and interlaced, in monogram. Sometimes the Würtemberg shield charged with three antlers appears as a mark. The presence of a crown has led to the erroneous name "Kronenberg" sometimes applied to this ware.

FRANKENTHAL CHINA—1755-1795

HISTORY. The hard paste porcelain factory of Frankenthal was established in 1755 by Paul Antoine Hannong, under the patronage of the Elector Palatine, Carl Theodor. In the account of French Chinaware we have already noted the circumstances that led to Hannong's removal from Strasburg where he had previously made hard paste porcelain.

Excellent china was made at Frankenthal, but there were financial difficulties and in 1762 the Elector bought the factory and continued the work under capable directors. Despite the high character of the products, the manufacture was not a success from a commercial point of view and the factory was at last closed in 1795.

THE BODY. The body at first shewed a slightly greyish tinge, but the paste was soon brought to a state of technical perfection in its whiteness and in all the other qualities that enter into the question.

THE GLAZE. The glaze likewise was technically perfect and of brilliant quality.

ARTICLES MADE AND CONTOUR. Table services of all sorts, tea, coffee and chocolate services, and all manner of decorative accessories were produced, and great stress was laid upon making the finest groups, figures and statuettes, glazed and in biscuit.

The work of Sèvres and Vienna to a great extent furnished models for emulation and the sequence of Rococo and Neo-Classic contours disclosed more or less resemblance to the individual interpretations of those factories.

TYPES OF DECORATION. Both the painted decoration and the gilding were of exceptionally fine character, and there was a remarkably full palette of colours in use. A deep royal blue ground colour, in imitation of the Sèvres *bleu du roi,* was highly favoured, and raised gilding, in the manner of Vienna, was successfully executed. A good underglaze black was also employed. Landscapes, figures, cameo subjects in medallions, landscapes in monochrome and polychrome, Classic subjects, birds and flowers in many manners supplied the *motifs.*

THE MARKS. The earlier pieces are marked with the crowned lion rampant of the Palatinate and the initials of Hannong (*J.*A.H.) in monogram. Later pieces bear the cypher of Carl Theodor surmounted by a crown.

THE LESSER GERMAN FACTORIES

The lesser German hard paste porcelain factories, such as Fulda, Cassel, Bayreuth, Ansbach, Wallendorf, Limbach and Kloster-Veilsdorf made some creditable china, but for the most part their wares exhibit no particular individuality. The factory at Fulda, in Hesse, patronised by the Prince-Bishop, was a notable exception and produced work of the greatest distinction, both in the way of table services and figures. The greater part of the work, however, put forth by these factories was of commonplace character and some of them indulged in the vicious practice of buying slightly decorated ware and revamping it with vulgar and over-loaded decoration.

Austrian Chinaware

VIENNA CHINA—1718-1864

HISTORY. The hard paste porcelain factory at Vienna was founded by a Dutchman, Claude du Pacquier, in 1718. This undertaking he accomplished with the aid of two runaway employees from Meissen, Samuel Stölzel an "arcanist" or expert in mixtures and mechanical processes, and Christoph Conrad Hunger, an enameller and gilder.

The factory produced work of admirable quality but du Pacquier was embarrassed by financial difficulties and eventually, in 1744, the factory with all its recipes was bought by the Empress Maria Theresa and thereafter conducted as a royal enterprise. The factory remained in the control of the State until 1864 when it was discontinued.

THE BODY. The paste of the early ware lacked the brilliance and whiteness of the Meissen body owing to the materials used, but after a supply of better material from Bohemia the body was brought to technical perfection according to the accepted standards of hard paste porcelain.

THE GLAZE. The glaze from the start was good and was soon brought to parallel quality with the Dresden glaze.

ARTICLES MADE AND CONTOUR. Besides the customary table services and objects of decorative purport, the Vienna factory produced a great quantity of the most elaborate vases and other ornaments and a large number of figures, groups and statuettes, glazed and in biscuit.

In the matter of contour, Dresden models and precedents appear to have supplied most of the impulse until the time when the Neo-Classic spirit began to assert itself, and consequently the Rococo forms flourished in florid exuberance. Even when the Neo-Classic influence became dominant, the Vienna factory without achieving any particular individuality in so doing managed to impart an ornate quality that often verged upon inconsistency. The advent of Empire forms gave greater scope for the display of sheer splendour and intricate enrichment.

TYPES OF DECORATION. Modelling in high relief, moulded ornaments in low relief impressed in the paste, piercing, fretwork, painting and gilding—all these decorative processes were freely employed. The subjects for painted decoration included polychrome Chinese *motifs;* Japanese birds and flowers; Imari red, blue and gold patterns; figures and landscapes; polychrome leafy scrolls with flowers, fruit, canopies, and figures, landscapes or scenes in cartouches; similar *motifs* painted in black with touches of gold; "German flowers," "Indian flowers," Sèvres "chintz" patterns, and hybrid flower forms; painting done over low reliefs; mythological subjects, battle scenes, and *putti* with their attendant embellishments. A number of good ground colours were also in use. In the latter part of the eighteenth century the practice of copying famous paintings as china decorations was followed to excess and many of the pieces of this time are terribly over-decorated.

In addition to the too lavish painted decorations, there was the further enrichment of raised gilding (PLATE 70, A), which required several coats of gold, each successive coat being fired and burnished. Further ornament was engraved on this elaborate gilding. The chemist Leithner devised a palette of enamel colours more extensive than was used by any other contemporary factory; he produced an underglaze black; and he also introduced the use of platinum as well as rich gilding. Altogether, the late eighteenth century was a period of the amplest technical resources at the Vienna factory, but while some of the china then produced commands admiration, not a little of it is characterised by vulgar ostentation and indicates unpleasantly decadent taste.

THE MARKS. During the period of du Pacquier's control most of the china was unmarked. After 1744, when the factory became Crown property, the Austrian shield was painted in underglaze blue. After 1827 it was stamped in underglaze blue with a wood block. From 1784 onward the pieces were dated by the last two figures of the year, impressed in the paste.

HEREND CHINA (HUNGARY)—c.1830
TO PRESENT DAY

HISTORY. About 1830, Moritz Fischer established an hard paste porcelain factory at Herend, in Hungary. He produced a very fine ware, anticipating Sèvres and Dresden in securing a full range of brilliant colours (PLATE 71, A) on hard paste.

Most of the product of this factory was in the form of clever copies of the finest pieces of Sèvres and Capo di Monte porcelain of earlier date and the later enamelled ware of China. Fischer's most brilliant triumph was with the jewel-like enamelled decoration of cups for the Oriental market. The Herend china is marked with the name "Herend" in very small letters and the Hungarian arms are sometimes applied over the glaze. The marks subjoined also appear on Herend china.

Swiss Chinaware

NYON CHINA

History. During the latter part of the eighteenth century, or at the very beginning of the nineteenth, a soft paste porcelain factory was established at Nyon, on the lake of Geneva. It was founded by a Frenchman named Maubrée and during at least a part of its career was directed by Robillard, who had previously worked at Sèvres. The factory was conducted according to French notions and French ideals prevailed, both in the fashion of the ware produced and in the matter of decoration. The influence of Sèvres was predominant.

The paste was white and translucent.

Only tableware and such small pieces as trays, candlesticks and inkstands were made at this factory.

Some of the earlier decoration, with landscapes, birds and tulips, shews a German influence, but most of the china was decorated with violets, roses, cornflowers and other small blossoms in a dainty and thoroughly French manner. Maubrée was himself at one time a flower painter at Sèvres. Some of the decoration was executed in Geneva.

The mark of the factory was a fish in underglaze blue. Manufacture was discontinued early in the nineteenth century, probably about 1813.

ZURICH CHINA—1763-1791

History. In 1763 an hard paste porcelain factory was established at Zurich by Heidegger and Korrodi who employed Spengler, an expert porcelain maker, along with some workmen, from Höchst to assist them in the undertaking. The traditions of the Höchst factory were followed.

The paste had a greyish tone. For a short period soft paste was tried, but was soon given up. The chief product consisted of tableware and some few decorative accessories, and a modeller from Ludwigsburg, Sonnenschein by name, modelled a certain number of figures.

The decorations were largely landscapes and flowers, the landscapes usually being of Swiss inspiration. Some of them were painted by the Swiss poet, Solomon Gessner. The best work of the factory was produced between 1775 and 1790.

The mark was a capital German Z in underglaze blue. The manufacture was not very profitable and the factory was discontinued in 1791.

Dutch and Belgian Chinaware

"AMSTEL" CHINA—1764-1810

WEESP—1764–1771
OUDE LOOSDRECHT—1771–1784
OUDE AMSTEL—1784–1799
NIEUWE AMSTEL—1799–1810

HISTORY. There are only two establishments to be taken account of in considering the china made in Holland. One of them began at Weesp and had a continuous existence under three other names and in three other places. The second was at The Hague.

Dutch china has always been overshadowed by the importance and sufficiency of Dutch Delft and, consequently, the wares produced during the eighteenth century never had the necessary stimulus to develope any distinctively national characteristics. Nevertheless, a considerable amount of very good china was made and much of it possesses a certain homely charm of "pleasant bourgeois character."

In 1764 Count Gronsfeldt-Diepenbrock acquired the plant of a bankrupt faïence factory at Amsterdam, removed it to Weesp, a little town near by, and established an hard paste porcelain works with workmen from Dresden, closely following Dresden tradition and practices.

The porcelain produced was of such excellent character that Count Gronsfeldt-Diepenbrock had no hesitation in proposing to Sèvres a scheme of amalgamation, since Sèvres was anxious to make hard paste porcelain and had not yet reached success in the experiments carried on there. The proposal was considered but not concluded as the management of Sèvres saw the many possibilities of international complications.

Then followed embarrassing difficulties for the factory at Weesp. Holland was flooded with Japanese porcelain at the time, thus affecting the market for native wares, and the German workmen were leaving and going home again. In the meantime, however, a Calvinist minister, by name de Mol, had become much interested in the factory at Weesp, regarded it as an opportunity and bought the works in 1771.

He thereupon transferred the establishment to Oude Loosdrecht and continued the manufacture of porcelain, devoting most effort to the production of "useful" ware. Under de Mol's direction the enterprise seems to have prospered and there was a very considerable output of china. After de Mol's death, in 1782, the business was carried on at Oude Loosdrecht by a limited company until 1784.

In 1784 the company removed the works to Oude Amstel and there continued to make the same quality of chinaware until 1799 when the ownership passed to another company.

The new company again moved the works, this time to Nieuwe Amstel, and at that place went on making porcelain until 1810 when the establishment was finally discontinued.

THE BODY. From the very outset, thanks to the experienced Dresden workmen who knew and followed the tried Dresden processes, the hard paste body was technically beyond all cavil, pure white and of the best quality, closely resembling the body of Dresden china.

THE GLAZE. The glaze was of the same, even, transparent brilliant quality as the Dresden glaze.

ARTICLES MADE AND CONTOUR. The china made consisted chiefly of tableware, breakfast sets, "useful" objects of various sorts, small boxes, pots and vases. Later a few more ambitious vases with intricate perforations were made and towards the end of the Oude Loosdrecht phase some busts in biscuit were produced.

The contours, for the most part, were borrowed from German and French sources. The shapes were partly Rococo in style but changed to Neo-Classic forms concurrently with the march of fashion. The leaning to French precedents and models became more pronounced towards the latter part of the Oude Loosdrecht period.

TYPES OF DECORATION. The types of decoration were as heterogeneous as the contours. All manner of *motifs* were used. Some of the china was wholly white with festoons, sprays, or other ornamental *motifs* in slight relief; the piercings of fruit baskets were often picked out with blue; there were moulded *motifs* with a sparing use of colour; cartouches contained small landscapes, birds, and polychrome flowers; sometimes there were Watteau-like subjects and scenes from Italian comedy; modelled fruits, leaves and birds, duly coloured, served as knobs or handles; landscapes and cupids were rendered *en camaïeu;* the cornflowers of Sèvres were frequent; and polychrome landscapes, birds and flowers were especially in favour.

THE MARKS. The Weesp mark consisted of the crossed swords of Dresden with two flanking dots. The Oude Loosdrecht mark was M:O L:, rendered in a variety of forms. The Oude Amstel mark was the name "Oude Amstel" or the letter A. The wares of all the four stages of this factory were so much alike that it is difficult to distinguish them.

THE HAGUE CHINA—1775-1785 (?)

HISTORY. The hard paste porcelain factory established at The Hague in 1775 by the Viennese Anton Leichner had only a short life, but during its career produced some very excellent work. Not only did this factory decorate its own ware, but it also decorated a great deal of the soft paste porcelain made at Tournay. This circumstance has sometimes led to the impression that The Hague factory made both hard and soft paste. Only hard paste was made at The Hague. The factory was given up at the end of about ten years.

THE BODY. The body was a fine, white hard paste of unexceptionable quality, produced according to the traditions of Dresden and Vienna and was virtually identical with them in character.

THE GLAZE. The glaze was also clear, even and brilliant like the glazes of Dresden and Vienna.

ARTICLES MADE AND CONTOUR. The preponderance of china produced consisted of tableware and the more usual objects of household adornment. There were, however, some elaborate vases made. There was no figure modelling and very little moulding in low relief was done, the china commonly presenting a perfectly plain, smooth surface. Energies were chiefly concentrated upon painted decoration which was of an high order. There were some late Rococo contours but most of the shapes were those of the Neo-Classic type.

TYPES OF DECORATION. Flowers in polychrome were, perhaps, the most usual decorative *motifs* employed at The Hague, but there were also "Boucher" children and cupids, with surrounding foliage and attributes, *en camaïeu;* birds of multi-coloured plumage; monochrome landscapes, sometimes in *grisaille;* and antique heads in profile, set in medallions with a pale pink ground. This last form of decoration was rendered with peculiar success.

THE MARKS. The mark was the city emblem—a stork holding a fish in its beak. This mark was painted in underglaze blue on the hard paste china made at The Hague; it was painted in on-glaze blue on the soft paste china made at Tournay but decorated at The Hague.

BRUSSELS CHINA
SCHAERBEEK, NEAR BRUSSELS—1784–1791
ETTERBEEK, NEAR BRUSSELS—1775–1803

HISTORY. The hard paste porcelain factory at Schaerbeek, near Brussels, was founded in 1784 by J. S. Vaume and continued in operation for only seven years.

The products consisted mostly of tableware and "useful" objects. It is possible that figures also may have been made. The Schaerbeek china was moderately decorated—landscapes like fine India ink drawings, small scattered flowers, landscapes in green, and scattered sprigs in conjunction with friezes and festoons of foliage formed the usual *motifs.*

The mark was a "B," with or without a crown, and sometimes with the words "Monplaisir près Bruxelles," in underglaze blue. The mark also occasionally occurred in other colours on-glaze.

The hard paste factory at Etterbeek, also near Brussels, was founded by Chrétien Kühne, from Saxony, in 1775. It made tableware, articles of household embellishment, and groups and single figures, both glazed and in biscuit. The decorations were of heterogeneous types, but birds, flowers and *genre* scenes predominated. The mark was E. B. in monogram. Little is known of the doings of this factory and it is said to have closed in 1803.

B

Swedish and Danish Chinaware

MARIEBERG CHINA—1758-1788

History. The porcelain factory of Marieberg, near Stockholm, is the first establishment in Sweden we have occasion to consider. It began its existence in 1758 under the management of a certain Ehrenreich, but succeeded in producing nothing save faïence until Pierre Berthevin became director in 1766. At one time or another various Frenchmen of talent were employed and, in nearly every instance, contributed materially to the improvement of the china produced. The factory passed through a number of vicissitudes and made numerous experiments with paste. Some of the china made was exceedingly beautiful, but the product was limited and the Marieberg ware is not plentiful. The manufacture came to an end in 1788.

The Body. The paste of Marieberg was an exceedingly variable quantity. Under Berthevin the body was a soft paste akin in composition to the French soft pastes. It was highly translucent, of a greenish yellow tone, and was sometimes marred by flaws. Between this and the white hard paste of fine, smooth texture, made for only two years, 1777 and 1778, under the Frenchman Dartou, there were many variations, but the most constant form was a semi-hard paste, white, slightly translucent, with a chalky or limy texture, and of uneven surface. The pieces made from this body are those that exhibit a peculiarly individual charm. The ware is attractive in appearance and highly prized, especially in Sweden, but it is very brittle.

The Glaze. The usual glaze, except the brilliant glaze on the hard paste that was made for two years, was soft and mellow and very like to that of Mennecy, which seems to have been regarded as a model.

Articles Made and Contour. The output at first consisted largely of custard cups. Other articles of tableware and sundry decorative accessories were gradually added until, at a comparatively late date, figures were included in the list of products.

The contours were almost wholly French and, for a great part of the time, were fashioned in a moderate Rococo manner. Towards the latter part of the factory's career the Neo-Classic trend became evident. Some of the early pieces were patterned so closely after the wares of Mennecy that they might almost be considered replicas.

Types of Decoration. As with the shapes of the early Marieberg china, so also was it with the manner of decoration. The methods of Mennecy decoration were so closely copied at the beginning that, without rigid scrutiny and an examination of the marks, it would be difficult to distinguish between the pieces.

Besides the Mennecy flowers and the Mennecy manner, other *motifs* of decoration employed included polychrome flowers of a more general character and diverse rendering, armorial bearings with garlands, medallions with wreaths and festoons, landscapes and *genre* subjects, coloured rims for plates with flowers in the centre, fretwork, piercings and modelled flowers that were naturalistically coloured, moulded low reliefs such as basket-work, foilage and ribbings, flowers in monochrome, small landscapes in iron-red, reddish purple or copper green, enclosed within panels, often of quatrefoil shape and, very frequently, only a few gilded lines on an otherwise undecorated body. Decoration with polychrome flowers was, perhaps, the most commonly used. The monochrome flowers were often painted in pure blue, in a strong bluish green, and in a full rich purple. The last named colour was especially characteristic of the factory.

The Marks. There are many variations in the Marieberg marks but the most usual mark is some form of the three crowns of Sweden, with or without MB. Occasionally the fleur-de-lys from the royal arms is added. The mark occurs in underglaze blue or in red on-glaze. Many pieces are altogether unmarked.

RÖRSTRAND CHINA—1880 TO PRESENT DAY

MARIEBERG—1782–1788

Rörstrand china is, in a certain sense, the offspring of Marieberg china, although the Rörstrand pottery works antedated the establishment of the Marieberg factory by many years and the Swedish Government had authorised Rörstrand to make fine porcelain as early as 1735. Nothing, however, but earthenware had ever issued from Rörstrand. After the Marieberg establishment had been transferred to Rörstrand in 1782, the Rörstrand works simultaneously continued making the earthen pottery they had always made.

When the making of Marieberg china came to an end in 1788, the Rörstrand factory kept on making earthen pottery of an high quality and maintained high standards of technique and distinguished traditions of decoration, in the formation of which the influences of Delft, Rouen and Mennecy are particularly noticeable for the earlier years, while those of Sèvres and Wedgwood appear later.

The six years of Marieberg china-making at Rörstrand added a tradition and an ideal to the Rörstrand heritage. The impulse to make fine porcelain had been renewed, although many years were to elapse before that impulse would bear fruit in realisation. In 1799, Geijer brought in new English methods. From 1825 to 1830, there was considerable reconstruction and a further adoption of English methods and English materials, especially English china-clay.

As early as 1780, the Rörstrand factory was producing admirable ironstone china or *flintporslin*. Characterised as it was by distinguished shapes and exquisite decoration, this ware found an excellent market both in Sweden and elsewhere, notwithstanding the competition of East India china and European porcelains of fine quality and great beauty. Along with the ironstone china or *flintporslin,* Rörstrand produced the kind of fine earthenware known in England and America as "white ware" or "Queensware," for which there was great demand.

In 1867, came a reorganisation and the Rörstrand Company was formed. At last, after sundry rearrangements, experiments and modi-

THE PRACTICAL BOOK OF CHINAWARE

fications of formulae, the Rörstrand works, in 1880, put forth a fine feldspar china whose quality entitles it to high regard.

While tableware is the chief output of the Rörstrand factory, vases and other articles of partially or wholly ornamental purpose form part of the product. The contours of all the pieces are notably good; traditional shapes are retained to a great extent but there are also modifications and adaptations to meet the preferences of the more modern-minded.

The methods of decoration employed include painting, gilding, transfer-printing, moulding and modelling. The manner of decoration at Rörstrand has naturally reflected the successive changes in popular taste through the many years of the factory's existence but has fortunately escaped the hideous excesses that obtained in many Continental and English potteries during the late nineteenth century.

During its entire period of operation, its has always been the policy at Rörstrand to retain the services of talented artists. In the creation of designs for the embellishment of the present chinaware, Rörstrand has a rich *répertoire* to draw from for both reproductions and for the adaptations Scandinavian artists have shown such facility in making. One should not forget either the gay but reticent polychrome types or the "blue and white" and also the creations *en camaïeu*.

The Rörstrand mark shows the three Swedish crowns, one above the name and two below.

GUSTAVSBERG CHINA—1827 TO PRESENT DAY

The story of the Gustavsberg pottery begins about the middle of the seventeenth century. Situated on the Island of Värmdö, although about only 15 miles from Stockholm at a small inlet of the Baltic called Farsta Bay, the pottery was in a spot so isolated, until the advent of the motor age, that it was necessary to provide housing for the workmen. Hence, a small town gradually grew up around the establishment, the factory the sole reason for the community's existence. Under the present enlightened management, this housing feature has been fully developed in accordance with the most comprehensive contemporary housing ideals.

Until 1827 the Gustavsberg product consisted wholly of various types of earthenware. In that year, however, the factory began to make chinaware and the manufacture of china has gone on ever since, along with the continued output of earthenware. The early period of china-making at Gustavsberg was inevitably a time of experiment, leading to the ultimate attainment of fine quality.

So far as shapes and types of decoration were concerned, the table-ware and decorative articles reflected the general trends of contemporary taste, with a strong leaning at first towards old English precedents. Throughout the nineteenth century, Gustavsberg china fortunately retained some of the typical Scandinavian restraint and reticence; in the last quarter of the century, conscious of the execrable taste generally rampant in Europe, the management made strenuous efforts to improve design.

The years aesthetically jejune were, nevertheless, years of marked technical advancement in the china-making world. In its technical progress, Gustavsberg was notably conspicuous. The task of converting the old Gustavsberg factory into a modern plant was well under way in 1937; since then the work has been completed.

In the beautifully translucent Gustavsberg body—the result of long-studied and nicely-adjusted formulae (modified upon occasion to meet special needs)—the kaolin or china-clay imported from Cornwall, and the ball clay also brought from England, are combined with Swedish feldspar and quartz. Besides the chinaware made from this felspathic body, the Gustavsberg factory likewise makes bone china, the formula for it derived from long-established English practice.

Gustavsberg china includes all manner of flat and hollow tableware and a great variety of bowls, jars, vases and other decorative articles. Manufacturing processes employed are throwing, "jiggering" on a spindle, turning on a lathe and moulding. The methods of decoration include painting, transfer-printing, gilding and modelling. The transfer decorations are those most generally used, and various printing techniques come into play. Underglaze and overglaze colours alike appear in the decorations, both painted and printed, as occasion may require.

For many years it has been the policy at Gustavsberg to retain the most able artists and allow them the utmost latitude in experimentation and the development of design. At the same time, the factory has been fortunate in avoiding the conflicts so often arising between the views of technical and commercial experts, on one hand, and the impulses to fresh and untrammelled expression by the designers, on the other. Thanks to this amicable give and take, Gustavsberg chinaware, both in shapes and decoration, displays a convincing quality combining straightforward simplicity with Northern vigour and imagery.

The Gustavsberg mark is an anchor with the name "Gustavsberg" in an arc above it.

UPSALA-EKEBY CHINA—1918 TO PRESENT DAY

One of the recent members of the Scandinavian porcelain family is the chinaware produced at the Karlskrona factory, a branch establishment of the Upsala-Ekeby factory that was founded in 1886, near the ancient university city of Upsala in Sweden. The Upsala-Ekeby factory itself was started for the manufacture of glazed earthenware tiles in accordance with a centuries-old craft tradition of the immediate neighbourhood. The Karlskrona Porslinsfabrik was started at the end of the first World War and since 1918 has been making fine feldspar china. In 1942, the Karlskrona china factory became affiliated with the Upsala-Ekeby Company and since then its chinaware has been known by the latter name.

The body is highly translucent and of white or ivory tones. The chief output of the factory consists of tea and coffee-sets and general domestic tableware of fine quality, although considerable attention is also paid to manufacturing a more robust type of tableware for hotel and restaurant use.

In the matter of decoration, the factory has specialised to some extent in monogram service, but other modes of decoration are also employed. The combined vigour and restraint commonly met with in Scandinavian decorative expression characterise both the surface embellishments and the contours of the Upsala-Ekeby ware.

The Mark of the Upsala-Ekeby china consists of the capital letters U and E, combined dipthong-wise and enclosed in a circle.

COPENHAGEN CHINA—1756 TO PRESENT DAY

HISTORY. About 1756 a porcelain factory was opened at Copenhagen with J. G. Mehlhorn, a former Dresden modeller, as director. Mehlhorn's directorship seems to have produced no tangible results in the shape of porcelain and only experiments were made. It was not until 1759, when a Frenchman, Louis Fournier, who had worked at both Sèvres and Chantilly, came to Copenhagen and succeeded Mehlhorn that a soft paste porcelain was made. This soft paste porcelain, whose body somewhat resembled that of Saint Cloud and Chantilly, was of pleasant quality and continued to be made till the end of 1765, when Fournier was succeeded by Frantz Müller. Although Müller continued for a while to make soft paste porcelain, he was experimenting with hard pastes of which he produced a sort by 1772 or 1773. This body was much improved by 1776 and perfected by 1780.

Under private management the establishment was beset by financial difficulties so that, in 1779, it was taken over by the King and then began an highly successful career.

ROYAL COPENHAGEN CHINA

The Royal Copenhagen china factory despite all the pressures of nineteenth-century public taste nevertheless always managed to maintain a degree of independence and freshness in its interpretations. When the twentieth-century "modernistic" revolt against gimcrackery came, the factory management and artists at Copenhagen refused to be rushed into illogical fads and extremes.

In Scandinavian countries the interpretation of modernism has been conspicuous for its sanity as well as for vigour of invention. To this statement every phase of creative design bears witness. In order to be modern, the Scandinavians have not thought it necessary to cast aside all tradition as a thing accursed. Their work shows that they consider modernism not a revolution nor an wholesale negation of all that has ever gone before, but rather a new phase of orderly evolution from the body of past experience, experience which generations of human endeavour, correction and selection have welded into a vital tradition.

This quality of well-poised assurance is inherent in modern Scandinavian ceramics no less than in architecture, silver-smithing or any other field of creative design. It is strongly in evidence in the recent porcelain fashioned at the Royal Copenhagen factory. Apart from the beauty of the hard-paste porcelain body—technically perfect, of mellow hue, and with a glaze of almost liquid softness in appearance—the cardinal features of appeal to the china-lover are contour and the manner of decoration. In these particulars, the Copenhagen china being made to-day displays a rich diversity of invention that can scarcely fail to enlist the interest of the most diverse tastes.

THE BODY. The soft paste body made during Fournier's management was translucent and of a creamy or more or less yellowish tinge while the soft paste made under the first part of Müller's *régime* had a greyish tone. The first hard paste made by Müller was darkish and somewhat grey. It was improved until, by 1780, it was hard, translucent and pure white.

THE GLAZE. The glaze of the first soft paste had a soft, lustrous brilliance and felt soapy to the touch. Müller's early glaze was imperfect and had a yellowish tinge. The final glaze for the hard paste body was smooth, perfectly transparent and brilliant.

ARTICLES MADE AND CONTOUR. Under Fournier the pieces produced were, for the most part, of small size and included bowls, powder-boxes, cups, custard cups, cream jugs, sugar-basons, breakfast sets and small vases. The list was gradually increased to include full sets of tableware, tea services, flower pots, tankards, tureens, punch bowls and a number of decorative accessories. From 1780 onward much larger, more "important" and elaborate vases, clock cases, mirror frames and sconces were added to the list, along with numerous figures, both glazed and in biscuit.

Although certain German influences in contour could be traced from time to time, the French influence was clearly predominant. The more restrained Rococo shapes were at first prevalent but were gradually supplanted by Neo-Classic forms. From 1780 onward the Neo-Classic types were universal and were later followed by the Neo-Grec shapes.

Besides all manner of tableware, and jars, vases, bowls, lamps and

other ornamental articles, the factory is still producing a great number
of exquisitely modelled and subtly coloured small *bibelots*—seals, mice,
birds, dogs and the like, as well as human figures. These justly celebrated figures are covered with a rich, limpid glaze that has long been
popularly associated with the Copenhagen factory.

TYPES OF DECORATION. Polychrome flowers (PLATE 71, B), in the
manner of Chantilly, supplied one of the earliest *motifs* and always
remained in favour. Besides these, the decorative scope included
modelling in high relief, fretwork, moulded ornamentation in low relief such as ribbings, flutings and foliage patterns, the use of ground
colours, wreaths, garlands, landscapes, flowers and landscapes *en
camaïeu* or in two colours such as purple and copper green, Classic
heads in wreathed and garlanded medallions, contemporary portrait
medallions, landscapes and heads in *grisaille,* Chinese subjects, a few
comics and battle scenes, and the minute later flowers such as the cornflower *motif* popularised by Sèvres. The gilding was good and used
in moderate amount. There was always a fondness for decorations in
blue and white and the *Strohblumen* and "onion" patterns borrowed
from Dresden were always great favourites and have remained so to
the present day. They are commonly known as "Copenhagen" patterns.

In tableware, the urge of modernism has furnished the Copenhagen
artists with some of their happiest inspirations. The old blue and
white "onion pattern" for table services has been so long identified with
Copenhagen that many find it hard to visualise Copenhagen china of
any other type. Nevertheless, the designers now at work have added
to the already immensely varied *répertoire* numerous highly individual
patterns that embody the best aspects of modern practice. As a rule,
they have achieved the most telling effects with the simplest imaginable
means. Oftentimes there are bands of strong colour and gilding, so
counterposed that they create incisive accent. Again, there are isolated
sprays of flowers or leafage in the middle of a plate or platter, with the
unadorned field of the creamy porcelain body surrounding them as a
foil to set them off and focus interest upon their perfectly wrought
details and the bold outline of their pattern. In many cases, whatever
restraint of colour or pattern may govern the design, there is such

spontaneity and buoyancy of invention that an impression of genial warmth and energy radiates from every one of these recent creations.

THE MARKS. The Copenhagen mark, three wavy lines in underglaze blue, is the same mark that was adopted May 1, 1775, when the factory was placed on a definite footing.

BING AND GRØNDAHL CHINA—
1853 TO PRESENT DAY

HISTORY. The Bing and Grøndahl china factory in Copenhagen started in 1853. The birthstory of this enterprise, and of the spirit that prompted it, must be told if one is to understand the subsequent history of the "Porcellansfabrik" and appraise the character of its products. The story is a tale of faith and adventure.

Grøndahl, an enthusiastic young figure-maker employed at the Royal Porcelain Works in Copenhagen, was bursting with ideas that he hoped might revolutionise that establishment. It was one of his darling ambitions to make small biscuit copies of Thorvaldsden's sculptures. The management, however, looked coldly on the "speculative genius of the factory." Thereupon Grøndahl left the Royal Porcelain Works, set forth to find someone more receptive to his scheme, and addressed himself to the Bing brothers, well-known Copenhagen merchants.

To quote from the illustrated brochure issued by the Bing and Grøndahl factory in 1910,

"Bing's business was founded in 1820 by H. J. Bing, a poor Dutch emigrant of Jewish faith. As a special mark of favour this man had . . . obtained a royal licence allowing him to deal in drawing and writing materials, maps and school articles. Against a bitter and obstinate opposition on the part of the Ironmongers' and the Grocers' Corporations, H. J. Bing and his two sons M. H. and J. H. Bing, who were first his partners and later on his successors, succeeded in working up this small stationery to an extensive and richly furnished fine-art repository and fancy-stationery, the object of which might, to a certain extent, justly be stated to be encouraging the public to decorate their dwellings with fine and artistically perfect articles by facilitating the purchase of the same."

The brothers Bing clearly understood that to make this commercial art venture "a paying concern, they had better go the whole length, founding the business not only on burning biscuit figures but on making glazed china . . . as well." Embracing Grøndahl's proposal and broadening the scope of his scheme, the brothers Bing established a pottery in Copenhagen, had the usual initial failures and discouragements in firing and glazing, and then entered upon a career of successful production. While putting forth "useful" chinaware—for which they had to create a market—they also made various types of art wares from the first.

In the factory's infancy, Grøndahl—the prime cause of the whole undertaking—died. This was a staggering blow, but other able artists were found who gladly threw in their lot with the fortunes of the new pottery and sustained an high order of merit in its products. Throughout its history, indeed, the factory has always retained a staff of exceptionally able artists—sculptors, modellers, painters.

The artists' work has reflected the sundry phases of taste current at the times at which they wrought. Nevertheless, while working in the spirit of their particular eras, along with perfect execution the Bing and Grøndahl artists showed rather more vigour and originality in their interpretations than was usual elsewhere, and the factory's technicians ably seconded the designers in mastering the problems the artists' intricate conceptions posed in body-composition, firing and glazing.

It has been characteristic of the establishment to experiment with and develop varied techniques. While its hard paste or "true" porcelain body is of the highest excellence, the factory has also produced a fine soft paste body of mellow hue and peculiar adaptability to decoration with overglaze enamel colours. At the same time, the artists and technicians have been notably successful in their control and management of underglaze colours and in developing the resources of this method of decoration. The technicians have likewise produced an especially satisfactory matt glaze to enhance the effect of certain types of ware. Another experimental departure from the usual activities of a china-factory has resulted in making stoneware an acceptable vehicle of new forms of decorative expression.

In both the utilitarian wares and in the numerous ornamental pieces, bibelots and figurines, reticence and restraint contribute an assured permanent value. The figurines have an especially fresh, virile and engaging quality.

It is worth noting that it is customary for the artists retained by this factory to sign the pieces for which they are responsible.

The Bing and Grøndahl china mark consists of three towers over the letters B and G, above the name "Kjøbenhavn" in a semi-circle.

Russian and Polish Chinaware

ST. PETERSBURG CHINA—1744

HISTORY. The Imperial Russian china factory was established in 1744 under Christoph Conrad Hunger who had managed the Vezzi factory in Venice for five years and had also gained his experience at Meissen, Vienna and elsewhere. Under his *régime* little was produced and he was soon succeeded by other directors. Until 1753 little was produced but small articles such as cups, saucers, jugs, and snuff boxes which were used as presents from the Court, although some statuettes were made as early as 1752.

A great change took place about 1763 when the products became partly commercial. The factory was continued under Imperial control.

There were two grades of ware made, the body of one being pure white and of the finest hard paste quality, the other being not pure white and of somewhat variable tinge. The glaze was good. Besides tableware and splendid vases, figures were produced both glazed and in biscuit. At first all the decoration was in the Dresden manner with "gold Chinamen," and monochrome landscapes and flowers in purple or green with gold or black. Later the range of colours increased and there were scenes from daily life, landscapes, animals, and multi-coloured birds and flowers. Most of the decoration was in a very gorgeous manner and highly elaborate, the best manners of Dresden and Sèvres being closely followed.

The china was marked with the Imperial Russian eagle and with the initials or monograms of the rulers, either impressed in the paste or painted in black or gold.

There were also china factories in Moscow and at Korzec in Poland where not a little good china was made and decorated in an acceptable and highly characteristic manner.

English Chinaware

BOW CHINA—1745-1776

HISTORY. Up to almost the middle of the eighteenth century, whatever experiments in porcelain-making may have been conducted previously, there was no established china factory in England. For her chinaware England had been dependent upon the Orient or else upon either the soft paste products of France or the hard paste china of Germany. Of all three kinds she had had abundant experience, and all three kinds were sufficiently represented throughout the length and breath of the Kingdom. The people knew and admired chinaware, and there was no danger of its being confounded with Delft earthenware imitations, no matter how cleverly they were made.

About the middle of the century there was a determined effort to establish china factories in England and to make wares for home consumption. There are fugitive notices of sundry ventures in this direction and some of them, in all likelihood, succeeded in producing tangible results of a more or less satisfactory nature, though scanty in quantity, before coming to an untimely and unrecorded end. The two earliest china factories to achieve an enduring foothold and put forth a substantial volume of finished wares of recognised commercial and artistic worth were Bow and Chelsea.

The early history of the Bow factory is wrapped in obscurity. It was at Stratford-le-Bow, in Essex, and at some early stage of its career—perhaps from the very outset—it was called "New Canton." In December 1744 a patent was issued to Edward Heylyn and Thomas Frye empowering them to engage in the manufacture of chinaware. A second patent was issued to Frye alone in 1749. What had been going on in the meantime is not certainly known, but it is not unreasonable to assume that attempts at china production had been made and rewarded with some measure of success. We shall probably not be far wrong in assigning 1745 as the date for the inception of the factory, and in regarding the years between then and 1750 as the period of small beginnings inevitable for a private enterprise of the sort, unaided by any princely patronage or royal subsidy, as were so many undertakings of a similar nature on the Continent.

At all events, by 1750 the mist of uncertainty clears away somewhat and we reach our first definite, authentic information which shews that the works then belonged to the Messrs. Crowther and Weatherby who had entered into partnership in that year. It was in 1750 that the first *known* piece of Bow china was made, although it was doubtless not the first fruit of the factory's existence. Thomas Frye, one of the original patentees, appears as manager, and in that capacity he continued till 1759, when he retired because of ill health. Much of our information regarding the Bow factory is gathered from the notebooks, diaries and memorandum books of John Bowcocke who was the commercial manager and traveller for the works.

The policy of the Bow factory seems to have been to place its chief reliance upon products of a distinctly commercial nature and to devote its efforts mostly to making and selling "useful" wares. In the announcements of the first auction sale of Bow china, held in 1757, is duly advertised "a large assortment of the most useful china in Lots, for the use of Gentlemen's kitchens, Private families, Taverns, etc."

It was customary in the eighteenth century for the china factories in England, besides maintaining shops or warehouses for the sale of their goods, to hold auction sales in London at certain intervals in order to dispose of any surplus stock they might have on hand, to popularise further their products, and to introduce any new creations they might have devised since the preceding sale. These sales sometimes covered a period of a fortnight or even longer.

The first London warehouse for the sale of Bow chinaware was opened in 1753 in Cornhill, near the Royal Exchange. Just after the first auction, in 1757, which took place at the rooms of Cock & Co., "in Spring Gardens, leading into St. James's Park," an advertisement announces the opening of a second warehouse:

"For the convenience of the nobility and gentry, their warehouse on the Terrace in St. James's Street is constantly supplied with everything new, where it is sold as at Cornhill, with the real Price marked on each piece without Abatement."

This West End venture, however, seems not to have met with the measure of success its promoters had hoped for it, and it was given up the following year, its stock of china being disposed of by auction.

From his memoranda and accounts, we learn that Bowcocke made journeys throughout the country to further the sales of the chinaware and, in 1758, the records shew that he was eight months in Dublin on the same errand, receiving frequent consignments of chinaware from the works and disposing of it by auction. The policy of relying mainly upon china of a more or less commercial description for profit seems to have brought success, for a period at least. Bowcocke's account book shews £10,000 cash receipts in 1753, and from the statement of T. Craft, a former employee, we learn that the works kept between two and three hundred people busy.

Frye's retirement from the works, it appears, marked the first stage in the course of decline. Weatherby died in 1762, and in 1763 Crowther, the remaining partner, became bankrupt. In May, 1764, the stock in trade of the Bow factory was sold by auction, but in some way, and probably on a greatly reduced scale, Crowther managed to carry on the business for some years afterwards. The London Directory for 1770–1775 records the warehouse of John Crowther, of Bow China Works, at number 28, St. Paul's Churchyard. In 1776 the entire business was sold for an inconsiderable sum to William Duesbury of Derby, the moulds, models and all other effects were removed, and thus ended the existence of the Bow factory. In 1777 Crowther was admitted an inmate of Morden College, Blackheath, and in that safe haven he spent the residue of his days free, let us hope, from carking business anxieties.

From the emphasis laid by its owners upon the commercial purveying of "useful" wares by the factory, it must not be inferred that Bow china was lacking in artistic merit, nor that the makers were at all blind to either the desirability or necessity of combining excellence of quality, grace of contour, and beauty and variety of decoration in the porcelain they put forth. While stressing the fact that their products were primarily useful as well as beautiful, they made not a few excursions into the realm of the purely ornamental, as the many statuettes and groups that issued from the Bow factory bear witness. In all likelihood these were made at Bow throughout the greater part, if not the whole, of the factory's career. If they could not be placed in the "useful" category, they had all the same a definite commercial value for they were most popular chimney-piece and table adornments, from the cottage and farmhouse to the manor and hall.

While some of the pieces made at Bow were not such as to commend themselves to the taste of every china-lover, and others would unquestionably be treated by nearly everybody with scant respect if they had been made only yesterday and not an hundred and seventy-five years ago, nevertheless the great bulk of chinaware that issued from "New Canton" was of a quality to command hearty admiration. All manner of articles were made, and they were made with great diversity of contour and decorated with a rich variety of patterns.

THE BODY. The body or paste of the Bow china was a variable quantity. Mr. Burton pertinently observes that "much trouble will . . . be saved collectors and others if they will look upon the Bow body as varying from time to time within fairly wide limits." The very early Bow paste was neither particularly white nor particularly translucent. It is obviously not a bone-ash body but the rich paste of glassy or soft paste porcelain, of similar quality with that of Chelsea. It has a distinctly warm, creamy tint and is translucent enough where the ware is thin, but quite opaque where it is thick. When fractured, it shews the dry, gritty or granular texture of other soft paste china and the break never exhibits the glossiness of partial vitrification characteristic of hard paste. It seems highly probable that the formulas for the early paste of both Bow and Chelsea were derived from a common source, and that the common source was someone well acquainted with the processes followed at Saint Cloud, Chantilly and Mennecy-Villeroy. It was in such a way that the knowledge of porcelain-making usually travelled.

Much of the Bow paste, especially the later paste, is exceptionally hard, a quality perhaps to be accounted for by the presence of the bone-ash or some of the other ingredients subsequently used in the course of experimentation. It was doubtless this continued experimentation, in the effort to achieve hard paste or its nearest approximate, that caused the differences in the Bow body. The late pieces are better potted than those of early make, thinner and of much whiter body, but they are poorer in substance; the pieces of the middle period are intermediate in quality.

THE GLAZE. The early Bow glaze, which is rich in lead, shews a slightly yellowish tinge and is apt to gather in the hollows of embossed patterns and at the base of the pieces. It is peculiarly soft, mellow and satin-like both to sight and touch. The glaze of the later ware is quite different in appearance, being perceptibly harder and more brilliant. For the blue and white ware the glaze was often slightly tinted with blue, a device adopted from the Chinese so as to bring the blue of the decoration and the colour of the body more harmoniously together and avoid any harshness of tone.

ARTICLES MADE AND CONTOUR. Besides the "useful" articles of chinaware made at the Bow factory, a category which included every description of tableware for all occasions and every accompaniment of tea tackle, there were vases, flower pots, candlesticks, sconces, "Girandoles and Branches for Chimney Pieces," inkstands, patch boxes and all the usual accesories for writing and dressing tables. There were also large numbers of the modelled figures and statuettes always in great demand.

The contours of the earlier china were perceptibly influenced by Chinese (PLATES 72, B and 73, B) and Dresden prototypes, but often displayed a good deal of independent interpretation. The figure work, of course, was in the first instance of Dresden inspiration but soon assumed a thoroughly English character. While the Oriental and Saxon influences were still strong in the expression of contours, the Rococo influence of Sèvres made a profound impression and Rococo shapes enjoyed marked popularity for a long time. The factory was discontinued before Neo-Classic tendencies became dominant.

TYPES OF DECORATION. The types of decoration employed at Bow were exceedingly varied and were inspired by both Chinese (PLATES 72, A and B; 74, A and B), and Japaneses examples, on the Oriental side, and by Dresden, Chantilly, Mennecy and Sèvres (PLATE 72, C) precedents, from the Continental angle.

The decorative processes included moulding, piercing (PLATE 74, A), modelling in relief, painting, transfer printing and gilding. The white Fuchien ware of China supplied the inspiration for the white pieces decorated with sprigs of "prunus" (PLATES 72, D and 74, B) or plum blossoms in relief, of which many were made. Other types, too, of relief floral ornament were moulded and luted on to the surface of the pieces (PLATE 75) they were meant to adorn. Much use, also, was made of moulded patterns impressed on rims of plates and other parts of table china. The prunus blossom supplied a frequent *motif* for this purpose as well as divers other floral items, and this moulded ornament, though left uncoloured itself (PLATE 74, B), was not seldom used in conjunction with painted decoration immediately beside it.

In surveying the coloured decoration, first of all must be mentioned the blue and white ware, painted in underglaze blue, obviously inspired by the blue and white K'ang Hsi porcelain of China (PLATE 72, A and B). If not made from the inception of the factory, its production began soon after and was continued in large quantities. The account books shew it was highly popular and constantly in demand. While the decorative inspiration of this ware was unmistakably Chinese—and many of the contours were Chinese, too—the execution was patently English. Powder blue ware was also imitated, with shaped white panels in reserve on which appeared various Chinese *motifs* either in blue or else with polychrome flowers, birds and butterflies. Some of the Chinese ware with solid dark blue glaze was imitated to a certain degree. A few of the *motifs* on the blue and white Bow china suggest a Delft origin.

Probably the most popular type of polychrome decoration, and one of the earliest produced, was the Kakiyemon mode or, as it was commonly called, the "old Japan" pattern. Even when it was not literally rendered, all sorts of adaptations from it made their appearance. Pieces painted in the Kakiyemon manner were frequently enriched with points of old dull gilding. The Japanese Imari decoration was also reproduced, though to a less extent.

Other Oriental *motifs* followed were the Chinese peonies (PLATE 74, B) and chysanthemums in polychrome, Chinese diapered borders for the rims of plates and edges of dishes, Chinese fighting cocks and other birds, and figures in the manner of the "Mandarin" china so esteemed about the middle of the eighteenth century.

Flowers scattered at random in the so-called Dresden manner, and flowers gathered in bouquets and bunches (PLATES 73, A and B), after the fashion of Chantilly and Mennecy, were common *motifs* of polychrome ornament, as also were small flowers gathered in garlands, wreaths and festoons, and likewise larger groupings of a few flowers or fruits painted with great naturalistic precision. The rims of dishes and plates that were adorned with this last-named sort of decoration were sometimes painted with a broad band of brownish grey. Other edges, especially on early pieces made before gilding was extensively practised, were often painted with a narrow line of reddish brown. There were, furthermore, plates and dishes moulded in the form of leaves; these were coloured according to nature.

Some of the china was enriched with heraldic bearings and further decked with little scattered multi-coloured flowers and diapered rims, much in the manner called "Lowestoft." Amongst the later wares were pieces with ground colours and reserved panels in which appeared figures, flowers, gaily-coloured birds, or Watteau-like groups in polychrome, very much in the manner of Sèvres. Occasionally decorations were executed altogether in gold on the white porcelain ground.

Still further, there were pieces decorated with landscapes, groups of figures, and country scenes, in grey, rose-violet or red *en camaïeu,* in the manner of Mennecy, Vincennes or Sèvres. These latter were not painted but printed with transfer designs. In some cases, where there was not so much elaborate detail, the outlines were printed in transfer and filled in with different colours painted on. The printing of transfer designs seems to have been done at Battersea. Oftentimes, where the centre of a plate or platter is filled with a transfer design, the border surrounding the rim is painted, thus indicating an early stage of the printing process.

Although in old sales lists and advertisements it is sometimes noted that the "old Japan" pieces were "most beautifully painted by several of the first masters from Dresden," it is much more likely that they were executed wholly by English hands. Thomas Frye, the manager, was an artist of no mean capacity and whether he himself did some of the painting or not, he was quite competent to direct all the operations without foreign assistance. Designs were gathered from all manner of sources and either adopted outright or else adapted to suit the circumstances. It was not an unusual thing for patrons to lend choice pieces of Oriental or Continental china in their possession to serve as models. As only one instance of this sort, may be quoted a memorandum in the factory records of 1756: "Patterns received from Lady Cavendish: a Japan octagon cup and saucer, lady pattern; a rib'd and scollop'd cup and saucer, image pattern; a basket bordered dessart plate; a Japan bread and butter plate."

The little Bow figures or statuettes, many of which are full of charm, were painted in bright colours in a manner appropriate to the subjects represented, although it is generally considered that their colouring was less satisfactory than the colouring done at the rival Chelsea works.

THE MARKS. A very large quantity of Bow china was unmarked. On the pieces marked, various devices occur. Of these, the anchor and dagger, usually painted in red or a reddish brown, it is important to remember. There is also sometimes found an arrow, with or without an annulet; likewise the monogram F. The caduceus and the bow and arrow marks are considered of doubtful import. Divers other marks, often mentioned in connexion with Bow, are of doubtful attribution.

CHELSEA CHINA—1745-1770

HISTORY. Like the early history of Bow, the earliest chapter of Chelsea's history is scant and involved in uncertainty.

What we *know* is that the Chelsea factory was working in, or slightly before, 1745 and that in that year were produced the celebrated "goat and bee" cream jugs with the legend "Chelsea, 1745" scratched in the paste before it was fired—sufficient evidence that the establishment was in existence and functioning. It is also recorded that a group of Staffordshire potters went to work in 1747 at the Chelsea China Manufactory. Becoming disgruntled, they left and returned to Staffordshire, an event which seems not to have affected the Chelsea works in the least for it went blithely on in its course of progress.

What we *believe* to be likely is that the factory was established by or, at least, managed by one Charles Gouyn, who is said to have been either a Fleming or a Frenchman, and that his skilled workmen came from France and Germany. Gouyn's identity and personality are largely conjectural. In his exhaustive book on Chelsea china, William King points out that "the strong resemblance between early Chelsea porcelain and that produced by the French soft paste factories renders it highly possible that Chelsea was started by some refugees from St. Cloud, Chantilly or Mennecy, and if this be so, Gouyn may well have been the individual in question." It is also likely that Sir Everard Fawkener was deeply concerned in the inception of the Chelsea factory and may have been responsible for financing and establishing it. He was at first a merchant and accumulated a comfortable fortune. Upon being knighted, about 1735, he was sent as ambassador to Constantinople; in 1744 he was made secretary to the Duke of Cumberland, and, in 1745, was given a lucrative post as joint postmaster-general. We shall meet with Sir Everard again further on.

Be all these things as they may, about 1749 Nicholas Sprimont appears on the scene and Charles Gouyn disappears shortly thereafter. Hence onward, the main facts of the factory's career are no longer obscure. Nicholas Sprimont, said to have been a Frenchman, but certainly some time a silversmith by trade with a shop in Compton Street, Soho, becomes manager and directs affairs so capably that the enterprise grows and prospers apace.

Sprimont directed the concerns of the factory with energy and discretion, and displayed great good taste in determining the character of the ware put forth. While not despising the manufacture of things of common use for which there was necessarily a constant demand, it must be confessed that Sprimont's efforts seem to have been more keenly bent in the direction of making elegant and elaborate articles and in multiplying the variety of products. Nevertheless, such was the distinction and charm of Chelsea china that the greater stress upon decorative considerations seemed not to prejudice financial returns.

Every conceivable thing that could be made of porcelain was made at Chelsea. Advertisments of sales and sales catalogues—some of the old sales catalogues have fortunately been preserved—acquaint us that "Epargnes and Services for Deserts, beautiful Groupes of Figures, etc., complete Table Sets of round and Oval Dishes, Tureens and Plates, with the greatest Variety of other useful and ornamental Pieces" are to be disposed of; that " a large and beautiful Lustre, richly ornamented with flowers and a fine figure of Fame sounding a trumpet," "a most significant Lustre in the Chinese taste," and "a most grand Lustre . . . with Flora and Cupids in the middle" are all within the reach of an eager public; that there are "several very curious Deserts, used at the most elegant and great Entertainments and now divided into proper Lots: Consisting of Domes, Temples, Triumphal Arches, Epargnes, etc., embellished with Trees, Arbors, Flowers, China Figures, Vauses, Girandols, Candlesticks, Branches and other Ornaments used at Desarts, with several sets of China Dishes, Plates and Tureens," awaiting purchasers; and that desirous customers may be accommodated with the "greatest choice of Branches with the best Flowers, such as were on the Chandelier at the last Sale; and upward of three thousand of those Flowers to be sold by themselves so that Ladies and Gentlemen may make use of them in Grottos, Branches, Epargnes, Flower-pots, etc., agreeable to their own taste." Nor were the foregoing by any means all. The catalogues include many other diverting conceits.

By 1754 the business was in a flourishing condition. There was a warehouse for the sale of Chelsea china in Pall Mall, as well as the shop at the factory. Also, in the spring of that year occurred the first sale by auction of surplus and special stock and this sale lasted fourteen days. Again, in 1755 and 1756, sales were held lasting sixteen days. Then came a period when Sprimont was ill and the production of the factory was diminished. By 1757 the warehouse seems to have been moved to Piccadilly. After Sprimont's recovery, or partial recovery, the Chelsea factory took on a new lease of life, many new and rarely beautiful decorations were put forth, and the annual sales were resumed. Sir Everard Fawkener died in 1758 and, about that time, Sprimont became owner of the works.

But Sprimont's health was failing. At the end of the advertisment for the sale of 1761 appeared this notice:

"The proprietor, *N. Sprimont,* after many Years intense Application, has brought this Manufactory to its present Perfection; but as his Indisposition will not permit him to carry it on much longer, he takes the Liberty to assure the Nobility, Gentry, and others, that next Year will be the last Sale he will offer to the Public."

As a matter of fact, there were other sales for some years. Sprimont continued to make periodic farewells, like a *prima donna,* for eight years longer and did not retire till the summer of 1769, during all which time the beautiful Chelsea wares appeared for sale. Finally, in August, 1769, he sold the factory and all its equipment to James Cox, and in February, 1770, Cox sold it to William Duesbury and John Heath of Derby. Thus ends the story of the Chelsea factory as an independent organisation.

Some years before this disposal of the Chelsea plant, despite the outward appearances of prosperity and the maintenance of brilliant achievement in the wares produced, it became evident that the financial affairs of the factory were going from bad to worse and that there was little likelihood of improvement. This was partly caused, no doubt, by the keen competition of other china factories that had been established, partly by Sprimont's failing health. Consequently, he was glad to relinquish the business and, after the disposal of stock by the 1769 sale, Cox got "the kilns, mills, models in wax or lead, all the manufactured or unmanufactured porcelain," and "all the materials and utensils," as well as the lease, for £600.

Although the factory had ceased to be a profitable concern, Sprimont retired in comfortable circumstances. He had an house in town and a country place in Dorset, and kept his own carriage. But he was not long to enjoy release from the anxieties of the porcelain works. He died in 1770.

Duesbury continued work at the Chelsea factory, using it as a branch of the works he had established at Derby in 1756. Upon this status the Chelsea works were kept in operation until 1783, when Duesbury decided to concentrate all his activities at Derby. The china made during this period of close association is known as Chelsea-Derby china. When the factory in Chelsea was finally given up, all the skilled workmen, along with the moulds, models and other trade appliances, were transferred to Derby. The kilns were demolished in 1784 and everything not deemed worth the cost of removal was destroyed.

THE BODY. The Chelsea body exhibited three distinct phases, the first from the beginning of the factory to about 1750, when Sprimont deemed it expedient to harden the paste. This second period lasted till about 1759, when renewed energy was manifested after Sprimont's illness. Then it was that the body was brought into closer conformity with the body produced at the other English factories.

The paste of the first period was soft, very translucent, of fine granular texture, warm creamy colour, and closely resembled the paste of Saint Cloud and Chantilly. The paste of the second period, introduced about 1750, was harder, less translucent, of a sandy, granular texture, but still of a mellow creamy tone. The earlier pieces of this period are apt to be heavy and thick and are occasionally warped in the firing; the surface, also, is sometimes uneven. It has been suggested that the change may have been caused by introducing finely ground Oriental porcelain into the composition of the mixture. Whether this was the case or not, the so-called "moons" in the body are characteristic of this period—small, moon-like discs, more translucent than the rest of the paste, visible if the piece is examined by transmitted light. The paste of the third period was modified by the addition of bone-ash, of which a large percentage was introduced into the composition. This bone china paste was still harder, of smoother and closer texture, white, and easier to manage in the firing.

THE GLAZE. The glaze of the first period was rich, soft, unctuous, mellow, and waxy to the touch. It often shewed minute pinhole flaws. The glaze of the second period was much more perfect in distribution, soft, mellow, and of pleasant waxy aspect. The glaze of the third period was harder and more brilliant.

ARTICLES MADE AND CONTOUR. As already mentioned, the articles made at Chelsea were of manifold diversity. Besides the table services, tea, coffee and chocolate services, the figures, the usual articles of household adornment, and the items mentioned in the catalogues quoted in the foregoing *History,* there were sundry pretty trifles such as buttons, bottle stoppers, trinkets for watch-chains, knobs for walking-sticks, thimbles, smelling bottles, snuff boxes, patch boxes, inkstands and divers other objects suggested by active inventive faculties.

In general, the contours of the articles produced were influenced by three chief sources of inspiration—Oriental forms (PLATE 78, B), types characteristic of Dresden manufactures, and the shapes in use at Sèvres. Just how and when these types were manifested, we shall see in the section on *Types of Decoration.* The Rococo influence, as might be imagined from the date of Chelsea manufacture, was most conspicuously in evidence.

TYPES OF DECORATION. While the types of decoration followed at Chelsea plainly point to the Orient, Dresden (PLATES 76, B; 77; 78, A and 79, A), and Sèvres as the three main springs of influence, the themes drawn thence were either imitated outright or else used as a basis for adaptation. Models of all three were carefully studied whenever the Chelsea designers could gain access to them. Pieces were sometimes borrowed from friends and patrons, as pointed out in the account of Bow, or sometimes the factory tried to buy good things outright for its own permanent collection. Of the latter course we have an instance on record in a letter written by Sir Charles Hanbury Williams, June 9th, 1751, to Henry Fox. Sir Charles Williams was then British Plenipotentiary at Dresden and while he was absent from England Fox was keeping his china at Holland House. This enlightening bit of correspondence was published in the *Burlington Magazine.*

The writer of the letter says:

"I received a letter about ten days ago from Sr. Everard Fawkner who is I believe concerned in the manufacture of China at Chelsea. He desired me to send over models for different Pieces from hence in order to furnish the undertakers with good designs; and would have me send over fifty or three-score pounds worth. But I thought it better and cheaper for the manufacturers to give them leave to take any of my China from Holland House and to copy what they like. I have therefore told Sr. Everard that if he will go to your house you will permit him and anybody he brings with him to see my China and to take away such pieces as they may have a mind to copy."

This letter not only indicates clearly the manner in which many of the best Chelsea designs were obtained, but also throws valuable light on Sir Everard's close connexion with the Chelsea factory. Sir Charles Williams had a valuable collection of china and that part of it to which his letter doubtless had special reference was a dinner set presented to him in 1748 by Augustus III, Elector of Saxony. It included "a dessert service with sweetmeat dishes in the form of artichokes, laurel leaves, sunflowers and double leaves, as well as tea and coffee sets, spoons and knife and fork dishes."

Vegetable-shaped dishes, leaf-shaped dishes and dishes made in the semblance of animals and birds were common in Dresden china of the period and the strong Dresden influence can be seen in such articles produced at Chelsea as well as in the figures and groups—some of which were direct copies—and in the extensive use of patterns moulded or impressed in low relief upon the paste in the form of basket-work, ribbing (PLATE 78, A), flowers, Rococo scrolls and other ornaments.

The direct Oriental influence was not extensive and, with few exceptions, was Japanese rather than Chinese. The most conspicuous Japanese influence is seen in the Kakiyemon and Imari designs of which much use was made. There is constant reference to the Kakiyemon styles under such names as "tyger and rock" pattern, "old Japan," "wheatsheaf and pheasant," "pheasant and border," and "lady pattern."

The Sèvres influence came later and was clearly indicated by the florid Rococo shapes, especially in the case of vases and other decorative pieces, the use of ground colours and reserved panels, the manner of gilding, and the *motifs* employed for the painted decoration.

The ground colours included a rich Mazarine blue, turquoise blue, pea-green, sea-green, red, yellow and a rich claret colour (PLATE 79, B), the last being quite distinctive of Chelsea and never produced anyhere else. With these ground colours there were reserved panels in which appeared well-painted naturalistic flowers, birds with gay plumage, fruits, landscapes, figures, pastoral scenes and scenes of gallantry after the manner of Watteau and Boucher. Besides these painted decorations in reserved panels, there were endless flower *motifs*—scattered flowers, flowers in organised compositions, garlands, wreaths and festoons.

There were also landscapes detached from any panel setting and to some extent both landscapes and flowers were rendered in monochrome, at a certain period a green *camaïeu* being much favoured for this purpose.

After William Duesbury bought the Chelsea factory and all its equipment in 1770 the Chelsea manner of decoration was continued, but certain changes became evident in this Chelsea-Derby period. For one thing, the elaborate Rococo shapes of vases and ornamental jars were discontinued and in their place appeared the more austere and simpler shapes inspired by Neo-Classic taste. *Motifs* from the "antique" were employed and all the painted decoration became much "tighter" and laboured. Also there was a tendency to over-decorate and load ornament on to excess. The rich claret-coloured ground, so distinctive of Chelsea, was discontinued, or when attempts were made to produce it it appeared diluted and washed out. The beautiful pea-green and turquoise grounds also experienced much the same sort of dilution.

THE MARKS. A very early mark, seldom met with, is an incised triangle. The usual early Chelsea mark is an embossed oval with an anchor in low relief. Occasionally the embossed anchor was touched with red enamel colour. Later it was customary for the anchor to be drawn by the painter or gilder when he had finished the decoration, and although it sometimes occurs in blue, it is generally to be found in red or a reddish brown. The gold anchor is generally found on the later pieces when very elaborate gilding was in fashion at the works. In a few cases, two gold anchors are found side by side.

In the Chelsea-Derby period, from 1770 to 1784, the mark consisted of the anchor of Chelsea in conjunction with the D of Derby. This combination of marks seems to have been used indifferently for the pieces produced both at Chelsea and at Derby during this period when both establishments were under the same ownership.

WORCESTER CHINA—1751 TO PRESENT DAY

HISTORY. About the middle of the eighteenth century, some prominent residents of Worcester were deeply concerned at the languishing industrial condition of the city. At the instance of Doctor John Wall, who had conceived the plan of establishing china manufacture as one means of remedy for the stagnation, in 1751 fifteen gentlemen incorporated a company entitled "The Worcester Tonkin Manufacture" to put the scheme into immediate operation.

The capital subscribed was apportioned in forty-five shares of £100 each, and five of these shares were presented to Doctor Wall and William Davis, apothecary, in recognition of "their discovery of the art and secrets of porcelain making" which they were making over to the company.

Whence these "secrets" were obtained is not recorded, but the actual working knowledge of formulas and processses was doubtless supplied by some experienced workmen who had gained that knowledge in another factory. It was only such intimate knowledge that could ensure immediate and satisfactory results and avoid a long period of costly experiments. A paragraph in the deed of incorporation named R. Podmore and J. Lyes, two skilled workmen, to whom special considerations were promised in the shape of occasional gratuities and a small percentage of profits in order "to ensure their fidelity." It is plain, therefore, that these two were to supply the technical experience.

In July, 1751, Warmstry House, an old mansion near the Cathedral, was leased and adapted to the purposes of a factory. Kilns were constructed and a staff of workmen got together.

In the *Gentleman's Magazine* of August, 1752, a sale of the newly made wares was advertised to commence on the 20th of September next following. Only small articles were made at first, for the kiln capacity was limited. But these small articles were of a useful sort, and the stock was soon increased to include the whole range of tableware. While aiming to produce chinaware of engaging appearance, the directors also endeavoured to put forth wares that would be thoroughly serviceable for table use and general domestic purposes. They were well aware that the china of Chelsea and Bow, however beautiful it might be, often came to disaster when brought into sudden contact with hot water. They knew that this shortcoming hindered its popularity and caused a preference for Oriental china that was not affected by sudden changes of temperature. They therefore tried to make a denser, harder body with better heat-resisting qualities and, at the same time, to follow Oriental models of shape and decoration that would compare favourably with the Chinese porcelain that was admittedly the standard.

Working to this double purpose, they succeeded in obtaining a paste that met the requirements of durability and resistance to heat, and also produced tableware so closely identical with the chinaware imported from the East that they advertised in the *Oxford Journal* in 1763 to inform the public that "services of Chinese porcelain can be made up with Worcester porcelain, so that the difference cannot be discovered." And what they promised, they were able to perform.

About 1768 a number of Chelsea decorators were employed on the staff at Worcester, and with their advent on the scene larger and more elaborate pieces were made and the scope of decoration was considerably broadened. Nevertheless, with all the improvements and beautiful as the Worcester china undoubtedly was, the sales did not come up to justifiable expectations and there seems to have been some radical defect in the business management.

Dissensions arose amongst the proprietors and there was a reorganisation in 1772 as a result of which the factory passed into the control of a smaller number of partners. After Doctor Wall's death, in 1776, the affairs of the factory sank into a discouraging state and, in 1783, Thomas Flight, who had been for a long time the company's London agent at their warehouse in Cheapside, bought the whole establishment for £3000 and his sons, Joseph and John, assumed the management of the works.

Very soon after the change of ownership, Robert Chamberlain, who had been the first apprentice of the Company in 1751 and had risen to the post of head decorator, left and with his son set up an independent china-decorating establishment near by in Worcester, obtaining his undecorated china from the Caughley factory.

He was so successful in this venture that in 1788–89 he built kilns at Diglis, in Worcester, and began to manufacture porcelain on his own account in opposition to the original factory at Warmstry House. Needless to say, there was keen rivalry and intensely bitter feeling between the two establishments, especially as they were both making virtually the same kinds of china.

In 1793 Martin Barr was taken into partnership with the Flights, the firm then being known as Flight & Barr. In 1807 Martin Barr the younger was admitted to partnership and the firm then became Barr, Flight and Barr. In 1829 the last of the Flights died and the factory was carried on by the Barrs.

Meantime, the rival factory of the Chamberlains had prospered and grown firmly established. New partners had been taken into the business from time to time, and there was no sign of abatement in the ruinous competition between the two concerns. Finally in 1840, the original china works and the Chamberlain factory were amalgamated and the china-making was carried on at the newer Chamberlain factory; the old works at Warmstry House were then devoted to tile-making. This arrangement continued until 1847. Upon the dissolution of partnership between Barr and Chamberlain in that year, the business of the Worcester factory almost ceased until 1850, when a newly-organised partnership took over the works and revived the business.

In 1862 a further re-organisation took place; the concern became a joint stock company under the name of the Worcester Royal Porcelain Company. This is the Company that has conducted the works ever since.

In 1800, a third china factory started up in Worcester—a schism from the Chamberlain factory owing to sundry dissensions. Thomas Grainger, a nephew of Humphrey Chamberlain, established this offshoot china-works and carried on his business under the firm name of "Grainger and Wood" until 1812, when the firm became "Grainger, Lee and Company." In 1839, George Grainger succeeded his father, and under his name the business continued until 1888, when the Royal Porcelain Company absorbed the Grainger establishment, thus unifying in a single organisation the making of porcelain in Worcester.

During the latter half of the nineteenth century, Worcester china did not escape the effects of the public taste.

Vases, ewers, dishes and other "shew-pieces," executed in the manner of the later Limoges enamels, were amongst the new products put forth by the reorganised company. The decoration of these pieces consisted usually of Classic subjects painted in white enamel on a rich Mazarine blue ground with, of course, an accompaniment of heavy gilding.

The Worcester factory also made extensive use of the Parian body for ornamental wares. The Worcester workmen were especially dexterous in their pierced work, for which, in their manipulation of the Parian body, they drew inspiration from old Chinese examples. The London Exposition of 1862 and the Paris Exposition of 1867 were the means of promoting a Japanese craze, and to this new impulse the Worcester factory responded by using the Parian body, in conjunction with a variety of coloured golds, for making jars, vases and the like in startlingly exact imitation of Japanese ivories and bronzes.

Ornamental ware of this description won such plaudits that it long remained a standard for the sumptuous Worcester output. With the same materials, including a rich palette of both ground and enamel-painted colours, elaborate creations in Persian, Indian and Italian styles were also put forth. These expensive and "splendiferous" pieces gained world-wide fame as typical Royal Worcester porcelain.

While such prize-winning *tours de force* of ceramic technical skill and too lavish embellishment were issuing from the Worcester ovens and kilns, a companion stream of "useful" chinaware was coming from the factory beside the Severn. Both tableware and decorative pieces are staple products of the Worcester factory. With the splendid technical traditions, and the rich *répertoire* of nearly two hundred years as an invaluable heritage, the works are now producing porcelain character-ised by tempered judgement and reasonable restraint in accord with the better disciplined tastes of our own day.

THE BODY. In all likelihood, the first paste was closely analogous to that first used at Bow and Chelsea—a fritted soft paste rich in glassy constituents. Very soon, almost from the first in fact, soapstone or steatite was used, a much harder and more infusible but less translucent paste resulting. The soapstone body continued in use till well towards the end of the century. Bone-ash may have been used in small quanti-ties as early as 1760. Between 1800 and 1810 numerous experiments were made to improve the paste, and about 1810 the bone porcelain body, composed of china-clay, china-stone and bone-ash, was finally adopted.

The earliest body was creamy in colour; the soapstone body was less creamy though mellow and not dead white; the bone-ash body was whiter, but not the dead, cold, glittering white of German porcelain.

THE GLAZE. The earliest glaze, rich in lead, had a soft luscious quality of surface; the glaze of the soapstone body was less fusible and had a certain amount of ground Oriental porcelain in its composition and some oxide of tin, which rendered it slightly opalescent or pearly and contributed to the Chinese-like quality of the blue and white ware; the final glaze was harder and more brilliant.

ARTICLES MADE AND CONTOUR. From the first, stress was laid upon the manufacture of useful articles rather than cabinet pieces. For a long time tableware was the chief product and elaborate vases and ornamental pieces were rarely made. Even as late as 1769, the catalogue of the auction sale in London, a sale that lasted for five days, mentions only four or five sets of covered jars and beakers.

After the coming of the Chelsea painters in 1768, however, there began a new development at Worcester and larger and more elaborate pieces began to be made, while even the ordinary tableware reflected the new influence in the manner of its decoration. Eventually, a cer-tain number of large and ornate vases (PLATE 85), covered jars, beakers, candelabra and the like were made, but the main emphasis of the factory was always placed on tableware and allied adjuncts.

At the very outset, Chinese types (PLATE 84) often served as models of contour, for Chinese porcelain was regarded as the standard to be emulated. At a later stage the shapes made at Sèvres exerted an appreciable influence, but there was never any approach to the exaggerated Rococo forms in use at that factory. Worcester Rococo was Rococo under restraint. From about 1770 onward the contours shew perceptibly the Neo-Classic trend and about 1800 and immediately afterwards the Neo-Grec influence was visible. Worcester never ran to extremes of contour, however, and Rococo, Neo-Classic and Neo-Grec interpretations were always moderate.

TYPES OF DECORATION. A very few of the earliest known Worcester pieces are in white, but they are so rare that it is hardly worth while enumerating them under Types of Decoration. Moulded decoration in low relief was largely employed in the shape of basket-work, ribbing, fluting, flowers, scrolls, and the favourite embossed pinecone or imbricated pattern. Modelling in high relief was little resorted to. Piercing and fretwork for such articles as fruit baskets were freely used. The moulded pieces also included such articles as the cabbage-leaf jugs with masques under the spouts, pickle dishes, artichoke cups in the form of leaves, and rockwork and shell stands for sweetmeats.

Chinese porcelain was more imitated (PLATES 81, A and B; 83, A and 84) at Worcester than anywhere else and nowhere else were the imitations so successful. During the first fifteen or twenty years all the best pieces of blue and white ware were (PLATE 83, A) produced, the designs being mostly Chinese. Transfer-printed decoration was first used about 1757 and the designs were engraved by R. Hancock. The printed pieces, as well as those bearing landscapes, figures and fanciful scenes, often displayed the portraits of popular heroes, such as the Marquis of Granby or the elder Pitt. These transfer designs (PLATE 87) were admirably wrought and appeared in black, blue, purple and red. The underglaze blue printing was not used before 1770.

After the coming of the Chelsea painters in 1768 the underglaze blue for the blue and white ware continued to be used but, in addition, we find underglaze blue in the form of powder-blue grounds and scale blue, with panels reserved for "plants, exotic birds, fruit and flowers in brilliant enamel colours" (PLATE 7). Besides the blue grounds there were apple-green (PLATE 88), pea-green, bright canary yellow, sea-green, French green, turquoise blue and a purplish crimson somewhat approximating the wonderful Chelsea claret colour. There were also radiating trellis and vine patterns, rose sprays, landscapes, Watteau pastorals and woodland scenes, patterns wholly in blue and gold, scattered flowers, flowers in bouquets, garlands and wreaths, designs adapted from the Japanese Imari ware (PLATES 81, 83, B and 86), and, from 1790 onward Classic figures executed in bat-printing which gives a delicate stippled effect, and designs taken from the work of Angelica Kauffmann, Cosway and Bartolozzi. During the Flight and Barr period the decorations were more precisely painted (PLATE 82) and gave an impression of "tightness"; there was also a tendency to over-decorate the pieces at this time. The so-called "dress services" with armorial bearings enclosed by overly ornate borders were good examples of this unfortunate trend.

THE MARKS. The earliest mark was a W in script. The usual mark was a crescent which may occur simply in outline, in solid colour, or with shaded lines. It is usually in underglaze blue, but is sometimes found in on-glaze red or gold. The early printed pieces had not these factory marks but generally had the inscription "R. H. Worcester" minutely engraved amidst the ornamental scrolls or on the groundwork. This mark was commonly accompanied by an anchor. "R. Hancock fecit" is likewise found on a few of the early pieces printed in black.

During the later periods from 1783 to 1840 the names or initials of the firm are impressed in the paste, painted in underglaze blue, and painted or printed in red on-glaze, thus: "FLIGHTS" or "FLIGHT," "FLIGHT & BARR," "FLIGHT, BARR & BARR," "BARR, FLIGHT & BARR," "F. B. B.," and "B. F. B." The earlier of these are occasionally accompanied by the crescent. After 1788 the mark is surmounted by a crown.

Chamberlain's factory generally marked their china with "Chamberlain's" in script, or with "Chamberlain's, Worcester," with or without the address of the London agency. The later Chamberlain marks are often printed.

DERBY CHINA—1755 TO 1848;
1848 TO PRESENT DAY

HISTORY. The Derby china factory was established by William Duesbury in 1755. Duesbury was the son of a Longton potter and for some years prior to the establishment of the porcelain factory he had been a china painter in London, executing commissions for Chelsea and Bow, now and again, purchasing undecorated wares and painting them, or painting special pieces to the order of private customers. About 1754 he seems to have been at Longton Hall helping Littler with his porcelain factory.

In 1755, with the financial aid of John Heath, he started the factory at Derby, converting a few cottages into workshops and erecting kilns. Comparatively little is known of the factory and its work until 1770 when Duesbury bought the Chelsea factory. As we have already seen, he kept both factories in operation until 1784, in the meantime buying out the establishment at Bow when it was offered for sale. After 1784 all the work was conducted at the Derby factory.

William Duesbury, who was apparently a clever business man and an able manager, died in 1786 and was succeeded in the conduct of the works by his son, the younger William Duesbury who carried on the business until 1795. In 1795, during the minority of the third William Duesbury the factory was conducted by his step-father, Mr. Kean and the firm was known as Duesbury & Kean. This partnership was dissolved in 1811, owing to family dissensions, and the business was sold to Robert Bloor who had been a clerk and salesman during the former partnership.

Bloor was altogether commercially minded and forsook the standards that had previously prevailed. For a while the factory was highly prosperous, but the cheapened wares and the lowered standard of decoration brought the inevitable nemesis and the business fell off sadly. In 1828 Bloor became deranged and the factory was carried on under a managing clerk, its fortunes sinking lower and lower until it was finally closed in 1848. The models and all the movable property were sold to a firm of Staffordshire potters and the buildings were soon afterwards demolished.

About 1848, a number of the old Derby staff, headed by Locker, banded together and carried on china-making in a small way, producing articles of the old type and character. Sampson Hancock was later at the head of this independent establishment.

In 1876, a new company, called the Derby Crown Porcelain Company, Limited, was formed to revive the industry on a large scale and met with very considerable success. In 1890, at the instance of the Duke of Devonshire, who was Lord Lieutenant of Derbyshire, Queen Victoria granted the company a Warrant of Appointment as Porcelain Manufacturers to Her Majesty and, at the same time, the right to incorporate the Royal Crown in their trade-mark. She likewise commanded that the company should thenceforth be called the Royal Crown Derby Porcelain Company, Limited.

During the last quarter of the nineteenth century, the prevalent taste of the period quite naturally was reflected in the decoration of Crown Derby china, as it also was elsewhere. As the twentieth century advanced, the vogue for over-elaboration subsided and reasonable restraint once more characterised the modes of embellishment. Certain patterns have always enjoyed popular favour, such as those in the "Old Japan Style," first introduced at Derby about the end of the eighteenth century during the Kean *régime,* and are still being produced.

The main output of the Crown Derby factory consists of "useful" chinaware, such as table services and tea sets. The bone-china body maintains the same excellence for which it has always been distinguished, and the decoration continues in accord with the traditions of a great past. It is interesting to note that, notwithstanding the insistent clamours of the ultra-modern protagonists, the great majority of purchasers manifest a decidedly conservative preference for chinaware embellishment of traditional inspiration.

THE BODY. While there is no definite information to be obtained respecting the body and glaze of the earliest Derby ware, it was almost certainly a glassy or soft paste like the body first in use at Bow and Chelsea. By 1764 experiments had evidently been in progress for improving the composition of the body. It was then that Richard Holdship, one of the partners of the Worcester company, in a most unprincipled and dishonest manner, betrayed the interest of his own organisation and engaged "to impart in writing to Duesbury and Heath his secret process for making china according to the proofs already made by him, and to supply them with all sufficient quantities of soapy rock at fair prices." Presumably the Derby body was improved and hardened as a result of this underhand deal. There seems also to have been a change about 1770 for one of the first things Duesbury did on buying the Chelsea factory was to send ten bags of bone-ash from there to the plant at Derby. About the end of the century the regular bone porcelain composition, comprising, china-clay, china-stone and bone-ash, was adopted. The early body had a mellow creamy tone, and this mellowness was never wholly lost, although in the later, harder body it was not so noticeable.

THE GLAZE. From the first the Derby glaze was good. The early glaze was soft and velvet-like; the later glaze was harder and more brilliant but not obtrusively so.

ARTICLES MADE AND CONTOUR. In the early days of the factory, besides the making of tableware and all the other distinctly "useful" items of chinaware, small figures were produced in large quantities and the establishment seems to have done a particularly thriving business in that direction. Before the absorption of Chelsea, figures and groups in biscuit were made. With the acquisition of the Chelsea works and Chelsea traditions, the Derby establishment continued to make all the diversity of wares produced under Sprimont. These have already been enumerated in the Chelsea section.

In the matter of contour, however, as already pointed out, Duesbury made a change and supplanted the exuberant Rococo forms by the soberer contours dictated by the Neo-Classic mode (PLATE 89, B). At a later date still, the Neo-Grec forms had their vogue in the Derby chinaware.

TYPES OF DECORATION. Under the Chelsea-Derby *régime* the Chelsea methods of decoration were continued so that, save for the evidence of marks, it would often be difficult to say whether a piece was Chelsea or Chelsea-Derby. Attention, however, has been called to the growing tendency to load on too much decoration (PLATE 89, A), and to a somewhat "tighter" and less spontaneous character in the painting. It is unnecessary to recapitulate all the characteristic forms of Chelsea decoration, but it must be pointed out in addition to these that a very rich and ornate adaptation of the Japanese Imari patterns (PLATE 89, B) was characteristic of the Derby factory and that, in the late period, a great use was made of flowing gold scrolls (PLATE 91) in conjunction with one or two rich colours to complete the scheme of arabesques. Under the second William Duesbury both the flower painting and the other painted decorations (PLATES 91 and 90, A) reached the height of excellence. At this time, too, not only figures and statuettes in biscuit were produced, but likewise very excellent portrait medallions in biscuit.

THE MARKS. The earliest mark of Derby was a script D, but it is of the rarest occurrence. The usual mark is a D beneath a crown and this was used down to about 1782. It was usually applied in underglaze blue, but is found also in purple, green, and rose. The Chelsea-Derby marks have already been given. Not long after 1782 crossed batons and six dots accompanied the crowned D. This mark is generally in purple or mauve, though it may occur in blue or in gold. While Kean was a partner the letter K occasionally appears in company with the D. When Bloor bought the works the pieces were marked "Bloor, Derby," with or without the crown. The Bloor marks were generally printed. A Gothic D crowned and printed in red belongs to the Bloor period, when the marks were commonly in red. Forged Dresden and Sèvres marks in underglaze blue are not uncommon on Derby pieces. The present Crown Derby mark, in use since 1890, shows the words "ROYAL

CROWN DERBY" in a semicircle over the Royal Crown, above two facing and interlaced D's, the interlacing of the bottoms of the D's resembling an heraldic torse.

LONGTON HALL CHINA—1752-1758

HISTORY. The china factory at Longton Hall in Staffordshire was a short-lived enterprise. It was established about 1752 by William Littler, the son of a Burslem potter, and came to an untimely end amidst financial difficulties in 1758. Littler and Aaron Wedgwood, who had entered into partnership with him, launched their business with insufficient capital and always suffered from this handicap until the end came. Their aim was to make china like that of Bow and Chelsea, but to produce it at a lower cost and sell it cheaper. During the few years of its limited production, Longton Hall china had a moderate sale in the Midlands. An auction sale in London, in 1757, failed to realise the proceeds expected. The entire stock was sold by auction in London and Birmingham, in 1758, and the factory was abandoned.

THE BODY. The Longton Hall body was a soft paste, granular in texture, full of specks and of a dingy, greyish white tinge. It has been called "the worst china ever produced in England."

THE GLAZE. The glaze was harder than the glaze of Bow and Chelsea; it was also thinner in its distribution and less likely to crackle and craze.

ARTICLES MADE AND CONTOUR. Tableware formed the principal output of the Longton Hall factory. Elaborate vases were never undertaken, but there were a few beakers, small vases and pomatum pots made. The figures mentioned in the sales advertisements were merely the table accompaniments of fruit baskets and similar dessert pieces. The shapes coincided with the Rococo phases (PLATE 114, B), interpreted at Bow and Chelsea.

TYPES OF DECORATION. Flowers, birds, and country or pastoral scenes with a few figures were *motifs* much employed. A bright underglaze cobalt blue was frequently used, either as a ground colour or in heavy masses. Reserved panels for bird or flower *motifs* were commonly enclosed with scrolled borders in raised white. In modelled ornament, acanthus leaves were especially favoured. There was little gilding.

THE MARKS. Longton Hall china was seldom marked and may easily be mistaken for inferior Bow or Chelsea ware. When marked, it had two L's crossed, or a device evolved from two L's.

LIVERPOOL CHINA—1800-1841

HISTORY. Although Liverpool was at one time an important centre of the ceramic industry, the quantity and quality of porcelain made there during the eighteenth century seems very problematical, despite the contention that four potters were engaged in making china, to wit, Richard Chaffers, Seth Pennington, Philip Christian and Reid & Company. It seems scarcely likely that there would be so few traces remaining had real china ever been manufactured at Liverpool in the eighteenth century in any appreciable quantity. Dillon suggests that some eighteenth-century soft paste porcelain that may have been made at Liverpool has been classified as Worcester or Salopian.

Further difficulties arise when one considers the readiness displayed by eighteenth-century manufacturers to label as porcelain articles whose composition is nearly identical with that of pottery. Much of the Delft ware made at Liverpool went by the name of porcelain, whereas its only actual resemblance to porcelain was its white colour.

Nevertheless, there are in the Liverpool Museum specimens, purporting to be of Liverpool manufacture, that shew a good quality of paste and glaze as well as creditable decoration. There are examples of transfer-printing, chiefly in black and brown, but also in green, deep purple, rose and red. Likewise there are Chinese designs, landscapes, rustic scenes, butterflies, red grounds, and also patterns in underglaze blue. Instances of bat-printing, too, occur.

Perhaps the most interesting figure connected with the Liverpool ventures at china-making was Richard Chaffers. Through the advice of Podmore, of the Worcester factory, Chaffers made an expedition into Cornwall in search of soapstone. The search was ultimately successful and Chaffers returned to Liverpool assured that he would be able to obtain all the soapstone necessary. The ware subsequently manufactured and sold by Chaffers & Co., as advertised in the *Liverpool Advertiser* in December, 1756, undoubtedly contained soapstone, but it seems not to have been a true porcelain.

At a more recent date (1800–1841) the Herculaneum works on the banks of the Mersey manufactured genuine porcelain. There is no difficulty in identifying its wares as they are plainly marked with the full name of the place, occasionally accompanied by the crest of the Liverpool Borough. There was no improvement in quality or decoration (PLATE 114, A), to distinguish the Herculaneum china from the products of other factories and while the decorations were pleasing, they were obviously adapted from types then in vogue at Davenport and elsewhere.

LOWESTOFT CHINA—c.1756–c.1802

HISTORY. Probably no one kind of china has ever stirred up so much contention or so much hot partisanship—or opposition, as the case may be—as the china that *was* made and the china that was *not* made at Lowestoft. Half the time, a violent Lowestoft partisan will ignore *facts* and claim an unlimited and elaborate production for a very small establishment; the violent opponent grudgingly admits that anything at all was made there. Both of them find the truth unpalatable.

As a matter of fact, most of the china that goes by the name of Lowestoft and that a great many people persist in calling Lowestoft, was never anywhere within miles of the place. On the other hand, there unquestionably *was* a porcelain factory at Lowestoft, and some very engaging chinaware was made there. All these facts are known and attested. But fallacies die hard, and it will probably be a long time before the admirers of chinaware will unite in giving the factory and its wares their just due without either addition or subtraction.

The factory was established by Messrs. Walker, Brown, Aldred and Richman and a considerable output of soft paste porcelain was produced so that it seemed worth while to have a warehouse in London. An advertisement in a London paper of 1770 acquaints the public that "Clark Durnford, Lowestoft China Warehouse, No. 4, Great St. Thomas the Apostle, Cheapside, London" will supply merchants, shopkeepers and others with the china made in Suffolk. They were, indeed, more china-*merchants* than china-*makers,* and must undoubtedly have sold more chinaware than their own small pottery could possibly have supplied. They were also ship-owners, engaged in the cross-Channel trade with Rotterdam, where they had a small warehouse.

It is known that in the latter decades of the eighteenth century other English potters were buying undecorated Chinese porcelain, having it decorated by their own painters, and then selling it "as the product of their own works." Apart from the china-painters employed at their own factories, "there were two celebrated china-painters in London, John Giles and Baxter," who "did most beautiful work on blank Chinese porcelain."

Ethical principles in the chinaware trade at this time were distinguished by extraordinary elasticity. The characteristic decorative types used in other English china factories and commonly regarded as peculiarly their property, the owners of the Lowestoft factory did not scruple to plagiarise for the soft paste china they actually did make in their own small establishment. Having "borrowed" the modes of decoration, they proceeded to mark the products, when so minded, with the same naïvely eclectic freedom. At times they employed symbols—to put it charitably—suspiciously like the Crescent of Worcester, the Crossed Swords of Dresden, or the well-known marks of other factories.

Under the circumstances, it is not unreasonable to assume that at least some of the stock on the shelves of the Lowestoft China Warehouse in Cheapside consisted of Oriental porcelain decorated in England—the vendors, indeed, may even have felt under no obligation to explain that it had not been wholly manufactured on the Suffolk coast. Many of the china-buying public were not squeamish about the source of embellishment on their purchases so long as the chinaware itself pleased them—and was, perhaps, cheaper than similar ware to be had through the East India Company.

The ship-owning Lowestoft china-factory proprietors exported "English clays and raw materials for the use of the Delft potters" and brought back pottery cargoes from Holland. Rotterdam received very considerable quantities of undecorated Chinese porcelain, for which less duty was paid on going into England than for chinaware already decorated. The wreck of one of their vessels with a "cargo of porcelain," together with the burning of their Rotterdam warehouse, caused the ruin of the Lowestoft Company. The shipload of porcelain was apparently destined for the London warehouse.

The sole nexus between Oriental chinaware and Lowestoft, the sole shadowy excuse for terming any of that Oriental chinaware "Lowestoft," is the *possibility* that a little of it may have been painted at Lowestoft, and the virtual *certainty* that, whether painted at Lowestoft or in London, it was sold as "Lowestoft China" at the shop in Cheapside.

The factory was closed about 1802 or 1803 after having continued in operation for nearly half a century.

THE BODY. The body was a soft paste with a yellowish tinge and is not very translucent.

THE GLAZE. The glaze was often slightly tinged with cobalt and was sometimes imperfectly fired so that it is a little dulled. There are often minute black points or specks in the glaze also. The Lowestoft glaze is strongly characteristic, not only because of this perceptibly bluish tinge that occurs on all pieces decorated in underglaze blue even when other colours in enamel are used with it, but also owing to its frequently thick and uneven distribution which is especially noticeable on the larger pieces. On pieces decorated only in enamel colours over the glaze, the glaze is apt to be more thinly applied and to shew a greenish tinge. The quality of the glaze on Lowestoft china with polychrome decoration contributes to the pearly appearance similar to that of Oriental china with decoration of the same sort.

ARTICLES MADE AND CONTOUR. The articles made at Lowestoft were largely tea services, punch bowls, cups and saucers, mugs, dishes, small plates, jugs, inkstands, basons, sauce boats, open-work fruit baskets and smaller ware generally. No large services or ambitious articles of a decorative nature seem to have been attempted.

The shapes were either copied from Chinese models or adapted from the wares of other factories such, for instance, as the cabbage-leaf jug of Worcester pattern.

TYPES OF DECORATION. At the beginning there seems to have been some imitation of Delft floral and scroll *motifs* in underglaze blue, but most of the early Lowestoft followed Chinese patterns. For a number of years all the decoration was in underglaze blue (PLATE 99, A and B), and it was not until about 1785 or 1790 that decoration in enamel colours began. In addition to the underglaze blue decorations there were moulded low reliefs in the form of ribbing, fluting, basket-work, scrolls (PLATE 99, A), rosettes (PLATE 99, B), and flowers. Piercing and fretwork also played an important part in the ornamentation.

In the polychrome decoration the favourite *motifs* were either Chinese subjects or else small flowers (PLATES 6, B and 98, B) in sprays or singly, and the colouring, though bright, was delicate (PLATE 98, A). Constant use was also made of fretwork (PLATE 99, C), scale or diapered borders or borders derived from the Chinese cord and tassel *motif*. Rose-colour was evidently much favoured by the Lowestoft china-painters (PLATE 98, A.)

Both Bow and Worcester workmen and decorators seem to have been employed at various times and this would account for some of the similarities in decoration to be found. So far as the blue and white ware is concerned, however, it should be borne in mind that Lowestoft has not the greenish tinge of Bow and Worcester when held against the light, nor has it the thin glaze with a greenish tinge displayed by the Caughley blue and white, but its glaze is thick and of distinctly bluish tinge.

In the blue and white ware also occasionally appear little local views, and in some instances these are set in panels and surrounded by a ground of powder blue which latter the Lowestoft makers seem to have been especially successful in copying from the Chinese. Straight and curved ribbings and flutings were often employed and on the pieces with narrow ribbing there was frequently a blue decoration of lines with minute sprays and flowers resembling the modern Copenhagen china, although the Lowestoft blue is deeper. The Chinese dragon in blue was obviously appropriated from the Worcester pattern. There was also apparently some attempt at transfer-printing in blue, in emulation of the Caughley willow pattern. A few black transfers, too, are said to have been made.

Designs prompted by the willow pattern or adapted from other Oriental *motifs* were executed in underglaze blue along with on-glaze red and gold, but the polychrome decorations were chiefly designs derived from the Chinese porcelain of the *famille rose,* or else the minute flower sprays and single blossoms usually associated with the name of Lowestoft, although decorations almost identical with the latter were also employed at New Hall, Wirksworth and elsewhere. The blue cornflower *motif* often appeared, there were occasionally pink or puce monochromes, there were "Mandarin" figures, doubtless inspired by Worcester, now and then cornucopias filled with flowers, while a very few instances of decorations with Classic figures have been attributed to Lowestoft, as well as a few instances of large flowers naturalistically painted. Armorial devices are known to have been executed but, so it seems, not often.

THE MARKS. There seems to have been no regular factory mark on the Lowestoft china and many pieces are altogether innocent of anything resembling a mark. Marks of other factories it appears, however, were now and again copied or approximated.

PLYMOUTH CHINA—1768-1770

HISTORY. The hard paste porcelain factory was established by William Cookworthy at Plymouth in 1768. Cookworthy was a Plymouth chemist who for years had been deeply interested in the subject of porcelain manufacture. He was persuaded that the materials requisite for making true hard paste porcelain, similar in the nature of its body to the porcelain of China or the hard paste porcelain of Dresden, could be found in England. He furthermore believed that those materials existed in abundant quantity in Cornwall. For a number of years he experimented with Cornish kaolin and felspar, or china-clay and china-stone, as they are usually called, and after discovering the most satisfactory sorts and the proper proportions for the composition, he established the Plymouth china factory with the aid and backing of Thomas Pitt of Boconnoc (afterwards Lord Camelford), having first secured a patent granting him exclusive right to the use of his composition for a term of years.

Cookworthy was sixty-three years old when he obtained his patent and founded the factory and he utterly lacked all experience in directing the mechanical processes and the details of management. The obstacles to be overcome were too great to admit of even moderate success for the venture and, in 1770, the Plymouth factory was abandoned and the business transferred to Bristol where Richard Champion, a young, capable and energetic man developed the enterprise into the famous Bristol china works.

THE BODY. The body of the Plymouth china was a true hard paste, the first that had been made in England. It was extremely hard, and was pure white and translucent, possessing all the qualities that good hard paste porcelain should have.

THE GLAZE. The glaze of the Plymouth china was often very imperfect, a circumstance caused by imperfect firing. It was frequently thick and uneven in patches and apt to be full of bubbles. In many cases it had a distinctly greyish tone from the smoke. This smoke stain was technically an imperfection, of course, but as a matter of fact it not seldom added to the charm of the china.

ARTICLES MADE AND CONTOUR. Much of the product consisted of the smaller sorts of tableware and tea services, although a number of excellent figures and groups and some admirable vases were also made. The shapes were more or less of a moderate Rococo fashion although a number of Chinese forms (PLATES 92 and 93), also were employed.

TYPES OF DECORATION. Modelling or moulding in low relief in the form of scrolls and leaf *motifs* (PLATE 94, B) formed part of the decorative system; also the modelling of shell-shaped salt-cellars, figures and other items in fuller relief or in the round contributed its share. A number of pieces appear in the white. Many pieces were decorated altogether in underglaze blue, but the blue was rather blackish where it had been thickly applied and was also apt to be streaky. The polychrome pieces shew brilliant and beautiful colouring (PLATES 92, 93 and 94, A), and the enamel-painted decoration is always in the form of sprays of flowers and detached birds and butterflies (PLATES 92 and 94, A). Ground colours were not used until after the business had been transferred to Bristol.

THE MARKS. When the pieces are marked they bear the alchemical symbol for tin which looks like a combination of the two Arabic numerals, 2 and 4. On the blue and white pieces the mark is in underglaze blue; on the polychrome pieces it is in red or reddish brown. On a few of the pieces where there is much gilding, the mark is in gold but it is not unlikely that some of these pieces may have been made at the Bristol factory.

BRISTOL CHINA—1770-1781

HISTORY. In 1770, when Cookworthy joined forces with Richard Champion and transferred the Plymouth factory to Bristol, the business was established in a building on Castle Green. From 1770 to 1773 this business was carried on under the firm name of Wm. Cookworthy & Co. In 1773 Champion bought Cookworthy's interest and patent rights and the firm then became Richard Champion & Company.

Champion was a merchant in the American trade and also an ardent supporter of Burke, and when the troubles incident to the American Revolution arose he sustained serious losses. In 1775, with Burke's support, he tried to obtain an extension of Cookworthy's patent, but the most he could secure was the sole right to use the china-stone and china-clay in making porcelain; others might employ the same materials so long as they did not manufacture porcelain within the time limit of the patent. Even though aided by Burke and other powerful friends in Parliament, litigation cost Champion dear for Josiah Wedgwood and the Staffordshire potters created a strong opposition to the renewal of the patent in any form. These charges and the losses occasioned by the war with the Colonies crippled Champion financially and he thought to extend the capital of the business but the times were not favourable.

A London warehouse, at 17 Salisbury Court, Fleet Street, was opened in 1776 and the best period of the enterprise seems to have been from 1776 to 1778, but at the end of that time Champion entertained the thought of selling the factory and his patent rights. A sale was effected in 1781 to a company of seven Staffordshire potters and Champion retired from the field of manufacture, going not long after to South Carolina where he died in 1791. The Bristol works were closed and the new company transferred the scene of their activity first to Tunstall and then to New Hall, at Shelton.

THE BODY. The paste was white, intensely hard, dense of texture, and translucent. In hardness and infusibility the Bristol body excels both Chinese and Dresden porcelain. Bristol china sometimes shews "wreathing," slight spiral ridges running round the piece from bottom to top, caused by imperfect manipulation in "throwing" and moulding the clay on the potter's wheel. When fractured or chipped the surface is more or less conchoidal with a waxy lustre.

THE GLAZE. The imperfections of the Plymouth glaze have already been noted. At Bristol the difficulties were overcome and an evenly distributed, clear, brilliant glaze was perfected. The simpler ware was glazed and fired at one operation, in the Chinese manner; the more elaborate pieces were first fired to a partial biscuit state, then dipped in the glaze and fully fired.

ARTICLES MADE AND CONTOUR. There were two grades of ware made at the Bristol factory—the "Cottage China" and the finer and more elaborate pieces. The cottage china included the ordinary "useful" tableware and a few small figures that were not carefully modelled. The shapes and decoration of the cottage china were simple. The finer tableware and the vases, jars and beakers were admittedly inspired by the Dresden manner. Figures (PLATE 96, B), and groups, excellently modelled, were made both glazed and in biscuit, and there were also in biscuit portrait medallions and plaques with armorial bearings, often surrounded by the most delicately fashioned wreaths of flowers. The fine tableware and tea and coffee equipages never displayed the exaggerated Rococo shapes of Dresden but rather tended to conservative Chinese shapes and the more sober forms of Neo-Classic derivation.

The catalogue of the 1780 sale of Bristol china notes "elegant patterns in Desert Services, Tea and Coffee Equipages, Cabinet and Caudle cups," and the contours of many of these articles distinctly bear the Neo-Classic impress.

TYPES OF DECORATION. The cottage china was simply decorated, generally with multi-coloured sprigs and sprays of flowers or with festooned ribbon borders. Very little of it was decorated with underglaze blue. Gilding was not used, and the glaze was applied before firing, in the usual Chinese manner. In the general output and finer sorts of Bristol china, ribbing, fluting, the embossed pine cone or scale pattern, scrolls and other moulded low reliefs were employed and some of the vases display considerable ornament modelled in high relief and applied. A brilliant on-glaze blue ground (PLATE 95) was used with reserved panels for multi-coloured flowers and birds, but the on-glaze blue usually has a mottled, smeary appearance. Yellow and various other ground colours were more successful. Festoons and wreaths of green leaves afforded a characteristic *motif* and these wreaths sometimes enclosed medallions with a chocolate ground on which appeared Classic figures in *grisaille*. The Bristol gilding was rich (PLATE 95), and often beautifully effective. The finer glazed figures were well decorated in enamel colours. The most successful and satisfying of the Bristol decorations were generally the multi-coloured flowers (PLATES 6, A; 96, A and 97, A and B), grouped in compositions, scattered, or disposed in garlands and festoons with or without ribbons. Champion was peculiarly successful with the green that appears in laurel leaves and festoons.

THE MARKS. While the factory belonged to Cookworthy & Co. the mark seems to have been the alchemist symbol for tin, the same as the Plymouth mark, painted in gold. The regular Bristol mark after Cookworthy's withdrawal, was a cross, incised in the paste, painted in blue underglaze or, more usually on-glaze, or in gold. The mark "B" was also used. When numerals occur they are the decorator's mark. The Dresden mark in underglaze blue was sometimes employed.

NEW HALL CHINA—1781-1825

History. When Richard Champion brought the Bristol china works to an end, he transferred his patent rights to a group of experienced potters who, in 1781, established a factory at Tunstall. Upon the withdrawal of two of their number, after some disagreement, in 1782 they removed the establishment to New Hall, at Shelton.

The members of the New Hall company seem unfortunately to have lacked the foresight to acquire either the experienced workmen or the invaluable collection of moulds of the Bristol company. Furthermore, although the New Hall organisation had been virtually established by Champion, the directors were unwilling to follow that worthy pioneer's example. Their ends were first and foremost commercial and they had little interest in maintaining the high standards and ideals of Bristol. At first they continued to make hard paste porcelain but soon made a change to a softer body and, eventually, adopted the bone standard. Content as the New Hall manufacturers were with a product, for the most part, inferior in the quality of its paste, mediocre in its ornamentation, and notable principally for its cheapness, it is not to be wondered at that New Hall china, coloured as it often was in gaudy enamels, with patterns of no particular distinction, failed to make either a wide or enduring appeal. The term of the patent ran out in 1796, and although an half-hearted attempt was made to improve the ware by the adoption of new methods in 1812, the end was stayed for only a short time and the factory was permanently closed down in 1825.

The earlier paste was milk white with a glittering glaze; the later paste was white or slightly greyish-white and had a thin glassy glaze with a somewhat greenish tinge.

The Bristol "cottage china" in all likelihood inspired a good deal of the New Hall product. The decorations were simple, sometimes crudely executed, and without gilding. Not a little of the unmarked china made at New Hall seems to have been attributed to Lowestoft, especially the sort embellished with sprays, sprigs or wreaths of small flowers and minute roses, joined together with little ribbons or lines of dots. In the better pieces produced, where the small flower wreaths or baskets of flowers were reasonably well executed (PLATE 106, A and B), the confusion with Lowestoft can be readily understood. The basket device appearing on the teapot is rather characteristic of New Hall. Moulded ornament was occasionally used and landscape subjects were now and again employed. Classic figures, too, may be found but are rare. The colours are often thick and heavy; again they are noticeably thin. In not a few instances the outlines of the design were transfer-printed and the colours were afterwards applied with a brush. For the china decorated with small flowers, in what is usually considered the "Lowestoft" manner, diaper patterns in deep pink or puce were often employed for borders. There were likewise adaptations of various sorts from the Chinese *famille rose* porcelain, and Japanese "Imari" patterns, too, were produced, the details of the design being commonly larger than those of the Derby "Imari."

When the New Hall china was marked, the earliest mark was the letter N incised in the paste; the later mark was the name New Hall in italics in a double circle, transfer-printed on the glaze.

PINXTON AND TORKSEY CHINA—PINXTON, 1796–1818; TORKSEY, 1803–1808

HISTORY. John Coke, brother of the Lord of the Manor of Pinxton in east Derbyshire, had developed a keen interest in the manufacture of porcelain as it was then conducted, and consequently when he discovered a fine white earth on the estate of Pinxton he was convinced that it could be used to advantage in making porcelain.

The first reports of trial specimens were unsatisfactory, but Coke, still determined, resolved to try his own hand. He secured the services of William Billingsley, a painter from Derby, built a factory at Pinxton in 1796 and set about establishing what he believed would be a prosperous business.

At first, all went well. The ware produced, while inferior in painting to the chief products of the day, was a fairly good commercial ware. It was mostly decorated with flowers rendered in a more or less realistic manner as this was the type of ornament for which Billingsley was famous. To some extent, however, ground colours were used (PLATE

107, B), with reserved panels and in these panels appeared either small landscapes or flower subjects.

As time went on, Billingsley paid less and less attention to the works. He took no active part in the painting and scarcely fulfilled John Coke's idea of an efficient manager. Such a state of affairs could not continue very long and finally they parted—Billingsley to wander about the country, engage in an abortive attempt to make china at Mansfield, and then be heard of later at Torksey; John Coke to recover his declining trade as best he could.

The factory was continued under the management of a Mr. Banks and, later, under a Mr. Cutts, but it never achieved any degree of success and the entire establishment was abandoned in 1818.

The Pinxton ware is sometimes marked with a cursive P in red. Occasionally the marks that appear at the end of the section are also found on china made at Pinxton.

After his failure at Mansfield, Billingsley retired to Torksey in Lincolnshire and, in 1803, established a porcelain factory with the help of his daughters who assisted him with the painting. The products of this venture met with even less success than those of Pinxton and the entire business was an utter failure. The year 1808 saw Billingsley fleeing from his creditors, never to be heard of again as an independent porcelain manufacturer. His Torksey wares are almost impossible to identify as they bear no mark.

$$\mathcal{C}* \qquad \mathcal{R}_{26}$$

CHURCH GRESLEY CHINA—1795-1808

HISTORY. Church Gresley must appear amongst the names of porcelain factories, in spite of the fact that no authentic piece of china emanating thence is known to exist.

This factory, started by Sir Nigel Gresley, seems to have had a tragic, and certainly had a brief, career. Sir Nigel, once Lord of the Manor of Burslem, fell upon evil days and had to retire to the family seat, Church Gresley, near Burton-on-Trent in Derbyshire.

Here, in 1795, he sought to recover his fortunes by the manufacture of porcelain, and although he superintended the work himself, employed his daughter as a decorator, and obtained the professional aid of W. T. Coffee, the Derby modeller, the venture was far from successful.

In 1800, Mr. Nadin, a local colliery proprietor, assumed the responsibilities of the concern, and even though he succeeded in obtaining from Queen Charlotte an order for a dinner service at £700, he was unable to execute the more important pieces such as the plates, platters, dishes and tureens which were all spoiled in the firing.

A third and final proprietor, Mr. Burton, of Linton in Derbyshire, met with no better success in the conduct of the works, and the year 1808 saw the factory definitely closed.

CAUGHLEY CHINA—c.1772-1799; 1799-c.1815

HISTORY. Thomas Turner, a man of some independent means and social standing, sometime an engraver at Worcester, went to Caughley in Shropshire about 1772 and there began the making of porcelain at a pottery that had been established near twenty years earlier but had hitherto made only earthenware.

For a number of years after Turner started the porcelain factory at Caughley, blue and white ware with printed transfer decorations was the chief article of manufacture and probably no establishment ever did more to popularise blue-printed china. Two characteristic patterns emanated from Caughley that have enjoyed vast popularity and are known the world over—the "willow pattern," and the "Broseley dragon." A London warehouse called the "Salopian China Warehouse" for the sale of Caughley chinaware was established in 1780 at number 5 Portugal Street, Lincoln's Inn Fields.

Thomas Turner retired from business in 1799 and sold the works to John Rose who continued to operate them in connexion with the Coalport factory nearby until 1814 or 1815 when they were closed and dismantled.

THE BODY. The Caughley paste was a good body both whiter and more translucent than the paste of the Worcester china.

THE GLAZE. The glaze was clear, perfectly transparent and of perfectly smooth and even distribution.

ARTICLES MADE AND CONTOUR. Tableware, tea and coffee services and all the "useful" items of chinaware were the chief products. Vases were made and a certain number of decorative items, but none of a large and elaborate character. The contours most favoured were either based on Chinese models or else followed the Neo-Classic impulse dominant at the period.

TYPES OF DECORATION. Until after 1780 the decorations consisted almost altogether of blue-printed transfer patterns, chiefly in Chinese designs, "but produced in a manner that no Chinaman ever dreamt of." Nevertheless, they were very good and the patterns were sharply engraved and cleanly executed. The blue was clear and strong and as the body was whiter than the Worcester body and the glaze perfectly transparent, the Caughley blue and white china never had the same mellowness of the Worcester blue and white which closely approximated the Chinese porcelain in quality. The Caughley blue and white china was sometimes painted in underglaze blue, as well as transfer-printed, although transfer-printing was usual for the willow pattern. In both cases the later Caughley blue and white was often enriched with bands of gilding and appeared not unlike much of the blue and white Chinese porcelain of the period that was made for export. The willow pattern appeared about 1780 and whole dinner services were made with this design which immediately achieved wide popularity. Dinner services were also painted in underglaze blue with "Chantilly sprigs" after the manner of some of the old Chantilly china.

Turner went to France in 1780 and is said to have brought back several French china-decorators. After that date there was greater variety in decoration. Small multi-coloured flowers (PLATE 8, B) were much used, either scattered or composed in bouquets, festoons or wreaths. One type of decoration that was very characteristic of Caughley consisted altogether of blue and gold (PLATE 100, A and B). The blue appears in bands or in flower shapes and all the delicate sprays, fine tracery and other minute details are done in gold. Besides a great variety of flower subjects, landscapes were employed and also birds with bright plumage. The later flower-painting in colours quite holds its own with the work of Worcester.

THE MARKS. The earliest Caughley mark was a C, commonly printed in blue, and closely resembling the Worcester crescent. S, painted or printed in blue, was also an early Caughley mark. Later, the word "SALOPIAN" was impressed in the paste and sometimes the painted S or C marks were used along with it.

COALPORT CHINA—(1780) 1790
TO PRESENT DAY

HISTORY. In 1780, John Rose, who had been trained at Caughley, established a small porcelain factory at Jackfield nearby. In 1790 he moved his establishment to Coalport, a mile farther down the Severn, and in 1799 bought the Caughley factory. In 1820, he also absorbed the Nantgarw and Swansea factories; in each case acquiring their moulds, patterns, wealth of experience and all their heritage of varied and valuable tradition.

Upon the death of John Rose in 1841, his nephew, W. F. Rose, and William Pugh continued the business under the previous firm name of "John Rose and Co." In 1862, William Pugh became the sole owner of the works and so continued until his death in 1875. Pugh's executors then threw the business into Chancery, with a receiver to manage the factory. At this time, a great accumulation of old stock at the Coalport factory was decorated and sold off in the process of estate settlement. When the business had thus fallen to a low ebb, an organisation styled the "Coalport China Company" bought the factory and not only revived the commercial prosperity of the establishment but also maintained an high standard of excellence in the products that "placed the Coalport works on a par with the most important factories of England." The Coalport China Company is still conducting the business on the original site of the factory established by John Rose.

THE BODY. The body was white and highly translucent and in every way very similar to the Caughley paste.

THE GLAZE. The Coalport glaze was of especially excellent quality. It had a felspathic basis, like the glaze of hard paste porcelain, but fused at a much lower temperature owing to the use of silicate of soda and potash and a large percentage of borax. When the enamel colours were fired on this glaze they readily fused with it and sank into it so that the mellow effect produced was similar to that of the softer lead glazes on the old soft paste porcelain.

ARTICLES MADE AND CONTOUR. The chief product of the Coalport factory was tableware along with the usual decorative accessories of an average type, although to some extent the more ambitious creations of Sèvres, Dresden and Chelsea were copied in the form of vases and other cabinet pieces.

In contour the Coalport productions in large measure followed the Caughley patterns, but also made direct imitations of the pieces produced at Sèvres and Dresden. Neo-Classic and, later, Neo-Grec impulses were plainly reflected in many of the shapes used.

The present Coalport output is mainly tableware. The factory has always had a catholic outlook on diversity of styles and likewise an extensive *répertoire;* technical excellence, coupled with these assets, ensures finished products comporting with Coalport's long record of high standing.

TYPES OF DECORATION. Besides continuing the Caughley manner of decorating, and emulating the manners of Sèvres and Dresden, painters from Worcester, Derby and the Staffordshire potteries were employed and these men brought with them all the current styles of those places. The deep Mazarine blue ground colour, so famous at Derby, was reproduced at Coalport and many other ground colours were also used, especially pink, apple-green, claret, a bright canary yellow, and grey, while a fine *rose Pompadour* was particularly esteemed. In the reserved panels with the ground colours, and also on china without ground colours, the widest variety of decorations were employed (PLATE 111, A), including all manner of floral subjects (PLATE 112, A), garlands, festoons, wreaths, landscapes, figures, gaily feathered birds (PLATE 112, B), and heraldic devices. Of common occurrence were basket borders with small flowers, birds and insects, in the Dresden manner; "Swansea roses"; the Brosely dragon in green as well as in blue; the "Bourbon sprig" or cornflower; blue underglaze flowers and sprigs in the old Chantilly fashion; the "worm sprig" pattern in underglaze blue; designs drawn from the Chinese *famille rose* porcelain; flowers, fruit, game and fish naturalistically painted; and moulded patterns in low relief as well as flowers modelled in high relief and coloured. After the Nantgarw factory was discontinued Billingsley migrated to Coalport and continued to paint his well-known roses and other exquisite flowers until the time of his death in 1828. During Rose's lifetime the factory was noted for its elaborate vases embellished with well-painted pictures set in panels.

During the latter part of the nineteenth century, Coalport chinaware —the "useful" sorts as well as vases and other ornamental objects— suffered from the prevailing atrocious taste and a persistent imitation of Sèvres, when Sèvres was equally a victim of decorative decadence. The Coalport dessert service, ordered by Queen Victoria for presentation to the Emperor Nicholas I of Russia, was one of the representative expensive ceramic "horrors" of the Victorian age.

When the twentieth century brought relief from the nightmare of perverted ideals in design, the Coalport factory could once again put its admirable technical equipment to the production of wares acceptable to a public with inclinations, generally conservative perhaps, but certainly more discriminating about inherent fitness in the forms and decoration of chinaware.

THE MARKS. On early pieces occurs the mark "Coalport." Later, the marks vary. We find *"Coalport,"* "JOHN ROSE & CO., COLE-BROOKDALE," "C. B. D.," and "C. D." On some later pieces C and S are combined and in the bows are the small letters C, S and N, for Caughley, Swansea and Nantgarw, the factories absorbed by Coalport. The modern Coalport mark is the name "COALPORT" in block capitals over a Crown; on one side of the Crown is the word "BONE," on the other side, "CHINA." Beneath, in an arc-shaped line, are the words "Made in England." Beneath that, is "A.D. 1750."

SPODE CHINA—c.1789 TO PRESENT DAY
(COPELAND'S)

HISTORY. Since 1770, the china-making firm now known as W. T. Copeland & Sons has been continuously in operation without even a shadow of interruption. It began as the Spode factory under Josiah Spode the first. The chinaware made to-day by the Copelands is called "Spode" quite as often as it is called "Copeland."

The first Josiah Spode, or "Old Spode," as he was frequently called, was both an exceptionally skillful potter and an astute business man. As a ready means of disposing advantageously of his wares, he opened a salesroom in London; this he put in charge of William Copeland, a London banker and tea merchant. Through his contacts with the Orient, "Copeland was able to supply Spode with innumerable Chinese designs. Many of the elaborately decorated papers in which tea was wrapped have been bequeathed to posterity as dinnerware decorations." So successful was the London venture that Spode sent his son Josiah to learn the selling end of the business under Copeland.

Josiah Spode I died in 1797, but not before he had achieved the great triumph of perfecting a bone-china body. "After years of experiment and failure . . . Spode drew from his oven the first piece of English Bone China" in 1794. This improvement of the porcelain body introduced by Spode was destined to have a profound effect upon all subsequent china-making in England.

Upon his father's death, Josiah Spode II assumed the management of the factory. Under his capable direction of the china-works at Stoke-upon-Trent, and with the able co-operation of William Copeland (now his partner) in London, the business rapidly increased until Spode chinaware was exported to every part of the civilised world. In 1805 Josiah Spode II produced his "Stone China," an exalted type of white earthenware or semi-porcelain so closely approximating real chinaware that it immediately became immensely popular. A strong incentive to putting forth this "Stone China" body was to make readily available replacements for breakage in table services of the so-called Chinese "Lowestoft" that had been imported from China. This same ware now being made goes by the name of Spode "Lowestoft" and reproduces both the shapes and types of decoration of the old East India china exported from Canton.

William Copeland died in 1826 and his son, William Taylor Copeland, succeeded to his place in the firm, which had been first "Spode and Copeland," and then "Spode, Copeland and Son." Josiah Spode II died in 1827 and, the Spode heirs being inactive in the business, in 1833 William Taylor Copeland bought out their interests and became sole owner of the business. "Alderman Copeland"—so called because he was an Alderman of the City of London and became Lord Mayor in 1835—took Thomas Garrett into partnership in 1835 and the firm was "Copeland and Garrett" until 1847, when the partnership was dissolved. From then until 1867 the title was "W. T. Copeland, late Spode." Since 1867 the firm name has been "W. T. Copeland and Sons."

THE BODY. Although bone-ash had been used in making English china before "Old Spode" entered the field of porcelain manufacture, it was at the Spode factory first that a correctly determined formula of calcined bones in combination with china-clay and china-stone was used, and this produced a body which, from the late eighteenth century, became the standard for nearly all subsequent English pastes. At one time Josiah Spode the Second made a venture in what he called "Felspar China," adding pure felspar while reducing the proportion of china-stone, but the previously determined bone porcelain remained the standard and the "Felspar China" was ultimately abandoned, even the formula being destroyed or lost.

The Spode body is a paste of rich tone, white and translucent, without being glassy.

To the Copeland firm is to be credited the first production of the Parian body—one of the very significant advances of the nineteenth century in porcelain-making.

"Sometime after 1840 a Derby figure maker named Mountford came to work for the firm of Copeland and Garrett, and, as the reputation of the Derby biscuit figures of the eighteenth century was still very great, experiments were set on foot to re-discover the Derby body. Similar experiments had been made at Derby, as the receipt had been lost, but without success."

The experiments at the Copeland factory resulted, not in the re-discovery of the old Derby biscuit formula, but in the fine Parian body, so named because of its resemblance to the famous old Greek statuary marble from the Island of Paros.

The Parian body was also often used as an ordinary porcelain body and glazed and decorated, in the same manner as the bone china. The glazed Parian ware has a rich creamy tint resembling that of the old glassy soft paste porcelains, such as may be seen in some of the Bow pieces.

THE GLAZE. The glaze is clear and transparent without being cold and glittering like some of the hard German glazes.

ARTICLES MADE AND CONTOUR. The articles produced consisted chiefly of tableware and the usual decorative accessories, although a number of "important" vases and cabinet pieces were made. Nor should we overlook the great variety of smaller objects such as inkstands, wafer boxes, bird baths and dishes, charming miniature sets, open work baskets and small figures.

The contours to a great extent followed the precedent of earlier-established factories and also reflected the Neo-Classic taste that was paramount when the factory was founded.

For about twenty-five years following the discovery of the Parian body, busts, statuettes and other ornamental pieces were produced in great numbers and to design and model them the Copeland factory engaged the most distinguished sculptors of the day. The other china factories followed the lead of Copeland's in producing Parian figures and the revived eighteenth-century vogue for biscuit statuary continued in great popularity until the fashion was vulgarised and done to death by eventually using the Parian biscuit for all manner of footling little trifles and do-dabs.

TYPES OF DECORATION. One of the most distinctive types of decoration employed in the early days of the Spode factory was what is sometimes known as the Crown Derby Japan Pattern, although the evidence of the Spode pattern books shews that Josiah Spode was devising Anglo-Oriental designs of this type (PLATE 105) long before the flood of Japanese designs with which the name of the Derby factory became so closely associated. These patterns, with their deep velvety blues and rich gold, were derived, as already pointed out, from the Japanese Imari porcelain.

Josiah Spode the Second was himself an accomplished designer and his well-matured judgement led him to a preference for a preponderance of Chinese design as appropriate for the decoration of china, although he by no means eschewed other types. The purely English type of decoration, and the French type were both represented very fully in the products of the Spode factory. In the interpretation of Spode Oriental designs there is often observable a strongly English flavour.

The decorations employed on Spode china include floral subjects, fruits, birds (PLATES 101, A; 102 and 103), landscapes and figures, along with rich gilding, and were used both in connexion with ground colours (PLATE 102) and on china without ground colours. Transfer-printing was also much used (PLATE 103) in black, blue and other colours and bat-printing was likewise employed in black and in colours. In not a few instances outline designs were transfer-printed and then filled in with colour by brush. This was particularly the case with much of the "Stone" china.

The ground colours frequently used on Spode china include dark blue, scale blue, apple-green, yellow, grey, marbled brown, turquoise, striped red and gold, crimson, marbled blue, salmon, green, lavender, canary and blue, solid gold and dotted or stippled gold, and gold scale on a blue ground.

In an enumeration of the types of decoration must be included raised flowers and birds, the willow pattern, flowers in Chinese taste, apple-green grounds with flowers in panels, views, raised fruit in colours on white grounds in the Dresden taste, bouquets of flowers on white stippled grounds, birds in the Chelsea manner, hunting scenes, bouquets and scattered flowers, numerous adaptations from the Chinese *famille rose* and *famille verte,* adaptations from the Japanese Hizen porcelain, landscapes with raised white flowers as accompaniment, medallions, vine leaves and grapes, butterflies, landscapes in *grisaille,* monochromes in sepia with gold borderings or maroon with gold borderings, and monochromes in other colours also, moulded decorations of various sorts amongst which must be mentioned the white flowers and other small *motifs* in low relief against such coloured grounds as pale lavender or green, Persian *motifs,* arabesques and seaweed patterns, blue and white willow designs, gold fruit and foliage on a royal blue ground, Van Hysum flowers and fruit in a salmon and gold setting, Classic figures inspired by the designs found at Pompeii and Herculaneum, clouds and cupids, Capo di Monte figures, "Mandarin" *motifs,* raised flowers, birds and figures in mat gold on coloured grounds, and the inimitable Billingsley roses and other flowers naturalistically painted on stippled gold grounds or plain gold grounds, besides the other forms of decoration before mentioned.

Spode "Stone China" is not porcelain and strictly speaking has no place in this volume but it was so near an approximation to porcelain and from 1805 onwards, when it began to be manufactured in company with the real china, it exercised such a profound influence and was so popular on account of its beautiful decoration, that it would be both unfair and ungracious not to give it at least a passing mention.

Spode's "Iron Stone Ware," as it was usually called, received colours and preserved their brilliance in a manner surpassing all other stone ware. Furthermore, it was a semi-porcelain and frequently translucent. It had a beautiful white body and the superiority of the products and their comparative cheapness built up their popularity on the Continent to such an extent that the French faïence-makers were well nigh driven out of business.

To a great extent Chinese designs derived from the *famille rose* were used for the decoration of the "Stone China" (PLATE 102, B), and such patterns as the Peacock design, the Parrot design, the Peony design, and others of similar character, all of which were truly remarkable for the beautiful freshness of their colouring and well-balanced composition, earned well-merited favour and became justly famous.

In the shapes of its vases, plateaux and other shew-pieces, and in the manner of decorating these and also much of its table chinaware, the Copeland factory inevitably reflected the unfortunate popular taste of the latter part of the nineteenth century. At the same time, however, a constant demand for chinaware decorated in one or another of the old favourites amongst traditional patterns (such as the "Old Japan" designs) ensured the continuance of types that command unabated appreciation at the present day.

Fully recognising the value and "merit of historic continuity," the Spode-Copeland factory consistently draws upon the immense store of tried and proved precedent contained in the pattern-books (treasured from the days of Josiah Spode I), deriving thence types of both shapes and decoration suitable for revival and, at the same time, *motifs* that a skilled corps of decorators happily employ in producing completely fresh expressions of chinaware embellishment.

THE MARKS. The marks on Spode china are plainly displayed and shew the various changes in the constitution of the firm at different dates.

SPODE   (SPODE)
                          Stone-China

MINTON CHINA—1798 TO PRESENT DAY

HISTORY. When Thomas Minton started to make china at Stoke-upon-Trent in 1798, his first porcelain body was of the "hybrid New Hall type," making extensive use of the china-clay and china-stone which had become available to all manufacturers at the expiration of Champion's rights in the Cookworthy patent. This body Minton soon abandoned for a body containing a large percentage of bone-ash in combination with china-clay and stone—a body that compared favourably with the bone-china body perfected by Spode about 1800. Whatever modifications in formula have been made since that time have always been in the direction of excellence.

The early china products of the Minton factory were limited to utilitarian articles of household service and small ornaments. With regard to the generally respectable but uninspired character of most of the chinaware emanating from Staffordshire in the fore part of the nineteenth century, Solon calls attention to a fact too often forgotten:

". . . that the making of porcelain—at Minton's, as well as in the other Staffordshire factories—was but a minor auxiliary to the manufacture of earthenware, to which the manufacturers devoted the larger share of attention."

As a matter of chinaware history, it is worth noting that Thomas Minton, the founder of the Minton establishment, studied as an apprentice-engraver under Thomas Turner at Caughley. There, according to tradition, he worked on the Caughley copper plate for engraving the first transfer-design of the famous "willow-pattern." At the end of his Caughley apprenticeship, he studied for several years in London, at the same time engraving transfer-printing plates for the Staffordshire potters; Josiah Spode, the first, was his chief patron at this period.

In 1789, he moved to Stoke-upon-Trent in order to be near the Spode factory and also to extend his professional connection. At Stoke, amongst other designs, he engraved for the Staffordshire earthenware potters the "willow" and "Broseley Dragon" patterns he had worked on at Caughley. The "willow-pattern" was an adaptation of a Chinese landscape derived from the decoration of the old Nankin blue and white china. The process of transfer-printing in underglaze blue, which Turner had so largely developed at Caughley, was then supplanting the earlier enamel or on-glaze printing in black on the Staffordshire earthenware.

There was a measure of improvement in the china at Minton's factory about 1825, when some of the former Crown Derby painters began to work for Minton, but the chief effect of their presence seems to have been a shift from Dresden to Sèvres as a source of imitation. At this phase of chinaware history, as Solon significantly points out,

"To make a good china body and drive a paying business were the all-absorbing considerations of the times; and it must be acknowledged that by adhering to this matter-of-fact doctrine the Staffordshire china-makers succeeded in establishing sound, profitable, and long-lived businesses."

From the outset of his china-making career, Thomas Minton shewed a firm determination to be second to none of the best of his competitors, either in the body of his ware or in its design and decoration. In the first aim, he achieved full success; in the latter, although he engaged the best artists obtainable, the public taste of the period precluded any successful essay at English individuality.

At Thomas Minton's death in 1836, his son Herbert succeeded him. Building on the sound foundations his father had laid, Herbert Minton's capable management brought the works to a "leading position among the porcelain factories of the world." In 1848, Léon Arnoux came to Minton's and continued as technical and art director until 1892. At his coming, an attempt was made to revive the manufacture of true hard paste porcelain, but local conditions and difficulties prevented successful work in that direction on any extended scale; the project was then abandoned and attention focussed on improving the bone porcelain body previously used. The improvements in formula then adopted resulted in a bone porcelain body of the highest quality, which has continued in use to the present day and contributed materially to the world-wide prestige of Minton china.

With a Frenchman as art director, it was natural that French artists should be employed and that the products of the factory should reflect French styles and taste, even though the earlier pro-French craze that affected the whole country had long since passed. For the execution of figures, the factory made a Parian body, and during the last half of the nineteenth century eminent French sculptors—Jeannest, Carrier-Beleuse and Protat—were engaged to model figures, vases and other fictile elegancies that rivalled similar works being put forth by the great Continental porcelain factories under royal or state patronage. Also, some of the best painters in Europe—Lessore, Boullemier, Müssil, Pilsbury and Thomas Allen—contributed to the renown of Minton chinaware decoration.

These elaborate achievements all ranked in the first order of excellence; they met the standards set and encouraged by the great international expositions of the period. The main fault that can justly be charged against this work, as Burton pertinently points out, is that "it is too learned and laboured, and lacks reticence and discrimination."

Far happier in conception, according to later canons of taste, were the products inspired by old Chinese porcelains. In the great variety of patterns for articles of everyday use, the Minton factory has maintained an high degree of excellence. In this respect it has strongly influenced other china-factories in England and also in other countries.

The present output of Minton china is characterised by sound judgement and restraint in shapes and decoration. The broad variety of patterns ensures adaptability to the manifold diversities of modern preference in either traditional or non-traditional vein.

THE MARK. The present mark on Minton china is a globe, surmounted by a crown, flanked at each side by a laurel branch, the name "MINTON'S" across the centre of the globe and, beneath the globe the inscription "EST 1793." The earliest mark, used until 1837, shewed an approximation to the two crossed "L's" of Sèvres with an "M" between them. After that, until about 1850, the mark was an "ermine spot" in enamel colour or gold. Since then there has been a succession of marks, the globe appearing about 1868 and continuing in one form or another until 1900, when the present mark was adopted.

DAVENPORT CHINA—c.1793-1887

HISTORY. The Davenport factory at Longport, a suburb of Burslem, was established by John Davenport about 1793; the business was continued by his descendants till 1887. The body, glaze and workmanship of the Davenport china are of the highest order, but the decorations, for the most part, possess no particular distinction and are exactly like those employed at all the contemporary factories. The influence of Derby, in this respect, is more noticeable than that of others. Elaborate dinner services, dessert services, tea and coffee services and vases were extensively produced. Great use was made of ground colours for rich decorations, an apple-green being particularly favoured. The marks were "DAVENPORT," "DAVENPORT, LONGPORT," sometimes alone and sometimes above an anchor. After 1806 the mark was occa-

sionally "DAVENPORT, LONGPORT, STAFFORDSHIRE," surmounted by a crown.

DAVENPORT

Ⓘ Ⓘ Ⓘ

WEDGWOOD CHINA—c.1804-1815
1878 TO PRESENT DAY

HISTORY. At the instance of Thomas Byerly, a nephew of Josiah
Wedgwood, the making of china at the Etruria works started early in
the nineteenth century as a "sideline" commercial venture; proving not
profitable, owing to the hard times following the Napoleonic wars, it
was discontinued in 1815, although the "useful" articles put forth during
this brief period—no better, no worse, than the average contemporary
bone china products of Staffordshire—bore favourable comparison with
similar output elsewhere. Before the discontinuance, however, the
Etruria works made a tea set for Napoleon at St. Helena in 1815.

There are in existence a few pieces of Wedgwood china, marked
with the word "WEDGWOOD" stencilled in blue or red over the
glaze.

The Wedgwood china had a fine light body with a brilliant glaze
whose surface was remarkably smooth and satin-like in appearance.
Decorations occur in both underglaze blue and enamel colours, the
underglaze blue displaying a purplish tinge. The designs often consist
of flowers and butterflies, either naturalistically painted or in a conventional Chinese manner with lattices. Butterflies and large flowers in
colours were sometimes used and a number of blue and white services
were made, enriched with heavy gilding.

The really important Etruria products, on which the makers focussed
their best efforts after 1815, were the justly-famed earthenware creations
launched during the lifetime of the "great" Josiah. One of these, the
white jasper ware, in its exquisite body so nearly approached porcelain
in "translucence, hardness and beauty of texture" that, as Burton, one
of the greatest ceramic authorities says, "it is . . . almost pedantic to
speak of Wedgwood's jasper as 'stoneware,' and not as 'porcelain.'"

Although the "great" Wedgwood "never made anything that has been called porcelain," his splendid creations exercised a profound influence on china-making not only in England but in most of the great Continental porcelain factories where the superbly graceful Classic shapes and type of decoration emanating from the Etruria pottery were eagerly seized upon for inspiration and freely copied.

Great proponent of the Neo-Classic style as he was, Josiah Wedgwood had the wisdom to engage the ablest artists of the day—Flaxman, George Stubbs, Tassie, Jochim Smith and Hackwood—to devise his shapes and decorations. With his own consummate technical skill and originality, and the co-operation of the artists whom he had enlisted in the service of industry, he laid his own and future generations under a debt of gratitude for his signal accomplishments in ceramic art.

In calling the first Josiah "the great Wedgwood," Mr. Gladstone well said, "That is the proper epithet for the greatest man who ever, in any age or any century, applied himself to the important work of uniting art and industry."

THE BODY. After the abandonment of porcelain-making about 1815, until 1878 the Etruria factory confined itself to making its varied earthenware products. In 1878, however, while continuing to produce all the former earthenware types of long-standing repute, it resumed china-making, with an excellent bone-porcelain body, a body that has always approved itself in England by its many desirable qualities. The present translucent, creamy body contains about 45% of bone-ash in its composition and is fired at about 1250° Centigrade. In 1936 an "Alpine pink" body was introduced, its composition being the same as for the white china but with the clay stained a shell pink before being fashioned into cups, plates and the like.

THE GLAZE. Lead glazes were formerly used, but the present glaze is of low-solubility type.

TYPES OF DECORATION AND CONTOURS. Etruria has consistently maintained the policy inaugurated by the first Josiah Wedgwood—invariably retaining able artists, whose work bestowed on wares produced with the highest technical skill ensures results of pre-eminent worth. One conspicuous result of this policy is to be seen in the elegant grace of the chinaware shapes employed, a characteristic for which all the Wedgwood wares have always been distinguished. It is worth noting that the contours in present use embrace both traditional derivations and also expressions of purely modern impulse. Such judicious combination of sources makes for healthy vitality.

Not long before World War I, a free-hand school of painting established at the factory began not only to reproduce from Josiah Wedgwood's pattern-book a number of eighteenth-century floral designs, but also to originate entirely new designs. The methods of decoration chiefly in use are transfer-printing and on-glaze enamel painting and, recently, multi-colour lithograph or decalcomania transfer-printing. Also, the "stencil and groundlay" process is used for certain types of decoration; the backgrounds are groundlaid colours, the detail outline of the design being stencilled on the china before the ground colour is dusted on to a receptive surface. The stencil material is then washed off, leaving the outline of the pattern white on the coloured ground, ready to be filled in by hand. Moulding and modelling are likewise to be reckoned subsidiary adjuncts to the processes of decoration.

Besides the "useful" wares, of various pleasing patterns and types of decoration put forth since the resumption of china-making at Etruria, several developments in the present century deserve mention. In 1908, the factory succeeded in reviving, on bone china, the old Chinese porcelain "powder blue" as a body colour in decoration. Not long afterwards, Etruria put forth lustred china with engaging iridescent colours. Not least interesting is the production, in recent years, of a series of commemorative view plates for a number of American universities and schools.

THE MARKS. The present Wedgwood mark (for chinaware only) was adopted in 1878. It consists of a small image of the two-handled Portland Vase, with the name WEDGWOOD underneath. Beneath WEDGWOOD, in smaller capitals, is "Bone China." Lowest of all is "Made in England"; this was added in 1891 to comply with customs regulations in the United States. Other marks, without the Portland Vase, are used for the non-porcelain Wedgwood wares.

NANTGARW CHINA—1811–1822

History. The Nantgarw porcelain factory was established at the little village of Nantgarw, near Cardiff, in 1811 by that vagrant porcelain-painter William Billingsley and a little group of associates who had been induced to support the scheme. The early efforts were marked by discouraging failures and by 1814 all the funds were exhausted. Mr. Dillwyn, a pottery manufacturer of Swansea, however, was persuaded that Billingsley could make good china if he had the proper facilities and the scene of operations was transferred to Swansea.

There the work was attended with more success, but the methods of manufacture were uncertain and the ware was often completely spoiled in the firing. In 1817 Dillwyn, exasperated at the loose methods and the constant waste, sent Billingsley and his assistants packing.

They then returned to Nantgarw where some other associates came to the rescue with fresh capital. Better results now rewarded the endeavours and the Nantgarw china achieved a sudden popularity. The leading London dealers engaged to take as much of it as the factory could make and the Prince Regent ordered a dinner service. The production was limited and a great quantity was spoiled in the firing. Finally, in 1819, the business broke down and the plant was sold at auction. W. Weston Young bought the plant and turned over the management to Thomas Pardoe of Bristol. In 1822 the ultimate collapse came and the factory was closed.

The Body. The body was a soft paste, very white and of exceptionally mellow appearance, and remarkably translucent—more translucent, in fact, than any of the other English porcelains.

The Glaze. The glaze was clear, soft and mellow, with a rich velvety quality.

Articles Made and Contour. Dinner services, tea and coffee services and dessert services were the articles chiefly made, although a certain number of small vases, inkstands and other decorative accessories were also fashioned. The contours were those of the Neo-Grec period and, while agreeable enough, shewed no especial distinction.

Types of Decoration. The most characteristic *motif* of decoration employed at Nantgarw consisted of flowers (PLATE 109, A and B). These flowers were painted in the Billingsley manner, so often seen on Derby china, where a number of blossoms grouped in composition are realistically rendered in rich colouring (PLATE 111, B), or else they were painted in the Young manner, single flowers being copied most meticulously as though intended to serve as illustrations of botanical specimens. Fruits were also treated in the same manner and, occasionally, birds supplied the theme. The favourite flowers were Billingsley's admirably painted double roses, along with tulips, lilies and other blooms of brilliant and contrasting colours. Very often butterflies and small insects figured in the decorations, and Pardoe painted birds on branches as well as flowers while, in some instances, single birds executed with the exactitude of ornithological coloured illustrations (PLATE 110) supplied the theme. The Billingsley roses and other flowers frequently occur massed in panels reserved on gold grounds (PLATE 111, B). For rims and borders ground colours were largely used, sometimes with reserved panels (PLATE 109, B) and sometimes without. Moulded ornament in low relief was often employed and, in many cases, the relief was left in the white, the coloured decorations occupying the smooth surfaces. A great deal of the Nantgarw china was decorated not at the works but in London, by Mortlock. Gilding was sparingly applied at Nantgarw; the pieces decorated in London are apt to exhibit much fuller gilding.

THE MARKS. The most usual mark was the name NANT-GARW, impressed in the paste, oftentimes accompanied by the letters C. W., also impressed. Any mark or marks other than this, or *not impressed in the paste,* should be regarded with distrust. Very rare marks are the name Nantgarw beneath a crown, name and crown both being painted in puce colour, or NANT-GARW, in capital letters, in gold, enclosed within a line. The name NANTGARW printed in red is a mark to excite suspicion. A great deal of spurious Nantgarw china is to be found.

NANT GARW
C.W.

Nantgarw

SWANSEA CHINA—1814-1823

HISTORY. Ever since 1764 there had been a prosperous little earthenware factory at Swansea and it was to this little plant that L. W. Dillwyn welcomed Billingsley, Walker and the rest of the disconsolate and ill-fated Nantgarw troupe in 1814, immediately after they were obliged to relinquish their first Nantgarw effort. Kilns were built alongside the earlier pottery and work commenced.

The early Swansea china, made on the first arrival of the Billingsley tribe, was the best and was precisely like that of Nantgarw. The great trouble, however, was that about ninety per cent. of it was regularly spoiled in the firing. To overcome this difficulty, Walker modified the composition of the body.

After 1817, when Dillwyn could no longer stand the frightful expense of these wasteful methods and sent the whole Billingsley contingent flying, the china was made of this modified body and the factory was carried on under the direction of Timothy Bevington, one of the shareholders. In 1820 Bevington became owner of the establishment and work was carried on a little longer, but the venture was not profitable and the factory was closed in 1823.

THE BODY. From 1814 to 1817, while the Billingsley *régime* lasted, the body was the same soft paste as used at Nantgarw—granular, exceedingly translucent, and very white, but with a faint greenish tinge when held up against the light. After Billingsley's departure from Swansea, modifications were made in the body in order to render it harder, denser and more durable. The later paste had a yellowish tinge, a more chalky texture, and was less translucent. Some of it, indeed, was opaque.

THE GLAZE. The glaze on the earlier Swansea china was the same as the Nantgarw glaze. The glaze on the modified body seems to have been softer and was distinguished by its peculiar dead whiteness.

ARTICLES MADE AND CONTOUR. Tableware, dessert services, tea services and the smaller decorative accessories were the products of the Swansea factory. The contours shewed all the usual Neo-Grec characteristics of the period.

TYPES OF DECORATION. The most characteristic decoration of Swansea china consisted of "Billingsley" flowers, that is to say, flowers painted in the manner affected by Billingsley whose methods were greatly admired by most of the china-decorators of his time and were closely imitated. For each flower he laid a flat ground of colour and then brushed out the high lights and usually juxtaposed light and dark flowers to intensify the effect. These multi-coloured flowers were sometimes small and arranged in bouquets, knots, garlands and festoons. Birds were often employed as decorative themes and, to a certain extent, low reliefs moulded in the paste were used in conjunction with colour and gilding for the enrichment of plate rims. Decorative scroll-work and ribbons, in colour or in gold, were likewise made use of. Incidentally, gilding was much more freely employed at Swansea than at Nantgarw. There were also wild roses, wild strawberries, and Henry Morris introduced elaborate fruit compositions. To a small extent figure subjects, with stippled grounds, and monochrome landscapes are to be included in the decorative catalogue. Ground colours were a good deal used, frequently of delicate tones, but besides these there were deep blue, pink, yellow, buff or biscuit colour and green. Oftentimes marbling or mottling appeared instead of a solid ground colour for the borders of plates and dishes, the marbled effect being produced by a network of lines of a deeper shade than the underlying ground colour or else by a network of gold lines. Figures were not made at Swansea but modelled flowers in high relief, not seldom in the biscuit (PLATE 107, A), were applied to embellish vases and similar objects, in conjunction with colour and gilding on their smooth surfaces.

THE MARKS. In all likelihood, much of the earlier china made at Swansea bore the Nantgarw mark. The Swansea marks were the name SWANSEA impressed in the paste or printed in red, DILLWYN & CO., BEVINGTON & Co., and, after 1817, a trident was often impressed in the paste along with the other marks.

ROCKINGHAM CHINA—1820–1842

HISTORY. The Rockingham china factory, at Swinton in Yorkshire, was established by Thomas Brameld about 1820 as an outgrowth of the potteries that had flourished for some time previously. The work was under the patronage of Earl Fitzwilliam, Marquess of Rockingham and, for this reason, was called Rockingham china. A few years after the start of the enterprise, Brameld was financially embarrassed, but the Marquess of Rockingham came to the rescue and continued generous support as long as the factory lasted. Despite the ambitious designs of Brameld, the excellence of the body and glaze, and the acclaim with which the ware was received, the works did not pay and were closed in 1842.

THE BODY. The body was bone porcelain of the best quality, dense in texture and creamy white in colour.

THE GLAZE. The glaze was clear, transparent, perfectly distributed and brilliant.

ARTICLES MADE AND CONTOUR. Besides the usual production of table services, dessert services, tea services and all the customary smaller decorative accessories, a number of large and exceedingly elaborate vases and cabinet pieces were made and also statuettes in biscuit, in the Derby manner. The contours were those that distinguished the period when a certain diluted remainder of Neo-Grec influence still survived. Although some of the shapes were fairly good, none of them possessed any real distinction. The best were survivals from former periods. Moulded edges were of common occurrence on dessert services.

TYPES OF DECORATION. Although all the technical processes of manufacture and decoration were perfect, and although no expense was spared to secure the services of the best artists and decorators of the period, the prevailing taste of the time was sinking to lower and lower levels, and the only distinction apparently left for Rockingham china to achieve was in the way of gorgeousness.

All the possible decorative processes, enumerated and explained in earlier pages, were understood and employed and all the earlier modes of decoration, as understood and interpreted at that particular time, were made use of. Ground colours with reserved panels (PLATE 113, B), in which were flowers, fruits, birds or landscapes, were particularly favoured, and lavish gilding was extensively practised. Elaborate dessert services with landscapes and still life subjects became a speciality of the works. Most of the pieces were very much over-decorated. Rockingham china is famed both for its beautiful ground colours and for the exquisite finish of its painting. Amongst the favourite ground colours were the noted "Rockingham green," popular for dessert and tea services, apple-green, a darker blue-green, deep Mazarine blue, bright blue, azure, three grades of pink, the darkest of which closely approached the famous Chelsea "claret," yellow somewhat deeper then the well-known Derby canary, buff or biscuit colour with gold for borders, pale orange, and a cool grey which, in conjunction with a little gilding, was favourably regarded by Quakers and was presumably devised for their use. Diaper patterns were also occasionally employed to good effect.

THE MARKS. The marks that usually occur are the words "Rockingham Works, Brameld," or "Royal Rockingham Works, Brameld," printed or else impressed in the paste, along with a griffin, the crest of the Fitzwilliam family, impressed or painted in red. The crest is said not to have been used till 1826. Sometimes a royal crown also appears.

WIRKSWORTH CHINA—c.1759-1777 (?); c.1804-?

HISTORY. In the second half of the eighteenth century soft paste porcelain was made at the Holland Manor House, at Wirksworth in Derbyshire. Although the history of the factory is obscure, there seems to be reason to believe that it was established about 1759, that one Gill was connected with it, and that it continued in operation till about 1777. It is believed that pottery was first made at Wirksworth and that porcelain-making was a subsequent venture; in what year the manufacture of porcelain began, it is impossible to say. From about 1777 till after the beginning of the nineteenth century there was apparently a cessation of work. Then, sometime subsequent to 1804, it is said that Billingsley revived the Wirksworth establishment for a brief period.

The paste, not of the softest variety, was of good quality, fairly translucent, smooth of texture and of a slightly warm-grey tinge. The products appear to have been chiefly tea equipage, dessert services and the usual sorts of tableware.

Bemrose mentions the similarity of the decorations to those in general use at Lowestoft, while the colouring was strong though not crude. A good deal of delicately moulded ornament in low relief was used—daisies, honeysuckle, roses and leaves. The subjects of decoration were chiefly flowers such as roses, pinks, cornflowers and bluebells, in small scattered sprigs and sprays, in knots and garlands attached with bows of ribbon or with rows of dots, and also occasionally in the form of larger blooms. The tasselled ornament to be found on Lowestoft borders was often employed, as well as dots, and the panels or cartouches for borders filled in with scale or diaper designs. The colours most used were crimson, pink, a reddish brown, puce, blue, green and yellow.

MADELEY CHINA—c.1827-1840

HISTORY. The manufacture and decoration of China at Madeley, in Shropshire, seems to have been the immediate outcome of the discontinuance of the Nantgarw and Swansea china. In its general character the Madeley china was virtually the direct successor of these wares.

The china factory at Madeley was established and conducted by Thomas Martin Randall who, prior to engaging in this enterprise, was a member of the firm of Robins and Randall, Burnsbury Street, Islington, china-decorators. During the great popularity of Nantgarw and Swansea china, Mortlock, the London china-dealer of Orchard Street, was ready to take every bit of it he could get, whether decorated or "in the white." As a matter of fact, a great deal of it was shipped to London in the white and there decorated, as already mentioned in the account of Nantgarw china. One of the firms that executed much of the decoration was that of Robins and Randall. A considerable amount of the Welsh china, when decorated in the Sèvres manner was profitably sold as "Old Sèvres," for its highly translucent, glassy body closely resembled the earlier French paste. Randall was well aware of the lucrative business to be done in both the Welsh and the old French chinaware, and this knowledge doubtless encouraged him to undertake his manufacturing scheme. Being an experienced chemist, as well as a capable decorator, he was thoroughly familiar with all the processes of making soft paste porcelain. When he severed his connexion with the London firm and went to Madeley, in 1825, he was well prepared for the making of soft paste porcelain.

Two kinds of china were made at Madeley and a third kind was decorated there. There was a soft paste china that was very like the porcelain of Nantgarw, Swansea and the earlier Sèvres; there was a china whose body was somewhat harder and this was produced in a more essentially commercial manner; and there was French chinaware imported in the white, or bearing only slight decorations that could be removed with acid, and of this large quantities were decorated.

In 1840 Randall, having acquired a comfortable fortune and being well advanced in years, retired from business and the Madeley factory was closed.

THE BODY. The china-dealers considered the Madeley body the nearest approximation to the old Sèvres soft paste ever made. It was just as translucent as the finest Nantgarw porcelain, but more creamy in tone and, therefore, possessed of the mellow quality characteristic of the best old Sèvres. The Nantgarw was often like snow in the whiteness of its tone; the Madeley paste was more like cream or rich milk. The harder paste had much the same appearance. There was no bone-ash used in the composition.

THE GLAZE. The glaze had the same general resemblance to the old French glaze as the body had to the Sèvres paste.

ARTICLES MADE AND CONTOUR. The articles chiefly made at the Madeley works were tea services, sweetmeat dishes, cake trays, wine coolers, candlesticks, spill vases, cabinet cups and covers, dishes, plates and general tableware and decorative accessories. Besides, there were occasional plaques for furniture inlay and a few statuettes and figures. The contours were both those characteristic of the period and those typical of Sèvres and the other Paris factories in the latter portion of the eighteenth century.

TYPES OF DECORATION. At Madeley the most capable decorators were employed and nearly all the decoration was distinctly in the French eighteenth-century manner, especially in the particulars more or less typical of Sèvres. This following of French fashions was so much the case that not a little of the Madeley china was habitually sold by the dealers at high prices as old Sèvres, and some of them were exceedingly annoyed at "the old Quaker," as they called Randall, because he would not forge the Sèvres marks. On both varieties of paste produced at Madeley the decorations included flowers, fruit, birds, *amorini,* delicately executed landscapes and pastoral scenes after the fashion of Watteau and the painters of his school, along with Rococo scrolls and other incidents of embellishment. The gilding was good and was often of an elaborate character. A number of good ground colours were used, the most successful of which were *rose Pompadour,* turquoise blue, apple-green, and pink.

THE MARKS. Neither kind of Madeley paste shews any marks. This absence of marks made it very easy for dealers when they wished to do so—as it seems a number of them did—to forge marks. Whatever marks were on the French china decorated at Madeley were allowed to remain.

LANE DELPH (MASON) CHINA—LATE EIGHTEENTH CENTURY—c.1850

MASON'S "IRONSTONE CHINA"—c.1804
TO PRESENT DAY

HISTORY. It has been pointed out in this book that although Spode's "Stone China" was not really china according to technical definition, it was nevertheless a *semi*-porcelain and so close an approximation to real china that it was entitled to consideration in company with products that were indubitably chinaware. The same may be said of Mason's "Ironstone China."

Miles Mason, who founded the business in the second half of the eighteenth century, was the son of a Cumberland yeoman who had built up an extensive Oriental porcelain-importing trade in London. From his shop in Fenchurch Street, he was one of the foremost purveyors of "crockery to the English Nobility and Gentry, who at that time used very little but Chinese Porcelain tableware." As a dealer in Oriental chinaware, he was constantly called upon to match patterns of table services in order to replace breakages.

By 1777, owing to high customs duties and delayed importations in war time, Mason's "matchings" had become so increasingly difficult that he determined to overcome the obstacle by making the required ware himself. He did "not set out merely to make acceptable tableware. His declared intention was to *match* the Chinese porcelain which he had supplied as importer." Knowing the difficulties that awaited him and "himself approaching middle age," he wound up his London business and went to study china-making in the factories at Worcester and Derby.

After several years of intense application, about 1780 Miles Mason set up a pottery at Lane Delph (now called Middle Fenton) near Longton, in Staffordshire. There he soon succeeded in making a fine true porcelain, specimens of which may be found in museums. Convinced, however, that this porcelain would not be a commercial success, he addressed his efforts to "the making of a ware comparable to hard porcelain in appearance and wearing qualities." The result was his "Ironstone China."

This ware, from the first, was of high excellence—"intensely hard" and "with the typical cold and brilliant porcelain glaze, white, or with a fine bluish colour" like much of the Chinese porcelain.

Miles Mason's sons, Charles J. and George, inherited the business which, from the outset, had been a marked success. Both of them inherited their father's mastery of technique. In 1813, Charles J. Mason patented the now perfected "Mason's Ironstone China." In 1851 the Mason descendants sold the business to Francis Morley, a Staffordshire potter, who moved all the moulds, patterns and other factory properties to Hanley, where the Mason Ironstone China is now made. In 1859 George L. Ashworth & Brothers bought the business and, in 1883, they sold it to John Goddard and it is still owned in the Goddard family.

Throughout all these changes in ownership, however, the use of the same moulds, patterns and technical processes has continued without interruption and the Mason traditions have remained unchanged. Not a little of the Mason ware is still decorated with patterns transfer-printed by the engraved copper-plate process, which gives the outline, and the enamel colours are afterwards filled in by hand. Many of the decorations are reproductions of engravings, some of which are an hundred years, or more, old. As the years have passed, improvements in mechanical equipment, of course, have been made in accord with the trend of manufacturing procedure everywhere else, and there have been certain technical modifications where they tended to general betterment.

THE BODY. Mason's Ironstone Ware has an hard vitreous body—according to the specification filed by Charles James Mason, when he took out the patent in 1813—consisting of "Scoria or Slag of Ironstone, pounded and ground in water in certain proportions with flint, cornwall stone, and clay and blue oxide of cobalt."

TYPES OF DECORATION. The original Miles Mason designs for decoration were notably excellent and were chiefly of Oriental character, especially of course those intended for the "matchings" to replace breakages in table services that had been imported from China. "Views" and floral subjects were also included in the repertoire. While the successive changes in popular taste have inevitably been reflected to some degree in the matter of decoration, nevertheless the old traditional patterns and adaptations made in their spirit, have always dominated the output of the Mason works.

THE MARKS. The Mason mark consists of the Royal Crown upon a cushion, the name "MASON'S" in Roman capitals above the crown, and "PATENT IRONSTONE CHINA," also in Roman capitals, on the front of the cushion. Below the cushion is the date "1813." This factory mark was adopted in 1813, when Charles James Mason took out the patent, and has remained the mark or "backstamp" ever since. The name "ENGLAND" is now printed beneath the mark to comply with American Customs requirements.

CAULDON (RIDGWAY) CHINA—1813-c.1858

The Cauldon Place Works, at Shelton, were established by Job Ridgway in 1813. These works continued in the control of the Ridgway family until 1858, when John Ridgway retired and sold out his interests. Earthenware of various sorts, stone-china and porcelain were all made at the Cauldon Place Works. The porcelain was of admirable quality and some of it displayed decorations that were both elaborate and rich. All the decorations were well executed, whether the subjects were flowers, fruit, birds, landscapes or figures. Green, deep blue and *rose Pompadour* were favourite ground colours and the gilding was both rich and excellently laid. Various marks were used, but nearly all of them clearly shew the source of manufacture.

ROYAL DOULTON CHINA—1877
TO PRESENT DAY

HISTORY. Although the history of the Doulton establishment begins with 1815, it was not until 1877 that china-making became one of the activities.

In 1815 two enterprising young men, John Doulton and John Watts, acquired an interest in a small pottery in Vauxhall Walk, Lambeth, a part of London whose potting associations go back to the time of Queen Elizabeth. By 1820, Doulton and Watts had become sole owners of their little business.

The unremitting industry and foresight Doulton and Watts displayed from the outset brought the reward of steady business increase and, "in 1826 they moved from Vauxhall Walk to other premises in Lambeth High Street, where there was more room for expansion." In 1835, John Doulton's second son, Henry, entered the business as a lad of fifteen, instead of studying for the Church or the Law, as his parents wished. Genuinely enthusiastic about potting and delighting in the creative nature of the craft, he made his first 20-gallon vessel before he was seventeen. His practical knowledge of potting, gained by experience from the ground up, was at the bottom of his subsequent brilliant success. Henry Doulton's inventiveness was responsible for the steam-driven potter's wheel—in adopting this mechanical improvement, the Doulton factory was ten years in advance of any other pottery.

By 1850, the call for Doulton stoneware and earthenware had so increased that additional factories had been opened at Dudley and St. Helen's. This process of expansion has steadily continued until now there are eight other establishments besides the original Lambeth foundation.

In 1877, encouraged by the success of the Lambeth wares, and under the impulse of Henry Doulton's high ideals, the firm decided to extend their interests to include the manufacture of fine china and fine earthenware. They bought an old-established pottery at Burslem, in Staffordshire, and set about bringing together a distinguished staff of designers, modellers and artists, who were given every opportunity to express their several talents.

So successful was this latest undertaking that in 1884 a new wing was built to give much-needed additional space for china-making; other additions soon followed to accommodate the ever-increasing staff of artists and craftsmen. In 1885, the Society of Arts awarded Henry Doulton the Albert Medal "in recognition of the impulse given by him for the production of artistic pottery," and in 1887 Queen Victoria knighted him for his ceramic attainments.

When Sir Henry Doulton died in 1897, his son Lewis succeeded to the control of the business which, in 1899, became a limited company. In 1901 the company received the Royal Warrant and thereby the right for the Doulton Potteries to use the word "Royal" in the official style of their manufactures.

THE BODY AND GLAZE. The Doulton bone china body, whose composition includes approximately 50% of bone-ash, is all that could be desired in hue, translucency and the other requisite technical qualities of good porcelain. The glaze—thanks to long and patient research that recovered some of the secrets of the old Chinese potters—is of unexceptionable quality.

ARTICLES MADE. The Royal Doulton chinaware is made at the Burslem factory and the output includes, besides a broad variety of fine tableware, vases and the like, a considerable number of china figures. During the mid-nineteenth century, ill-considered and excessive decoration had brought into disrepute the whole tribe of china figures, porcelain ornaments to which Bow and Chelsea had once imparted such compelling charm. The Doulton revival of figurines, conceived in simpler and more ingenuous vein, was greeted with immediate success.

TYPES OF DECORATION. While both shapes and the decoration of tableware have been considered with due respect to all shades of conservative and traditional taste and preference, there has been also a sufficient response to the "modernistic" urge in the production of a number of well-considered forms and embellishments of non-traditional type.

THE MARK. The Doulton mark is four "D's" interlaced in the manner of a quatrefoil, encircled by the words "Royal Doulton" (above) and "England" (below), the whole surmounted by the Royal Crown and the British Lion.

BELLEEK CHINA—IRELAND, 1857 TO PRESENT DAY

HISTORY. The only porcelain factory in Ireland is in the town of Belleek, at Lough Erne in County Fermanagh. China-clay and felspar were found in the neighbouring hills in 1851 and, in 1857, the factory was established. The Parian body used at Belleek is composed of the same ingredients used in "true" or hard-paste porcelain, but in different proportions—less kaolin or china-clay and a larger quantity of felspar or china-stone. No bone-ash is used. Some of the Belleek porcelain contains as much as 72% of the local felspar. The Belleek paste can be fired so that the biscuit has a dull sheen. When glazed, the usual English type of china glaze melts onto the biscuit body at a lower temperature than it takes to fire the biscuit.

One of the chief decorative aims in the early days of the factory seems to have been the closest possible imitation of "natural shells and coral." To further this over-stressed naturalism, the surface of the ware was often covered with a "pearly lustre," produced by a film of bismuth compound fired on at a low temperature. Besides the shells and coral creations, dolphins, tritons, sea-horses, nereids, aquatic plants and sea-urchins figured largely amongst the favourite marine subjects. These pieces occurred in biscuit and also in the creamy, ivory-like glazed ware of Parian body, some of the "glittering iridescent glaze" recalling mother-of-pearl.

The Belleek factory also put forth "useful" chinaware, such as breakfast, dinner and tea services—with the same Parian body—very thin and translucent and often referred to as egg-shell china. The shapes of the various articles were generally graceful. From the very nature and mellow colour of the body and the character of the glaze, there is no occasion for additional decoration in enamel colours. In a way, Belleek china holds a place comparable in this respect to the Oriental *blanc de Chine*.

Belleek china met with keen admiration on this side of the Atlantic and, in the latter part of the nineteenth century, several American factories began to copy it. In 1883, the Etruria pottery, in Trenton, secured some of the men from the Belleek fatcory in Ireland, started making both ornamental and "useful" Belleek egg-shell china in a large way, and won considerable reputation for this product. In 1886, the Bennett factory, in Baltimore, started to make Belleek, but soon discontinued the manufacture because it interfered with the more lucrative branches of the business.

Several other factories also essayed Belleek manufacture from time to time; the Ceramic Art Company, of Trenton (v. LENOX CHINA), rather specialised in it and achieved some very acceptable results.

The Belleek china now being made has the same Parian body as used from the outset of the industry. Tableware is the factory's chief output, along with vases, jars and other moderate-sized elegancies. The ware is characterised by delicacy, exquisite modelling and the deft craftsmanship displayed in such details as the pierced work. In recent years, some slight enamel colour decoration has occasionally been applied but, as already noted, Belleek china needs none. The most successful use of colour is in the shamrock pattern—scattered shamrock leaves of a realistic green. Generally speaking, however, one rather regrets the employment of colour for this ware as superfluous and apt to detract from the effect of a naturally beautiful creamy body fashioned in a distinguished shape.

The Belleek mark shows an Irish round tower, the harp, the greyhound and the three-lobed shamrock printed or stencilled in red, brown or green.

American Chinaware

To many it may appear strange that more space is not devoted to American china. As a matter of actual fact, very little china was made in America prior to 1840. Most of the old china in America, with the exception of the products of one exceptional china factory, is either china made at one of the factories already enumerated in England or else china imported from the East. The china of the British factories forms part of the common Anglo-Saxon heritage, along with language, laws and customs.

The plates, platters, dishes, tureens, jugs and tea services with American buildings, views and public personages printed in blue as decorations, were, almost without exception, made at Liverpool or the Staffordshire potteries for the American market. Comparatively few of them are really chinaware at all. Most of them are an excellent quality of white earthenware or stone-china and, therefore, strictly speaking, do not come within the purview of this volume which deals with porcelain of both the soft paste and hard paste types and the bone-porcelain, which stands mid-way between the two.

As pointed out, in the earlier sections, the chinaware of Oriental and English origin can be studied and collected in America just as well as in England, for it was brought to America in the Colonial period and in the early years of the Republic by ship-loads.

NORTH CAMBRIDGE CHINA—c.1769

HISTORY. One of the earliest attempts to make china in the Colonies appears to have taken place in Boston. We know almost nothing of its beginnings, and less of the results it achieved. Whether any soft paste porcelain was actually produced, it is impossible to say.

In the *Boston Evening Post,* of May 15, 1769, appeared an advertisement asking for samples of white clays and fine white sand, to be submitted for examination. On the 16th of October, 1769, appeared the following advertisement:

"Wanted immediately at the new Factory in New Boston, four Boys for Apprentices to learn the Art of making Tortoise shell, Cream and Green Colour Plates, Dishes, Coffee and Tea Pots, Cups and Saucers, and all other Articles in the Potter's Business, equal to any imported from England."

What was the outcome of this venture we know not.

PHILADELPHIA (SOUTHWARK) CHINA— 1769–1772 OR 1773

HISTORY. In December 1769, the following card or handbill notice was circulated in Philadelphia, then the largest and most important city of the Colonies:

"NEW CHINA WARE. Notwithstanding the various difficulties and disadvantages, which usually attend the introduction of any important manufacture into a new country, the Proprietors of the China Works, now erecting in Southwark, have the pleasure to acquaint the public, they have proved to a certainty, that the Clays of America are productive of as good Porcelain, as any heretofore manufactured at the famous factory in Bow, near London, and imported into the Colonies and plantations, which they will engage to sell upon very reasonable terms; and as they purpose going largely into this manufacture as soon as the works are completed, they request those persons who choose to favour them with commands, to be as early as possible, laying it down as a fixed principle, to take all orders in rotation, and execute the earliest first; dealers will meet with the usual encouragement, and may be assured, that no goods under Thirty Pounds' worth, will be sold to private persons out of the factory, at a lower advance than from their shops. All workmen skilled in the different branches of throwing, turning, modelling, moulding, pressing and painting, upon application to the Proprietors, may depend on encouragement suitable to their abilities; and such parents, as are inclined to bind their children apprentices to either of these branches, must be early in their application. . . . All orders from the country, or other provinces, inclosed in letters, postpaid, and directed to the China Proprietors in Philadelphia, will be faithfully executed, and the Ware warranted equal to any, in goodness and cheapness, hitherto manufactured, or imported from England."

The promoters of this enterprise were Mr. Gousse Bonnin, who had probably learned his trade at Bow, and Mr. George Anthony Morris. Later they advertised for bones, so that it is evident they made use of bone-ash in the paste. In 1772 they advertised again for apprentices to learn the various branches of making and decorating china.

Like many others who had before them embarked on the making of porcelain, the undertakers of the Southwark china factory found to their sorrow that it was a very expensive business and beset with difficulties. In 1771 they appealed to the Assembly of Pennsylvania for financial assistance in the form of a subsidy or else of a loan, and they also had recourse to a lottery in order to raise badly needed funds. What success they met with in these directions we know not, but after running the factory for a little more than two years they were obliged to close it, the real estate was sold, and Bonnin went back to England.

THE BODY. The body was a soft paste porcelain of granular texture and of a mellow cream colour.

THE GLAZE. The glaze was clear, soft and of a velvety quality.

ARTICLES MADE AND CONTOUR. The articles made were of the "useful" sort and included dinner services, dessert services with fretwork fruit baskets, tea services and all the small table accessories. The shapes were those then current in England and were patterned on those of Bow, Chelsea and Worcester.

TYPES OF DECORATION. The types of decoration included moulded devices in low relief and painted flowers and leaves in underglaze blue.

THE MARK. The mark was a small P in underglaze blue.

In the Philadelphia Museum of Art there is a piece (PLATE 119, A) of this ware, belonging to the Franklin Institute, which once formed part of a dinner and dessert service. It is of good quality and compares favourably with the early work of Bow or Worcester.

BERGEN (NEW JERSEY) CHINA—c.1825

HISTORY. "The Jersey Porcelain and Earthenware Company," was incorporated in the town of Bergen, New Jersey, on the 10th of December, 1825. "In the following year," we are told by Dr. Barber, "the products of the factory were awarded a silver medal at the exhibition of the Franklin Institute, Philadelphia, as being the 'best china from American materials.'" In the Trumbull-Prime Collection in Philadelphia there is a bowl of good body and glaze made at Bergen. The manufacture of porcelain did not continue, however, more than a couple of years and seems never to have produced any appreciable results.

NEW YORK CHINA—c.1816

HISTORY. Porcelain is said to have been made in New York City early in the nineteenth century, probably by Dr. Mead, and it is believed that ware of an excellent quality was produced from American materials, but data concerning this venture and authenticated pieces, with one or two exceptions, are lacking. In the Philadelphia Museum of Art there is a vase fifteen inches high, of soft paste body and exceedingly white glaze marked "finished in New York, 1816." There is no gilding and it is without coloured decoration.

PHILADELPHIA (TUCKER) CHINA—
1825–1838

HISTORY. From 1816 to 1822, Benjamin Tucker, a Philadelphia Quaker, had a china shop in Market Street. His son, William Ellis Tucker, who had a talent for drawing and painting, often decorated the china and his father built for him a kiln in the back premises wherein to fire it. The younger Tucker was obsesssed with the notion of making porcelain and carried on numerous experiments to that end. At length, having satisfied himself that he could achieve his purpose, he established a china factory in 1825, his younger brother Thomas being associated with him. In 1828, Thomas Hulme became a partner and in 1832 Judge Joseph Hemphill became a member of the firm. William Ellis Tucker died in 1832 but the business was carried on with great success until 1838, when it was discontinued.

THE BODY. The body was neither the same as the French soft paste porcelain nor was it the same as the bone porcelain made in England, but it had characteristics common to both. It was, indeed, more nearly allied to the Oriental hard paste porcelain. It had great heat-resisting qualities and fire tests shewed that it would stand an higher degree of heat than the Sèvres hard paste porcelain of the same period.

At first the paste had a yellowish tinge, but before long it was brought to a creamy mellow white.

THE GLAZE. The glaze was clear, transparent and of beautiful quality with a bluish tinge wherever it accumulates in thicker masses near mouldings or in flutings.

ARTICLES MADE AND CONTOUR. Table services, dessert services, tea and coffee services, inkstands, jardinières, vases and all the usual decorative accessories were made extensively. Some of the shapes were quite original, but the majority of them shewed a strong Neo-Grec influence and many of them were close copies of Sèvres forms. Pitchers and jugs seem to have been a speciality (PLATES 116, A; 117 and 118, B).

TYPES OF DECORATION. The Tucker china may be divided into three decorative periods. During the first period, from 1825 to 1828, the decorations consisted of crude monochrome landscapes, or butterflies, flowers and fruits painted in sepia or brown (PLATE 116, A and B). There was no transfer-printing, and gold was employed only to a very limited degree.

In the second period, from 1828 to 1832, Thomas Hulme very materially improved the character of the decoration, which now included sprays or groups of flowers, well executed (PLATE 115, A and B), with an appropriate degree of gilding. Roses were conspicuous in the bouquets and floral decorations, and birds also supplied *motifs*. There were also decorations entirely in white and gold (PLATE 118, B), executed with great distinction.

In the third period, from 1832 to 1838, more ambitious decorations (PLATE 117) were employed and so well carried out that a great deal of the Tucker and Hemphill china has frequently been mistaken for Sèvres until the marks were examined. Sepia landscapes, with gilding, were continued, and all the flower and bird types of the second period, but, in addition, there were table services and vases with compositions of festoons, wreaths and medallions. Medallions, enclosed within foliage bands, flower wreaths or gold tracery, displayed monograms, initials or armorial bearings. Occasionally portraits, also, made their appearance. In the compact bands and festoons of flowers of many colours, roses, tulips and forget-me-nots were especially in evidence.

THE MARKS. When the Tucker china was marked it was plainly marked with the names of the makers, the mark varying with the different changes in the personnel of the firm. A great deal of the china, however, is altogether without marks but in nearly every instance it can be identified beyond all question by comparison with the pattern-books, which have been preserved.

LENOX CHINA—1889 TO PRESENT DAY

HISTORY. Lenox chinaware is named—and very rightly—for Walter Scott Lenox, who devoted his whole life to realising the ideal of making fine china in America equal to the best made in Europe. In 1889, when he began to manufacture china,

". . . many American manufacturers were in the habit of stamping their wares with English marks in order to sell their goods. No one dreamed that an American factory could turn out china of the first quality. The public of the United States believed that foreign ware alone was worth purchasing and domestic china was given scant consideration."

Spurning subterfuge and fraudulent labels, Lenox was determined his porcelain should win recognition for its own intrinsic worth, unsmirched by any shadow of deception. In spite of the blindness and paralysis that fell upon him, in the face of the most disheartening obstacles he kept on with unflagging zeal and maintained his ideals and standards until "he had effectually eliminated American prejudice against native china and had established the prestige of American-made goods."

Born in Trenton, New Jersey, in 1859, from boyhood Walter Scott Lenox was fascinated by the craft of pottery. In due time, as an apprentice he mastered the practical details of china-making, devoting whatever leisure he had to the study of decoration, and subsequently became art director at the Ott and Brewer factory.

Eventually, convinced that he would have to have his own factory in order to realise his dream of making a "grade of china equal to the finest created abroad," in 1889 he formed a partnership with Jonathan

Coxon, Sr., in the Ceramic Art Company. In this connection, it is interesting to note what Dr. Barber, writing in 1893, said of the Ceramic Art Company in his *Pottery and Porcelain of the United States:*

"They are rapidly making a name by their constantly increasing patterns, many of which are exquisitely conceived and show the touch of thorough artists. Their specialities are Belleek ware and 'Indian China,' . . . They have secured the best designers and painters that can be found and employ both the overglaze and underglaze processes in decorating. Their egg-shell ware is furnished in the white to decorators."

In 1894 Lenox acquired his partner's interest and carried on the business alone till 1906, when he organised Lenox, Incorporated, the present style of the company.

The history of the establishment and successful achievements of the Lenox china factory is chiefly the personal history of Walter Scott Lenox. His unflinching determination, resolute fidelity to the highest ideals, and dogged perseverance won out over all discouragements, of which there was no lack. The sharpest blow of adversity fell in 1895, just as success was beginning to reward his efforts. He was stricken with both blindness and a paralysis that destroyed the use of his legs, a twofold calamity that might well have quenched the spirit of a less courageous man. Thanks to the *esprit de corps* he had evoked in his whole staff and the loyalty he had inspired, and thanks above all to the unswerving devotion and co-operation of Harry A. Brown (at that time secretary of the company), who not only assumed all the burden of business management but became virtually "eyes" for his friend and chief, the programme laid out continued without recession and Lenox's cherished ambitions were fulfilled, although for twenty-five years (until his death in 1920) he could "see" the results of his labours only by touch.

THE BODY. The ivory-cream, translucent body of Lenox chinaware is a "true" or hard paste porcelain, the meticulously selected ingredients for which are prepared with the utmost care and exactitude of which modern scientific methods and equipment are capable.

ARTICLES MADE. The Lenox factory in Trenton, besides the tableware whose production is a major consideration, also makes bowls, vases, figurines and other articles of use or ornament, and it has to its credit a commission for the first American-made dinner service for the White House, in 1918, several White House table services since then, and Embassy and Legation dinner services as well as Presidential services for Cuba and Venezuela.

TYPES OF DECORATION. The methods of decoration employed include freehand painting by skilled artists, with such *motifs* as birds, flowers or fruit; body colouring; the use of both underglaze and overglaze ground colours; transfer-printing, much of it by a multi-colour decalcomania process; modelling; relief moulding for borders and rims; and several types of gilding. The *répertoire* of designs is exceptionally rich and is constantly being added to by talented designers.

THE MARKS. The mark is a script capital "L" within a laurel wreath; beneath is printed LENOX, with "Made in U.S.A." below the name.

SYRACUSE CHINA—ONONDAGA POTTERY COMPANY—1888 TO PRESENT DAY

HISTORY. The Onondaga Pottery Company, the makers of Syracuse China, trace the story of their establishment back to 1850 when W. H. Farrar, "who had some experience in making butter crocks and whiskey jugs," set up a pottery at what is now the company's Fayette Plant. There "Farrar's Rockingham and Yellow Ware Pottery" turned out "bean pots, pie plates, mixing bowls, tea pots, clay dogs, cats, frogs, lions, etc." and other earthenware oddments.

A few years later, the Empire Pottery Company was formed and took over "Farrar's Rockingham and Yellow Ware Pottery." The new company added an indifferent sort of "white ware" for table use to the factory's output, but led a precarious existence until the summer of 1871, when the Onondaga Pottery Company was organised and assumed control of the works.

The Onondaga Pottery Company, too, had a struggling infancy until, at the end of four years, they could actually show a small profit, chiefly derived from the manufacture of a white granite ware they had started to make in 1873. In 1875, James Pass entered the employ of the Company, and his advent was the harbinger of better fortune. "The zeal and skill of James Pass was undoubtedly the largest single contributing force to the development of the Company. A student of chemistry, he experimented with the qualities of many minerals and with new methods of manufacture until about 1890 he developed the product now known as Syracuse China." In later years, when Mr. Pass had become President of the Company, it was truly said of him that "he could do or had done everything in a pottery from a bit of modelling to carrying a saggar."

Since 1888, when the labours and zeal of James Pass resulted in the production of thin, translucent china, the steady growth of the Onondaga Pottery Company has called for many extensions to keep pace with manufacturing requirements, until now there are large and completely equipped modern factories at the original Fayette Plant and at the Court Plant, started in 1921 on a 300-acre farm east of the City of Syracuse. To the credit of the Onondaga Company it should be noted that (in 1897) they were the first in America to establish their own lithograph decalcomania plant and (in 1908) their technicians were the first, either in America or abroad, to produce and develop underglaze multi-colour decalcomania printing for china decoration.

While the Onondaga Pottery Company spared no efforts in making fine tableware, they also pioneered in vitrified hotel china of high quality for hotels, restaurants, steamships, railway diners and other public places where the tableware was subjected to hard usage. In 1928 they perfected their Ivory Hotel China (necessarily of heavier body than domestic chinaware) and saw to it that the decoration should be of really excellent and interesting character.

The beautiful felspathic body of Syracuse china is thoroughly vitrified, highly translucent, and gives forth a clear, ringing tone when struck; the glaze is in keeping with the quality of the body. While the designers and decorators make use of all the varied *répertoire* of techniques for embellishment of the factory's output, the company's forward-looking Art Council have furnished the impulse for some significant developments. They have, for instance, inspired the production of a paper-thin type of featherweight china, with appropriate shapes and decorations, for use on airliners where every ounce of weight in the equipment must needs be a matter of careful consideration. Nor is the Art Council heedless of the claims made by the exponents of modernism in the particulars of both contour and decoration, though corporate common-sense exercises a tempering restraint.

Since the beginning of china-manufacture at Syracuse, there has been a succession of marks to distinguish the special products that have appeared from time to time. The present mark is the name "SYRACUSE" in large Roman capitals, with the word "China," in much smaller script, beneath it to the right.

PICKARD CHINA—1938 TO PRESENT DAY

HISTORY. Pickard china, made at Antioch, Illinois, is one of the most recent members of the chinaware family in America.

The Pickard factory began in Chicago, in 1897, as a decorating establishment and, over a period of more than forty years, achieved an high reputation for painted and gold decorations on fine table china obtained in the white from other china factories.

In 1930 it was decided to make chinaware as well as decorate it, and an addition to the Chicago plant was built for the express purpose of conducting experiments with the manufacturing end in view. After five years of experimenting with clays and minerals, a satisfactory porcelain formula was reached. Next, followed two and an half years of test production, during which the initial obstacles of manufacture were successfully surmounted and a larger plant was established at Antioch.

At last, in the summer of 1938, chinaware manufactured and decorated by the Pickard factory made its appearance, and its quality has ever since ensured general public approbation.

The Pickard china is characterised by a fine felspathic body of ivory tone, highly translucent and completely vitrified, with an excellent lustrous glaze. The decorations, both in gold and in colours, are skillfully executed and the designs employed attest the presence at the factory of a corps of able artists. The output of the establishment is virtually confined to fine tableware. The floral decorations—both those treated in a fully naturalistic manner and those expressed in conventionalised simplicity—display an engaging fertility of invention and a freshness of interpretation.

The Pickard mark consists of a lion *gardant* supporting a shield with a fleur-de-lys above a scroll bearing the name Pickard; immediately beneath is the word "CHINA" over "Made in U.S.A."

LAMBERTON CHINA—1939 TO PRESENT DAY

HISTORY. Lamberton china is made by the Scammell China Company in Trenton, New Jersey. Although Lamberton china is a relatively recent production, the establishment whence it comes, which "has always been known, more or less informally, as the Lamberton Works," dates its foundation in 1869.

In that year three Quakers, George Comfort, Thomas Bell and Jonathan Stewart—"respectively a farmer, a grocer, and a shoe manufacturer"—attracted by the prospect of lucrative returns, determined to go into pottery-making. Their pottery, which they started with only two kilns, was in that part of Trenton called the Port of Lamberton, where the canal joins the Delaware River, and hence the name Lamberton Works. There they made hotel ware, which they called "Trenton China."

The pottery grew in extent and in volume of profitable business, but the owners eventually sold it and, for a short time before 1892, the new proprietor made porcelain electrical supplies. In 1892, a fire in the Maddock factory obliged that Trenton firm to find new quarters and they bought the Lamberton Works, where they made porcelain sanitary equipment until their new plant was finished. However, to turn their investment in the older pottery to good use, they formed a new company, the Maddock Pottery Company, and made hotel ware at the Lamberton Works.

In 1901, D. William Scammell, who had been connected with the Trenton factory where they made Belleek china, joined the Maddock Pottery Company and gradually, in the course of years, bought out the Maddock holdings until he owned a controlling interest in the concern. At last, in 1922, Mr. Scammell and his five brothers bought the last remaining Maddock interest and formed the Scammell China Company, which continued the extensive manufacture of hotel ware.

In the spring of 1938, Messers Bruce and Mannal, of the Philadelphia firm of Fisher, Bruce and Company, aware of the steadily increasing demand for fine dinnerware and bent on sponsoring a type of American-made table china they were convinced would meet with popular favour, entered into negotiations with the Scammell China Company as a pottery establishment particularly well equipped to translate their inspiration into reality. "What they wanted was a thin, hard, translucent china of excellent quality at a moderate price—made from the same materials and produced in the same manner as the fine chinas from the Old World," fashioned in shapes of suitable character and with well-designed and well-executed decorations.

In accordance with these requirements, work started in the autumn and Fred D. Farrell, one of the foremost ceramic designers in the country, supplied a series of decorations. In January, 1939, the happy collaboration between sponsors and manufacturer resulted in the public appearance of the new Lamberton china, its fine, translucent, true porclain body of a delicate ivory tone, with a clear and exceptionally hard glaze.

The Lamberton china output is confined to all varieties of tableware. The decorative processes employed are moulding, modelling, painting, transfer-printing and gilding. Capable artists are retained as designers and the Scammell factory is one of the few American potteries that make all their own decalcomania for transfer-printing.

The Lamberton Mark is a square enclosing the words

LAMBERTON
Ivory
CHINA
Made in America.

CASTLETON CHINA—1941 TO PRESENT DAY

HISTORY. Castleton china, made by the Shenango Pottery Company, is comparatively a newcomer in the field of American chinaware. It first appeared in the market as a finished product in 1941. Its beginnings, however, antedated this *début* as a mature creation by about thirty years.

When James M. Smith, Sr., acquired the Shenango Pottery, at New

Castle, Pennsylvania, he found a small weatherbeaten plant and old equipment of doubtful quality. Mr. Smith threw himself whole-heartedly into the task of reconstructing an outworn establishment, fully aware that great difficulties confronted him before he could hope to realise his ideal of making fine china that would command favourable comparison with the best wares produced anywhere.

Tireless research and unflagging experimentation filled the years; "the bottom drawer of his desk became the custodian of his secret hopes —the sample plates therein changed with each new formula, each achievement a little 'closer to the heart's desire,' until at last, towards the end of 1939, a body had been reached that satisfied the eye and touch."

At this point, another man with "an equally extravagant imagination and high-reaching hopes," Louis E. Hellmann, joined forces with Mr. Smith. "With a deeply rooted knowledge of porcelains, and fully cognisant of the possibilities America with its vast resources offered," Mr. Hellmann had combed the United States "for a pottery that would share his enthusiasm in creating fine china." The result of their combined efforts was the Castleton china that made its public appearance in 1941.

The Castleton body is of admirable Parian quality, highly translucent and of soft ivory tone. Besides the fine tableware, which is the chief output of the factory at New Castle, the articles produced embrace bowls, trays, plaques, vases and other objects of mainly decorative intent.

The decorations employed cover a wide range of types extending all the way from the time-honoured and much-esteemed flower sprays to *motifs* of ultra-modern inspiration. The processes used include painting in enamel colours, transfer-printing, gilding, moulding and modelling. Following the worthy precedent set by the famous and long-established china factories of the Old World, Castleton has founded a Contemporary Artists Group and invited some of the foremost artists of the present day to contribute to the repertoire of decorations. Paintings by Thomas Hart Benton, Ernest Fiene, Georges Schreiber and Lee Townsend have been reproduced on sundry bowls and trays, and Vertés, Dali, Montenegro and Bemelmans have been commissioned to create designs for the embellishment of dessert services, vases and service plates.

The shapes of Castleton chinaware vary from conservative and traditional forms to contours devised to meet the tastes of the most modern-minded and, in this latter particular, the Museum of Modern Art in New York has collaborated.

The Castleton Mark consists of a lyre, with a festoon band from one support to the other and the name "Castleton," as shown below.

CASTLETON

Bibliography

1. "THE NEW CHAFFERS": MARKS AND MONOGRAMS ON EUROPEAN AND ORIENTAL POTTERY AND PORCELAIN, WITH HISTORICAL NOTICES OF EACH MANUFACTORY: * William Chaffers, 13th Edition. Reeves & Turner, London, 1912.
2. ENGLISH PORCELAIN: Arthur Herbert Church, Chapman & Hall, London, 1885.
3. PORCELAIN, ORIENTAL, CONTINENTAL AND BRITISH: R. L. Hobson, E. P. Dutton & Co., New York, 1906.
4. OLD ENGLISH CHINA: Mrs. Willoughby Hodgson, G. Bell & Sons, London, 1913.
5. POTTERY AND PORCELAIN: A HANDBOOK FOR COLLECTORS; Translated from the Danish of Emil Hannover, with notes and appendices, by Bernard Rackham, E. Benn, Ltd., London, 1925.
6. A HISTORY AND DESCRIPTION OF ENGLISH PORCELAIN: William Burton, Cassell & Co., London, 1902.
7. A BRIEF HISTORY OF OLD ENGLISH PORCELAIN AND ITS MANUFACTORIES: M. L. Solon, Bemrose & Sons, London, 1903.
8. CHELSEA PORCELAIN: William King, Benn Bros., London, 1922.
9. CATALOGUE OF THE SCHREIBER COLLECTION OF PORCELAIN: Victoria and Albert Museum, South Kensington; His Majesty's Stationery Office, London, 1915.
10. CATALOGUE OF THE HERBERT ALLEN COLLECTION OF ENGLISH PORCELAIN: the Victoria and Albert Museum, South Kensington, Bernard Rackham, His Majesty's Stationery Office, London, 1917.
11. CATALOGUE OF THE COLLECTION OF ENGLISH PORCELAIN IN THE DEPARTMENT OF BRITISH AND MEDIAEVAL ANTIQUITIES AND ETHNOGRAPHY OF THE BRITISH MUSEUM: R. L. Hobson, London, 1905.
12. CONTRIBUTIONS TOWARDS THE HISTORY OF EARLY ENGLISH PORCELAIN: J. E. Nightingale, Bennett Bros., Salisbury, 1881.

* This compendious book is veritably the china-lovers' and collectors' "Bible," so to speak. It contains an enormous quantity of data regarding every aspect of both pottery and porcelain and is an indispensable source of reference for the student.

13. THE CERAMIC ART OF GREAT BRITAIN: Frederick William Llewellynn Jewitt, J. S. Virtue & Co., London, 1883.
14. ENGLISH POTTERY AND PORCELAIN: Edward Andrews Downman, London, 1918.
15. THE FIRST CENTURY OF ENGLISH PORCELAIN: W. Moore Binns, Hurst & Blackett, London, 1906.
16. SPODE AND HIS SUCCESSORS: Arthur Hayden, Cassell & Co., London, 1925.
17. OLD SPODE: T. G. Cannon, F. A. Stokes & Co., New York, 1924.
18. THE CERAMICS OF SWANSEA AND NANTGARW: W. Turner, Bemrose & Sons, London, 1897.
19. WORCESTER PORCELAIN: R. L. Hobson, B. Quaritch, London, 1910.
20. A CENTURY OF POTTING IN THE CITY OF WORCESTER: Richard William Binns, London, 1877.
21. THE CHEYNE BOOK OF CHELSEA CHINA AND POTTERY: Reginald Blunt, London, 1924.
22. THE POTTERY AND PORCELAIN OF DERBYSHIRE: Alfred Wallis and W. Bemrose, Junior, Bemrose & Sons, London, 1870.
23. LONGTON HALL PORCELAIN: William Bemrose, Bemrose & Sons, London, 1906.
24. OLD BOW CHINA: Egan Mew, T. C. & E. C. Jack, London, 1909.
25. CHELSEA AND CHELSEA-DERBY CHINA: Egan Mew, T. C. & E. C. Jack, London, 1909.
26. BOW, CHELSEA AND DERBY PORCELAIN: William Bemrose, Bemrose & Sons, London, 1898.
27. THE OLD DERBY CHINA FACTORY: John Haslem, G. Bell & Sons, London, 1876.
28. CHATS ON ENGLISH CHINA: Arthur Hayden, F. A. Stokes & Co., New York, 1904.
29. THE A. B. C. OF COLLECTING OLD ENGLISH CHINA: J. F. Blacker, G. W. Jacobs & Co., Philadelphia, 1910.
30. THE CHINA COLLECTOR: H. William Lewer, D. McKay, Philadelphia, 1914.
31. A HISTORY AND DESCRIPTION OF FRENCH PORCELAIN: E. S. Anscher, Translated by William Burton, London, 1905.
32. PORCELAIN: William Burton, London, 1906.
33. ROBERT HANCOCK AND HIS WORKS: A. R. Ballantyne, London, 1885.

34. POTTERY AND PORCELAIN IN THE UNITED STATES: Dr. Edwin Atlee Barber, New York, 1901.
35. CHINESE PORCELAIN BEFORE THE PRESENT DYNASTY: S. W. Bushell, Pekin, 1886.
36. CHINESE ART: S. W. Bushell, Handbook, Victoria and Albert Museum, South Kensington, 2 VOLS. 1906.
37. CHINESE POTTERY AND PORCELAIN, BEING A TRANSLATION OF THE T'AO SHUO: S. W. Bushell, Oxford, 1910.
38. LA MANUFACTURE DE PORCELAINE DE CHANTILLY: Paris, 1892.
39. HISTOIRE DES MANUFACTURES FRANÇAISE DE PORCELAINE: Comte de Chavagnac, Paris, 1906.
40. LES ORIGINES DE LA PORCELAINE EN EUROPE: Baron J. C. Davillier, Paris, 1882.
41. PORCELAIN: E. J. Dillon, London, 1904.
42. HISTOIRE DE LA CÉRAMIQUE, POTERIE, FAÏENCES ET PORCELAINS CHEZ TOUS LES PEUPLES: E. Garnier, Tours, 1882.
43. THE SOFT PASTE PORCELAIN OF SÈVRES: E. Garnier, London, 1892.
44. DICTIONNAIRE DE LA CÉRAMIQUE: E. Garnier, Paris, 1893.
45. DISCORSO SULLA FABBRICA DI PORCELLANA STABILITA IN VINOVO: Vittorio Amadeo Gioanetti, Torino, 1859.
46. CHINESE PORCELAIN AND HARD STONES: Edgar Gorer and J. F. Blacker, London, 1911.
47. LA CÉRAMIQUE CHINOISE: E. Grandidier, Paris, 1894.
48. CHINESE PORCELAIN: W. G. Gulland, London, 4th Edition, 1918.
49. ROYAL COPENHAGEN PORCELAIN: Arthur Hayden, London, 1911.
50. PORCELAIN OF ALL COUNTRIES: R. L. Hobson, London, 1906.
51. HISTOIRE ARTISTIQUE, INDUSTRIELLE ET COMMERCIALE DE LA PORCELAINE: A. Jacquemart et E. Le Blant, Paris, 1862.
52. HISTORY OF THE CERAMIC ART: A. Jacquemart, Translated by Mrs. Bury Palliser, London, 1873.
53. HISTOIRE ET FABRICATION DE LA PORCELAINE CHINOISE: Stanislas Julien, Paris, 1856.
54. HISTORY OF THE COALPORT PORCELAIN WORKS: Frederick William Llewellynn Jewitt, London, 1862.
55. THE GARLAND COLLECTION IN THE METROPOLITAN MUSEUM, NEW YORK: Laffan, New York, 1907.
56. THE SÈVRES PORCELAIN OF BUCKINGHAM PALACE AND WINDSOR CASTLE: Guy Laking, London, 1907.

57. La Manufacture de Porcelaine de Sèvres: Gaston de Breton, Paris, 1882.

58. Pottery and Porcelain: Frederick Litchfield, London, 1912.

59. A History of Pottery and Porcelain: J. Marryat, London, 1868.

60. History and Description of Chinese Porcelain: W. C. Monkhouse, Notes by S. W. Bushell, London, 1901.

61. La Fabbricagione della Porcellana in Napoli e dei Prodotti Ceramici Affini: G. Novi, Napoli, 1879.

62. Relics of William Cookworthy: Prideaux, 1853.

63. Lowestoft China: W. W. R. Spelman, London, 1905.

64. Continental China: C. H. Wylde, London, 1907.

65. China Collecting in America: Alice Morse Earle, New York, 1907.

66. Old English China with American Views: Edwin Atlee Barber, Indianapolis, 1899.

67. The Old China Book: N. Hudson Moore, F. A. Stokes & Co., New York, 1903.

67. Oriental Lowestoft: J. A. Lloyd Hyde, Scribner, 1936.

68. Pottery and Porcelain in the United States: Edwin Atlee Barber, Putnam, 1893, 1901, 1909.

INDEX

Ahrenfeldt, Charles, 175; Charles Jules, 176; china, 175, 176
Albrechtsburg, 180, 181
Alcora, 178
Alençon, 165
Allen, Thomas, 273
Alluaud, factory, 174; M., 171
Saint Amand-les-Eaux, china, 154
American Colonies, attempts at china-making, 34; chinaware in, 27, 28, 293; orders from, 70
American, factories, 292; Revolution, 255; universities, 277; views of buildings, scenery and personages, 293
Amorini, 286
Amsterdam, 202
"Amstel" China, 202-204
d'Angoulême, China, 164; fabrique du Duc, 155
Ansbach, 196
Antheaume, 125
Antonibon, Pasquale, 115
Antioch (Illinois), 302
Antonio, Maestro, 109
d'Argenson, Memoirs, 132, 142
Arita, 95, 97; China, 98, 99
Armand, 151
Armorial, bearings, 66; china, 70
Arnoux, Léon, 273
Arras, China, 153, 154
Artists, Sèvres, 151
d'Artois, Comte, 155, 156; China, 157-159
Ashworth, George L., 287
Aubert, 151
des Aubiez, Maurin, 156
Augustus, III, Elector of Saxony, 234; the Strong, King of Poland, 179

Bachelier, 151
Baltimore, 292; china-making, 36
Banks, —, 260
Barber, Dr. E. A., 36, 295
Barbin, François, 127
Baroni, Giovanni, 115
Baroque, contours, 54; manner, 123
Barr, Martin, 238
Bartolozzi, 242
Bat-printing, 248, 269
Battersea, 227

Bavaria, Elector of, 190
Baxter, —, 250
de Baynal, 125
Bayreuth, 192, 196
"Beach" China, 33
Bell, Thomas, 303
Belleek, China, 291, 292; factory, 292; town, 291
Bellevue, 144
Bemelmans, 305
Bengraf, 192
Benjamin, —, 158
Bennett, factory, 292
Bennington, 36
Benton, Thomas Hart, 305
Bergen (N.J.), China, 295, 296
Berlin, 181; China, 186-188
Berthevin, Pierre, 207
Bevington, Timothy, 280
de Beyerlé, Baron Jean Louis, 168, 169, 170
Billingsley, flowers, 281; roses, 179; tribe, 280; William, 259, 260, 265, 278, 280, 284
Bing, brothers, 216, 217; H. J., M. H. & J. H., 216; & Grøndahl, China, 216-218
Birmingham, 247
Biscuit, definition of, 39
Blanc de Chine, 69, 71, 84, 292
Bleu du roi, 129, 135, 139, 150, 195
Bloor, Robert, 243, 246
Blue and white, Canton, 76; Nankin, 272; ware, 65, 225
Blue, Mazarine, 86, 235, 239, 264, 283; Mohammedan, 63; powder, 66; underglaze, 63
Body, Amstel, 203; d'Artois, 158; Berlin, 186, 187; Bow, 224, 225; Bristol, 256; Capo di Monte, 112; Caughley, 261; Chantilly, 125; Chelsea, 232; Chinese, 76; Saint Cloud, 121; Coalport, 264; Courtille, 160; Derby, 245; Dresden, 182; Frankenthal, 195; Fürstenberg, 192; Ginori, 106; Hague, 204; Höchst, 189; Japanese, 96; Lenox, 299; Longton Hall, 247; Lowestoft, 251; Ludwigsburg, 194; Madeley, 285; Marieberg, 207; Mason's Ironstone, 288; Meissen, 182; Mennecy-Villeroy, 127, 128; Nant-

311

garw, 278; Niederviller, 169; Nymphenburg, 191; Orléans, 140; Philadelphia (Southwark), 295; Plymouth, 254; Reuilly, 161; Rockingham, 282; Royal Copenhagen, 214; Royal Doulton, 290; Sceaux, 137; Sèvres, 147, 148; Spode, 267, 268; Strasburg, 167; Swansea, 280; Tournay, 138, 139; Tucker (Philadelphia), 296, 297; Venice, 110; Vienna, 197; Vincennes, 132, 133; Wedgewood, 276; Worcester, 240
Boileau, M., 143, 156, 167
du Bois, Madame, 28
Boizot, —, 151
Bone, ash, 240, 245, 267, 295; china, 35, 211, 244, 266, 271, 276, 277
Bonnin, Gousse, 295
Boston, 68, 293, 294; china-making, 36; *Evening Post*, 299
Böttger, Johann Friedrich, 179, 180, 182, 183
Boucher, pastorals, 235
Bouchet, —, 151
Bouillat, —, 151
"Bourbon sprig," 265
Bourdon-Desplanches, 157, 158, 159
Bourg-la-Reine, China, 153
Bow, 53, 70, 105, 113, 192, 193, 237, 240, 245, 247, 252, 294, 295; China, 221-228
Bowcocke, John, 222, 223
Brameld, Thomas, 282, 283
Brancas-Lauraguais, Comte de, 165
Brandenburg, Elector of, 188
Bristol, 70, 258, 278; China, 255-257; works, 254
British Museum, 62, 70, 83
Brodel, Giovanni, 116
Brooklyn, 74
Brongniart, 106, 147
"Broseley Dragon," 261, 265, 272
Brown, Harry A., 299
Brunswick, Dukes of, 192
Brussels, China, 205, 206
Buen Retiro, China, 177, 178
Burke, Edmund, 255
Burlington Magazine, 233, 234
Burslem, 247, 274, 290; Manor of, 260
Burton, William, 40, 42, 46, 47, 224, 261, 273, 275
Byerly, Thomas, 275

Caen, China, 172
Caffieri, —, 151
Cairo, 30
Camden (N.J.), 68
Camelford, Lord, 254

Canton, 31, 71; China, 76; decorations, 61; "Factories," 68
Capo di Monte, 177, 199; China, 108, 111-115; factory, 105; figures, 270; mark, 105
Cardiff, 278
Carl, Eugen, Duke of Würtemberg, 193, 194; Theodor, Elector Palatine, 195
Cassel, 196
Casting, 45, 139
Castle Green, 255
Castleton, China, 304-306
Caughley, 252, 272; China, 261-263; factory, 238, 263; patterns, 264; "willow-pattern," 253
Cauldon (Ridgway), China, 289; Place Works, 289
Cavendish, Lady, 228
Caxon, Jonathan, Sr., 299
Celadon, China, 96; ware, 49
Centennial, 1876, 74
"Ceramic Art Company," 292, 299
Chabry, —, 151
Chamberlain, factory, 239, 242; Humphrey, 239; Robert, 238
Champion, Richard, 254, 255, 256, 258, 271
Chaffers, Richard, 248, 249
Chanou, 161, 162
Chantilly, 53, 105, 108, 128, 129, 130, 140, 143, 213, 224, 226, 227, 228, 232; China, 124-127; "sprigs," 262, 265
Chapelle, Jacques, 136, 137
Charles Théodore, Archduke, 167
Charles III, King of Naples, 111; King of Spain, 177; VII, 30
Charleston, 68
Chartres, Duc de, 156
Cheapside, 238, 250, 251
Chelsea, 105, 192, 193, 221, 224, 237, 240, 245, 247, 291, 295; China, 228-236; "claret," 242, 283; -Derby, China, 232; manner, 269; -Derby, period, 235; régime, 246
Chêng Te, reign, 64
Ching-tê Chên, 66, 68, 69, 75, 76, 80, 95, 96; factories, 61, 65, 77; town of, 69
Chia Ching, reign, 64
Chicago, 302; World's Fair, 74
Chicanneau, MM., 120; Pierre, 121
Ch'ien Lung, 66, 77; reign, 65
China, Canton, 76; Chinese characteristics, 76; -clay, 40; export, 76; "Fitzhugh," 76; Fuchien, 48; Hall, 71; ingredients, 77; Japanese, 53; "Jesuit," 88; "Mandarin," 87; "China-Mania," 25-37; "Medallion," 76; Nankin, 75, 76; nature

of, 39; -painters, London, 250; Trade, 68, 71, 72, 75

Chinaware, Ahrenfeldt, 175, 176; Saint Amand-les-Eaux, 154; American, 293; "Amstel," 202-204; d'Angoulème, Rue de Bondy, 164; Arita, 97-99; Arras, 153, 154; d'Artois, 157-159; Belleek, 291, 292; Bergen (N.J.), 295, 296; Berlin, 186-188; Bing & Grøndahl, 216-218; Bourg-la-Reine, 153; Bow, 221-228; Bristol, 255-257; Brussels, 205, 206; Buen Retiro, 177, 178; Caen, 172; Capo di Monte, 108, 111-115; casting, 45; Castleton, 304-306; Caughley, 261-263; Cauldon (Ridgway), 289; Chantilly, 124-127; Chelsea, 228-236; Chelsea-Derby, 232; Chinese, 56-95; Church Gresley, 260, 261; Clignancourt, 162, 163; Saint Cloud, 119-123; Coalport, 263-266; colours, 48, 49; contours, 52; Courtille, 160, 161; Davenport, 274, 275; decoration of, 47-49; Derby, 243-247; Doccia, 102-109; Dresden, 179-186; egg-shell, 292; Este, 116, 117; experimentation, 35; firing, 45; Frankenthal, 195, 196; French, 118-176; Ginori, 33, 102-109; Gustavsberg, 210-212; Hague, 204, 205; Haviland, 173-175; Herend, 199; Hirado, 99, 100; Höchst, 188, 190; Imari, 87, 97; Ironstone, 209; Italian, 102-117; Japanese, 95-101; Kaga, 100; Kakiyemon, 87; Kioto, 100; Kutani, 100; Lamberton, 303, 304; Lane Delph, 286; Lauraguais, 165, 166; Lenox, 298-300; Lille, 123, 124; Limoges, 170; Liverpool, 248, 249; Longton Hall, 247, 248; Lowestoft, 249-253; Ludwigsburg, 193, 194; Madeley, 284-286; Madrid, 177, 178; making of, 44-49; Marieberg, 207, 208; marks, 52; Marseilles, 170; Mason, 286-288; Mason's "Ironstone," 286-288; Medici, 102, 109; Meissen, 179-186; Mennecy-Villeroy, 127-130; Mikawachi, 99, 100; Minton, 271-274; moulding, 44; Nabeshima, 99; Nantgarw, 278, 279; nature of, 38; New Hall, 258, 259; New York, 296; Niederviller, 168-170; North Cambridge, 293, 294; Le Nove, 115; Nymphenburg, 190-192; Nyon, 200; Okawachi, 99; Oriental, 56-101; Orléans, 140, 144, 165; Paris, 154-156; St. Petersburg, 219, 220; Philadelphia (Southwark), 294, 295; Pickard, 302, 303; Pinxton and Torksey, 259, 260; Popincourt, 165; Portuguese, 178; Plymouth, 253-255; Reuilly, 161, 162; Rockingham, 282, 283; Rome, 116; Rörstrand, 209, 210; Rouen, 118, 119; Royal Copenhagen, 213-216; Royal Doulton, 289-291; Rue Thiroux, 163, 164; Sceaux, 136-138; Sèvres, 141-152; shipments, 80; Spode, 266-271; Strasburg, 166-168; Swansea, 280, 281; Syracuse (Onondaga Co.), 300-302; throwing, 44; Tournay, 138-140; Treviso, 116, 117; Tucker (Philadelphia), 296-298; Upsala-Ekeby, 212; Valenciennes, 171, 172; Vaux, 160; Venice, 109-111; Vienna, 197, 198; Vincennes, 130-136; Vincennes (Hannong), 156, 157; Vinovo, 116; Wedgwood, 275-277; Wirksworth, 283, 284; Worcester, 236-243; Zurich, 200, 201

Chinese, porcelain, 30

Ch'ing, Dynasty, 65-95

Church Gresley china, 260, 261

Chocolate-drinking, 26, 31

Christian, Philip, 248

"Cincinnati" dinner-service, 72

Cirou, Ciquaire, 124, 125

City Troop, Philadelphia, 73

Clignancourt china, 155, 162, 163

Saint Cloud, 54, 105, 118, 127, 129, 166, 213, 224, 229, 232; Château de, 120; china, 119-123; factory, 124

Coalport, china, 263-266; China Company, 263; factory, 261

Cock & Co., 222

Coffee-drinking, 26, 31

Coffee, W. T., 261

Coke, John, 259, 260

Colours, 48, 49; decoration, 61; enamel, 48, 49, 64; of glaze, 70; underglaze, 48, 49, 64, 85

Comfort, George, 303

de Condé, Prince, 124, 125

Connecticut, Academy of Arts & Sciences, 71

Contours, characteristic, 52, 53, 54; Chinese, 79-82; Japanese, 97; Neo-Classic, 169, 183; Neo-Grec, 169; Rococo, 113, 183

Cookworthy, patent, 254, 255, 271; & Co., 255, 257; William, 253-255

Copeland, "Alderman," 267; William, 266, 267; William Taylor, 267; W. T. & Sons, 266

Copenhagen, 183, 216; china, 253

Cornflower, decoration, 145, 170, 204, 253, 265, 284

Cornhill, 222, 223

Cornwall, 211, 249, 253

Corporation, City of New York, 74

Cosway, 242

Courtille, china, 160, 161; factory, 155
de Coussy, Mathieu, 30
"Cottage" china, 36, 256, 258
"Cow" china, 72
Cox, James, 231
Craft, T., 223
Crown Derby, 272
Crowther, and Weatherby, 222; John, 223
Crusaders, 30
Cumberland, Duke of, 229
de Custine, Comte, 169, 170
Cyfflé, 169

Dali, Salvador, 305
Dartou, 207
Davis, William, 236
Davenport, 249; china, 274, 275
Decalcomanias, 175, 277, 300, 305
Decoration, 47-49; *en camaïeu,* 30, 108,
    136, 139, 143, 151, 159, 169, 170, 204,
    205, 210, 215, 227, 235; establishments,
    37; polychrome, 64, 107, 129; *grisaille,*
    205, 215, 257; Kakiyemon, 125, 184,
    226, 234; types, Chinese, 83-94; types,
    Japanese, 96-98
Deleneur, 153
Delft, 202, 209, 226, 248; potters, 251;
    pottery, 26
De Moitte, 162
Denmark, 183
Derby, 223, 231, 232, 259, 261, 264, 274,
    279; biscuit, 268; "Canary," 283; china,
    54, 243-247; factory, 287; manner, 282
Derbyshire, 260, 261, 283; Lord Lieuten-
    ant of, 244
Deruelle, Pierre, 162, 163
Devonshire, Duke of, 244
Diaper, Chinese patterns, 88-91; "par-
    tridge-eye," 129, 150; patterns, 283
Dickens, Charles, 37
Dietrich, 181
Diglis, 238
Dihl, 164
Dillon, 248
Dillwyn, L. W., 278, 280
Directoire, 149, 152; mode, 150
Doccia, 104, 105; china, 102-109; factory,
    102, 105
Dodin, 151
Dorez, Barthélemy, 123; brothers, 123
Dorset, 232
Doulton, china, 289-291; factory, 290; Sir
    Henry, 289, 290; John, 289; Lewis, 290
Dresden, 53, 105, 106, 108, 109, 110, 131,
    177, 180, 194, 197, 199, 202, 203, 204,
    213, 215, 219, 225, 226, 227, 228, 233,
    246, 253, 256, 257, 264, 265, 269, 272;

china, 142, 179-186; crossed swords,
    250; manner, 126, 134
Dryander, M., 169
Dublin, 223
Dubois, brothers, 130, 131, 132, 133
Duesbury, and Kean, 243; William, 223,
    231, 232, 243, 245, 246
Duplessis, 131, 134, 148, 151
Durnford, Clark, 250

East India Company, 31, 80, 251; Com-
    panies (English, Dutch and French), 29,
    67
East Liverpool (Ohio), 36
Egg-shell china, 62, 292
Ehrenreich, 207
Emblems, Chinese, 91-93
Empire, fashion, 150; First, 149, 152; Pot-
    tery Company, 300; style, 107
"Empress of China," 71
Enamels, Limoges, 239
d'Entrecolles, Père, 69, 77, 84
Este china, 116, 117
Etruria, factory, 276; (Trenton, N.J.), 292;
    works, 275
Etruscan, features, 108
Etterbeek, 205, 206
d'Eu, Comte, 153
Export china, 76

"Factories," Canton, 68, 69
Falconet, 151
Famille, noire, 66, 87; *rose,* 66, 87, 253,
    259, 265, 269, 270; *verte,* 65, 66, 87,
    270
Farrar, W. H., 300
Farrell, Fred D., 304
Fauquez, Sieur, 171
Fawkener, Sir Everard, 229, 231, 234
la Fayette, Marquis de, 75
Federal Era, 71
Felspar, 40; "Felspar China," 267
Ferdinand, IV, King of Naples, 112
Ferrara, 116
Fiene, Ernest, 305
Figures, Bow, 228; Chelsea, 230; "Man-
    darin," 253; Royal Copenhagen, 214,
    215
Firing, 45, 46, 47
Fischer, Moritz, 199
"Fish House," punch, 75; punch bowl, 74
"Fitzhugh," borders, 72, 75; china, 75,
    76; description, 75; medallions, 75;
    name, 75; pattern, 72
Fitzwilliam, Earl, 282; family, 283
Flaxman, 276
Fleet Street, 256

Flight, and Barr, 238; "Flight and Barr" period, 242; John, 238; Joseph, 238; Thomas, 237
Florence, 102, 103, 109; china, 32
Fontainebleau, 144
La Fontaine, fables, 169
Foo Chow, 75
Forms, Neo-Classic, 241, 246; Neo-Grec, 241, 246; Rococo, 241, 246
Fourniers, 171, 174; Louis, 213, 214
Fox, Henry, 233
Francesco I, de Medici, 102
Francis I, 30
Frankenthal, 156, 167; china, 195, 196
Franklin Institute, 36, 295, 296
Franks, Sir Wollaston, 83, 91
Frederick, Augustus, Elector of Saxony, 131; the Great, 181, 186
French, chinaware, 118-176; East India Company, 124
Frye, Thomas, 221, 222, 223, 228
Fuchien, china, 48; factory, 61; province, 69; "white ware," 61, 77, 108, 113, 122
Fulda, 196
de Fulvy, M., 130, 131, 132, 135
Fürstenberg china, 192, 193

Garrett, Thomas, 267
Gentleman's Magazine, 237
Gérin, 130, 131
Saint Germain, 144
Gerona, 178
Gerréault, Sieur, 140
Gessner, Solomon, 201
Gilding, 129, 135, 136, 138, 143, 152, 153, 158, 159, 168, 170, 172, 175, 198, 208, 210, 211, 215, 257, 262, 269, 275, 279, 281, 283, 286, 289, 297, 300, 305
Giles, John, 250
Ginori, Mchse. Carlo, 102-105; china, 43, 54, 102-109; family, 106; marks, 108, 109; Marquess, 33
Gioanetti, Dr., 116
San Giobbe, factory, 110
Gladstone, Hon. W. E., 276
Glaser, —, 192
Glaze, 45-47; Chinese, 78, 79; colours of, 70; crackled, 78; definition of, 39; Japanese, 97; "orange-peel," 70; "transmutation," 79
Glot, Richard, 137
Gloucester Fox Hunting Club, 73
"Goat and bee" cream jugs, 229
"Gold Chinamen," 183, 219
Gombroon, 31; ware, 26, 31
Gotzkowski, 186, 188
Gouyn, Charles, 229

Grainger, George, 239; Lee and Company, 239; Thomas, 239; and Wood, 239
Granby, Marquess of, 241
Gravant, 130, 131, 133, 135
Greenpoint (L.I.), 36
Grellet, 171, 174
Gresley, Sir Nigel, 260
Grisaille decoration, 205, 215, 257
Grøndahl, 216, 217
Gronsfeldt-Diepenbrock, Count, 202
Guerhard, 164
Gustavsberg china, 210-212
Gwynne, Nell, 31

Hackwood, 276
Hague, The, 202; china, 204, 205
Halle, 186
Hancock, R., 241, 242; Sampson, 244
Hannong, family, 156; Joseph Adam, 167, 168; Paul, 166, 167, 168; P. A., 116, 157, 158, 160, 166, 195
Haviland, Charles, 171; Charles Field, 174; china, 173-175; David, 173, 174; Theodore, 174, 175
Heath, John, 231, 243, 245
Heidegger, 200
Saint Helen's, 290
Hellmann, Louis E., 305
Hellot, 131, 133, 135
Hemphill, Hon. Joseph, 296
Herbo, Dorchies, 154
Herculaneum, 113, 114, 270; china, 249; works, 249
Herend china, 199
Herold, Johann G., 181, 184
Hettlinger, 145
Heylyn, Edward, 221
Hirado, porcelain, 99, 100
Hizen, 95; porcelain, 270
Höchst, 166, 186, 192, 200; china, 188-190
Hohenzollerns, 188
Holdship, Richard, 245
Holland, 71, 202, 251; House, 233, 283
"Hongs," 68
van Braam-Houckgeest, Andreas Everardus, 71, 73, 74
Huet, 158
Hulme, Thomas, 296, 297
Hungary, 199
Hunger, Christoph Conrad, 109, 110, 111, 197, 219
Hyakken, 95
Hyde, J. A. Lloyd, 72

Imari, china, 87, 97, 99, 125; decoration, 184; patterns, 246, 259; ware, 78, 242
Indian, styles, 239

Ireland, 291, 292
Ironstone china, 209, 270
Islington, 284
Italian, china, 33, 102-117; styles, 239

Jackfield, factory, 263
Jacques, M., 127, 128, 137; Jacques et
    Jullien, MM., 153
Saint James's Park, 222
Japanese, china, 53, 87; decoration, 96
Jasper ware, 275
Jersey City, Porcelain and Earthenware Co.,
    36, 295; Pottery, 36
"Jesuit" china, 83, 88
Jullien, M., 127, 128, 137

Kaga, china, 100; factory, 95
Kakiyemon, china, 87, 95; decoration, 125,
    184; manner, 129; pattern, 226
Kändler, Johann, 181, 182
K'ang Hsi, 66, 68, 77; china, 226; reign
    of, 65
Kaolin, 40, 41, 77, 95, 106, 165, 168, 169,
    172, 211, 253
Karlskrona, factory, 212
Kauffmann, Angelica, 242
Kean, régime, 244
King, William, 229
Kioto, china, 100; factory, 95
Kloster-Veilsdorf, 196
Korrodi, 200
Korzec, 219
Kühn, 181
Kühne, Chrétien, 206
Kutani, china, 100

"Lady Pattern," 234
Lallement, 125
Lamberton, china, 302, 304; Port, 303;
    works, 303
Lambeth, 289
Lambrequins, 129
Lamoniary, M., 171
Lancret, 129
Lane Delph, china, 286, 287
Lanfrey, François, 169, 170
von Langen, Baron, 192
Lassia, 161, 162
Latourette, K. S., 71
Latrobe, 71
Lauraguais, china, 165, 166
Leboeuf, Andrè Marie, 163, 164
Lecot, 151
Le Guay, 151
Leichner, Anton, 204
Leipzig, 180
Lemaire, M., 156, 165

Lemire, 169
Lenox, china, 298, 300; Walter Scott, 298,
    299
Le Riche, 151
Levaux, 151
Lewis, Joseph Saunders, 74
Lille china, 123, 124
Limbach, 196
Limoges, 148, 172, 173, 175; china, 171;
    enamels, 239
Lisbon, 178
Lister, Dr. Martin, 120
Littler, William, 243, 247
Liverpool, 293; china, 248, 249; Museum,
    248
Locker, —, 244
Locré, 160, 161
London, 237; auctions, 222, 240, 247;
    china-painters, 250; dealers, 278; Lord
    Mayor of, 267; warehouses, 250, 251,
    256, 261
Longport, 274
Longton, Staffs, 287
Longton Hall, 243, 247; china, 247, 248
Lough Erne, 291
Louis, XIV, 29, 31, 118, 121, 123; XV, 54,
    127, 144, 149; XVI, 145, 146, 148, 149,
    154, 155, 157, 159, 165; Philippe, 156
von Löwenfinch, A. F., 188
Lowestoft, 258, 259, 284; armorial, 70;
    china, 249-253; Chinese, 66-76; China
    Warehouse, 250; legend, 9; manner,
    227, 259; name, 67; Oriental, 66-76;
    period, 72; Spode, 267; town of, 66
Ludwigsburg, 201; china, 193, 194
Lunéville, 169
de Luynes, Memoirs of Duc, 131
Lyes, J., 236

Marks, authenticity of, 52; chinaware, 52;
    Chinese, 94; Japanese, 98
Macquer, 135
Maddock, Pottery Co., 303
Madeley, china, 284-286; factory, 284
Madrid china, 177, 178
du Maine, Duchesse, 137
Mainz, Archbishop-Elector, 188; Prince-
    Bishop, 189
Manchu Dynasty, 65, 95
"Mandarin," china, 87, 227; figures, 85,
    253; motifs, 270
Mann, Sir Horace, 32
Mansfield, 260
Marcolini, Count, 181, 186
Maria Theresa, Empress, 197
Marie Antoinette, 145, 154
Marieberg, 209, china, 207, 208

Marie-Josèphe, Dauphine, 131
Marly, 144
Marseilles china, 170
Maryland, 68
Mason, Charles James, 287, 288; china, 286-288; George, 287; "Ironstone China," 286-288; "matchings," 287; Miles, 286, 287, 288
Massié, 171, 174
Masso bastardo, 106
Mathieu, King's enameller, 131
Maubrée, 200
Max Joseph III, of Bavaria, 190
Mazarine blue, 86, 235, 239, 264, 283
Mead, Dr., 296
"Medallion" ware, 76
Medici china, 9, 30, 102, 109
Mehlhorn, J. G., 213
Meissen, 166, 180, 181, 186, 188, 189, 197, 219; china, 179-186; "posies," 70
Melchior, Johann Peter, 189, 191
Mennecy-Villeroy, 125, 140, 143, 153, 170, 208, 209, 224, 226, 227, 229; china, 54, 127-130
Mérault, 151
Le Mercure Galant, 120
Meudon, 144
Mikawachi china, 99, 100
Milano, 106
Ming, dynasty, 64; period, 61, 63, 64, 68, 77, 80
Minton, china, 271-274; Herbert, 272; Thomas, 271, 272
Modelling, 108, 113, 151, 241, 277
Modernism, Scandinavian, 213
de Mol, 203
Moncloa, 178
Mongol dynasty, 62
Monochrome decoration, 126
Monograms, 66
Montenegro, 305
"Moons," 232
Moreau, Sieur, 160
Morden College, 223
Morley, Francis, 287
Morris, George Anthony, 295; Henry, 281; Captain Samuel, 73
Morristown, (N.J.), 74
Mortlock, 279, 284
Morton, Gen. Jacob, 74
Moscow, 219
Motifs, Chinese, 129; cornflower, 253; Egyptian, 152; Etruscan, 152; Imperial, 152; Japanese, 129; Pompeian, 159, 161; Roman, 152; Oriental, 134
Moulding, 44, 256
Müller, Frantz, 213, 214

Munich, 191
Museum, advice of, 55; use of, 51; British, 62, 70, 83; Liverpool, 248; of Modern Art (N.Y.), 306; Philadelphia, 295, 296; Sèvres, 151; Victoria and Albert, 121

Nabeshima, china, 99
Nankin, blue and white, 272; china, 75, 76
Nantgarw, 281, 284, 285; china, 278, 279; factory, 263, 265; troupe, 280; village, 278
Naples, 105, 107, 111, 112, 177
Nast, 165
Naudeck, 190
Neo-Classic, forms, 54, 183, 241, 246; manner, 107, 110, 149
Neo-Grec, forms, 54, 241, 246, 297; manner, 107, 149, 282
"New Canton," 221, 224
New Hall, 253, 256, 271; china, 258, 259; decoration, 258
Newport, 68
New York, 68, 71, 173, 175; china, 296; city arms, 74; Corporation punch bowl, 74
Nicholas I, Emperor of Russia, 265
NThe recherchederville china, 168-170
Nieuwe Amstel, 202, 203
de Noailles, Maréchal, 167
North Cambridge china, 293, 294
Le Nove china, 115
Nymphenburg china, 190-192; Palace, 190
Nyon china, 200

Okawachi china, 99
"Old Japan" pattern, 226, 228, 234, 244, 271
"Old Spode," 266, 267
"Onion" pattern, 183, 215
Onondaga Pottery Co., 300
Oporto, 178
"Orange-peel" glaze, 70
"Oriental Lowestoft," 72
d'Orléans, Duc, 120, 124; china, 140, 141; factory, 155, 165
d'Osson, Marquis, 157
Oude Amstel, 202, 203, 204
Oude Loosdrecht, 202, 203, 204
Owari, factory, 95
Oxford Journal, 237

du Pacquier, Claude, 181, 197, 198
Padova, 116
Pajou, 151
Pardoe, birds, 279; Thomas, 278
Pall Mall, 230

Parian, body, 239, 267, 268, 273, 291, 292, 305; figures, 268; ware, 36
Paris, 120, 140; china, 154-156
Parrot pattern, 270
"Partridge-eye" diaper, 129, 150, 151
Pass, James, 300, 301
Passau, 186, 192
Paste, definition, 39; hard, 39; soft, 39
Patent, Cookworthy's, 254, 255
Pattern, books, 269, 271, 277; "Broseley Dragon," 261, 265, 272; Caughley, 264; "Chests," 70; Diaper, 283, (Chinese), 88-91; Imari, 246, 259; "Lady," 234; "Old Japan," 226, 228, 234, 244, 271; "Onion," 183, 215; Peacock, 270; Parrot, 270; Peony, 270; "Pheasant and border," 234; "Strohblumen," 215; "Tyger and rock," 234; "Wheatsheaf and pheasant," 234; "willow," 253, 261, 262, 272
Pélissier, Pierre, 123
Penn, William, 28, 68
Pennsylvania, Assembly, 295; Hospital punch bowl, 74
Pennington, Seth, 248
de Penthièvre, Duc, 137, 140
Percier and Fontaine, 152
Perrotin, 151
Persian, cobalt, 63; styles, 239
Peterinck, 138
Saint Petersburg, china, 219, 220
Petuntse, 40, 41, 46, 77, 95
Pewter, tableware, 26
Philadelphia, 36, 68, 72, 74; china, 34; (Southwark) china, 294, 295; Museum of Art, 295, 296
Phyfe, Duncan, 71
Piccadilly, 231
Pickard, china, 302, 303; factory, 302
Pigalle, 151
Pinxton, 259, 260; and Torksey china, 259, 260; Lord of Manor, 259
Pithou, 151
Pitt, Thomas, 254
Plymouth china, 253-255
Podmore, 236, 249
Poland, 219
Polychrome decoration, 107
du Pompadour, Marquise de, 132, 137, 141, 142
Pompeian motifs, 108, 152
Pompeii, 113, 114, 270
de Pontchartrain, M., 118
Popincourt, china, 165; factory, 155
Porcelain, acquaintance with, 31; bone, 43; casting, 45; character of, 43; Chinese, 41, 56-95; colours, 48, 49; decoration of,

47-49; different sorts, 39; discovery of in England, 43; firing, 45; German, 41; Japanese, 87, 95-101; Oriental, 42, 56-101; manufacturing processes, 41, 44-49; moulding, 44; nature of, 38, 39; throwing, 44; trade in, 30, 31
Portici, 111; Villa Reale, 112
Portland, Duke of, 120; Vase, 277
Portugal, 178
Portuguese china, 178
Poterat, Louis, 118, 121
Potters, Delft, 251; Staffordshire, 244, 255, 264
Pouyat, 171
Powder blue, 66, 226, 277
Prince Regent, 278
Providence, 68
Pugh, William, 263
Punch bowls, 73, 74

Queen, Anne, 120; Charlotte, 261; Elizabeth, 30, 289; Mary, 27, 32; Victoria, 244, 265
Queensware, 209

Randall, Thomas Martin, 284, 285, 286
Raphael, frescoes, 152
Reichard, 186
Reid and Company, 248
Reine, *fabrique de la,* 155; *porcelaine à la,* 164
Renaissance, arabesques, 70
Reuilly, rue de, china, 161, 162; factory, 155
Reverend, Charles, 118
Revolutionary War, 71
"Rice-grain" china, 48, 62
Richard, Champion & Co., 255; Company, 106
de Richelieu, Duc, 132
Ridgway, family, 289; Job, 289; John, 289
Ringler, Joseph Jacob, 190, 193
Robert, J. G., 170
Robillard, 200
Rockingham, china, 282, 283; "green," 283; Marquess of, 282
Rococo, forms, 54, 113, 183, 225, 233, 246; manner, 107, 110, 128, 149
Rome china, 116
Roosevelt, Theodore, 34
Rörstrand china, 209, 210
Rose, John, 261, 263, 265; W. F., 263
Ross, Capt. Charles, 74
Rosset, 151
Rotterdam, 250
Rouen, 121, 209; china, 9, 118, 119

Royal, Copenhagen china, 213-216; Crown Derby Porcelain Company, Limited, 244; Doulton china, 289-291; Exchange, 222; Porcelain Company (Worcester), 239
Rue Thiroux china, 163, 164
Ruffinger, 160

Salopian, 248; China Warehouse, 261
Saxony, 109, 179, 188; Elector of, 131; porcelain-making, 34
Scammell, China Company, 303, 304; D. William, 303
Scandinavian, modernism, 213
Sceaux, 140, 153; china, 136-138
Schaerbeek, 205
Schreiber, George, 305
Sesto, 102
Severn, 239, 263
Sèvres, 35, 41, 107, 125, 126, 127, 129, 132, 134, 154, 155, 156, 159, 163, 170, 171, 177, 185, 187, 188, 195, 199, 200, 202, 209, 213, 215, 219, 225, 226, 227, 233, 241, 246, 264, 265, 272, 285, 297; artists, 151; china, 141-153; Museum, 151
Shapes, 54; American, 173; Chinese, 52, 79-82, 123; European, 69; "imitation," 53; Neo-Classic, 225; Neo-Grec, 297; Oriental, 107; Persian, 80; Rococo, 225, 233; tableware, 72
Shelton, 256, 258, 289
Shenango Pottery Co., 304
Shropshire, 261, 284
Silesia, 186
Silver, table-services, 26
Sims, Capt. Walter, 71
Sioux, 151
Smith, James M. Sr., 304, 305; Jochim, 276
Soapstone, 240, 249
Solon, m., 272
Sonnenschein, 201
Soulavie, Memoirs, 132
South Carolina, 36, 256
Southwark (Philadelphia) china, 295
Spain, 111, 112; throne of, 111, 112
Spengler, 200
Spode, china, 266-271; Josiah I, 266, 269, 271, 272; Josiah II, 266, 267, 269; "Stone China," 286
Sprimont, Nicholas, 229, 230, 231, 245
Spring Gardens, 222
Staffordshire, 247, 287; factories, 272; potters, 229, 244, 255, 256, 264, 272, 293; tableware, 10, 11
"State in Schuylkill," 74
Stewart, Jonathan, 303
Stockholm, 207, 210

Stoke-upon-Trent, 266, 271, 272
Stölzel, Samuel, 197
"Stone China," 266, 267, 269
Strasburg, 156, 195; china, 166-168
Stratford-le-Bow, 221
Strawberry Hill, 32
"Strohblumen" pattern, 183, 215
Stubbs, George, 276
Styles, Indian, 239; Italian, 239; Persian, 239
Sung, factories, 61; period, 62
Swansea, 278, 284, 285; china, 280, 281; factory, 263; roses, 265
Sweden, 207
Swinton, 282
"Symbols," Chinese, 91-93
Symbolism, Chinese, 94

Table, services, 26; silver, 26; pewter, 27; ware shapes, 72
Tassie, —, 276
Tea, drinking, 26; introduction of, 31; tackle, 26
Têhua, 69; factory, 61
"Throwing," 44, 256
Torino, 116
Torksey, 260
Tournay, 153, 154, 204; china, 138-140
Townsend, Lea, 305
Trade, "China," 67, 68, 72, 75; Egyptian, 65; European, 65; Indian, 65; Persian, 65
Transfer-printing, 188, 210, 211, 227, 241, 253, 259, 262, 269, 272, 277, 300, 305
Translucence, 39
Trenton (N.J.), 292, 298, 299; china-making, 36
Treviso china, 116, 117
Trollope, Mrs., 37
Trianon, 144
Tschirnhausen, 179, 180
Tucker, Benjamin, 296; china, 34, 36, 296-298; William Ellis, 296
Tunstall, 256, 258
Turner, Thomas, 261, 262, 272
Tuscany, Grand Duke of, 102
"Tyger and rock" pattern, 234
Types of decoration, Chinese, 83-94; Japanese, 98

United States, 67, 71
Upsala-Ekeby china, 212

Valenciennes china, 171, 172
Van Hysum, flowers, 270
Varick, Col. Richard, 74
Vaume, J. S., 205

Vaux, china, 160; factory, 155
Vauxhall Walk, 289
Versailles, 120, 144, 145; porcelain room, 31
Venice china, 109-111
Vezzi, brothers, 109; china, 109; factory, 219; Francesco, 110; Geminiano, 110
Victoria and Albert Museum, 30, 121
Victorian Era, bad taste of, 35
Vienna, 105, 106, 107, 109, 190, 195, 204, 219; china, 197, 198
Views, English and American, 10
de Villeroy, Louis François de Neufville, Duc, 127
Vincennes, 105, 127, 137, 141, 147, 150, 155, 166, 167, 227; china, 130-136; Vincennes (Hannong) china, 156, 157
Vinovo china, 116
Virginia, 68
Voyages of American Ships to China, 1784-1844, 71

Walker, Brown, Aldred and Richman, 250
Wall, Dr. John, 236, 237
Wallace Collection, 151
Wallendorf, 196
Walpole, Horace, 32
Wandhelein, Karl, 104
Wan Li, Emperor, 65
War between the States, 36
Warehouse, London, 251, 256, 261; Lowestoft China, 250
Warmstry House, 236, 238

Washington, Association of New Jersey, 74; Mrs., 73
Watteau, subjects, 129, 184, 204, 227, 235, 242, 286
Watts, John, 289
Weatherby, 223
Wedgwood, 177, 193, 209; Aaron, 247; china, 275-277; Josiah, 255, 275, 276, 277
Weesp, 202, 204
Wegeli, Wilhelm Caspar, 186, 188
Wellington, Duke of, 178
White House, 34, 74; dinner-service, 300
"Wheatsheaf and pheasant" pattern, 234
Williams, Sir Charles Hanbury, 233, 234
"Willow" pattern, 10, 261, 262, 272; Caughley, 253
Wirksworth, 253; china, 283, 284
Worcester, 53, 107, 238, 248, 249, 252, 253, 261, 263, 264, 295; china, 35, 236-243; crescent, 250; factory, 287; Royal Porcelain Company, 238; Tonkin Manufacture, 236
"Worm sprig," 265
Würtemberg, Duke of, 193

Yorkshire, 282
Young, W. Weston, 278
Saint Yrieix, 106, 148, 169
Yung Cheng, reign of, 65
Yung Lo, 63; reign of, 62

Zurich china, 200, 201

PLATE 1

LARGE CHINESE "IMARI" PLATTER
Glaze of distinct bluish tinge; flowing pattern of peonies, chrysanthemums and Japanese "brocade" *motifs* in blue, red and gold

Courtesy of the British Museum

PLATE 2

A. EIGHTEENTH CENTURY *FAMILLE ROSE* OCTAGONAL
PLATE

Rim of characteristic rose pink; polychrome centre on white ground,
with "Mandarin" figures, vases, jars and table

B. EARLY EIGHTEENTH CENTURY PLATE

Decoration in characteristic *famille verte* colouring; diaper border enclosing inner border composed of emblems and flowers; centre, in shaped panel,
shewing steps, house and flower vase

Courtesy of the British Museum

PLATE 3

LARGE JAPANESE IMARI PLATTER
Flowered and foliated border, enclosing garden scene and "long Eliza" figures; decoration red, dark
blue and gold; glaze of greyish tone

Courtesy of the Victoria and Albert Museum, South Kensington

PLATE 4

A. **SCEAUX ICE-PAIL, POLYCHROME FLOWER DECORATION**
Courtesy of the Victoria and Albert Museum, South Kensington

B. **GINORI OVAL PLATTER,** c.1760
Shaped moulded rim, polychrome flower decoration in manner of **Mennecy**

Courtesy of Factory Museum at Doccia

PLATE 5

A. DRESDEN CHINA PLATE WITH KAKIYEMON
DECORATION
Decoration and colouring characteristic of Kakiyemon mode

B. SÈVRES SMALL COVERED JAR
Characteristic apple green ground colour, with reserves and flowers

Courtesy of the British Museum

PLATE 6

A. BRISTOL TRAY
Shaped edge and slightly moulded rim; garland and scattered flower decoration

B. LOWESTOFT CUP AND SAUCER
Moulded flutings and small flower decoration

Courtesy of the Victoria and Albert Museum, South Kensington

PLATE 7

WORCESTER PLATTER

Scale blue border, exotic multi-coloured birds, butterflies and insects in shaped reserved white panels edged with gilt Rococo scrolls. Centre white, with birds

Courtesy of the British Museum

PLATE 8

A. EIGHTEENTH CENTURY CHINESE POWDER-BLUE VASE
erved and shaped panel in white bearing multi-coloured symbols or emblems

Courtesy of the British Museum

B. CAUGHLEY MUG
With scrolls and bands of characteristic deep blue and gold

Courtesy of the Victoria and Albert Museum, South Kensington

PLATE 9

BAROQUE	ROCOCO	NEO-CLASSIC	NEO-GREC

Teapots

Cups

Various

TABLE OF CHARACTERISTIC CONTOURS

A. K'ang Hsi, Baroque; B. Worcester, Rococo; C. Derby, Neo-Classic; D. Derby, Neo-Grec;
E. Chinese, Baroque; F. Chelsea, Rococo; G. Sèvres, Neo-Classic; H. Sèvres, Neo-Grec;
I. St. Cloud, Baroque· J. Mennecy, Rococo; K. Spode, Neo-Classic; L. Vienna, Neo-Grec

PLATE 10

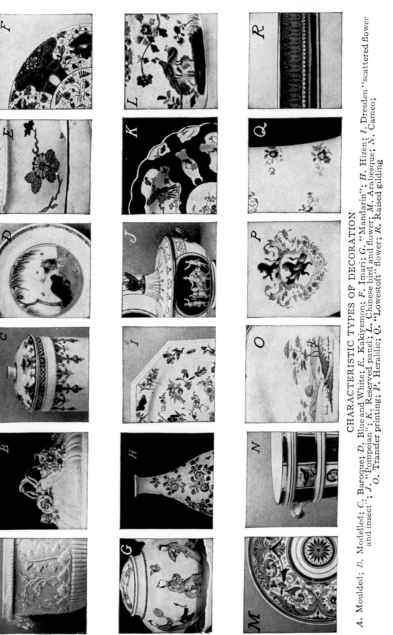

CHARACTERISTIC TYPES OF DECORATION

A. Moulded; B. Modelled; C. Baroque; D. Blue and White; E. Kakiyemon; F. Imari; G. "Mandarin"; H. Hizen; I. Dresden "scattered flower and insect"; J. "Pompeian"; K. Reserved panel; L. Chinese bird and flower; M. Arabesque; N. Cameo; O. Transfer printing; P. Heraldic; Q. "Lowestoft" flower; R. Raised gilding

PLATE 11

COVERED BLUE AND WHITE JAR OF MING PERIOD
Glaze of faint bluish tinge; flowing pattern in light blue and two shades of dark blue

Courtesy of the British Museum

PLATE 12

A. BLUE AND WHITE BOWL OF MING PERIOD, LATE 16TH CENTURY
Greenish blue tinge in glaze; figures in house, trees, scrolls and inner diaper border in light and dark blue

B. LARGE BLUE AND WHITE DEEP PLATTER OF MING PERIOD
Greenish tinge in glaze; decorations in many varying shades of blue with dark blue line work; shaped panels in border containing emblems and flowers; landscape in centre; Persian and Indian influence

Courtesy of the British Museum

PLATE 13

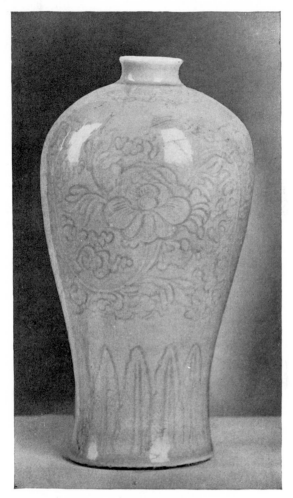

CELADON VASE, SEA-GREEN GLAZE
Engraved underglaze flowing pattern of peonies above a band of
water-leaves at the base

Courtesy of the Victoria and Albert Museum, South Kensington

PLATE 14

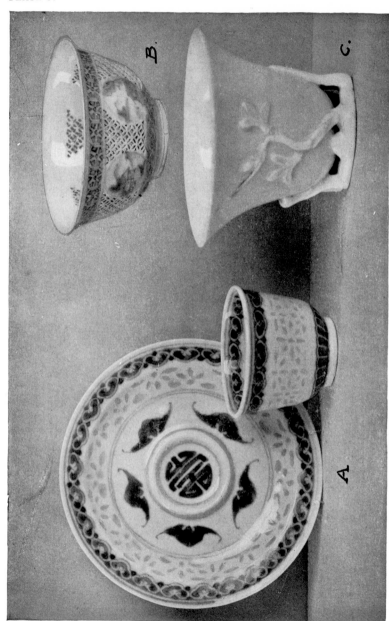

A. BLUE AND WHITE CUP AND
SAUCER

Rice-grain decoration in the paste; border of
jou-ee heads in several shades of blue; five
blue bats and mark in centre of saucer

B. BLUE AND WHITE CUP

Sides pierced with interlacing coin fretwork

C. "BLANC DE CHINE" CUP

White ware of Fuchien, with prunus-blossom
decoration in relief

Courtesy of the Victoria and Albert Museum, South Kensington

PLATE 15

BLUE AND WHITE COVERED JAR

Deep blue crackled ground, with large crackles, the blossoms and stems of the prunus decoration reserved in white

Courtesy of the Victoria and Albert Museum, South Kensington

PLATE 16

VASE OF THE SO-CALLED "BATAVIAN" WARE

Glaze of slightly greenish tinge; body a yellowish brown or "dead-leaf" brown with four circular reserved white panels containing peony and leaf decoration in underglaze blue; neck tall with Persian pomegranate or flame pattern in underglaze blue

Courtesy of the Victoria and Albert Museum, South Kensington

PLATE 17

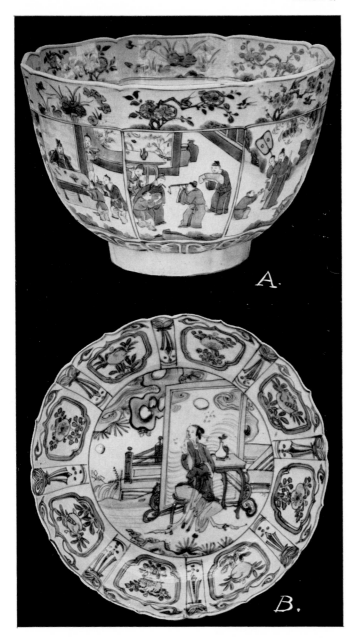

A. EIGHT-SIDED BLUE AND WHITE BOWL OF K'ANG HSI REIGN
(1662–1722)

Glaze of slight bluish tinge; decoration in many shades of blue

B. DEEP BLUE AND WHITE PLATE OF LATE MING PERIOD

Glaze of very pale bluish tinge; decoration in several shades of greyish blue outlined in dark blue; "long Eliza" and house scene in centre; waved or shaped rim and border of shaped panels containing flowers and emblems

Courtesy of the British Museum

PLATE 18

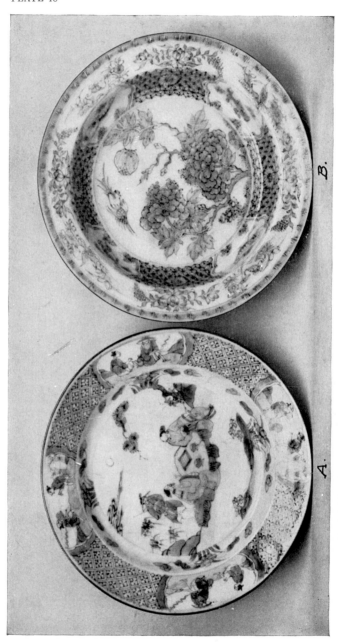

TWO EARLY EIGHTEENTH CENTURY BLUE AND WHITE PLATES (CH'ING PERIOD)

Broad rims for export to Europe; glaze of bluish tinge; decoration in two shades of light blue and two shades of dark blue; light brown edge to rim

A. Figures in centre with sparse, suggested landscape; diapered rim with four reserved panels containing figures

B. Peony centre with flower-scroll rim

Courtesy of the British Museum

PLATE 19

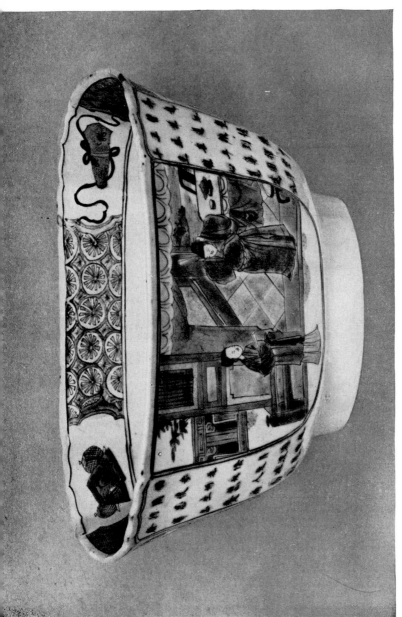

EIGHT-SIDED K'ANG HSI BOWL (1662-1722)

Four long sides and four short sides; figures and interiors on long sides, inscriptions on short sides; inside rim chrysanthemum-diapered with four white reserved panels on short sides containing emblems; decoration in several shades of green, pale yellow, smoke, violet and vermilion, line work in black; glaze of slight greenish tinge

Courtesy of the British Museum

PLATE 20

EARLY EIGHTEENTH CENTURY (CH'ING PERIOD) LARGE CIRCULAR
PLATTER OR TRAY

Raised rim; central *motif* of peonies, twigs and birds shewing Kakiyemon influence,
surrounded by border of *jou-ee* heads; rim diapered with four reserved panels containing
lobsters and fishes; decoration in green, vermilion, mauve and pale yellow, line work black,
and touches of gold on red flowers; glaze slightly bluish

Courtesy of the British Museum

PLATE 21

K'ANG HSI BOWL (circa 1700)

Exterior Nankin yellow ground with fan-shaped reserved panels containing flower, twig and leaf *motifs*; floral decoration, inside and outside, in brilliant green, vermilion, light blue, pale yellow and pale mauve; glaze slightly bluish

Courtesy of the British Museum

PLATE 22

A. K'ANG HSI PLATE WITH FLOWER-SPRAY BORDER

Broad rim for Western export; centre, finely drawn birds and flower sprays; decoration in gold, pale green, greenish blue, pink, black and vermilion, the gold and vermilion predominating, with line work in black; greyish glaze

B. K'ANG HSI PLATE

With broad rim for Western export; border of *jou-ee* heads in vermilion, blue, green and gold; partridge and flower decoration, shewing Kakiyemon influence, in same colours with the addition of light yellow; bluish tinge in glaze

Courtesy of the British Museum

PLATE 23

B.

A.

A. EARLY EIGHTEENTH CENTURY PLATE WITH FIVE BATS
White ground surrounding mark in centre; decoration in shaded red with dark line work

B. EARLY EIGHTEENTH CENTURY OCTAGONAL PLATE
Alternate sectors of dark blue and white; decoration in green, gold, vermilion and pale yellow; gold diaper and chrysanthemums on dark blue grounds, flowers and vases in centre and white sectors

Courtesy of the British Museum

PLATE 24

A. EIGHTEENTH CENTURY CUP AND SAUCER, DECORATED AT CANTON
Decoration in deep cobalt blue with superimposed gilding; white glaze

B. SEVENTEENTH CENTURY CUP AND SAUCER
Border of emblems and emblems on outside of cup; decoration in brilliant green, light blue,
vermilion and pale yellow; glaze nearly white

Courtesy of the British Museum

PLATE 25

A. K'ANG HSI PLATE (1662–1722)

Herring-bone diaper rim edge and border of empanelled flower groups, enclosing centre with "Mandarin" figures; decoration in light and dark vermilion with touches of gold; bluish glaze

B. EIGHTEENTH CENTURY "JESUIT" PLATE

Border of flower scrolls and winged cherubs, and centre depicting the baptism of Christ; decoration in dull vermilion and gold; greenish glaze

Courtesy of the British Museum

PLATE 26

A. EIGHTEENTH CENTURY PLATE WITH MOULDED AND WAVED RIM

Decoration akin to manner of so-called "Lowestoft" china; six panel border of small figures and flowers, elephant and rider in centre, enclosed by Rococo scrolls, Western influence in design; decoration green, deep pink, light blue, gold and vermilion; glaze slightly greenish

B. "LOWESTOFT" MUG, MADE TO WESTERN ORDER

Small scattered "Dresden" flowers and English inscription enclosed in Rococo scrolls; decoration pink, brown, dull blue, gold, vermilion and light green; glaze slightly greenish

Courtesy of the British Museum

PLATE 27

A. BEAKER VASE *B.* COVERED JAR
Part of eighteenth century "Lowestoft" mantel garniture with armorial bearings and small
scattered "Dresden" flowers, made to Western order; decoration cobalt blue, light pink,
bluish green, gold, black and dull vermilion; glaze of greyish tone

Courtesy of the British Museum

PLATE 28

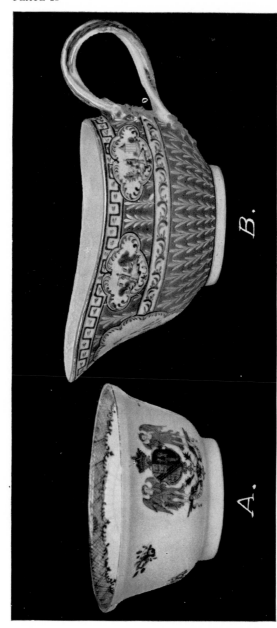

A. SMALL EIGHTEENTH CENTURY "LOWESTOFT" BOWL
Made to Western order with armorial bearings, small scattered flowers, and diapered border inside rim; decoration green, pink, gold, vermilion, cobalt blue, and deep violet; glaze slightly bluish

B. EIGHTEENTH CENTURY GREEN "LOWESTOFT" SAUCEBOAT
Western shape and Western manner of design; decoration deep rich green, deep pink, gold, and touches of deep cobalt blue; glaze slightly bluish

Courtesy of the British Museum

PLATE 29

CHINESE "LOWESTOFT," HELMET CREAM PITCHER AND SUGAR BASON c. 1790
Paste white, glaze faintly bluish; orange ground colour, Classic figures in black; gilding

Courtesy of the Philadelphia Museum of Art

PLATE 30

A. EIGHTEENTH CENTURY CHINESE
"LOWESTOFT" CUP
All decoration finely drawn in black

B. EIGHTEENTH CENTURY CHINESE
"LOWESTOFT" SAUCER
Decoration finely drawn in black in imitation of the Worcester
transfer prints engraved by Hancock and others

Courtesy of the Philadelphia Museum of Art

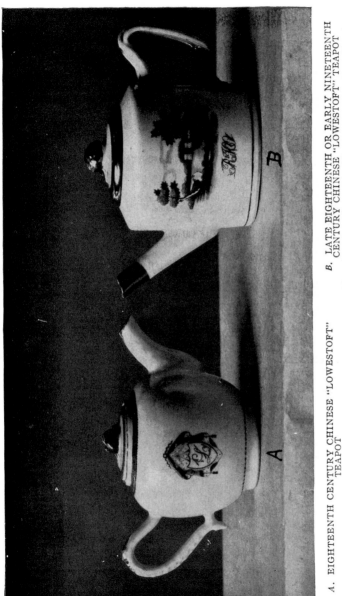

PLATE 31

A. EIGHTEENTH CENTURY CHINESE "LOWESTOFT" TEAPOT

Made to Western order, with shield, monogram and heraldic man-tlings; decoration deep blue, red and brown, with gold bands and small gold stars powdered on deep blue ground

B. LATE EIGHTEENTH OR EARLY NINETEENTH CENTURY CHINESE "LOWESTOFT" TEAPOT

Monochrome landscape in Western manner; decoration brown and gold

Courtesy of the Philadelphia Museum of Art

PLATE 32

A. CHINESE "LOWESTOFT" PLATTER WITH DECORATIONS
IN APPLE GREEN

Courtesy of the Philadelphia Museum of Art

B. CHINESE "LOWESTOFT" COVERED DISH WITH
UNUSUAL DECORATION OF STRAWBERRIES

Courtesy of the Philadelphia Museum of Art

PLATE 33

CHINESE "LOWESTOFT" PLATTER

Decorations in black; gold-lined at edge. Part of large "Cow" pattern china table-service. Design drawn in Philadelphia; service made and decorated to order in China c.1810

Courtesy of Dr. John B. Carson

PLATE 34

"MEDALLION" PUNCH BOWL

This polychrome "Medallion" decoration on Chinese porcelain came into use about 1820 and continued in fresh favour for many years

PLATE 35

A. JAPANESE EIGHT-SIDED BOWL; EIGHTEENTH
CENTURY

With polychrome flower decorations inside and out; decorations
in cobalt blue, light bluish green, vermilion, gold and creamy
yellow; glaze of slightly bluish tinge

B. JAPANESE KUTANI PEAR-SHAPED BOTTLE OR
VASE; EIGHTEENTH CENTURY

With polychrome flowers; decoration in dark blue, green, vermilion, pale rose and yellow; glaze of slightly greyish tinge

Courtesy of the British Museum

PLATE 36

BOWL OF MEDICI CHINA; LATE SIXTEENTH CENTURY

Decorations in blue, paste creamy white, glaze soft and waxy with slight bluish tinge

Courtesy of the Victoria and Albert Museum, South Kensington

PLATE 37

GINORI PLATTER, 1737; THE FIRST PIECE WITH POLYCHROME DECORATION MADE
AT DOCCIA

Cream-coloured waxy paste: slightly raised moulding at edge of rim, with guilloche of mulberry and green,
thin orange band, polychrome flower sprays on rim. figure with purple over-robe, green sleeves and coral
red under-robe

Courtesy of Factory Museum at Doccia

PLATE 38

A. GINORI ICE PAIL, c.1760

Waxy paste, clear glaze; polychrome flower sprays scattered in Dresden manner, rose mulberry band at rim

B. GINORI SOUP PLATE, c.1760

Shaped rim with pineapple or basketwork moulded ornament and moulded ribbings; polychrome flowers in Mennecy manner, with scattered flowers and fruits in centre

Courtesy of Factory Museum at Doccia

PLATE 39

A. GINORI OVAL PLATTER, c.1775
Shaped moulded rim; Chinese peony decoration with prevailing red, blue and gold

B. GINORI COVERED DISH, 1770
Without coloured decoration, cream-coloured waxy paste, clear glaze; Louis XV. contour shewing Rococo influence, moulded pineapple or basketwork ornament about rim, and moulded
gadrooning; delicately modelled flowers, leaves and stems applied

Courtesy of Factory Museum at Doccia

PLATE 40

A. GINORI PLATE, c.1815
Very hard, white body, clear glaze; ground of rim a deep red, charged
with elaborate gilt decoration in French Empire *motifs*

Courtesy of Factory Museum at Doccia

B. GINORI PLATE, c.1780
Shaped moulded rim; paste hard and white; decoration of Oriental
origin, chiefly in red, blue and gold

Courtesy of Factory Museum at Doccia

PLATE 41

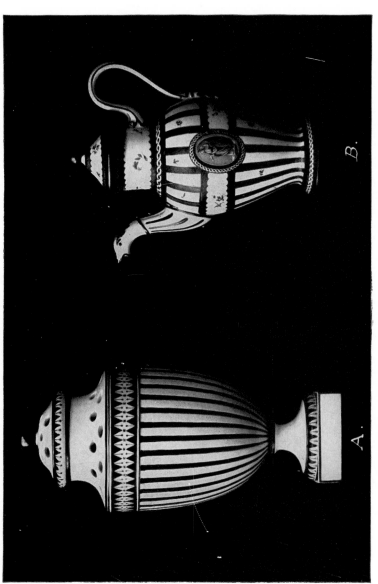

A. GINORI URN-SHAPED VASE OR JAR, c.1790
Paste hard and white; vertically striped decoration shewing contemporary French influence

B. GINORI CHOCOLATE POT, c.1790
Classic impulse seen in oval medallion and guilloche bandings; French vertical stripings and other items interpreted in characteristic Italian manner

Courtesy of Factory Museum at Doccia

PLATE 42

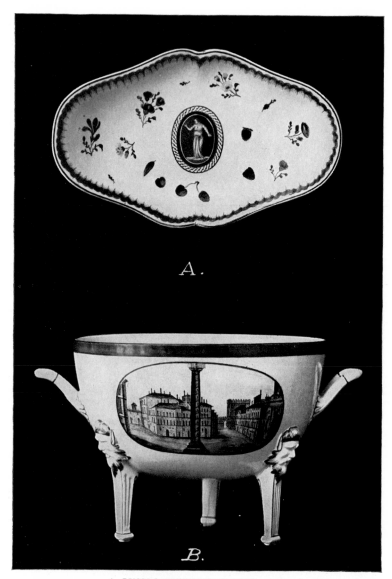

A. GINORI SWEETMEAT DISH, c.1780

Wedgwood influence in central medallion, scattered polychrome flowers and fruits in Dresden manner; hard, white paste, clear glaze

B. GINORI TUREEN ON LEGS, c.1780

Paste hard, slightly creamy in colour; Neo-Classic influence seen in oval shape, straight, fluted legs and collared feet

Courtesy of Factory Museum at Doccia

PLATE 43

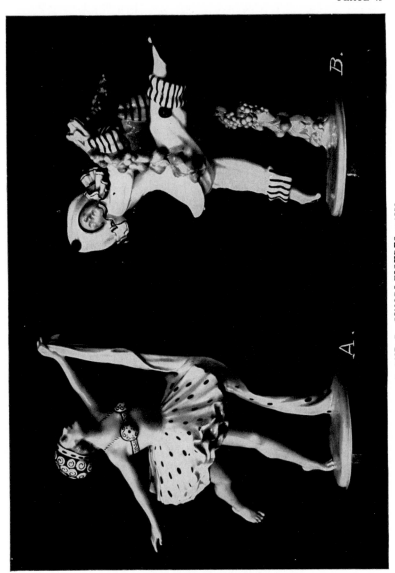

A. AND *B.* GINORI FIGURES, c.1775
Creamy white paste, clear glaze; exquisite modelling, partial polychrome decoration
Courtesy of Factory Museum at Doccia

PLATE 44

A. AND *B*. GINORI CUPS AND SAUCERS, c.1765
Decorations *en camaïeu*

Courtesy of Factory Museum at Doccia

C. GINORI REPRODUCTION OF
CAPO DI MONTE FIGURE
From Capo di Monte mould; flesh tints
and partial coloured decoration

Courtesy of Factory Museum at Doccia

PLATE 45

A. CAPO DI MONTE CUP
Modelled decoration in relief, strong polychrome treatment; creamy soft paste
Courtesy of the British Museum

B. NAPLES PLATTER AND TUREEN IN POMPEIAN MANNER
Hard, white paste, clear glaze; gold decorations, pale green figures on black ground
in medallion
Courtesy of the Victoria and Albert Museum, South Kensington

PLATE 46

LE NOVE JARDINIÈRE

Bands in yellow-green with gold diaper, flowers in dull madder, blue, yellow, violet and vermilion; glaze slightly uneven and of yellowish tinge

Courtesy of the Victoria and Albert Museum, South Kensington

PLATE 47

A. VENETIAN CUP AND SAUCER

Heraldic devices in dull Indian red; decorations in gold, violet and a little green; glaze
cold white

B. VENETIAN TRAY WITH SHAPED RIM

Floral decoration in light violet, yellow, deep green and Indian red; cold white glaze

Courtesy of the Victoria and Albert Museum, South Kensington

PLATE 48

A. SAINT CLOUD FLOWER POT, IN THE WHITE

Gadrooned rim and base, moulded flower and foliage decoration in low relief, modelled handles; creamy white soft paste, slightly greenish glaze

Courtesy of the Victoria and Albert Museum, South Kensington

B. SAINT CLOUD TEAPOT, IN THE WHITE

Moulded prunus-blossom *motif* in relief, modelled handle and spout; creamy white soft paste, slightly greenish glaze

Courtesy of the Victoria and Albert Museum, South Kensington

PLATE 49

A. SAINT CLOUD COVERED JAR
Decoration in underglaze blue, *motifs* in Louis XIV manner;
creamy soft paste, glaze slightly bluish

B. SAINT CLOUD COVERED JAR
Moulded decoration in relief coloured, pink, yellow,
blue and violet, stems and leaves green and blue
green; creamy paste and glaze

Courtesy of the Victoria and Albert Museum, South Kensington

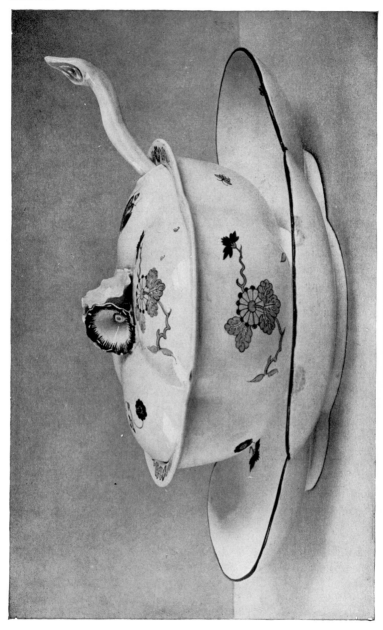

CHANTILLY GRAVY BOAT

Characteristic lobate form with modelled flower knob Kakiyemon decoration in light blue, light green, pale yellow and vermilion; creamy soft paste, glaze slightly bluish

Courtesy of the Victoria and Albert Museum South Kensington

PLATE 51

A. AND *B*. CHANTILLY FLOWER POT AND LOBATE COVERED DISH
Creamy soft paste, slightly greenish glaze: decorations light and dark greyish underglaze blue

C. CHANTILLY OVAL FRUIT DISH

Edges of perforations in mulberry, light blue ribbons on handles, flower sprays in mulberry
yellow and green; creamy soft paste, glaze nearly white

Courtesy of the Victoria and Albert Museum, South Kensington

PLATE 52

MENNECY-VILLEROY VASE

Characteristic flower decoration in rose, mulberry, yellow, green and dull blue; rim line of burnt Siena; soft paste of creamy ivory tone, clear glaze

Courtesy of the Victoria and Albert Museum, South Kensington

PLATE 53

B.

A.

A. MENNECY-VILLEROY COVERED JAR

Characteristic flower decorations in deep green, rose, yellow and light
purple; soft paste of creamy ivory or amber tinge, white glaze

B. MENNECY-VILLEROY COVERED DISH

Flower decorations in blue, purple, rose and olive green; characteristic mauve or mulberry lines at edges and rims; soft paste, of creamy
ivory tinge, white glaze

Courtesy of the Victoria and Albert Museum, South Kensington

PLATE 54

THREE VINCENNES VASES

Painted and modelled decoration, gold, yellow, pink and mulberry, leaves cold green; creamy white soft paste, glaze creamy and slightly uneven

Courtesy of the Victoria and Albert Museum, South Kensington

PLATE 55

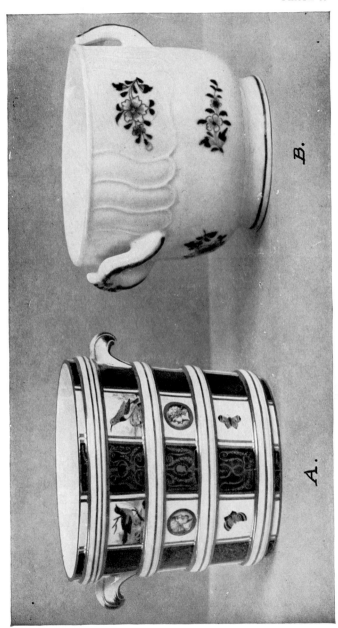

A. TOURNAY FLOWER POT

White paste, clear glaze; bands dark blue with gold arabesques, medallions in smoky violet, birds naturalistic colouring

B. ARRAS FLOWER POT

Moulded ornament, decorations in dark underglaze blue; creamy paste,
glaze slightly greenish

Courtesy of the Victoria and Albert Museum, South Kensington

PLATE 56

A. SÈVRES CUP AND SAUCER

Typical Directoire shape; creamy paste, clear glaze; decorations in gold and polychrome, flower knots in brilliant pinks, blues, violets, greens and yellows

B. SÈVRES CUP AND SAUCER

Typical diapered *motif*, bands in yellow-pink and gold, flowers in yellow, mulberry and blue, medallions naturalistic, paste creamy clear glaze

Courtesy of the Victoria and **Albert** Museum, South Kensington

PLATE 57

SÈVRES TEAPOT

Typical vine and trellis design; white paste, clear glaze; top and base uneven deep blue, columns shaded madder, leaves grey green, red berries, gold banding

Courtesy of the Victoria and Albert Museum, South Kensington

PLATE 58

A. SÈVRES OCTAGONAL PLATE

Hard white paste, clear glaze; Classic figure in medallion and arabesque border with *putti*; decorations deep green, rose, yellow, light purple and gold

B. SÈVRES CUP AND SAUCER

Hard white paste, clear glaze; decorations blue, purple, rose, olive green and gold

Courtesy of the Victoria and Albert Museum, South Kensington

PLATE 59

SÈVRES JUG

Characteristic Empire shape; ground burnt Siena, Classic arabesques in deep brown, panels
highly naturalistic in colour, bands, spout and handle gilt

Courtesy of the Victoria and Albert Museum, South Kensington

PLATE 60

A. SÈVRES CUP AND SAUCER

Typical Empire shape; hard white paste, clear glaze; decorations gold, black, pale green, shades of brown and dull blue, ground biscuit coloured or buff

B. SÈVRES CUP AND SAUCER

Hard white paste, clear glaze; gold arabesques on rim of saucer and cup, flower decorations light green, light yellow and deep shades of rose, blue and violet

Courtesy of the Victoria and Albert Museum, South Kensington

PLATE 61

LATE EIGHTEENTH CENTURY BOWL AND EWER

Made at one of the porcelain factories near Paris; decorations in very deep blue and pure gold; white, hard paste, clear, transparent glaze

Courtesy of the Victoria and Albert Museum, South Kensington

PLATE 62

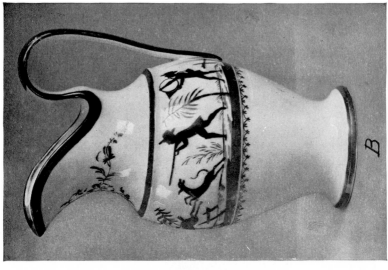

B. EMPIRE JUG WITH GOLD DECORATION

Made at one of the porcelain factories near Paris; white paste, clear white glaze; silhouette hunting scene in gold

A. CAEN JUG, EMPIRE SHAPE

Paste white, glaze of slightly greenish tinge; oblong medallions in sepia with black border, other decorations in gold with light greenish grey leaves

Courtesy of the Victoria and Albert Museum, South Kensington.

PLATE 63

A. NIDERVILLER FLOWER POT
White paste, glaze of slightly bluish tinge; decoration *en camaïeu* in
smoky violet, gold handles and bandings

B. VALENCIENNES COVERED SUGAR BASON
White paste, cold white glaze; decorations in gold, blue, pale bright
violet and light green

Courtesy of the Victoria and Albert Museum, South Kensington

PLATE 64

A. DRESDEN "ONION PATTERN" SOUP PLATE
Hard white paste, cold white glaze; decoration in deep blue

B. DRESDEN CUP AND SAUCER
Hard white paste, cold white glaze; typical Dresden flower decoration in two shades of green, mulberry, vermilion, greenish yellow and dull blue

Courtesy of the Victoria and Albert Museum, South Kensington

PLATE 65

A. EARLY DRESDEN CHOCOLATE POT

White paste, cold white glaze; decoration *en camaïeu* in rose mulberry, red and gold banding, Louis XIV, arabesque *motif* around neck

B. EARLY DRESDEN JUG

White paste, cold white glaze; gilding and polychrome flower and insect decoration in light yellow, mulberry, dull bluish green and vermilion

Courtesy of the Victoria and Albert Museum, South Kensington

PLATE 66

A. DRESDEN FIGURE OF LACE MAKER*

White paste, glaze slightly bluish; decoration in pale yellow, deep violet, light blue, green and viridian

*This figure represents Barbara Ottman who introduced pillow lace-making into Germany in 1561

DRESDEN JARDINIÈRE

White paste, glaze slightly bluish; modelled ornament and moulded ornament in paste; decoration in gold, mauve, yellowish green, vermilion and mulberry

Courtesy of the Victoria and Albert Museum, South Kensington

PLATE 67

A. NYMPHENBURG FLOWER POT
Paste cold white, clear white glaze; gold and blue arabesque border, flowers in mauve, pale yellow, dull blue, vermilion and two greens

B. HÖCHST SAUCE BOAT WITH MOULDED ORNAMENT
Paste white, cold white glaze; decoration in mulberry, pale blue, green, yellow and vermilion

Courtesy of the Victoria and Albert Museum, South Kensington

PLATE 68

A. BERLIN TEA CADDY

White paste, clear white glaze; decoration in gold, varying shades of brown, violet, vermilion and dull greens

B. ANSBACH TEAPOT

Moulded ornament at base of spout; cold white paste, white glaze; decoration in light green, vermilion, pale blue, deep and light violet

Courtesy of the Victoria and Albert Museum, South Kensington

PLATE 69

LUDWIGSBURG TUREEN

Paste of greyish tinge, clear white glaze; modelled and applied ornament, and ornament moulded in paste about rim of lid
and body; deep coloured flower and insect decoration in blue, violet, vermilion, red and deep yellowish green

Courtesy of the Victoria and Albert Museum. South Kensington

PLATE 70

A. VIENNA EMPIRE-SHAPED MILK JUG.

White paste, clear glaze; decoration in gold, mulberry, pale
yellow, grey and flesh colour

B. NYMPHENBURG CUP AND SAUCER.

White paste, excellent clear glaze; decoration in vermilion, pink,
pale green, dull blue and violet

Courtesy of the British Museum

PLATE 71

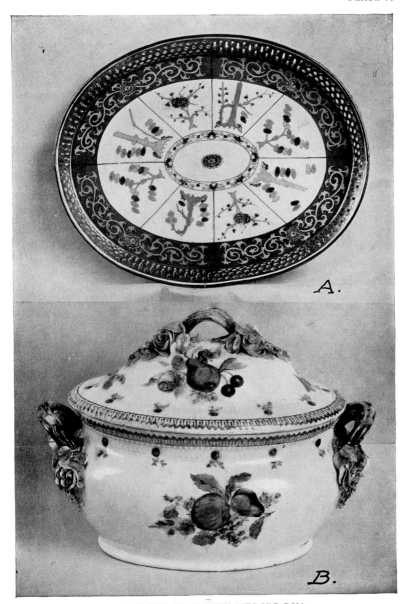

A. HEREND TRAY WITH PIERCED RIM
White paste, smooth, clear glaze; deep Indian red border with gold arabesques, light centre
with vari-coloured decoration

B. COPENHAGEN TUREEN
White paste, excellent clear glaze; decoration in blue, pink, yellow, vermilion and varied
shades of green; modelled and applied flower handles

Courtesy of the Victoria and Albert Museum, South Kensington

PLATE 72

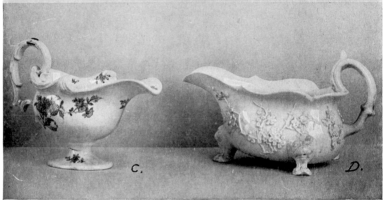

A. BOW BLUE AND WHITE PLATE IN CHINESE MANNER
Creamy paste, slightly bluish glaze; decoration in deep, dull blue

B. BOW BLUE AND WHITE SAUCEBOAT IN CHINESE MANNER
Same paste, glaze and colouring

C. BOW SAUCEBOAT, FRENCH ROCOCO MANNER
Creamy paste, slightly yellowish glaze; moulded ornament impressed in paste, decoration
pink, yellow, light blue and bluish green

D. BOW SAUCEBOAT WITHOUT COLOUR DECORATION
Prunus blossoms in relief on sides; moulded feet and handle; creamy paste, glaze of yellowish tinge

Courtesy of the Victoria and Albert Museum, South Kensington

PLATE 73

A.

B.

A. BOW MUG WITH BULGING BASE

Creamy paste, slightly bluish glaze; flower decoration in mulberry,
dark bluish green, light yellow and cobalt blue

B. BOW GLOBULAR TEAPOT

Same paste, glaze and colour characteristics as *A*

Courtesy of the Victoria and Albert Museum, South Kensington

PLATE 74

A. BOW PERFORATED FRUIT DISH

Creamy paste and glaze; decoration in vermilion, cobalt blue, gold and bluish green

B. BOW PLATE

Creamy paste, slightly yellowish glaze; prunus blossoms, without colour, moulded in relief on rim, Chinese peony decoration in green, deep pink, pale blue and bright yellow

Courtesy of the Victoria and Albert Museum, South Kensington

PLATE 75

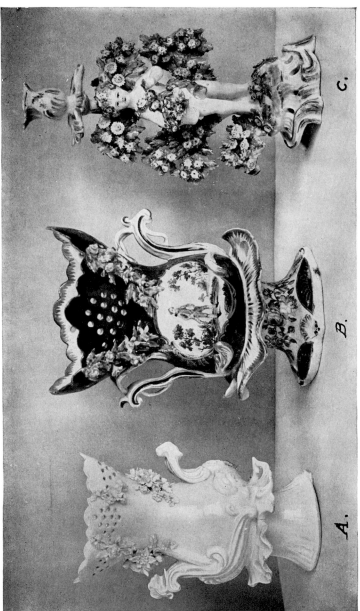

A. BOW VASE IN THE WHITE

Creamy paste, greyish glaze; modelled and
applied, moulded and perforated ornament

B. BOW VASE WITH DEEP COBALT
GROUND

Creamy paste, greyish glaze; modelled and applied, moulded and perforated ornament; decoration in reserved panel on cobalt ground
colour, in gold, mulberry, yellow, green and
vermilion

C. BOW CANDLESTICK WITH MOD-
ELLED FIGURE

Creamy paste, greyish glaze; modelled **flowers** and moulded ornament; decoration in
deep rose, green, vermilion, blue, **yellow**
and gold

Courtesy of the Victoria and Albert Museum, South Kensington

PLATE 76

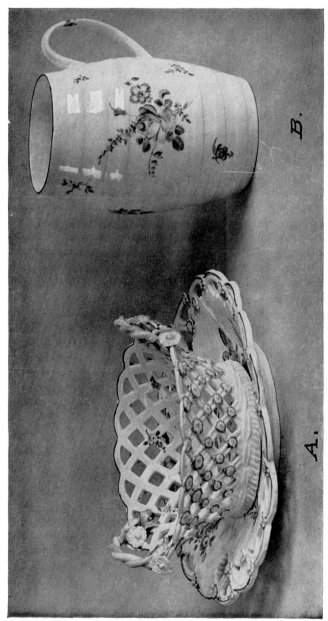

A. BOW PERFORATED FRUIT DISH AND STAND

Creamy paste, slightly greyish glaze; modelled and applied, moulded
and pierced ornament; decoration in mauve, yellow, yellowish green,
light blue and vermilion

B. BARREL-SHAPED CHELSEA MUG

Creamy paste, slightly greyish glaze; scattered flower decoration
Dresden manner in the same colours as noted for *A*

Courtesy of the Victoria and Albert Museum, South Kensington

PLATE 77

CHELSEA OBLONG OCTAGONAL PLATTER

Creamy paste, clear white glaze; moulded rim; scattered flower, butterfly and insect decoration in pale yellow, several shades of mauve and mulberry, two shades of green, dull blue and dead vermilion

Courtesy of the Victoria and Albert Museum, South Kensington

PLATE 78

A. CHELSEA FLUTED CHOCOLATE POT

Creamy paste, slightly greenish glaze; moulded fluting; decoration pale yellow, dull vermilion, mulberry and several shades of green

B. CHELSEA EIGHT-SIDED VASE

Creamy paste, clear white glaze; semi-Kakiyemon decoration in cobalt blue, turquoise blue, pale yellow, deep vermilion and gold

Courtesy of the Victoria and Albert Museum, South Kensington

PLATE 79

A. CHELSEA FLOWER HOLDER WITH SCALLOPED
FLARE TOP

Creamy paste, clear white glaze; moulded bands and shape; decoration in violet, light blue, pale yellow, green, vermilion and
biscuit colour

Courtesy of the Victoria and Albert Museum, South Kensington

B. LATE CHELSEA COVERED SUGAR BASON

Creamy paste, clear white glaze; claret coloured ground with reserved white panels; decoration in gold, green, blue, pale
Venetian red and deep mulberry

Courtesy of the Victoria and Albert Museum, South Kensington

PLATE 80

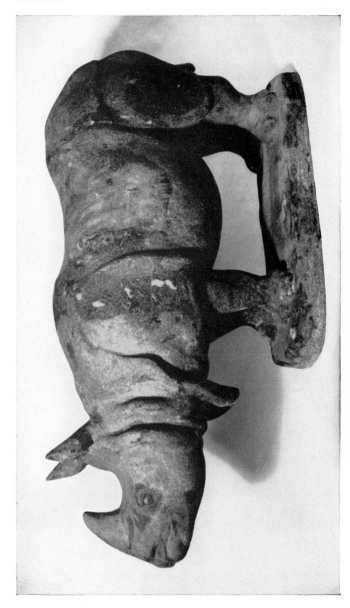

BING AND GRØNDAHL PORCELAIN RHINOCEROS FIGURE

Modelled by Jean Gauguin. Made by the Bing & Grøndahl Porcelain Factory, Copenhagen

PLATE 81

A. WORCESTER TEAPOT

White paste, **excellent** clear glaze; decoration adapted from the Japanese Imari brocade patterns in red, gold, green and blue

B. WORCESTER PLATE

White paste, clear glaze; decoration inspired by Japanese Imari patterns, in red, deep
blue and gold

Courtesy of the British Museum

PLATE 82

LATE WORCESTER PLATE

White paste, clear glaze; Empire style decorations in gold on ground-coloured rim, naturalistically
coloured landscape in centre.

Courtesy of the Museum, Royal Worcester Pottery

PLATE 83

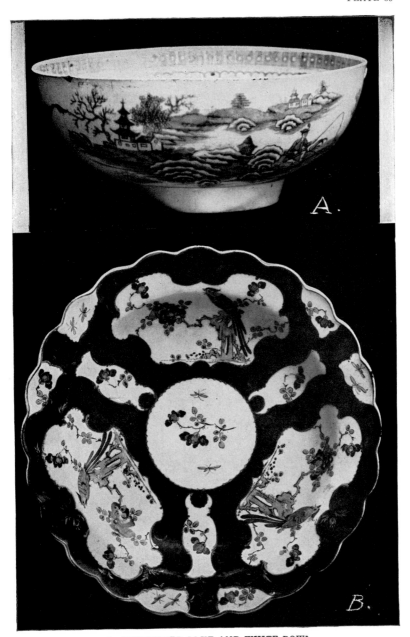

A. WORCESTER BLUE AND WHITE BOWL
Decoration in deep blue in the Chinese manner; white paste, clear glaze

B. WORCESTER PLATE WITH DEEP BLUE GROUND
Paste white, clear glaze; shaped white panels reserved in deep blue ground colour, reserved
panels containing multi-coloured *motifs*; remote Japanese Imari influence

Courtesy of the Museum, Royal Worcester Pottery

PLATE 84

WORCESTER CHOCOLATE POT WITH SWELLING BASE
White paste, clear glaze; attenuated Mandarin figures in pale but varied colours

Courtesy of the Museum, Royal Worcester Pottery

PLATE 85

WORCESTER VASE OF LATE PERIOD
White paste, clear glaze; moulded ornament; gold decorations with figures in naturalistically coloured landscape with panel reserved in ground colour

Courtesy of the Museum, Royal Worcester Pottery

PLATE 86

WORCESTER CHOCOLATE POT WITH DOMED LID
White paste, excellent clear glaze; decoration in semi-Imari manner with red,
deep blue and gold predominating

Courtesy of the Museum, Royal Worcester Pottery

PLATE 87

WORCESTER SOUP PLATE

White paste, clear, smooth glaze; engraved and transfer printed design in dull green
monochrome

Courtesy of the Museum, Royal Worcester Pottery

PLATE 88

EARLY WORCESTER MUG OF DR. WALL PERIOD

Creamy white paste, clear transparent glaze; bright apple green ground colour with shaped
and reserved white panel bearing polychrome flower decoration

Courtesy of the Museum, Royal Worcester Pottery

PLATE 89

A. DERBY OVAL BUTTER DISH WITH SHAPED LID

Creamy paste, clear glaze; gilded feet, handles and bandings; ground colour bluish grey, festooned flowers in burnt orange, yellow, pale green, and rose colour for the ribbons

B. DERBY VASE

White paste, clear glaze; deep blue ground colour with elaborate gilt decorations and reserved naturalistic landscape panels on the sides

Courtesy of the Victoria and Albert Museum, South Kensington

PLATE 90

B.

A.

A. DERBY PLATE WITH FLOWERED BORDER

Creamy paste, glaze slightly greenish; spirally divided rim, with decoration in vermilion, deep blue, gold and light green

B. DERBY PLATE WITH IMARI DECORATION

Creamy paste, glaze slightly greenish; Japanese Imari inspiration modified with pattern carried out in light and dark blue, pale greenish
yellow and pale yellowish green, deep Venetian red, deep violet and gold

Courtesy of the Victoria and Albert Museum. South Kensington

PLATE 91

A. DERBY CUP AND SAUCER

Paste white, clear colourless glaze; arabesque decoration in gold, deep
yellow, deep vermilion, light green and violet

B. DERBY BOWL

Paste white, faint greenish tinge in glaze; decoration in bright rose,
yellow, light green, blue, burnt Siena and gold

Courtesy of the Victoria and Albert Museum. South Kensington

PLATE 92

PLYMOUTH COVERED GARNITURE JAR OF CHINESE SHAPE
White paste, glaze slightly greyish or smoked; decoration in yellow,
green, mulberry, purple and deep Venetian red

Courtesy of the Victoria and Albert Museum, South Kensington

PLATE 93

PLYMOUTH MUG WITH SWELLING BASE

Paste white, glaze slightly greyish or smoked; decorated with Chinese *motifs* in brilliant
colours, green, vermilion, dull blue, bright yellow and mulberry

Courtesy of the Victoria and Albert Museum, South Kensington

PLATE 94

A. PLYMOUTH MUG WITH SWELLING BASE

White paste, glaze slightly bluish grey or smoky; flower bouquet and spray decoration in gold, violet, vermilion, blue, green, and yellow

B. PLYMOUTH SAUCEBOAT OF ROCOCO SHAPE

Paste white, glaze slightly bluish grey or smoky; moulded ornament in paste; colour decoration in black, Venetian red, mulberry and grey green

Courtesy of the Victoria and Albert Museum, South Kensington

PLATE 95

BRISTOL CHOCOLATE POT WITH DOMED LID

Hard white paste, clear, colourless glaze; bright marbleised or stippled cobalt ground, rather
harsh; elaborate scroll and band gilding of excellent quality; reserved white panels with
polychrome flowers in green, mulberry, yellow, purple and deep Venetian red

Courtesy of the Victoria and Albert Museum, South Kensington

PLATE 96

A. BRISTOL PEAR-SHAPED CHOCOLATE POT

Creamy paste, clear glaze; flowered decoration in Dresden manner in
pale pink, yellow, deep cold green, smoky violet, Venetian red and gold

B. BRISTOL FIGURE OF *AUTUMN*

Creamy paste, clear, colourless glaze; decoration in green, yellow,
vermilion, dull blue, pale mulberry and gold

Courtesy of the Victoria and Albert Museum, South Kensington

PLATE 97

B. BRISTOL PLATE WITH SHAPED AND MOULDED RIM

Hard white paste, faint bluish tinge in glaze; interlaced blue ribbon border, flower spray decoration in blue, violet, pink, green, greenish yellow, vermilion and gold

A. BRISTOL PLATE WITH SHAPED AND MOULDED RIM

Hard white paste, faint bluish tinge in glaze; decoration in green, rose, brown, blue shading to purple, vermilion, yellow and gold

Courtesy of the Victoria and Albert Museum, South Kensington

PLATE 98

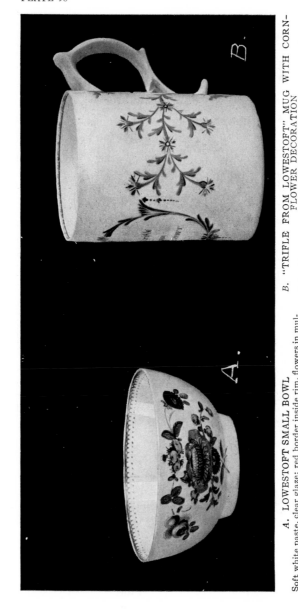

A. LOWESTOFT SMALL BOWL

Soft white paste, clear glaze; red border inside rim, flowers in mulberry, yellow, dull blue, vermilion and green

B. "TRIFLE FROM LOWESTOFT" MUG WITH CORN-FLOWER DECORATION

Soft white paste, glaze faintly bluish; decoration in blue, mulberry, bluish green and touches of vermilion, green border

Courtesy of the Victoria and Albert Museum, South Kensington

PLATE 99

A. LOWESTOFT BUTTER BOAT
Soft white paste, distinctly bluish glaze;
moulded ornament impressed in paste; decoration in deep dull blue

B. LOWESTOFT CREAM PITCHER
Soft white paste, bluish glaze; moulded ornament impressed in paste; decoration in
deep dull blue

C. LOWESTOFT PIERCED FRUIT BASKET
Soft white paste, very bluish glaze; moulded ornament; decoration deep blue

Courtesy of the Victoria and Albert Museum, South Kensington

PLATE 100

A. CAUGHLEY SAUCER

Creamy paste, clear glaze; decoration in gold and very deep blue

B. CAUGHLEY COVERED CUP WITH TWO HANDLES

Creamy paste, clear glaze; characteristic decoration in gold and very deep blue

Courtesy of the Victoria and Albert Museum, South Kensington

PLATE 101

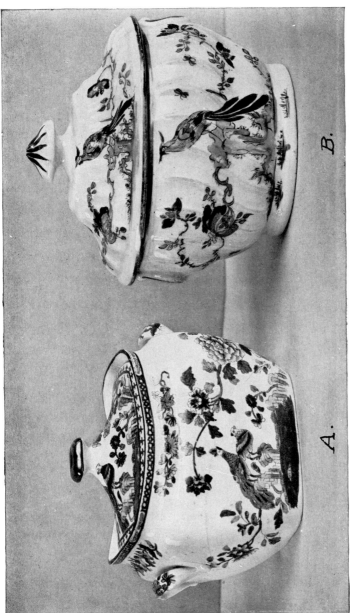

A. SPODE OBLONG SUGAR BASON
Creamy paste, clear glaze; typical Chinese decoration in shades of
brilliant green, pink, yellow, deep blue, biscuit and gold

B. OVAL, SPIRAL FLUTED CAUGHLEY SUGAR BASON
Creamy paste, faintly bluish glaze; moulded flutings; Chinese decoration in pale green, light and bright yellow, vermilion and cobalt

Courtesy of the Victoria and Albert Museum, South Kensington

PLATE 102

A. SPODE COVERED BUTTER DISH

Creamy paste, glaze of faintly greenish tinge; light grey blue ground with rich gilding, flowers in pink, vermilion, cobalt, yellow and green

B. SPODE STONE-CHINA PLATE

White paste, glaze slightly bluish; rose-coloured diapered border, rest of decoration in rose, biscuit, vermilion, green and deep violet

Courtesy of the Victoria and Albert Museum, South Kensington

PLATE 103

SPODE OVAL DISH WITH SHAPED RIM

Creamy paste, clear glaze; transfer printed decoration in warm grey, gilded rim and handles

Courtesy of the Victoria and Albert Museum, South Kensington

PLATE 104

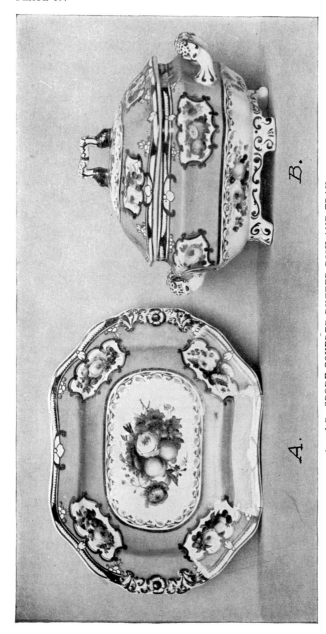

A. and *B*. SPODE COVERED BUTTER DISH AND TRAY

Cream paste, clear glaze bright cobalt ground with reserved panels in white, rich gilding, flowers in pink, blue, burnt orange, deep violet and light green

Courtesy of the Victoria and Albert Museum, South Kensington

PLATE 105

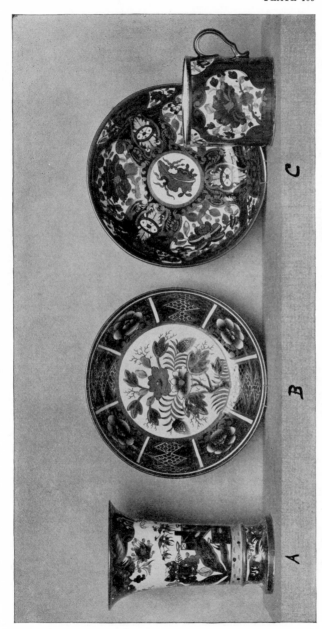

A. SPODE VASE IN JAPANESE IMARI MANNER   *B.* SPODE SAUCER AND *C.* SPODE CUP AND SAUCER, IN
Creamy paste, clear glaze; decoration in rich gold, biscuit, brilliant   DIFFERENT VERSIONS OF JAPANESE IMARI MANNER
green, very deep blue and vermilion   Creamy paste, clear glaze decoration in gold, very deep rich blue.
vermilion and yellowish green

Courtesy of the Victoria and Albert Museum, South Kensington

PLATE 106

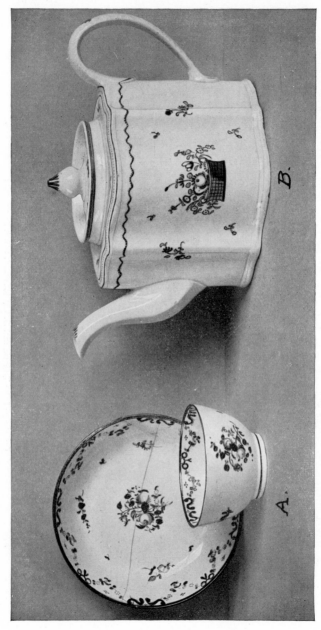

A. NEW HALL CUP AND SAUCER

White paste, glaze of faintly bluish tinge; flower spray, festoon and
ribbon decoration in pale bluish green, dull Venetian red, deep pink,
deep violet and touches of blue

B. NEW HALL STRAIGHT-SIDED TEAPOT

White paste, glaze of slightly bluish tinge; decoration in pale bluish
green, deep pink, deep violet and Venetian red

Courtesy of the Victoria and Albert Museum, South Kensington

PLATE 107

A. SWANSEA VASE WITH MODELLED AND APPLIED FLOWERS IN BISCUIT
White paste, glaze transparent; decoration in gold, light blue, pink, black, vermilion and pale yellow

B. PINXTON JARDINIÈRE
White paste, glaze slightly greenish; buff ground colour, decoration in green, sepia, yellow and gold

Courtesy of the Victoria and Albert Museum, South Kensington

PLATE 108

WEDGWOOD IVY PATTERN PLATE AND BOUILLON CUP AND SAUCER
Porcelain dinner-service. A modern product of the Wedgwood factory

Courtesy of Josiah Wedgwood & Sons, Inc.

PLATE 109

A. NANTGARW PLATE WITH SHAPED RIM   B. NANTGARW PLATE, SHAPED RIM

Paste white, clear glaze; brilliant flower decoration in yellow, blue,   Paste white, clear glaze; light blue ground colour in rim, with rich pink, vermilion, purple, shaded greens and gold   gilding, panels in green, yellow, brown, mauve, pink, blue and yellow

Courtesy of the Victoria and Albert Museum. South Kensington

PLATE 110

NANTGARW PLATE

Paste creamy, clear glaze and brilliant: richly gilded rim, decoration in bright yellow and orange, shades of yellow, yellowish green and brown

Courtesy of the Victoria and Albert Museum, South Kensington

PLATE 111

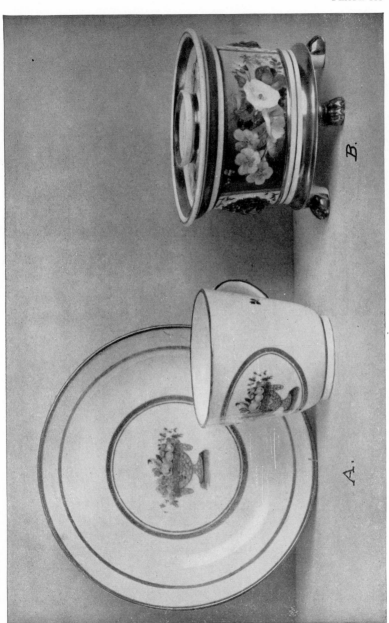

B.

A.

A. COALPORT CUP AND SAUCER   **B. EMPIRE-SHAPED NANTGARW INKPOT**

Paste white, glaze slightly bluish; gold banding, monochrome decora-   Paste white, glaze brilliant; highly naturalistic flower panels in
tion in warm grey   yellow, blue, pink, green and rose, heavy brilliant gilding

Courtesy of the Victoria and Albert Museum, South Kensington

PLATE 112

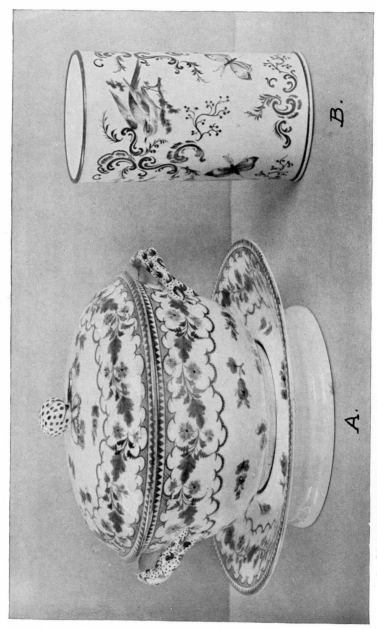

A. COALPORT BUTTER DISH IN TRAY   *B.* COALPORT CYLINDRICAL VASE

Paste white, glaze clear and brilliant; decoration in blue, deep pink   Paste creamy, glaze brilliant; decoration in lgold, light grey-blue, light
and light green   pink and yellow

Courtesy of the Victoria and Albert Museum, South Kensington

PLATE 113

A. ROCKINGHAM SUGAR BASON   *B.* ROCKINGHAM JUG

Paste white, glaze clear and mellow; decoration in green, blue, pink and gold   Paste creamy, glaze clear; biscuit-coloured ground, heavy gilding, flowers in reserved panels in deep orange, light blue, yellow and green

Courtesy of the Victoria and Albert Museum, South Kensington

PLATE 114

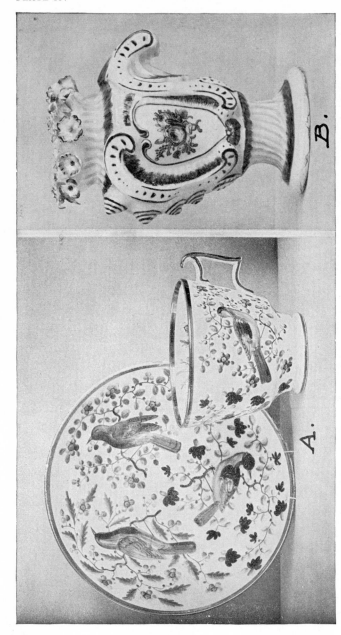

A. LIVERPOOL CUP AND SAUCER

Paste white, glaze cold white; decoration in bright blue, bluish and yellowish greens, light Indian red and dark vermilion and varied browns

B. LONGTON HALL VASE

Paste white, glaze slightly greyish; decoration in deep mulberry, yellow, pink and green

Courtesy of the Victoria and Albert Museum, South Kensington

PLATE 115

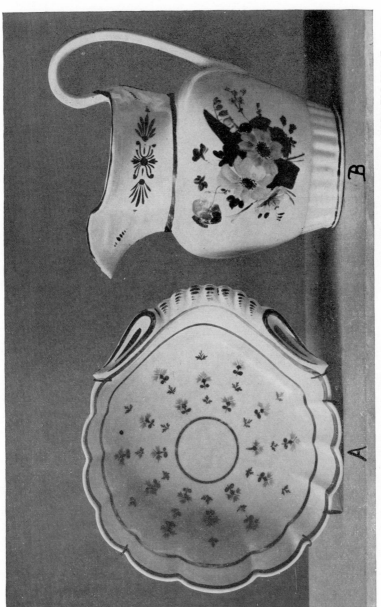

A. TUCKER SHELL-SHAPED DISH
Milky white paste, clear glaze; decoration in deep blue, light green and gold

B. TUCKER JUG OF CHARACTERISTIC SHAPE, c.1830
Milky white paste, glaze slightly bluish; moulded ornament at base, lip and handle: flowers in natural colours, brilliant gilding

Courtesy of the Philadelphia Museum of Art

PLATE 116

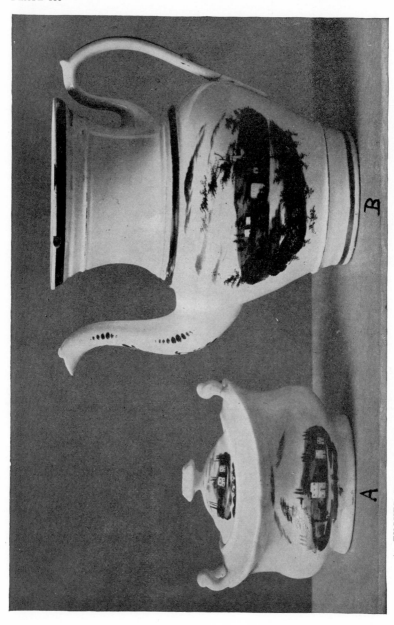

A. TUCKER SUGAR BOWL, c.1830
Milky white paste, clear glaze; monochrome landscape decoration
in dark brown

B. TUCKER COFFEE POT, c.1830
Milky white paste, clear glaze; all decoration in brown

Courtesy of the Philadelphia Museum of Art

PLATE 117

LARGE TUCKER WATER JUG OF CHARACTERISTIC SHAPE, c.1835
Paste milky white, clear, brilliant glaze; typical flower decoration in natural
colours, brilliant gilding

Courtesy of the Philadelphia Museum of Art

PLATE 118

A. SMALL TUCKER PLATE

Milky white paste, clear, brilliant glaze; decoration wholly in gold "spider" pattern

B. VASE-SHAPED TUCKER JUG

Milky white paste, clear, brilliant glaze; moulded ornament in body, gold decoration

Courtesy of the Philadelphia Museum of Art

PLATE 119

A

B

A. FRAGMENT OF SOFT PASTE PORCELAIN, c.1770
Made at Southwark, Philadelphia. Creamy paste and glaze; decoration in blue

Courtesy of the Philadelphia Museum of Art

B. SMALL TEAPOT AND TEACUPS OF ORIENTAL CHINA
One of a set from which William Penn drank tea in Philadelphia

Courtesy of Mrs. H. Genêt Taylor

PLATE 120

A. BLUE STAFFORDSHIRE PLATE
Transfer printed in underglaze blue; made for the American trade,
view of the old waterworks in Philadelphia

B. LIVERPOOL JUG, c.1800
Transfer printed in black, made for the American trade

Courtesy of the Philadelphia Museum of Art